Deleuze and Contemporary Art

Deleuze Connections

'It is not the elements or the sets which define the multiplicity. What defines it is the AND, as something which has its place between the elements or between the sets. AND, AND, AND – stammering.'

Gilles Deleuze and Claire Parnet, *Dialogues*

General Editor
Ian Buchanan

Editorial Advisory Board

Keith Ansell-Pearson
Rosi Braidotti
Claire Colebrook
Tom Conley

Gregg Lambert
Adrian Parr
Paul Patton
Patricia Pisters

Titles Available in the Series

Ian Buchanan and Claire Colebrook (eds), *Deleuze and Feminist Theory*
Ian Buchanan and John Marks (eds), *Deleuze and Literature*
Mark Bonta and John Protevi (eds), *Deleuze and Geophilosophy*
Ian Buchanan and Marcel Swiboda (eds), *Deleuze and Music*
Ian Buchanan and Gregg Lambert (eds), *Deleuze and Space*
Martin Fuglsang and Bent Meier Sørensen (eds), *Deleuze and the Social*
Ian Buchanan and Adrian Parr (eds), *Deleuze and the Contemporary World*
Constantin V. Boundas (ed.), *Deleuze and Philosophy*
Ian Buchanan and Nicholas Thoburn (eds), *Deleuze and Politics*
Chrysanthi Nigianni and Merl Storr (eds), *Deleuze and Queer Theory*
Jeffrey A. Bell and Claire Colebrook (eds), *Deleuze and History*
Laura Cull (ed.), *Deleuze and Performance*
Mark Poster and David Savat (eds), *Deleuze and New Technology*
Simone Bignall and Paul Patton (eds), *Deleuze and the Postcolonial*

Forthcoming Titles in the Series

Laura Guillaume and Joe Hughes (eds), *Deleuze and the Body*

Deleuze and Contemporary Art

Edited by Stephen Zepke and
Simon O'Sullivan

Edinburgh University Press

© in this edition, Edinburgh University Press, 2010
© in the individual contributions is retained by the authors

Edinburgh University Press Ltd
22 George Square, Edinburgh

www.euppublishing.com

Typeset in 10.5/13 Sabon
by Servis Filmsetting Ltd, Stockport, Cheshire, and
printed and bound in Great Britain by
CPI Antony Rowe, Chippenham and Eastbourne

A CIP record for this book is available from the British Library

ISBN 978 0 7486 3837 6 (hardback)
ISBN 978 0 7486 3838 3 (paperback)

Contents

Acknowledgements

The editors would especially like to thank all those who gave their labour to this project for free, most notably the contributors, and the translators Juan Fernando Mejía Mosquera, Tim Adams, Robin Mackay, Victor Faessel and Brian Holmes. We would also like to thank Anita Fricek, Leonardo Kovačević, Tom Medak, Petar Milat, Hannah Neighbour, Ralph Paine, Nick Thoburn and Carol Macdonald at EUP.

List of Illustrations

Deleuze and Guattari *and* Contemporary Art

Stephen Zepke and Simon O'Sullivan

> The artist stores up his treasures so as to create an immediate explosion.
>
> Deleuze and Guattari, *Anti-Oedipus*

Conjunction *Versus* the Relational

Deleuze and Guattari *and* Contemporary art. Our emphasis lies squarely on the conjunction, on what it might mean and what it might be able to do. How can we articulate or even explode this conjunction, now and for a future to come? What is at stake is an actualisation of Deleuze and Guattari's 'logic of the AND'; an actualisation in action, a pragmatics that is not a 'localisable relation going from one thing to the other and back again', but a 'transversal movement that sweeps one *and* the other away, a stream without beginning or end that undermines its banks and picks up speed in the middle' (Deleuze and Guattari 1988: 28). Following this 'stream' that erodes its own banks, we cannot imagine that this relationship, this *and*, could be articulated by either 'philosophy' or 'art', at least in their traditional forms. As many of the essays here argue, Contemporary art is a field that seems to attack the very ground of this old distinction. Indeed, perhaps Contemporary art is a field of production (we would say a *future*) that ignores the line Deleuze and Guattari draw between concepts and sensations. In this sense then, the volume offers a cross-section of the encounter of Deleuze and Guattari and Contemporary art, an encounter that might irradiate our 'present' with the 'crepuscular light' of an *and* in which they become indistinct. Under these conditions the shifting qualities of a 'to come' emerge, in the eruption of an atemporal and untimely *contemporary*. . .

Gathered together here are a collection of transversal experiments with the *and* between art, in its contemporary and visual form, and

Deleuzo-Guattarian philosophy. In fact, we do not necessarily hold that Contemporary art need always be visual art, but according, perhaps, to the law of the market, many of our essays are concerned with the latter. Nevertheless, other essays in our collection address the pictorial imaging of music, software art, the life of 'scenes', or more strictly philosophical 'images of thought', and those essays concerned with Guattari's 'aesthetic paradigm' clearly include all forms of artistic activity. We have also endeavoured to include authors who come from outside the Anglo-American world, and others working primarily as artists rather than scholars. In this we hope the collection might act as a gust of fresh air blown into the often stale closed halls of the Academy and its rather insular Discourse.

But before we get too blown away let us take a breath and recompose our own academic demeanor. . . Clearly, neither Deleuze nor Contemporary art need the other, and their relation is not especially obvious given that Deleuze and Guattari did nothing much more than mention contemporary artists in passing.[1] Nevertheless, the last decade of the twentieth century and the first of the twenty-first could perhaps, in relation to the world of Contemporary art, be called 'Deleuzian'. Why, then, this increasingly familiar conjunction: Deleuze *and* Contemporary art? Without wishing to be overly cynical about the fashion economy of the art world, and its voracious hunger for ever new theoretical 'product', the incredible proliferation of 'rhizomatic', 'nomadic' and of course 'relational' artists and artworks that have recently inundated the art world is perhaps a symptom of a much wider transformation that is not specific to art, but which has certainly included the latter as a willing partner. Globalisation and the concurrent explosion of information technology have created a ubiquitous internationalism, where local discourses and styles are frequently reduced to 'colour' justifying the seemingly endless parade of biennales, trienalles, art fairs and other such 'mega-events'. Contemporary art and theory encompasses the globe, but often expresses little more than a global homogenisation. In this sense, both Contemporary art *and* the philosophy of 'D&G' face the same problem, that of avoiding what Guattari called the 'promotional operations' of the (art) world, and its continual creation of 'fads' that maintain themselves through publicity (Guattari 1996: 109). Here art *and* philosophy have become sadly satisfied by their 'success' in the markets of the culture industry. Deleuze and Guattari explicitly condemn this commodification of art: 'There is no such thing as commercial art. It's a contradiction in terms' (Deleuze 2006: 288). 'The art market perverts aesthetic creation' (Guattari 1996: 265).

In fact, as Eric Alliez argues here, the philosophy of Guattari has already been instrumentalised by the contemporary art market in the form of 'relational aesthetics'. This art 'movement', named as such by the curator and art critic Nicolas Bourriaud, is now ubiquitous. It presents a precise instance of the problem: claiming a contemporary political efficacy – in the name of Guattari – for 'an art form where the substrate is formed by inter-subjectivity, and which takes being-together as a central theme' (Bourriaud 2002: 15). But, Alliez asks, does this 'inter-subjective substrate' really represent a break with contemporary forms of subjection, or does it simply produce 'a populism of the multitude, or more exactly a populism of which the multitude would be the (post)aesthetic subject and the object of "re-aestheticisation"? Where the aestheticisation of dissensus would become the post-political form for the exhibition of a postmodernist consensus affirming its "open" and "relational" qualities, self-affirming the value of conviviality beyond antagonism and/or radicality.' In today's 'relational' culture the aesthetics of 'being-together' turns 'militancy' into 'little services rendered' (Bourriaud 2002: 36). We are faced with a contemporary art eager to stage a panel discussion on the 'relational fabric' of what Bourriaud tellingly calls 'inter-human commerce' (36, 17).

Against this dispiriting vision of artistic practices we raise Nietzsche's banner: 'Art and nothing but art! It is the great means of making life possible, the great seduction to life, the great stimulant of life' (Nietzsche 1967: 452). Contemporary art is a social 'probe-head' creating micropolitical mutations and inhuman becomings within contemporary subjectivity, 'existential events' opening new possibilities to life. Artists and art, Guattari tells us, offer us the most advanced models for 'a chaosmic plunge into the materials of sensation', and so 'constitute the final lines along which primordial existential questions are folded. . . . How are sounds and forms going to be arranged so that the subjectivity adjacent to them remains in movement, and really alive?' (Guattari 1995: 90, 133).

Politics

The essays in this volume answer this question in a variety of ways. There are those who understand the Life that is at stake here in directly political terms. Gustavo Chirolla, for example, argues that the 'question of the relation of modern art to the people has changed, the artist has ceased to address or invoke the people as a "constituted force". This is still the case for Contemporary art, unless the invocation of the people

4 Deleuze and Contemporary Art

is considered to be the reproduction of a consensus.' In *Treno* (2007), a video installation by Clemencia Echeverri, Chirolla hears a 'scream' lamenting the 'forced disappearances' happening in Colombia. A collective voice sings the names of the dead thrown into the waters of the Cauca River, and in so doing defiantly calls forth a people to come. Similarly, Suely Rolnik enters Cildo Meireles' installation *Red Shift* (1967–84), where 'the diffuse and omnipresent experience of oppression becomes visible and/or audible in an environment where the brutality of state terrorism provokes the reaction of a voluntary blindness, deafness and dumbness, as a matter of survival'. In the context of the Brazilian dictatorship (1964–85), Rolnik argues, this work shows how the affective 'event' of oppression makes politics and poetics 'absolutely inseparable within the precise formation of one single gesture and in the intensive diagram of its inflammatory potential'. Like Chirolla, Rolnik sees the artistic act as a micropolitical explosion of Life that escapes what Chirolla (following Agamben) calls 'thanopolitics'. Both Chirolla and Rolnik remain strongly commited to the position of the 'artist', which despite its autonomy, and even because of it, enables the aesthetic 'gesture' to enter political 'life' and to make real changes. In this their work follows Deleuze's assertion: 'There is no other aesthetic problem than that of the insertion of art into everyday life' (Deleuze 1994: 293).

But there are other ways of understanding this assertion, and we have recently seen a rise in more committed forms of aesthetic production that have turned a revitalised institutional critique against the global commodity of 'art'. Gerald Raunig, for example, argues that the 'inserting' of Contemporary art into processes of social production requires its removal from 'art' in its institutional sense. This operation allows artists to develop 'aesthetic' strategies of both intervention and organisation within militant political movements. Raunig sees this aesthetic activism at work in Marcelo Expósito's videos, which 'draw a line of flight from conventional documentary practices (historiographic, artistic and activist), and at the same time are interventions into those political practices that have abandoned the old figure of the opposition and separation of politics and aesthetics.' Such art activism would merge politics and aesthetics in the production of militant affects.

One further way of approaching the politics of our *and* would be to explore and extend Deleuze and Guattari's own writings on art and aesthetics into the realm of Contemporary art. This would be to expand upon Deleuze's interest in, and one might say insistence on, colour as the medium of aesthetic signs-forces. This approach, while affirming the necessity of Contemporary art introducing radical alterity into the machines of subjective production, seeks these breaks within the exist-ing traditions of art, in sensations which already experiment with an intimate inhuman 'outside'. Stephen Zepke, for example, explores the work of Anita Fricek as a 'critical' practice in Nietzsche's sense, one that uses painting to 're-value' the institutionalised forces-sensations circu-lating in the 'semio-economy'. This, Zepke argues, 'extends Deleuze's rejection of Kant's transcendental conditions of possible experience to Greenberg's account of modernist abstraction, and develops a painted sensation whose real conditions (qua individuation) go beyond the "aes-thetic", to become directly "political". . . . This would be to "paint with a hammer", to engage with (institutional) forces such that their value is *created* by a critical evaluation. Here we enter into the realm of a *critical* sensation, one in which it attains value as *high* or *low, noble* or *base*.' Fricek's paintings, as she puts it, 're-boot' our institutional conditions.

The Aesthetic Paradigm

Indeed we might well wonder whether the disappearance of 'art' into 'life' is something Deleuze and Guattari themselves would advo-cate, given the fact that their texts are full of references to painters, writers, musicians and filmmakers who lie squarely within the Western canon. As we have already suggested, the lack of direct references to contemporary art practices, the rigorous distinction of philosophy's concept from art's sensation, and their rejection of Conceptual Art in *What is Philosophy?* already makes Deleuze and Guattari's uptake by Contemporary art something that could seem rather in excess of their own intentions. The 'concept' is now clearly one of Contemporary art's tools, and in fact art today cannot claim to be 'contemporary' without some sort of theoretical reference, be it explicit or implicit. Deleuze and Guattari's insistence on sensation as art's ontological realm of opera-tion therefore seems to us one of the fundamental 'problems' that their conjunction with Contemporary art raises. Nevertheless there does seem to be some room to move offered by Guattari's comment in a 1992 interview that 'conceptual art produces the most deterritorialised sensa-tions it is possible to create . . . In the place of working with painting, with colours, with sounds, it works with a material that is the concept. But it's not a concept made for creating concepts, it's a concept that creates sensations' (Guattari 1994: 53). Following this line of thought, which is also clearly applicable to the way a 'concept' operates through the 'affect industry', we could argue that Contemporary art consti-tutes a new 'expanded field' that utilises and critiques the sensations produced by cognitive 'immaterial labour'. Maurizio Lazzarato, arguing precisely this point, sees such an expanded field as offering new political opportunities to launch an 'immanent critique' of contemporary capital, inasmuch as the aesthetic composition of material and immaterial production is the ground shared by art and politics. Contemporary art in this sense, Lazzarato argues, 'does not signify the disappearance of hand-work or physical labour, but the constitution of another assemblage in which manual labour and intellectual labour, "material" labour and "immaterial" labour are caught up in a "machinic" process, which can be found not only in the "actions" of the broader "public," but also in artistic institutions, the state, business, local collectives, criticism and the media'. The 'event' of this invention was, Lazzarato argues, Duchamp's readymade, which was the moment the art object dissolved into the 'creative act'. In these machinic processes 'where neither time nor space reigns', it is possible to both 'problematise and experiment with the modes of constitution of the work of art (and the artist) and with the commodity (and the labourer) by examining the forces, principles and *dispositifs* which institute and consolidate them as values'. Contemporary art's use of the strategy of the readymade is a red thread leading away from 'art' and into Capital's unconscious.

Many of the essays in the volume attempt to assess the achievements and potentials of Contemporary art within this 'expanded field' of the 'aesthetic paradigm'. Jussi Parikka, for example, looks specifically at the new information machines increasingly running our lives, attending to the question of coding within recent software art. He argues that such work turns away from dominant signifying regimes and restricted economies on two fronts. First, 'software is not (solely) visual and representational, but works through a logic of translation' and 'what is translated (or transposed) is not content, but intensities, information that individuates and in-forms agency'. Second, 'software art is often not even recognized as "art" but is defined more by the difficulty of pinning it down as a social and cultural practice'. Here the invisible and viral nature of code exemplifies the new aesthetic paradigm where, as Parrika points out, a politics of practice can only operate through 'experimentation geared towards the unexpected, the imperceptible'.

Johnny Golding, in perhaps the most philosophically orientated essay of our collection, maps out this new aesthetic realm in relation to philosophy. Here, Hegel, but also Heidegger (and others) are utilised as perhaps unexpected resources in reconstructing a non-dialectical and complex Deleuzian aesthetics, one in which the contemporary – the 'right "here" and right "now"' – is at stake. As Golding points out, Deleuze and

Guattari thus 'present a peculiar – but utterly profound – reconditioning of "the becoming-x", of philosophy itself' in 'the algorithmic encodings of the zeros and ones, torn from the usual binaric either/or casings, and cast instead as, on the one hand, the rhizomatic bodies without organs, and, on the other, the refrain'. Golding calls this 'fractal philosophy', or, following Deleuze, simply 'the task of art': an 'algorithmic hearing, a learning how to "take note"'. Beyond the tracking through of different philosophical positions, Golding's implicit argument is for a certain kind of practice – a 'media-arts-philosophy' – that is equal, yet resistant, to the contemporary times we inhabit.

Scenes and Encounters

Many contemporary artists and art theorists use *all* of Deleuze's writings – whether on art or not – in confronting the new materials and logics of contemporary practice beyond painting. Deleuze and Guattari's writings call forth this kind of pragmatic construction, and, as such, they might well be understood as *the* artist's philosophers. Certainly their conceptual invention, coupled with an affirmative and affective intensity, especially in the *Capitalism and Schizophrenia* project, makes Deleuze and Guattari an attractive 'resource' for those working in the field of Contemporary art. An example is David Burrow's imaginative use of Deleuze's *Foucault* to explore the seeable and the sayable of the art world's 'logic of scenes'. Burrows argues that art scenes in general, and more specifically recent London art scenes, should be understood as diagrammatic, as '*movements* producing mutant statements and a basis for a praxis of art and life'. For Burrows, a scene is defined less by its size (indeed, an individual might be a scene) than by the 'durational quality' of its 'affective and intensive encounters', which testify to a non-dialectical avant-garde that remains the creative motor of art production.

Robert Garnett attends to an even more particular moment in the London of the early 1990s, when he identifies 'the kind of virtual–actual "buzz" or "vibe", that "something in the air-ness", which is constitutive of the energetic intensity of a "scene" in its becoming'. Garnett uses Deleuze's work on humour to contrast this emergence to the more ironic practices that still dominate much of the art world today. Here Contemporary art's logic is seen to be that of the joke; a disruptive affect rather than an ironic commentary. Simon O'Sullivan's point of departure is a particular Contemporary art practice in which he identifies a new attitude, no longer the 'critique of originality and authenticity' that dominated 'postmodernism' (and led, as Guattari acerbically notes, to the 'prostitution' of art 'to the values of the most retrograde neo-liberalism' [Guattari 1996: 110]), but a repetition of 'the modern impulse', which O'Sullivan characterises as 'the desire for, and production of, the new'. Following Deleuze, O'Sullivan identifies a logic of 'future-orientation' within Contemporary art that runs counter to the postmodern 'linguistic turn'. As he suggests: 'the operating field of these practices is the future', the artists here operate 'as kind of prophets, and specifically *traitor* prophets (traitors to a given affective/signifying regime). Traitor prophets offering up traitor objects perhaps?'

O'Sullivan is not alone in drawing a line between postmodern allegorical practices and art discourses and more contemporary practices that have moved beyond the critique of representation. Edgar Schmitz's essay constructs a Deleuzian logic of the trap around the sculptures of Andreas Slominski, exemplifying the desire to explore art's abstract machines without thinking about signification. Slominski's work captures an 'ambient' mode of and for Contemporary art in which, as Schmitz remarks, 'encounters with the object occur under unclear terms because any possible critical distance makes way for an involvement for which form is simply permeable: traps include smoothing out transitions, blurring the edges of different realms to such an extent that it becomes a near-impossibility to designate an inside and an outside in relation to them'. Here Schmitz begins to rethink art's operating logics using (as does Garnett) Deleuze's *Logic of Sense* to suggest an art of surfaces and of non-discursive surface humour.

Technologies

It is well known that Guattari and Deleuze were fascinated by machines. Their work constantly invokes a technological 'plane of immanence' composing the organic and inorganic, material and immaterial, and actual and virtual realms of our 'operating system'. In their processual complexity these machines have a particular relation to aesthetic procedures inasmuch as they construct, and are constructed by, sensations. 'The machine is the affective state', Deleuze and Guattari argue, 'and it is false to say that modern machines possess a perceptive capacity or a memory; machines themselves possess only affective states' (Deleuze and Guattari 1995: 128). Artistic machines explode in the middle of our contemporary 'Mechanosphere', they are creative lines of flight emerging from capitalism's schizo-unconscious. In this way Deleuze and Guattari's work not only clearly describes our contemporary cybernetic reality, but also offers ethical and aesthetic mechanisms that might influence the ongoing production of our collective subjectivities. As they write: 'All these machines are already there; we are continually producing them, manufacturing them, setting them in motion, for they are desire, desire just as it is – although it takes artists to bring about their *autonomous* presentation' (Deleuze and Guattari 1995: 137, italics added). Some of our contributors specifically address this technology of desire, and its artistic operation within the 'aesthetic paradigm'. Claudia Mongini's essay on the composer Anestis Logothetis offers a precise mapping of a musical machine, drawing not only on Deleuze's work but also on Gilbert Simondon. Mongini explores Logothetis' compositional technique and experimental form of musical notation as an 'aesthetic and implicitly ethico-political engagement, [which] consists in the creation of *dividual* refrains: complex human and nonhuman assemblages defined not by the sum of the people, signs or devices involved, but by the simultaneous and successive interplay of affective forces able to individuate and form a *transient* multiplicity'. Artistic compositions such as Logothetis' are, Mongini argues, cybernetic and improvisational 'scores' for collective experimentation. In such 'machines', as Guattari says, subjectivity remains 'really alive', overflowing the form of the subject in an emergent process of subjectivation.

Taking the concept of the machine and of the artist in a quite different sense, Elisabeth von Samsonow offers us the figure of 'becoming-girl' as a post-Freudian feminist 'anti-Elektra'. She convincingly argues that the girl 'is in possession of a logos of creation' because she controls the means of production of the human itself, 'whether we discuss the imaginary of birth or the potency of artistic production'. The girl in this sense utilises a unique schizo-technology composed of what von Samsonow calls 'Daedalian objects'; 'sculptural things with the quality of living machines'. Of particular interest here are the girl's 'gadgets', her mobile phone, laptop and other devices that express and construct (in von Samsonow's vocabulary they 'give birth to') a *schizosomatic quadrant of pre-oedipality*. 'Being online' is the 'production logos of the girl', von Samsonow suggests, and this is 'in exact accordance to the ideal of contemporary art'.

Barbara Bolt offers us a different slant on the question of technology and art production. Bolt is a painter, or perhaps better, she is part of a 'painting-machine', one in which, as Deleuze and Guattari say, 'the mechanic is the most deterritorialized part' (Deleuze and Guattari 1995: 135). In this sense Bolt describes her own practice as a 'materialist philosophy of painting [that] no longer places the artist at the centre, as the one who displays technical mastery in the handling of the material means, but gives material a privileged position'. Through this materiality of colour and its medium, she argues, 'art is able to wrest the percept from the perception and the affect from affection'. The fluid fields of liquid colour infusing her paintings are only the end points of her practice, which for Bolt is an inorganic athleticism, a 'performance' composing a 'complex assemblage' of forces that ultimately produces something 'true to life' beyond representation.

Finally, in perhaps the most experimental take on the conjunction of our collection, the artists Neil Chapman and Ola Stahl offer us a poetic fiction that dramatises a number of Deleuzian concepts, 'lived' by their cast of invented *conceptual personae*. Chapman and Stahl's work brings together art *and* philosophy, sensation and the concept, in a pragmatic experiment calling forth a new earth, and a new people. No other essay in this collection captures so well the unnerving and untimely but also abstract beauty of truly transversal production. In this way Chapman and Stahl foreground the *heterogenesis* of the world, and the necessity of actively constructing it. They offer us a schizo-art for a schizo people, a poetic-delirious disjunctive-conjunction: a 'BLOODCRYSTALPOLLENSTAR' in which our *and* finally becomes a 'mutating centre'.

References

Bourriaud, N. (2002), *Relational Aesthetics*, ed. C. Schneider, trans. J. Herman, New York: Lukas and Steinberg.
Deleuze, G. (1994), *Difference and Repetition*, trans. P. Patton, New York: Columbia University Press.
Deleuze, G. (2006), 'The Brain is the Screen', in *Two Regimes of Madness: Texts and Interviews 1975–1995*, ed. D. Lapoujade, trans. A. Hodges and M. Taormina, New York: Semiotext(e).
Deleuze, G. and F. Guattari (1988), *A Thousand Plateaus*, trans. B. Massumi, London: Athlone Press.
Deleuze, G. and F. Guattari (1994), *What is Philosophy?*, trans. H. Tomlinson and G. Burchell, London: Verso.
Deleuze, G. and F. Guattari (1995), 'Balance-Sheet Program for Desiring Machines', in Félix Guattari, *Chaosophy*, ed. S. Lotringer, trans. R. Hurley, New York: Semiotext(e).
Guattari, F. (1994), 'Félix Guattari et l'art contemporain', in *Chiméres*, 23 (Summer).
Guattari, F. (1995), *Chaosmosis: An Ethico-Aesthetic Paradigm*, trans. P. Bains and J. Pefanis, Sydney: Power Publications.
Guattari, F. (1996), *The Guattari Reader*, ed. G. Genosko, Oxford: Blackwell.
Nietzsche, F. (1967), *The Will to Power*, ed. W. Kaufmann, trans. W. Kaufmann and R. J. Hollingdale, New York: Random House.

Note

1. The exceptions being the painter Gerald Fromanger, about whom Deleuze, Guattari (and Foucault) wrote essays, the performance artist Jean-Jacques Lebel, the artist Yagoi Kasuma and the photographer Keiichi Tahara, about whom Guattari wrote.

POLITICS

Chapter 1

The Politics of the Scream in a Threnody

Gustavo Chirolla Ospina

> We do not feel ourselves outside of our time but continue to undergo shameful compromises with it. This feeling of shame is one of philosophy's more powerful motifs. We are not responsible for the victims but responsible before them.
> Gilles Deleuze and Félix Guattari, *What is Philosophy?*

Deleuze is interested in the scream.[1] He asks about the importance of the scream when he thinks about Francis Bacon's painting. How to paint the scream? It is about making visible, not just a particular sound, but those invisible forces that make it come about. The same problem arises with music, it is Alban Berg who knew how to 'make music out of the scream' and he put the sonority of the scream in a relationship with the sound-less forces of the Earth, as with Marie's scream in *Wozzeck* and with the soundless forces of Heaven in *Lulu* (Deleuze 2002: 60). In cinema, Straub and Huillet value the scream; it becomes both a speech act and an act of resistance (Deleuze 1987: 289). Which movement of art will make the scream an act of resistance, and take us from the aesthetics to the politics of the scream?

This text will revolve around Colombian artist Clemencia Echeverri's work *Treno*. From the Greek *threnos*, meaning lament, and *oide*, meaning song, *Treno* is, quite precisely, a funeral song, an audiovisual threnody. This funeral song ends with a scream, what Deleuze calls a 'cry against death' (Deleuze 2002: 61). It is not about picking an artwork as a paradigmatic example in order to think the relationship between Deleuze and contemporary art, so that we can comfort ourselves with the application of a number of his concepts to the interpretation of such work. Rather, the selection of *Treno* for this essay responds to a series of questions this work raises from its very specific way of thinking, and that provokes our own thought in turn. These questions relate to the political realm, and particularly to the notion of the people. The question of the scream will be my guide in this investigation.

Deleuze has pointed out that both philosophy and art are related to the people. In *What is Philosophy?* he writes with Guattari:

> The artist or the philosopher is quite incapable of creating a people, each can only summon it with all his strength. A people can only be created by abominable sufferings, and it cannot be concerned any more with art or philosophy. But books of philosophy and works of art contain their sum of unimaginable sufferings that forewarn of the advent of a people. They have resistance in common – their resistance to death, to servitude, to the intolerable, to shame, and to the present. (Deleuze and Guattari 1994: 110)

Deleuze won't stop saying that artists like Mallarmé, Kafka or Klee – rather than more populist ones – insist that art needs a people but, nevertheless, that the people is what is missing. As a result, there is nothing they can do but summon it with all their strength, summon a people that do not yet exist, a people to come. This will be my subject then, the specific relationship between art and politics, a relationship with the people that is missing, the one that is to come. Maybe there we will also be able to find keys to think about how that relationship exists with regard to philosophy.

What does it mean to think about this subject from a concrete geographical and historical situation? For reasons that I will come to, this situation may be described as a thanatopolitics.[2] Let's stress for the moment that, as Deleuze and Guattari say, 'A people can only be created by abominable sufferings.' It is precisely these kinds of situations that lead us to write about thanatopolitics and the funeral song, the audiovisual threnody by Clemencia Echeverri. Yes, it is a lament! But let's remain calm; if there is something we have learned from Deleuze's aesthetics it is, as he says, that 'Any work of art points a way through for life, finds a way through the cracks' (Deleuze 1995: 143).

A Shame at Being Human

Before continuing our commentary on the politics of the scream in Echeverri's installation, let us recognise that there are philosophical screams also. 'Shame! Shame!' is what we seem to hear everywhere in Deleuze's late works. In an interview with Antonio Negri, referring to *A Thousand Plateaus*, after listing a number of problems that, in his view, the book's 'amazing will to theorise' seems to leave open, the Italian philosopher notes: 'I seem sometimes to hear a tragic note, at points where

1.1: Clemencia Echeverri, *Treno*. Multiscreen projection in the *Actos del Habla* exhibition, Art Museum of the National University, Bogota, Colombia, 2009. Image courtesy of the artist.

it's not so clear where the "war machine" is going'. Deleuze answers: 'You say there is a certain tragic or melancholic tone in all this. I think I can see why. I was very struck by all the passages in Primo Levi where he explains that Nazi camps have given us "a shame at being human"' (Deleuze 1995: 171–2).

Let's leave the subject of the war machine aside, as this may distract us, although in his answer Deleuze says that 'artistic movements are war machines in this sense' (Deleuze 1995: 172). Levi's expression, 'A shame at being human', is taken beyond the fields of extermination by Deleuze, for we experience this feeling in 'utterly trivial situations, too: in the face of too great a vulgarization of thinking,' because what shames us in today's capitalism is that 'we've no sure way of maintaining becomings, or still more of arousing them, even within ourselves' (173). In *What is Philosophy?*, at the end of the fourth chapter, the reference to Primo Levi is repeated and the tragic tone becomes more evident. Geophilosophy is the relationship of philosophy to the present because, they say: 'We don't lack communication, we have too much, we lack creation. *We lack resistance to the present*' (Deleuze and Guattari 1994: 108). 'A shame at being human' becomes a leitmotiv; shame in the face of all the circumstances that haunt the existence of today's democracies, shame in the face of the 'ignominy of the possibilities of life that we are offered' (107–8). In accordance with such a tragic fate, Deleuze and Guattari heroically declare: 'This feeling of shame is one of philosophy's most powerful motifs' (108). Evidently, in order to resist this present what we need is creation, both the creation of concepts and the creation of beings of sensation: 'Art and philosophy converge at this point: the constitution of an earth and a people that are lacking as the correlate of creation' (108).

May '68 is behind us,[3] and between *Anti-Oedipus* in 1972 and *A Thousand Plateaus* in 1980, eight years have past. The interview with Negri and the publication of *What is Philosophy?* take place in the early '90s, and there are no reasons for thinking that the tragic tone is strange or new: 'We are in a weak phase, a period of reaction' (Deleuze 1995: 121). There is, then, a very close link between 'a shame at being human' and the people that is missing, and all that surrounded by a tragic atmosphere, even a melancholic one. The spirit of the times is polluted by reaction, and we live in a conservative age. 'And there is no way to escape the ignoble but to play the part of an animal (to grow, burrow, snigger, distort ourselves): thought itself is sometimes closer to an animal that dies than to a living, even democratic, human being' (Deleuze and Guattari 1994: 108).

Deleuze's reading of Primo Levi goes beyond any humanist commitment, because shame is what leads us to interrogate our own present, and is not the result of an injustice that reveals, in a negative way, an aspiration to an ideal of the human. If that were the case Deleuze would be an undercover humanist, just a critic of the human as a value that remains a prisoner of a certain faith in humankind, a melancholic humanist. But that melancholy is precisely the situation of humanity today, that which man has become, from the most extreme to the most insignificant, so that which makes any humanism possible is the possibility of a distinction between the human and the nonhuman, as Agamben would say, being eliminated. Deleuze's vitalism actually moves away from that melancholy.

Deleuze's philosophy is evidently anti-humanist; it contains a rejection of any moral or political doctrine centred on human nature, and on the human in itself as a value. It is not surprising that, since *Kafka: Toward a Minor Literature*, written in 1975 with Guattari, Deleuze will insist on the nonhuman becomings of humans and especially on the concept of animal-becoming, as a way of facing and displacing the ancient ontological question that has been the cornerstone of every humanism, the relationship between the human and the animal. This anti-humanism is finally stated with a lapidary formula in *What is Philosophy?*: It is the brain that thinks and not man – the latter being only a cerebral crystallisation of the former (Deleuze and Guattari 1994: 210). In a similar way we find there an aesthetics that goes against every humanist theory of art; works of art are not conceived as the highest expression of human spirit. When Deleuze and Guattari claim that art as a form of thinking is the creation of beings of sensation, affects and percepts, they define these terms in an anti-humanist way; affects are precisely these nonhuman becomings of man, just as percepts – including the town – are nonhuman landscapes of nature (169).

The Scream and the Horror

Francis Bacon meant to paint the scream rather than the horror. For Deleuze it is necessary to distinguish between these two kinds of violence: that of the spectacle, which belongs to horror and the order of figuration; and that of sensation, which belongs to the scream and to the realm of the figural, where the figure has abandoned both narration and representation. Choosing the scream and not horror Bacon remains faithful to modern art's motto as stated by Paul Klee: 'not to reproduce the visible but to make visible'. With the scream the invisible

1.2: Clemencia Echeverri, *Treno*. Two-screen projection, Alonso Garces Gallery exhibition, Bogota, Colombia, 2007. Image courtesy of the artist.

forces that produce it become visible, forces of darkness become visible through the convulsion they produce in the body, forces of death that make us falter. That visibility takes place 'when, like a wrestler, the visible body confronts the powers of the invisible' (Deleuze 2002: 62). Then, the forces of life become visible, the forces of the body that resist death: 'life screams at death'. The scream concentrates all those forces into one action, an action that is the sign of the struggle. Deleuze calls these affirmative forces that are liberated in the combat the powers of the future (61). All the violence in contemporary art moves between the scream and the horror, between the being of sensation and the sensationalist show; however, the violence of the latter is found more often than that of the former.

Let us turn to the work of Clemencia Echeverri. *Treno* is an audiovisual installation in which two very large projection screens facing each other fill the whole exhibition space. Here we experience, as the title states, a threnody: a funeral song for the victims of a political catastrophe. As in Krystof Penderecki's *Threnody for the Victims of Hiroshima*, the victims are the reason of the song. In this case, the lament is audiovisual; the space between the screens becomes filled with images and sounds, silences and shadows. We see the image of a river, its current grows on one of the screens until it is filled, then the current fills the opposite screen until an alternation of flows is created and repeats itself at variable intervals; we hear the sound of the current, along with frogs and crickets, which increases and decreases as it runs through the gallery space. At a given moment voices are heard, voices that call out names, names of people, screams that are carried by the current of the river across the exhibition space. These names are calls from one side of the river (not necessarily to someone on the other side), voices that cry out to summon an other (perhaps, the absent one); finally we see the river tainted red, and as the only answer to the previous calls we see a few clothes, appearing like ghosts, being taken out of the river, spectres of a suffering people. The place of the spectator in *Treno* is paradoxical, both on one and on the opposite side of the river, while also being in the middle of the current, amongst the flowing waters. It is there where the spectator is reached by the calling voices; the scream itself reaches the dimension of a song as it circles the space. The peasants use the strategy of calling out a name, like a *Sprechgesang*, to communicate across long distances, and in this way they establish a bridge of sound between one shore of the river and the other. In Echeverri's installation, the spoken/sung words become a lament that finds no answer on the opposite shore, the bridge is broken and the tumultuous river drowns out the calling voices.

Even as a funeral song, it is a mistake to try to interpret this work as a representation of mourning, or as a symbol of a given form of violence and the way it is suffered by a person or people; as if the propitiatory experience of art extended a bridge between the representation of a conflict and the abominable suffering it causes, between understanding and feeling. In both cases we would get nothing but a dramatisation and an aestheticisation of the victim. This work is born out of the impotence, the unbridgeable abyss, experienced in the face of the event of violence, and of a singular form of violence: forced disappearance. 'I don't know what are we going to do, madam. They took my son away', the artist remembers a phone call, a female voice coming from the shore of the Cauca River that, according to her own words, made evident 'a clamour and a search without an answer'. The impossibility of speaking on behalf of the victim imposes itself on the artist with all its strength; we can no longer confer such declaratory power on art, on the contrary, artistic practice has to be confronted with the very impossibility of testimony. We'll return to this.

As we have seen, there is yet another side to the problem of representation: the sensational. How to avoid the spectacle of violence? How to escape the mediatic clichés of violence and its representations? I think *Treno* stays on Bacon's line, but it gives a collective and political character to the scream that is not evident in the work of the Irish painter. In her audiovisual installation the Colombian artist places the spectator between the two large projections of the river, with no need to use images of horror or extreme cruelty. As the stream of the river grows, she manages to produce a drowning sensation in the viewer who is placed in the middle of the scene. Only at the end, and as a hint, do we find the traces – clothes – of a thanatopolitics, carried by the river. The point is not to avoid such representations on moral grounds but to produce something else, leaving the sensational and the spectacle of death aside. *Treno* is the scream, the cry, without the horror.

What we need now is to find the way in which the scream becomes collective, political. Let us remember that in order to state the political character of the human being, Aristotle, in his *Politics*, drew a distinction between voice (*phone*) and speech (*logos*). By means of the voice animals and humans are able to express a sensation of pleasure or pain; with *logos*, which belongs only to humans, they can express what is right and what is wrong, the just and the unjust. For Aristotle the very nature of politics lies in being able to establish the measure of justice by means of the word. *Treno* is a lament, a funeral song in which every word has become a scream, and, precisely, the whole exercise of art in this case consists in turning the voice (*phone*) into a political expression. This is the politics of those voices that have been deprived of *logos*.

On the one hand the scream implies a corporal dimension, as we have pointed out, a combat between the forces of the body and those of death. On the other there is an implication in the order of enunciation, the calling and laments as speech acts. The scream begins in the field of mixed bodies, amongst their actions and passions, but then becomes a clamour in the field of enunciation. We may say that it is about these two aspects of the very same assemblage that are irreducible to each other, the visible and the enunciable (Deleuze 1988: 70–93), the machinic assemblage of bodies and the collective assemblage of enunciation (Deleuze and Guattari 2004: 97–8). Let us remember that for Deleuze and Guattari enunciation is neither informational nor communicative. Here the physical scream increases its illocutionary power as a call, as a collective clamour, and therefore it constitutes an especially political assemblage. As a result, we no longer remain inside the Aristotelian orbit, because the scream is an assemblage of bodies and the clamour has a linguistic nature; instead the scream intrudes into the word, it invades the speech act with an intensive power. The scream is not political because it is discursive, but because it is the signature of the body, it is a speech act signed by the depths of the body.

In *Treno* several voices follow each other in the same stream of sound, two masculine voices call for Nazareno and Orfilia, one feminine voice calls for Victor. Each one of these particular voices, begging for a proper name, becomes a clamour against death, a simultaneous scream of suffering and resistance, of mourning and demand. In each voice multiple voices resound, each scream is a collective assemblage of enunciation. In the whole work of Straub and Huillet, Deleuze says, the scream has been revalued precisely as speech act, as a speech act that is also an act of resistance (Deleuze 2006a: 323). Let us resume the path that leads us from how to make the scream to how to make the politics of the scream. First we have the question of making the scream, both in music and painting, but also for cinema and video-installation; the point is to try to make the forces that produce the scream perceptible in each realm. Second we run in to a scream that concentrates a relationship of forces in itself, forces of life that resist death; there the point is to make perceptible the forces that collide in this uncertain combat. Finally this scream against death and no other becomes a speech act that is an act of resistance.

The Visible and the Enunciable

Deleuze shows how Carmelo Bene makes a statement go through a continuum of variations. 'You make me feel terror. . .' The scream by Lady Anne in Bene's *Richard III* goes through a number of variations and through a variety of speech acts that make it 'grow into a woman of war, come back as a child, reborn as a maiden'. It is a kind of *Sprechgesang*. Different to the song in which one tries to keep a constant tone (*tessitura*), 'in *Sprechgesang* we keep suppressing it with a fall or a rise' (Deleuze 1979: 105). Carmelo Bene overloads the script of *Richard III* with indications that diminish the importance of the content, a set of precise operations are effectuated in relation to the variables that the statement goes through, making it, Deleuze says, 'just like a musical script'. Words don't form a text anymore, the theatre-man stops being an actor or director to become an operator in an experimentation-theatre (89).

Clemencia Echeverri dispossesses the words of the song from their alleged communicative function. In principle it may proceed according to that function, as the voice climbs above the waters waiting for an answer, but as communication fails, the call mutates into a lament that resounds throughout the room. The lament is a kind of *Sprechgesang* incorporating each and every one of the voices. However it is the whole work, the consolidation of all its heterogeneous elements, not only the voices, which properly constitutes the lament, as the audiovisual assemblage of a scream. In this sense the audio-video installation establishes a relationship between the linguistic and non-linguistic elements.

In order to speak about the visible and the enunciable Deleuze and Guattari borrow terms from Hjelmslev when they speak about the form of content and the form of expression. As they use them, these belong to certain aspects of the machinic assemblage of bodies and the collective assemblage of enunciation. Let us stop for a moment on the plane of content. It is important to be precise, as Deleuze is regarding Foucault, about the meaning of the visible, which does not designate simply what we see or what we generally perceive. 'Visibilities are not forms of objects, nor even forms that would show up under light, but rather forms of luminosity which are created by the light itself and allow a thing or object to exist only as a flash, sparkle or shimmer' (Deleuze 1988: 52). According to this interpretation the visible that belongs to artistic practices does not consist in reproducing what we see, but in the form in which the invisible forces become visible, in the form of visibility in which such forces subsist as a flash, sparkle or shimmer. From a more general perspective, that of the percept, we may say that under one form of the content non-perceptible forces become perceptible. This form of the content is comprised of both luminosities and sonorities, visual and sound images, making up, finally, a compound of sensations.

Have we introduced an ambiguity? How can we talk about form in this context if the task of art resides in making visible, from each domain, non-perceptible forces? The relationship that is established is no longer that of matter and form, but that of material–forces. The answer to this objection is that in the latter relationship form does not disappear; instead it is the result of the material–forces relationship, which is more direct and profound. In *The Fold* Deleuze explains that form in the baroque is not a mould but the emergence that is produced through a process of modulation or permanent moulding. 'Baroque is informal art par excellence . . . but informal is not a negation of the form' (Deleuze 1993: 35, translation modified). Something similar happens in modern baroque artists from Klee to Dubuffet. The infinite fold affects all matters and makes the Form appear, so that: 'In the baroque the coupling of material–force is what replaces matter and form' (35). On the other hand, according to the use that Deleuze and Guattari make of Hjelmslev, in addition to formed matter there is a non-formed matter of the content and a non-formed matter of expression. We find this articulation in art in what Deleuze and Guattari call 'a passage from the finite to the infinite, but also from territory to deterritorialization' (Deleuze and Guattari 1994: 180–1). The form of content or expression obeys an 'interlocking of differently oriented frames . . . The frames and their joins hold the compounds of sensations, hold up figures, and intermingle with their upholding, with their own appearance' (187). But beside the system of frames a kind of deframing operates, where some lines of flight traverse the territory and open it to the infinite, allowing flows of non-formed matter to follow a line of absolute deterritorialisation. The coupling material–forces passes from the finite to the infinite, from the form of content or of expression, from compounded material or consolidation of heterogeneous elements, to the abstract plane of composition, a diagram of non-formed matter.

We have discussed the scream as a collective assemblage of enunciation in *Treno*, and we must now turn to the form of the content to discuss the machinic assemblage of bodies. Echeverri's installation presents a whole compound of visual and sound sensations, to install means here to operate with the heterogeneous components of a material, and to experiment through very precise operations. First: the spectator is placed, as we have pointed out, between two large projection screens where the same sequence of images of a river are projected at different intervals of time; the current grows on one side as it decreases on the other, the sound of the current also becomes louder and diminishes as it circles the space. Being a compound of light and sound we may characterise it as vibration, a simple sensation 'that implies a constitutive difference of level' whose intensity rises and falls (Deleuze and Guattari 1994: 168). Second: a body-to-body tension (a clinch) operates between the intensities – vibrations – of the voices and the sound and visual forces of the turbulence of the river, 'when two sensations resonate in each other by embracing each other so tightly in a clinch of what are no more than energies' (168). Third: through the play of lights and shadows, cried rumours, noises and silence, a space-time is created; a space populated with voices. Fourteen minutes of the coexistence of multiple durations, from the discontinuous intervals in which images succeed each other to the variations and nuances of the colour of the changing surface of the river. By these means a sensation is produced in the spectator, a bizarre feeling of drowning in the middle of the scene she is participating in, bizarre because 'sensation refers only to its material' (166). This is an audiovisual drowning, the violence of the compound of sensations and not of the spectacle.

When Deleuze, also in *Foucault*, explains the way in which discursive practices and non-discursive practices, the visible and the enunciable, the form of content and of expression, are interwoven, he claims that even in a relationship of knowledge where the privilege of the enunciable over the visible is essential, such privilege never implies a reduction (Deleuze 1988: 49). The experimental operations we have pointed out show that this is even more evident in the realm of art. On the one hand there is an intensive use of language, and on the other, there is no need to privilege the enunciable over the visible. It is not certain, however, that this is true for every type of contemporary practice. Stephen Zepke shows the existence of at least two lines of development that evolve from the *readymade*; either a conceptual development that privileges the enunciable over the visible and the discursive over the sensible, or a development outlined by Guattari's '*aesthetic paradigm*' where the readymade as a being of sensation is animated by the forces of life. This second line of development, in which any privilege of the conceptual-discursive implies the 'despotism of the signifier' and the inclusion of a *transcendent* dimension, is presented as a politics of resistance. From

1.3: Clemencia Echeverri, *Treno*. Photograph of the Cauca River. 0.90 × 0.69 m. 2008. Image courtesy of the artist.

this point of view Zepke sees certain avant-garde movements, such as the work of Brazilian artist Hélio Oiticica, as using the *readymade* as a mechanism of 'sensorial-corporeal participation'. Oiticica attributes to this expressive mechanism the power to contribute to the creation of a people (Zepke 2008: 33–9).

If we want to escape both the 'despotism of the signifier' and the generalised consensus it enforces, it is necessary to understand that in artistic practices there is a functional independence between the form of the content and the form of the expression, between the visible and the enunciable. There is also a constant movement that goes from one to the other, because of resonance, juxtaposition or disjunction. Deleuze and Guattari named this relationship of mutual affect that nevertheless conserves the terms' irreducible nature, *reciprocal presupposition* (Deleuze and Guattari 2004: 87). In the work of Straub and Huillet, for example, there is a disjunction between seeing and speaking, a voice speaks about something while we see something different, 'the voice rises, it rises, it rises and what it is talking about passes under the naked, deserted ground that the visual image was showing us, a visual image that had nothing to do with the sound image' (Deleuze 2006a: 323).

The artistic task of making enunciable the non-enunciable is what Deleuze and Guattari call *fabulation*. Fabulation owes nothing to a memory; instead it refers to a complex material made up of words and sounds (Deleuze and Guattari 1994: 171). It has no other object than to work on language from inside, to work on its very phonological, syntactic and semantic components to produce a permanent variation. Examples of this appear all through Deleuze's work, and include Kafka, Beckett, Gherasim Luca, Jean-Luc Godard, Pasolini, Bene, etc. Fabulation can be summed up in the formula: 'to make language stutter', which must not be confused with stuttering as a speech impediment. On other occasions the formula refers to Marcel Proust: 'to speak one's own tongue as a foreigner'. To stutter, or to speak as a foreigner, consists in putting language into continuous variation. On the other hand, *fabulation is the creator of giants*. For Bergson, from whom the notion comes, it corresponds to a visionary power different from imagination that is in charge of 'creating semi-personal forces or efficacious presences' (Deleuze 1979: 173). We need, says Deleuze, to recuperate this notion and invest it with a 'political content'. In this way, his proposal continues, the idea of utopia should be substituted with that 'of a "fabulation" in which a people and art both share' (Deleuze 1995: 174). The non-enunciable that comes to be enunciated is precisely that excessive and gigantic power that carries abominable sufferings along with it, but at the same time these are 'efficacious presences' that confront the cause of those sufferings. Suffering therefore gives rise to a struggle against death that becomes a political enunciation shared by art and the people.

Let's return to the subject of the people that is missing to art to see how it connects with fabulation. 'We are not referring to popular or populist artists', Deleuze and Guattari write, 'Mallarmé said that the Book needed a people. Kafka said that literature is the affair of the people. Klee said that the people is essential yet lacking' (Deleuze and Guattari 2004: 381). The question of the relation of modern art to the people has changed, the artist has ceased to address or invoke the people as a 'constituted force'. This is still the case for contemporary art, unless the invocation of the people is considered to be the reproduction of a consensus. If art does not stop summoning a people that is lacking it is because it is addressing a people that does not yet exist, a possible people or a people to come. How is this lack of the people connected to the fabulation that we say is common to both art and the people itself? First, if the people are not a constituted force neither is art capable of creating a people, for 'a people can only be created by abominable sufferings'. Second, when art appeals to a people that is lacking it does not mean that they do not exist, rather that they do not exist yet, that they are in the process of becoming. Third, fabulation is common to both the people and art because they have suffering and resistance in common. As a result, there is creative fabulation when the non-enunciable becomes enunciated, when suffering and resistance to ignominy become a political enunciation; a politics of life against death.

Let us go back to *Treno* now, and consider it from the point of view of the reciprocal presupposition between the plane of content and the form of expression. In the work the scream appears in both planes, passing from one to the other, because the scream is both a relation of forces and a speech act at the same time. To scream means to make perceptible what is not perceptible and to make enunciable what is not enunciable in a lament, a threnody. The visual and sound sensations are composed in the form of content, and create the installation's audiovisual space-time. What remains to be explained is how the relationship between visible and enunciable operates in this work. We see a river, we see its current growing, we hear voices soaring, soaring above the waters. . . A movement takes place; it goes from the deterritorialisation of the scream as a call or signifier, to its reterritorialisation as a lament. What imperative does this movement obey? What does this clamour now produce? Through a transformation of the speech act into a scream/lament non-enunciable forces become sound, forces we do not see, the forces of an abominable *thanatopolitics*. Visually imperceptible forces become perceptible though the scream's sonority. The problem is still to catch the forces that produce the scream itself, to place the sound of the scream in a relationship with the forces of darkness. In this case the scream does not answer to visible forces that may be exerted directly on one's own body, the scream calls for the other, against its forced disappearance, against the production of corpses that the river makes invisible. This is what *thanatopolitics* means, the concerted organisation that attributes to itself a power over life, over the decision of life and death, and executes a systematic plan of *making die* (*hacer morir*) (Giorgio Agamben explores this relationship between the fabrication of corpses and thanatopolitics [see Agamben 1999: 85–9]). This plan makes the river a place of invisibility, the place of the disappearance of the corpses. As much as we see the current growing and the voices soaring over the waters, we hear through the scream what we do not see in what we see. But the scream does not offer to us only the sound of the invisible (the imperceptible) forces that produce it, the scream is also a lament that makes enunciable the non-enunciable, a clamour that enunciates a suffering and a resistance, that pronounces itself against this *making die* in its act of mourning. The speech act of pronouncing the unpronounceable takes place in a given situation, in the space created by the composition of the visual image and the sound image. The current of the river we see, whose turbulent sound we hear, is perceived as a medium of invisibility, as a hideaway that we perceive in this way only through the screams and laments. Only in the end do we see what we did not see before: 'corpses' (the ragged clothes that the turbulence reveals). Hence the clinch between the form of content and the form of the expression: the continuous variation of sound that floods the room, the intervals of different times in which the visual image is projected on one screen and then on the other, each voice in the manner of a *Sprechgesang* falls or climbs. In the end everything fades, there is nothing left but silence and darkness surrounding the spectator.

   Enunciate the unenunciable. How can such an enunciation be understood? We say that it is testimony. The word that comes from the scream is the true testimony of a *thanatopolitics*. The subject of the *phone* is then the witness. He is the *superstes*, a Latin word used to refer to the witness, not any kind of witness (*testis*), but the one who has survived an event of which they are called to offer testimony (Agamben 1999: 17). The survivor is a paradoxical kind of political subject, they are the one that is called to offer testimony with their scream, with nothing but their scream because they have been excluded from the authorised record of

1.4: Clemencia Echeverri, *Treno*. Multiscreen projection in the *Actos del Habla* exhibition, Art Museum of the National University, Bogota, Colombia, 2009. Image courtesy of the artist.

the *logos* and therefore excluded from politics. Properly speaking 'there is no subject of the testimony . . . Every testimony is a process or a field of forces incessantly traversed by currents of subjectification and desubjectification' (Agamben 1999: 121).

Finally we must ask: What is the relationship between art and testimony? We can't pretend that the work is the symbol of an abominable suffering and that the artist can erect himself or herself as the one who speaks on behalf of the other, in the place of the victim; art has abandoned such declarative power. The testimony belongs exclusively to the victim who speaks for herself. The work of art is not 'addressed to. . .' neither is it 'on behalf of'. It is 'before'. It is a question of becoming (Deleuze and Guattari 1994: 109). It is precisely this impossibility of testimony, the impossibility of being instead of, in the place of. . ., that makes the work of art possible. The point is neither that it is *about* testimony, nor that it reflects on testimony, the point is to make the scream and to make a politics of it. What the work accounts for is making, by its own means, the non-perceptible perceptible, making enunciable the non-enunciable. The work does not bear witness but shows the possibility of the scream as testimony. It does not represent a conflict, it actualises a power. Therefore, it makes evident the need of a people even if that people is what is lacking: 'we are not responsible for the victims but before the victims' (108). Let us remember that in *What is Philosophy?* Deleuze and Guattari say that philosophy books and works of art have resistance in common with a people. 'Their resistance to death, to servitude, to the intolerable, to shame, and to the present' (110). In this sense, through this common resistance, there might be in the philosopher, the thinker or the artist a becoming that links them to a people, a becoming-people of the thinker. It is a matter of becoming and not of identification: 'The people is internal to the thinker because it is a "becoming people," just as the thinker is internal to the people as no less unlimited becoming' (109).

Translated by Juan Fernando Mejía Mosquera

References

Agamben, G. (1998), *Homo Sacer I: Sovereign Power and Bare Life*, trans. D. Heller-Roazen, Stanford: Stanford University Press.
Agamben, G. (1999), *Remnants of Auschwitz: The Witness and the Archive*, trans. D. Heller-Roazen, New York: Zone Books.
Deleuze, G. (1979), 'Un manifeste de moins', in C. Bene and G. Deleuze, *Superpositions*, Paris: Minuit.

Deleuze, G. (1988), *Foucault*, trans. S. Hand, London and New York: Continuum.
Deleuze, G. (1993), *The Fold, Leibniz and the Baroque*, trans. T. Conley, Minneapolis: The University of Minnesota Press.
Deleuze, G. (1995), *Negotiations 1972–1990*, trans. M. Joughin, New York: Columbia University Press.
Deleuze, G. (2002), *Francis Bacon: The Logic of Sensation*, trans. D. Smith, London and New York: Continuum.
Deleuze, G. (2006a), 'What is a Creative Act?', in *Two Regimes of Madness, Texts and Interviews 1975–1995*, ed. D. Lapoujade, trans. A. Hodges and M. Taormina, New York: Semiotext(e).
Deleuze, G. (2006b), 'May '68 Didn't Happen', in *Two Regimes of Madness: Texts and Interviews 1975–1995*, ed. D. Lapoujade, trans. A. Hodges and M. Taormina, New York: Semiotext(e).
Deleuze, G. and F. Guattari (2004), *A Thousand Plateaus*, trans. B. Massumi, London and New York: Continuum.
Deleuze, G. and F. Guattari (1994), *What is Philosophy?*, trans. H. Tomlinson and G. Burchell, New York: Columbia University Press.
Zepke, S. (2008), 'The Readymade: Art as the Refrain of Life', in S. O'Sullivan and S. Zepke (eds), *Deleuze, Guattari and the Production of the New*, London and New York: Continuum.

Notes

1. This essay is a product of the research project 'The Spatial Turn in Contemporary Philosophy', developed by the Núcleo de Investigaciones en Estética of the Pontificia Universidad Javeriana, Bogota.
2. I use this term in the sense that Giorgio Agamben gives it in his *Homo Sacer I: Sovereign Power and Bare Life*. In today's societies biopolitics may be mistaken for thanatopolitics, where control of and decisions on life are transformed into decisions about death (Agamben 1998: 150).
3. For a more detailed view of this period, see Deleuze (2006b: 233–6).

Chapter 2

A Shift Towards the Unnameable

Suely Rolnik

> West of Tordesillas, metaphor has no value of its own. It is not that I dislike metaphor. I want all works to be seen some day not as objects for sterile flights of fancy, but as marks, memories, and evocations of real and visible conquests.
>
> Cildo Meireles

Having decided to experience Cildo Meireles' *Red Shift*, I take the first available flight to Belo Horizonte.[1] Arriving at Inhotim, I head straight for the work, installed in a building especially constructed for the installation and conceived by the artist himself.[2] A fourth wall has been added to the structure that did not exist in previous versions, which allows a separation from the external space. This is no trifling matter; free from the distracting murmur of exhibitions and with no time limit, I enter the installation, shut the door and let myself go.

First environment: furniture, domestic appliances, carpets, paintings, but also porcelain penguins on a fridge, fish in an aquarium, parakeet in a cage, and all types of knick-knacks and trinkets cluttering the space. Not to mention an LP spinning endlessly on the turntable, a constantly illuminated television and just a few books, all pompously bound, displayed on the shelf as if they too were trinkets. Signs of the passion for consumption propelled by industrial modernity, mingled with nostalgia for everyday objects of pre-modern existence. Were it not for a computer, this would be a typical Brazilian middle-class living room of the 1960s and '70s. An ordinary scene of ordinary lives.

Two elements nevertheless diverge from this condensed normality; one is the colour (everything is red, in different tones; one cannot help seeing it), the other is the sound (the constant flow of water which composes the soundtrack of a video of the installation itself, playing in a loop on a television; one cannot help hearing it). I let myself be guided by the sound and follow on.

Second environment: in some sort of non-specific in-between space a thick red liquid has apparently been spilt from a small glass bottle that has fallen to the floor. It spreads through the rest of the house in an immense stain totally disproportionate to the size of the flask. I let myself be guided by this colour that inundates the floor and move on.

Third environment: the colour is lost in pitch-blackness. Beneath the beam of a light installed precariously at the back of the room, a single object can be seen in the impenetrable darkness. It is a white sink, tilted as though falling; from the tap gushes a red liquid that splatters over its entire surface. As the only scene fraught with drama, it seems to suggest there is a hidden narrative, which if deciphered would reveal a supposed meaning of the work. Complete mistake; as my intimacy with the installation increases, this expectation disappears.

In Search of the Shift

The artist did not give the red in the first environment to the objects, it arrived along with them. Colour constitutes these objects to such a degree that it seems to emanate from them, contaminating the atmosphere of the room and of my own body; my eyes, my ears, my skin, my breath. . . my subjectivity. It is not by chance that Meireles calls this first space *Impregnation*. Little by little, I begin to lose the references that the objects offered when I first arrived. In the second environment (called *Entorno* in Portuguese), the red seems to have detached itself from things in order to present itself as such; a dense redness that overflows to occupy the entire environment. Meireles named this part of the work *entorno*, meaning both 'overflowing' and 'environment', as here I can no longer hang on to any certain reference. There is nothing logical here: between the bottle and the spilt liquid there is a total disproportion; it is impossible to find any recognisable function for this space in the normal residence I had supposedly entered. My disorientation intensifies.

In the last environment, *Shift*, the colour finally merges with the sound. If from the start and till that moment there is a strong presence of both, they nevertheless run parallel without any relation. In the gushing tap at the centre of that precariously balanced sink however, they are articulated, and produce some kind of meaning; the incessant noise of a flood of red water that nothing can staunch. The relief is short-lived; the topsy-turvy logic that would unite these elements does not hold up, it dissolves beneath the impact of the deep darkness. What takes place, in fact, is a *Shift* – as the artist calls this last room and the installation as whole.

Every time a logic appears to take bodily form, it deconstructs itself with the next step taken. It is a process that functions as a loop, like the video image that we watch in the first room, in which the installation itself eternally returns – as does our own unrest while we remain there. 'The work functions in a circle', argues Meireles himself, referring to another moment of the work characterised by the same kind of logic:

> The second spot contains a plausible explanation – in this case even a literal one – for the red of the first. At the same time, this spot introduces another aspect: the question of the perfect horizon resulting from the surface of the liquid at rest. Caused by this horizon one gets the impression of walking towards the third, and last part. The detour, properly speaking, that deconstructs the previous part, precisely because it casts doubt on the fact that you are on a plane surface. However, at the end, the colour red is introduced and you're again connected to the beginning.

With rigorous precision tempered by a subtle humour, the artist plays with elements susceptible of recognition, either in terms of meaning or of form (the 'extensive' dimension of the work). These elements promise tranquillity, just as, simultaneously, the artist pulls the carpet out from under our feet, leaving us ungrounded and thrown into the chaos of the field of forces that are actualised in the work (its 'intensive' dimension). This paradoxical back-and-forth movement seems to constitute one of the essential elements of the thoughtful poetics that permeates *Red Shift*.

But it doesn't stop there. During the afternoon I spent in *Red Shift*, and after several comings and goings within it, I began to feel the pulse of a diagram of forces, vaguely familiar and yet strangely inaccessible. Might this not announce the shift that operates in the work? Yet still I know nothing about it. I must wait until the experience settles.

Some days after my visit, the disquiet gains its first words: fainting. . . desolation. . . despondency. . . collapse. . . paralysis. . . fear. . . An endless sense of apprehension, absolute impotence, exhaustion. What gradually takes shape is the daily sensation of living under Brazil's military dictatorship – precisely the period in which the diverse ideas that led Meireles to conceive the installation first crystallised and came together. This has nothing to do with a metaphor of the regime's brutality in its visible and representable face (which is the usual interpretation, hackneyed by repetition according to the artist himself). Instead, it relates to the sensation of an invisible atmosphere that impregnates everything – the regime's intensive diagram of forces – and is implacable in its subtlety and intangibility. The impression is that under or behind that excessive pathological 'normality' permeating life in those decades of state terrorism, an incessant bleeding of the vital flows of Brazilian society is in process, day after day. All is overtaken, as the sound and colour of flowing red liquid takes over the whole installation.

It is well known that colours are fields of forces that affect our bodies, and of them red has the smallest frequency and the longest wavelength of the spectrum. These qualities make it shift less as it moves in space and give it the capacity to attract other colours, imposing itself upon them. Indeed, red in this installation imposes itself onto the singularity of things and makes them uniform. This physical experience of the work actualises within my body the sensory mark of the omnipotence of military power over subjectivities, which homogenises everything under the impact of terror, restraining the vital movement (understood here as the potential of creation, differentiation, shift). There is no single space that escapes such omnipresence – no home, school, workplace, street, bridge, square, bar, restaurant, shop, hospital, bus, taxi. . . not even the air itself. An arc of tension is formed, extending itself to the limit: nerves standing on end, a state of permanent alert. A total impossibility of rest, but also of making 'shifts' as we move through time and space.

It is no easy matter to connect with such sensations and overcome their denial; more difficult still is to actualise them, whether visually or in any other language, whether verbal, cinematic, musical or even existential. And yet exactly this is required to re-appropriate and activate the vital flow that has bled away (or in less serious cases, has been staunched). If any artistic effort in this direction is effectively worthwhile – and if it is equally worthwhile to let oneself be contaminated by its creations – the aim is certainly not to remain within the memory of the trauma, to substantialise and historicise it, glorifying oneself in the role of the victim. On the contrary, such an effort is valuable because it becomes a way of reactivating and re-inscribing in the present what was there before the trauma, and has been drained away on account of it – a 'real and visible conquest' that overcomes the toxic effects inscribed in the body's memory. In this installation, Meireles manages to materialise such a shift towards the unnameable, actualised here as 'marks, evocations' of this conquest. If we are able to let ourselves go, this shift can become equally possible in our own subjectivity.

Politics and Poetics

The wider context in which Meireles' ideas for this installation originated was the movement of institutional critique that developed internationally in art during the 1960s and '70s. The major focus of that movement – the nerve centre of its poetics – was to problematise the power of the 'art system' over the work. In general, the factors at stake ranged from the spaces devoted to the works to the categories that 'official' art history used to qualify them, by way of the media that could be employed and the genres that could be recognised. But in South American countries during that same period, the political dimension was added as a central element of the institutional territory of art to be problematised.

The specificity of these South American practices has been recognised in (official) Art History by grouping them together under the categories of 'ideological or political conceptual art'. However, this does not mean, as that history mistakenly asserts, that the artists have converted themselves into activists conveying ideological messages. What made them incorporate the political dimension into their poetic investigation was the fact that the dictatorship's oppression was experienced at the core of their creative activity. The most obvious manifestation of this constraint was the outright censorship of the products of the creative process. Far more subtle and harmful, however, is its impalpable effect of inhibiting the very emergence of this process – a threat that continues to hover in the air, due to the inexorable trauma of the experience of humiliation. This is a nodal aspect of the sensible tensions that mobilise the need to create, in order to give them bodily form in a work of art.

The 'basic core' of Meireles' work, according to the artist himself, 'is an investigation of space in all its aspects: physical, geometrical, historical, psychological, topological and anthropological'. This artistic investigation is an action inserted into the transversality that composes the very territory of art, upturning many of its layers, including the political one. It is understood here however, in a sense that is very different from the ideological, pedagogical or militant one that some people insist on attributing to the work of this artist, a sense that the artist does not recognise (we will see later which is the other sense of politics we are talking about) (Meireles 1999: 136). This is the case with *Red Shift*, in which the diffuse and omnipresent experience of oppression becomes visible and/or audible in an environment where the brutality of state terrorism provokes the reaction of a voluntary blindness, deafness and dumbness, as a matter of survival (Meireles 1999: 136).

In this context, the conditions are given to overcome the scission existing between micro and macropolitics, which in turn is reproduced in the scission between the classical figure of the artist and the political activist. A compound of these two types of acting upon reality seems to have been sketched within the artistic propositions of the period in Latin America. It is this singularity that has been missed by (official) Art History. Before considering the implications of this lapse, it is necessary to ask exactly what differentiates micro and macropolitical actions and why their integration is important.

Let's begin with what they have in common; both have as their starting point the urgency of confronting the tensions of human life in the places where its dynamic is interrupted or at least weakened. Both have as their aim the liberation of vital movement from its obstructions, making both of them essential activities for the 'health' of a society (understood here as the affirmation of the inventive potential for change, when life demands it as a condition of its continuity). However, the orders of tension that each confronts are distinct, as are the operations behind their confrontations and the subjective faculties they involve.

On the side of macropolitics we find ourselves confronted by conflictual tensions in the cartography of visible and speakable reality: conflicts of class, race, religion, gender, etc., as the effects of the unequal distribution of established places in a given social context. This is the plane of stratification that outlines subjects and objects, as well as the relation between them and their respective representations. With micropolitics, we are confronted by the tensions between this plane and what is announced in the diagram of sensible reality, invisible and unspeakable: a domain of fluxes, intensities and becomings.

The first type of tension is accessed through perception, the second through sensation. The first approaches the world as a map of forms on which we project representations and attribute meaning to them. The second approaches the world as a diagram of forces that affect our senses in their capacity for resonance. The irreducible paradox between these two capacities of the sensible provokes collapses of meaning and forces us to think and to create. The classic figure of the artist tends towards the side of micropolitical action while that of the activist tends towards macropolitics. It is this separation that began to dissolve in Latin America during the 1960s and '70s. Acknowledging this, we can begin to answer the question about the damage caused by Art History's lapse with regard to this type of practice.

Ideological Conceptualism?

Right from the start, official history failed to do justice to these practices by designating them as 'conceptual'. A different name would have distinguished them from the artistic practices thus categorised in the United States and Western Europe, where even what is meant by 'concept' differs. Worse still was to describe such a conceptualism as 'ideological' or 'political', as has been attempted in certain accounts (not coincidentally, by North American or Western European authors who did not live through this experience). The fact is that we find in these artistic proposals the seeds of the integration between politics and poetics, experienced and actualised in artistic creations, but still impossible to label. To call them 'ideological' or 'political' denies the state of estrangement that such a radically new experience produces in our subjectivity. The operation is quite simple; if what we experience is not recognisable as art, then in order to protect ourselves from this disturbing noise we categorise it as politics, and everything retains its rightful place. The abyss between micro and macropolitics is maintained; the process of their fusion is aborted, along with all that might have come forth (though in the best of cases, the seed remains dormant). In reality this state of estrangement constitutes a crucial experience because, as suggested above, it is the symptom of the forces of alterity reverberating in our own body. These reverberations put into crisis the current cartography and lead us to create. Ignoring them means that the problematising potential that fundamentally characterises artistic action will be blocked.

The artistic interventions that retain their inherent political force are those drawn out from the manner in which the tensions of the present affect the artist's body, and it is this quality of relating to the present that such actions can stimulate in those who perceive them. The formal rigour of the work, in its physicality, becomes indistinguishable from the rigour of its actualisation of whatever provoked the tension, as lived in the body. The more precise the form, the stronger the pulse of its intensive quality and the greater its power to insert itself in its surroundings (*entorno*). When such an insertion takes place it brings to existence a new politics of subjectivation, which will perhaps proliferate, generating new configurations of the unconscious within the social field, and breaking with the dominant references.

What this kind of practice can elicit is not just the consciousness of that which generates tension (in this case, overpowering oppression), and the awareness of its visible, representational side, but instead the experience of this state of things in one's own body, its invisible, unconscious side, which intervenes in the process of subjectivation at exactly the place where it falls captive and loses potency. In the face of such an experience, it becomes much more difficult to ignore the sense of uneasiness that the current cartography provokes in us.

What is gained is a more precise focus, in contrast to the reduction of everything involving social life to macropolitics, making of the artists who operate on this terrain mere scenographers, graphic designers and/or publicity agents of activism – although these have their function and undoubtedly characterised certain forms of practice during those decades, and led to them being described as 'political' and/or 'ideological'. It was the extension of such a qualification to the entire group of Latin American artistic proposals during the 1960s and '70s that produced the unfortunate misunderstanding of Art History, and meant it lost sight of the irreversible shifts occurring in that context. Meireles himself insists on the difference on several occasions: 'I had problems with that kind of political art in which the emphasis was on the discourse, leaving the work looking like mere propaganda' (Meireles 1999: 136). Or when he states that if his work has actually been permeated with some political orientation it has happened unconsciously.[3] Or when he tells us about how when he was asking artists for works for the *Impregnation* room in its first version, Raymundo Colares brought him a badge with the image of Che Guevara. The only white object on display, it was different from the rest not only because of its colour but also for its reference to an external, metaphorical representation.[4] The image of Che symbolises political resistance operating in the extensive dimension, and contrasts with the political status of its intensive dimension. This dimension is integrated into a poetics that characterises the work and it is precisely where its power to question its surroundings resides. Is it not precisely what Meireles is aiming at when he characterises the political orientation of his work as 'unconscious'?

The work of Meireles is certainly one of the most striking examples of this kind of practice. Its vigour is not found in its representational content, based upon a referent external to its poetics (ideological or otherwise). This kind of interpretation is founded upon false clues, placed there by the artist as an anecdotal dimension that his work supposedly has, but whose very function is, on the contrary, to be destroyed. Faced with the irredeemably implausible, we create an apparently plausible imaginary articulation, guidelines that misguide our insistence on maintaining our distance from experience, blind, deaf and mute. But when these are shown to be non-operative we are forced to face the intolerable.

The equivocation starts with the idea that we are within the domain of symbols, metaphors and narratives. But neither does the work's vigour lie in the physicality of form itself, supposedly autonomous and disassociated from the experience of the world. In both these interpretations

– these 'sterilised flights of fancy', as Meireles would no doubt call them – the body of the one who interprets is absent in its vulnerability to the forces of the world and thus of the work; nor is the world there in its potential to affect that body. The work, in short, is not there in terms of its potential to infect its interpreters, nor in its power to intervene in the state of things.

In contrast to these absences, the vigour of Meireles' *Red Shift* is found in its intensive content of world-forces as they reach the artist's body, and are indissoluble from the extensive form of their actualisation in the work. Hence its status as 'event'. If there is politics here and if there is also poetics, they are absolutely inseparable within the precise formation of one single gesture and in the intensive diagram of its inflammatory potential. This is why Meireles' work – as with many other works by Brazilian and other Latin American artists of the period – possesses the power to keep our bodies awake. It depends only on our desire.

Translated by Brian Holmes

Reference

Meireles, C. (1999), 'Artist's Writings', in *Cildo Meireles*, London: Phaidon Press.

Notes

1. This is a reworked and retranslated version of a text written for an exhibition by Cildo Meireles at the Tate Modern, London, 2008.
2. *Red Shift* is permanently installed at Inhotim – Centro de arte contemporáneo, Brumadinho, Minas Gerais, Brazil.
3. Telephone conversation with the artist.
4. Ibid.

Chapter 3
The Heterogenesis of Fleeing

Gerald Raunig

In everyday usage fleeing is something for cowards. The virtue of manfully throwing oneself with a weapon into the midst of a fight is opposed to the flight and withdrawal typical of a dishonourable attitude. In the hetero-normative everyday the sanctified mode of subjectivation for the honourable and manly fighter is a decision to take one of two sides, followed by a fight for the sublation [*Aufhebung*] of this division, and the final reestablishment of unity. Movement may only develop in this striated and stratified space between division and unity.

Yet within our narrow geopolitical-discursive space shaped by occidental-dialectical thought we find residues of a figure that affirms flight, cunning elusion and subversion, while evading the constraint of division and sublation. There are various recent approaches in philosophy, in political practice and in art production that have developed and tested a non-dialectical notion of resistance that goes beyond the concepts of contradiction, negation and reaction. These conceptual developments stretch from various figures of flight to nomadism, desertion and destitution, to disappearance, betrayal and diverse concepts of exodus.[1]

I would like to draw out a specific genealogical line of this ensemble of conceptual creations which have gained special meaning in the last thirty years, not least in the field of art, where they – and this is what I wish to problematise here – have often been interpreted in an abusive manner. On the other hand my discussion will thematise the figure of fleeing in its. actuality, which I would like to try to exemplify with reference to three video works by the Spanish artist and activist Marcelo Expósito.

Lines of Flight: Some Conceptual Components

Already in the course of the 1970s, submerged within Gilles Deleuze and Félix Guattari's practice of conceptual invention – as well as in

Deleuze's collaboration with Claire Parnet – the notion of a line of flight begins to appear more and more frequently. In 1980, at the climax of Deleuze and Guattari's collaboration – the second volume of *Capitalism and Schizophrenia* with the title *A Thousand Plateaus* – the line of flight finally became a central concept within a bundle of conceptual creations, in vicinity to and interference with other new concepts such as deterritorialisation, the body without organs, smooth space and nomadology. Whereas those notions seem to have become almost ubiquitous in certain discourses over the last decades, their specification has never reached an appropriate clarity. The effect of this inaccuracy in the adaptation of Guattari and Deleuze's concepts is on one hand a depoliticisation of these concepts (which were developed within highly political contexts), and on the other hand – and as a result – an extensive denunciation of its authors as 'postmodern relativists', 'hippies' and 'quixotic theory-poets'.

Against this backdrop I would like to start by sketching the seven most important conceptual components of the line of flight as they appear in the writings of Deleuze and Guattari. These components have in common that they all point to a specific and central strategy, described in the introduction of their last book *What is Philosophy?* as a *creatio continua* of concepts. This is how Deleuze and Guattari understand the function of philosophy, and I want to add to this proposition two possible forms of its actualisation. On the one hand there is the continuous practice of creating *new* concepts 'that are aerolites rather than commercial products' (Deleuze and Guattari 1994: 11). The creation of concepts functions in this first mode as a radical linguistic break that consciously creates misunderstanding and irritation. Besides this strategy of sending celestial bodies into everyday language there is also a second, no less disturbing possibility of conceptual creation: the radical *dislocation* of concepts, which I would like to discuss in connection to the figures of fleeing.

1) The concrete quality of the word 'flight' has to be investigated against the background of its manifold and misleading connotations of escapism, artistic hermeticism or political withdrawal.[2] This misunderstanding implies that the invocation of the word flight means a personal withdrawal of the subject from the noise and chatter of the world. In the philosophical perspective on the spheres of art production, the exemplary protagonist of flight, for both Deleuze and Giorgio Agamben, is Herman Melville's Bartleby. In Paolo Virno it is the figure of the 'virtuoso' pianist Glenn Gould. In the rapid digestion of these figures by art

discourse they are often quickly reduced to personifications of individual resistance and, in the case of Bartleby, of individual withdrawal. Luckily this appropriation of the concept of flight was anticipated by Deleuze and Guattari, who unambiguously answered it. In the short eighth chapter of *A Thousand Plateaus*, about the novel and its incisions, its breaks and lines of flight, they state: 'As for the line of flight, would it not be entirely personal, the way in which an individual escapes on his or her own account, escapes "responsibilities," escapes the world, takes refuge in the desert, or else in art. . .? False impression' (Deleuze and Guattari 2004: 225).

Fleeing here does not mean something escapist or pacifying, on the contrary it is an extremely active affair involving the continual search for the newest weapons – exemplified in the quotation from the Black Panther activist George Jackson in *A Thousand Plateaus*:[3] 'To flee, but in fleeing to seek a weapon' (Deleuze and Parnet 2002: 102). The connection between flight and weapon undermines the dichotomy of active fight and cowardly flight. Flight here means neither defence nor individualism but an inventive form of offence. 'Lines of flight, for their part, never consist in running away from the world but rather in causing runoffs, as when you drill a hole in a pipe; there is no social system that does not leak from all directions, even if it makes its segments increasingly rigid in order to seal the lines of flight' (Deleuze and Guattari 2004: 225).

2) Lines of flight are not phantasms, nor chimeras. 'The great and only error lies in thinking that a line of flight consists in fleeing from life; the flight into the imaginary, or into art. On the contrary, to flee is to produce the real, to create life, to find a weapon' (Deleuze and Parnet 2002: 36). *To produce the real*, this sounds like an anticipatory answer to the criticism Deleuze and Guattari received in the decades after *Capitalism and Schizophrenia* when they were brushed off as stoned hippie poets and kings of metaphor. Contrary to these denunciations and allegations a militant, sometimes revolutionary tone blows through Deleuze and Guattari's writings in the 1970s, but by excerpting quotes out of context this aspect often gets intentionally lost both in academic and art writing. But the metaphoric is truly the very last thing Deleuze and Guattari would tie up with the business of creating and inventing: 'it is always on a line of flight that we create, not, indeed because we imagine that we are dreaming but, on the contrary, because we trace out the real on it, we compose there a plane of consistence' (Deleuze and Parnet 2002: 102).

3) As if fleeing alone isn't suspicious enough, it is regularly accompanied with further vocabulary from the arsenal of denunciation found in military language: Flight means desertion, fleeing means betraying. But in appropriating the concept of betrayal a radical reassessment takes place, a radical shift first of all concerning the object of betrayal: 'We betray the fixed powers that try to hold us back, the established powers of the earth' (Deleuze and Parnet 2002: 30). Fixed and established powers do not form an outside; they traverse our bodies, our relations, our worlds. The traitor therefore betrays her own realm, her own gender, her class, and her majority. To betray one's own majority means to drop out of one's own dominant normality. 'For it is difficult to be a traitor; it is to create. One has to lose one's identity, one's face, in it. One has to disappear, to become unknown' (33). At the beginning of betrayal is the movement of disappearance, of becoming-nobody as a break with loyalty to the logic and to the terror of identity, representation and visibility. Yet, as an absolute act that would result in *being*-nobody, to loose the face, to abandon identity, to disappear is perhaps not only difficult but not even imaginable, least of all in the business of art and writing with their manifold modes of accumulating symbolic capital. Rather, betrayal as a creative act has to be imagined and actualised as a tendency of disappearance, as a movement that constantly has to be instituted, which again and again starts anew and thwarts the institutions, the structures, and the state apparatuses of representation.

4) The concept of the line is also removed from its everyday meaning within the conceptual assemblage of the flight-line. According to Deleuze and Guattari, lines of flight are not continuous lines, unbroken and straight, but combinations of flows and incisions, a continuous stuttering, a stumbling, often beside the usual tracks. There is nothing regular in the lines of flight, nothing divine, nothing that commands over territories, over possessions, over striated spaces dominated by straight-ahead movement. Instead a line of flight implies a demonic multitude, hopping from one interval to the next, jumping over intervals (Deleuze and Parnet 2002: 30 ff.).[4]

Even though the concept of flight seems to assume a movement from one place to another, which is also suggested by the mathematical definition of the line, this is in fact not the case with the line of flight. 'The line is between points, in their midst, and no longer goes from one point to another' (Deleuze and Guattari 2004: 298). The line runs through points, between points, as a flow through the middle, a rampant middle without beginning or end. As a result, lines of flight can have a specific movement (although not from one point to another), but they can also take place on the spot as a motionless journey, a flight without changing place. Deleuze (and on this point he is not entirely in personal accordance with Guattari) repeatedly quotes in this context (where he also says that becoming shouldn't be frightened off) the philosopher of history and universal historian Arnold Toynbee, on the surprising quality of the nomadic:

> Toynbee shows that nomads in the strict, geographical sense are neither migrants nor travellers, but, on the contrary, those who do not move, those who cling onto the steppe, who are immobile with big strides, following a line of flight on the spot, the greatest inventors of new weapons. (Deleuze and Parnet 2002: 28)[5]

Such paradoxes of nomads not moving from their spot, or fleeing as marking time, seem to me especially helpful in dealing with the all too flowery traditions of interpreting Deleuze and Guattari: from the nomadological pathos of the cosmopolitan intellectual to the figure of migration as a new revolutionary subject.

5) In contrast to traditional left, particularly Marxist, political theory, there are no concepts of the individual and of society in Deleuze and Guattari. Not so much in their place, but rather undermining this specific axis of striating thought, both authors use notions like singularity and event. Like these, lines of flight are not only non-escapist and non-individual, they cross the binary logic of collective and individual. For Deleuze and Guattari such oppositions don't describe a relevant reality:

> It is possible for a single group, or a single individual even, to exhibit all the lines we have been discussing simultaneously. But it is most frequently the case that a single group or individual functions as a line of flight; that group or individual creates the line rather than following it, is itself the living weapon it forges rather than stealing one. (Deleuze and Guattari 2004: 226)

6) Fleeing is not simply an empty movement of one or more people escaping. In place of a subject–object relation between the one who draws a line of flight and the line of flight as such, between the one forging a weapon or appropriating it and the weapon as such, fleeing *becomes* at the same time an invention, and therefore a productive, creative, inventive weapon. Instead of understanding fleeing and taking up a weapon as contrasting poles and referring to them as neatly separated modes of subjectivation, for example the (effeminate) coward and the

(manly) hero, we must understand flight and weapon as being inter-linked. Creation takes place precisely in this concatenation of fleeing and inventing. Different possible worlds are created precisely on the lines of flight. Creating worlds also means fleeing the idea of only one possible world, and at the same time it means creating ever new ones. Flight as *de*stitution overlaps with a *con*stitution of new social concatenations, with a constituent power, with an *in*stituent practice.

7) Finally the line of flight is *primary*. Not in the sense of a chronology or an eternal universality but rather as constitutive for the social plane of immanence. Here it is necessary to once again read the notion of flight against its everyday use, against the idea of flight being a reaction to an antecedent situation, an antecedent attack. 'One might say in a certain sense that what is primary in a society are the lines, the movements of flight. For, far from being a flight from the social, far from being utopian or even ideological, these constitute the social field, trace out its grada-tion and its boundaries, the whole of its becomings' (Deleuze and Parnet 2002: 101).[6] If we consider this primacy of lines of flight as a mode of subjectivation that does not just simply react to something, then the final semantic consequence is a necessary shift from a 'flight from. . .' to fleeing as an absolute concept.

'The Year in Which the Future Ended (Began)'

In his video *The Year in Which the Future Ended (Began)* (12 min., 2007) Marcelo Expósito draws two lines of flight that thwart the dichotomies of a politics of remembrance. Here fleeing carries us beyond conven-tional forms of documentary practice in order to actualise the remains of a traumatic history in a very different way.[7] Instead of burying the future by burying the past under the cover of pseudo-objective represen-tations, Expósito introduces memory work as a *twofold* archaeological practice. Whilst the past often becomes petrified in the procedures of writing history and in the classical forms of documentary, here a present-becoming is to be worked out that emerges *in-between* the images, and at the same time *in-between* the archaeological findings. *Worked* out, yes, because memory does not just come about simply through contem-plation: 'memory is work, not something you can just contemplate'.[8]

The point of flight for Marcelo Expósito's video is the year 1977, the year when the first democratic elections took place in Spain, and according to the official history the high point of the democratic process in Spain. For Expósito, however, speaking thirty years later, it was 'the

3.1: Marcelo Expósito, video still from *The Year in Which the Future Ended (Began)*, 12 min., 2007. Image courtesy of the artist.

year in which the future ended (began)'. Much could be said about the emptiness of this sanctioned date, much also about the continuities of the Franco regime beyond this threshold and up to today. Similar to the way the notion of 'transition' is used for the neoliberal transformation process taking place in the ex-communist countries of Europe, the phrase 'transition towards democracy' is also of great significance in Spain. And as this notion serves to test new forms of neoliberal exploitation under the cover of democratic promises in the post-communist countries, there are also indications that the late introduction of democracy in Spain is not only an adjustment to Western European normality. Yet, Expósito's interest is initially less about the thirty years that have since passed and about the accumulated layers of repression that have congealed in this time. In fact, he draws his line of flight back to forty years before 1977. In a dreamlike and accelerated rewind he accumulates representative images of the Franco period's clerical fascism, but also the resistance against it, from the attacks of ETA in the early 1970s via the various insurgencies of the 1960s and 1950s. The frenzied rush into the past then encounters the years of purging and isolation after the war, and finally the Civil War and revolution. The assumption of the video is that the 'official accounts of the transition to democracy are largely naturalised through a form of visual representation based on over-codified images that, paradoxically, increasingly show less and at the same time increasingly hinder the possibility of understanding the historical events that they supposedly represent'.[9]

The canonical repetition of the images, especially in the case of jubilee events, halts the past and rudely decontextualises it. This is why Expósito invents his first line of flight trying to betray the dominant representation, to revive the images of the past. On this first line Expósito over-affirms the rude form of official documentation by accelerating the sequences of the canonised images in a rampant rewind, so that they completely lose their representational connotations. The memory and dream work of the images serve here to connect past and future, which lose their linear alignment and melt into a flow, a line of flight, which cleaves a new way between the points of dominant history.

In the video's final passages, however, a robust archaeological practice is added to this first line of flight, which is an archaeology of images. The motto of the video, 'to stir up the underworld', not only refers to an archaeology of *visual* representation, but also to a concrete undertaking, to the small but effective social movements of those who dig up the bones of hundreds of Civil War fighters and anonymous victims of the Franco regime in the here and now. In the meticulous work of excavation, sorting, labelling and documentation, 439 bodies of Republican soldiers of the Civil War, as well as victims of Franco's reprisals in the early years after the war, were exhumed in the central Spanish commune Uclés between 2005 and 2007.[10]

This specific form of memory work finds itself embedded in a social movement working underground like a mole, which stirs up the official politics of the Spanish state, or, as Marcelo Expósito puts it, creates 'a truly micropolitical earthquake':

Since the end of the 90s some people decided: if the law and the state does not take any decision in terms of what to do with our relatives buried like animals everywhere around the country, we are just gonna go and take them out – that means that an impressive social process has taken place: dozens of what are officially called *asociaciones por la recuperación de la memoria histórica* [associations for the recovery of historical memory] have been created, with the main aim to locate where corpses are buried, and start the process of exhuming the corpses (individually or collectively), trying to identify the relatives, and burying them again with honours and with a proper name, when possible.

Some of these associations are linked to the communist party, others are close to the CGT [the anarcho-syndicalist union], others are independent; some are connected in networks, others not so much, but the interesting question is how they operate: They profit from the fact that they move in 'a-legality' – normally they are started by people who are relatives (often the grandchildren of those who were repressed and assassinated) – and they are joined by more and more people: those who give testimonies of the shootings or the burials, local historians, lawyers, archaeologists, politicians sometimes who can give 'unofficial' shelter to some of the activities, forensic scientists, volunteers who give a hand in several kinds of activities: excavations, driving cars. . .

Hundreds of people joining their very different knowledge and competencies in order to construct a network of practical activities in order to . . . what to say? just exhuming corpses? – not only that – it's a kind of taking the phantom out – like a real return of the repressed, which totally puts in question, on nearly a preconscious level, in my opinion, the psycho-social basis of the democratic transition and our present political order.[11]

Here the concrete archaeological movement complements the other line of flight, the one of visual representation, with a material memory work that subverts the underground connections between fascist history and today's governmentality. Material and immaterial memory work overlap, developing complementary strategies of commemoration in becoming and so refute collaboration with oblivion. Whereas the official account of the democratisation process disconnects the future from any relation to the past, in Expósito's work the relation between past and future is actualised in both lines of flight, it is put into a disquieting tension within the present becoming. To not let the past rest, but rather to speed it up, to put it into a state of unrest, this is what lines of flight mean here.

The Deleuzianism of Antonio Negri

Whereas 1977 marks a dubious turning point or 'transition' in Spain, the same year in Italy was one of both revolt and the beginning of the *anni di piombo*, the leaden years. The genealogy of (post-) operaist thought was an important strand of the struggles developing in Italy during the 1960s and '70s; from the labour struggle taking place in the big factories to the non-institutional strategies of the *autonomia operaia*, and to the early theoretical and practical ways of contesting the transformations of the capitalist mode of production that continue today. In these experiences of the *autonomia*, flight was already a familiar idea, mainly in terms of a flight from the factories. Antonio Negri, who significantly contributed to the formation of the operaist movement from the beginning of the 1960s, founded the group *autonomia operaia* in 1969. This group developed notions like *operaio sociale*, social worker and *fabbrica diffusa*, all of which no longer understood the factory as the centre of production and conflict, but more diffuse spaces and intersections, potentially the society as a whole.

After his arrest on the charge of terrorism, and following his denunciation as *cattivo maestro*, Negri fled to Paris and linked the (post-) Marxist operaist theory more strongly with those of the poststructuralist colleagues in his French exile. Negri and Guattari wrote a book together (*Nouvelles espaces de liberté*, 1985),[12] while his relationship to Deleuze could be inferred from an interview Negri conducted with Deleuze called 'Control and Becoming'. There Deleuze repeats his dissociation from the traditional Marxist concern with contradictions, and returns to the notion of the line of flight: 'First, we think any society is defined not so much by its contradictions as by its lines of flight, it flees all over the place, and it's very interesting to try and follow the lines of flight taking shape at some particular moment or another' (Deleuze 1995: 171). Negri seems not to have forgotten the stimulation of the time in Paris; a few years later he even describes his choice in 1997 of returning to Italian prison from exile in Paris as a 'line of flight' (Negri 1998: 17).

That's how the figure of fleeing as a specific form of 'being-against' was finally and prominently taken on in the political manifesto *Empire* that Negri co-authored with Michael Hardt around the turn of the millennium. With the concepts 'nomadism', 'desertion' and 'exodus' Hardt and Negri continued conceptualising the non-dialectical form of resistance by flight begun by Deleuze and Guattari.

> Whereas being-against in modernity often meant a direct and/or dialectical opposition of forces, in postmodernity being-against might well be most effective in an oblique or diagonal stance. Battles against the Empire might be won through subtraction and defection. This desertion does not have a place; it is the evacuation of the places of power. (Hardt and Negri 2000: 212)

Migrant exodus appears in *Empire* as a dismissal of the national state's logic of borders and as an expression of the right to freedom of movement. Besides this exodus from peripheries suffering from new forms of exploitation in the global post-Fordist regime, three further categories of exodus appear in the books of Hardt and Negri: The old figure, developed in the *autonomia*, of the exodus of workers from the factories, and therefore also from the patriarchal and hetero-normative conditions of labour; the decline of the state and representative democracy as exodus from an obsolete form of government and being governed; and finally an exodus from the narrow boundaries of the anthropological scheme that wants to determine humans as the centre and confine them within the boundaries of their gendered bodies.

Whereas the all too sympathetic propagation of migration as a revolutionary subject poses a problem in the writings of Hardt and Negri,[13] the punch line of Negri's concept of exodus lies in an activist turn of the figure of flight towards the militant. This connotation is also inherent in Deleuze and Guattari's concept of the line of flight, but in Negri both the analysis of the revolutionary past and the promise of a new communism get a tactical touch of a wild flight that provokes the accumulation of desire rather than its loss: 'For me, exodus sometimes requires force.'[14]

'Radical Imagination'

Such a culmination, such an activist twist, can be traced in another video by Expósito. *Radical Imagination (Carnivals of Resistance)* (61 min., 2004)[15] presents the experiences of Reclaim the Streets, one of the most important groups from the 1990s that worked with new, partly artistic forms of political activism.[16] Reclaim the Streets found their highly diverse origins in the ecological and rave movements of the early 1990s, and organised numerous radical occupations of public spaces in London and other British cities. Expósito's video focuses mainly on the occupation of the financial centre in London, one of the main actions that took place on the 'Global Action Day Against Capital', 18 June 1999, which became known as 'J-18' and 'Carnival against Capital'.

One component of the becoming-aesthetic of the new political practices is their emphasis on questions of form: forms of organisation, forms of action, non-representational forms of representation. In this context carnival functions less as a simple antagonism – '*against* capital' – and more as a figure fleeing such dichotomies and overcoming classical forms of protest. Radical carnival does not enact a Dionysian freak-out that would enable us to work more efficiently afterwards. Here being *against* is not a transgressive gesture trying to run against a border or overcome it. Rather, in this carnivalesque flight the inventive power of new forms of political organisation and action become important, forms which do not separate politics and aesthetics, but develop a new political aesthetics.

Marcelo Expósito not only shows that 'Carnival against Capital' anticipated or developed the most important forms of action for the anti-globalisation movement, his video also refers to the historical forerunners of the carnival as insurgence. These forerunners had one thing in common: contrary to orderly strikes and demonstrations where protest masses tend to be homogenised into a structure from the beginning, in the carnival a formation emerges that I call a *non-conforming* mass. Against the denunciation of the mass as grey, indifferent and homogenous, against the negative connotations of the mass that can also be found in leftist discourses, the concept of a *non-conforming* mass suggests that it cannot be understood as *uni-form*. Such a non-conforming formation organises itself in heterogeneity and difference, as a permeable, fluctuating, diffused mass. Its non-conformity is double: The mass signals its non-conformity by not agreeing with the form of how it is governed, and its unity remains exclusively negative, based on the rejection of the specific forms of being governed. On the other hand, non-conformity is the negation of every positive description of community and means the permanent differentiation of the singular. The non-conforming mass is not locked into *one* form, but moves itself, its space and its sociality.

In the non-conforming form of the radical carnival the most problematic separation in aesthetic as well as political representation, the separation between active and passive components, is dissolved. This is shown in a statement of Mikhail Bakhtin, quoted in the video: 'Carnival ignores any distinction between actor and spectator, it does away with the stage, the spectators don't go to a carnival, they are the carnival.'[17] If crisis and insurgency, confusion and protest, emerge in the un-formed, formless, non-conforming flows of radical carnival, then this is not about the effect of an inside on an outside, an 'outside effect', achieving the education or involvement of those positioned outside – the anonymous art audience or the revolutionary subject, persons aesthetically and politically yet to be enlightened. What is important is a new mixture of bodies and signs that does not want to present itself to an outside, that wants to be different and excessive, as excessive and different *as possible* – even if only for the short time of the event, the rupture, inventing ever new tricks to avoid being counted, striated and divided by a state apparatus. The 'Carnival against Capital' enables not only the event, the rupture, the flight, but also social recompositions, the emergence of desiring machines by which the striation of space is disrupted. This double movement, these parallel lines of flight and weapon, of suspending rupture and social recomposition, inform the quality of transgression on the plane of immanence as it shapes the radical carnival. This form of *immanent transgression* means that there is no spatial beyond of transgression, but also no temporal beyond, no succession of flight and invention, of fleeing and constituent power. The space where immanent transgression takes place is the only possible space of transgression. The time of immanent transgression is the actualisation of two temporalities of the line of flight, the event of protest in fleeing and the duration of the inventive constituent power. In the words of Reclaim the Streets activist John Jordan: 'We want to get away from a traditional confrontational protest situation and prefigure our imagined world in the moment of protest itself.'[18]

Paulo Virno and the Grammar of Exodus

Paolo Virno is a philosopher who mainly works on the philosophy of language. This philosophy, like that of Antonio Negri – although less obviously – also emerges from the Marxist background of Italian operaist and post-operaist theory. As a young man in the 1970s Virno was active in the group *Potere Operaio*, and spent three years, up to his acquittal, in prison because of it. Unlike Negri, Virno has no personal relations or theoretical filiations to Deleuze and Guattari, and his work shows no explicit references to the French line. Yet the resonances between the different European flows of political philosophy, as they shaped the late twentieth century, also appear in Virno's central concepts.

Virno develops his own concept of flight and exodus very early, and as a direct result of his experiences of the *autonomia* in the 1970s. In September 1981 he published the short essay 'Il gusto dell'abbondanza' ('The Taste of Abundance'), where he clearly outlines his concept of exodus.[19] Beginning from an image already described by Marx as the crisis of the capitalist accumulation process, the desertion of workers from the factory, Virno offers an interpretation of the difficulties of implementing capitalism in the United States. Low property prices, an almost inexhaustible reservoir of land, and a situation of overabundance enabled a mass flight from work under the wage lords. According to Virno, the cult of mobility emerging in the 1970s, the desire to escape unambiguousness, and the desertion from the factories were repetitions of this early American crisis of capitalism: 'Nomadism, individual freedom, desertion, and the feeling of abundance nourish the contemporary social conflict' (Virno 2002: 181). Already in 1981 Virno concludes his essay about exodus with the following sentences, which have remained his 'program' until today:

Disobedience and flight are not in any case a negative gesture that exempts one from action and responsibility. To the contrary, to desert means to modify the conditions within which the conflict is played instead of submitting to them. And the positive construction of a favourable scenario demands more initiative than the clash with pre-fixed conditions. An affirmative 'doing' qualifies defection, impressing a sensual and operative taste on the present. The conflict is engaged starting from what we have constituted through fleeing in order to defend social relations and new forms of life out of which we are already making experience. To the ancient idea of fleeing in order to better attack is added the certainty that the fight will be all the more effective if one has something else to lose besides one's own chains. (Virno 2002: 181)

In his most well-known book, *A Grammar of the Multitude*, Virno returns after almost twenty years to the figure of (radical) disobedience and flight (Virno 2004: 69–71). There he describes, amongst other things, the migration of the political from the 'public sphere' into the realm of production. He explains the subsumption of political acts by the work process, and particularly by virtuosity. In it Virno sees the essential premise of contemporary production connected with the emergence of a new historical-political 'subject': the post-Fordist multitude. Certainly, upon reading *A Grammar of the Multitude*, the impression might arise that Virno, in contrast to the older Negri, is more interested in the grammar than in the multitude. His interest in questions from the philosophy of language, and his emphasis on language as an undefined score common to all humans, confirms this interpretation. But it is the continuous quality of Virno's writing to connect by surprising breaks and bridges these questions of language and intellect as a transindividual basis of cooperation and as 'general intellect' to components of political philosophy.

In Virno's latest book, *Motto di spirito e azione innovativa* (*Wit and Innovative Action*), this theoretical strategy of politicising linguistic grammar is repeated once again. Initially the book offers a basic discussion of the 'essence', 'structure' and 'logic' of the joke in relation to the emergence of creativity and innovative action. The book's starting point is Freud's study of the joke, published in 1905. Virno sees this book as a significant attempt to interpret the various kinds of joke in a quasi-*botanical* way, and he proceeds in a similar, although – like Deleuze and Guattari – strictly anti-Freudian manner.

But Virno is not interested in the joke *per se*. According to him the joke is a diagram of innovative action. In its grammar macrocosmic changes of life forms are mirrored in miniature. In extensive philosophical elaborations, mainly about Aristotle, Wittgenstein and Carl Schmitt, Virno tries to show that it is the joke that demonstrates that the world can be changed, and indeed *how*. After these elaborations about, amongst other things, the difficulty in applying a rule and its relation to the exception and the state of exception, he finally and quite surprisingly returns to two of his most well-known figures from *A Grammar of the Multitude*. In *Motto di spirito e azione innovativa* these figures appear first of all as two basic types of joke. For Virno these are the multiple, ambivalent use of concepts and sayings, and the dislocation of meaning. All jokes as well as all human undertakings to change their form of life nourish themselves, according to Virno, *either* from the unusual combination of existing elements *or* from an abrupt deviation. In this context jokes become the microcosm where we experience the unexpected combination and shift of meaning as the basis of a change in forms of life. These are exactly the two modes of *creatio continua* of concepts that I referred to at the beginning of this text: the new combination, the recomposition that consciously creates misunderstanding and irritation and the radical dislocation of concepts from their familiar contexts. But we find this basic typology on the macroscopic level as well, as innovation and exodus – or, to return to the key concepts of this text, as inventing and fleeing, weapon and flight, rupture and recomposition, destitution and instituent practice.

Virno writes about the link between jokes as dislocations and the oldest stories of exodus: The logical-linguistic resources needed for finding a way out of Egypt are exactly those that jokes feed upon. These are characterised by deferral and dislocation, that is, by an abrupt deviation from the axis of the discourse. On a linguistic level this deviation means instantly changing the subject if a conversation proceeds as if on train tracks. In the political field it is actualised as a collective defection, as exodus. Confronted with the question of whether they should be subordinate or openly rebel against the pharaoh's domination, the Israelites invent a possibility no one previously reckoned with: they flee. Instead of treating the problem as a decision between given alternatives, exodus changes the context this problem appeared in. This opens, Virno argues, a side road not yet inscribed into existing political maps, and so changes the very grammar determining the options of thinkable choices:

> Exodus is the transmission of the heuristic procedure the mathematicians call data variations, onto political practice. By preferring secondary or heterogeneous factors we gradually move away from a specific problem, namely the question of submission or insurrection, to a completely different

problem: How can we actualise a movement of desertion and simultaneously test forms of self-administration which previously were unthinkable? (Virno 2005: 79)[20]

From Virno's first political writings on exodus to the language philosophy of the recent books, this Deleuzo-Guattarian figure reappears: there is a concatenation between flight and weapon, between the movement of fleeing, of deserting, of suspending, and the virtuosic, inventive, constituent power of social recomposition that emerges anew in the setting of post-Fordist capitalism.

'The City Factory': To Escape the City as Factory

So what score are present-day virtuosos playing from? I suggest the following answer: every day, contemporary virtuosos (taking virtuosity as an activity without a finished work, in need of a public space) . . . are following that specific and peculiar score which is the 'general intellect', the whole ensemble of human intellectual abilities.[21]

With a great deal of political and aesthetic intuition, Marcelo Expósito approaches the actualisation of Virno's conceptual assemblage in his video *First of May (the City-Factory)* (62 min., 2004). The video offers a complex introduction to the transformation from the Fordist paradigm of the factory to the post-Fordist paradigm of virtuoso cognitive and affective work. With the example of the Fiat factory at Lingotto, once a proud centre of automobile production and now a hotel and conference centre and example of the *fabbrica diffusa*, Expósito shows in meaningful and detailed images those transformations of the political and of the means of production described by Virno. Parallel to this a discussion of forms of resistance runs through the video, from strikes to interventions into the city as the space of the post-Fordist factory, from clogs thrown into the machinery to the figure of the hacker disrupting the machinery of communication, from the striking workers of the Fordist factory to the contemporary practice of the ChainWorkers and the Euromayday movement as a transnational renewal of the political practice of the 1st of May.[22]

In post-Fordist capitalism, labour increasingly develops towards a virtuoso performance without product. It demands a space that is structured like the public. It demands the presence of others, which Hannah Arendt recognised as the basic category of the political. It demands that one exposes oneself to the gaze of others, and as a result cooperation and communication become basic qualities of labour, and virtuosity and performativity become necessary inter-subjective competences.[23] Virno's example comes from the field of virtuosity in the narrow everyday sense: Glenn Gould hated to perform in front of the public and therefore retreated to the recording studio. Of course, this retreat is by no means a simple withdrawal to the artist's ivory tower. In his video Expósito shows Glenn Gould's practice in an astonishing way: Virtuosity takes place here as a suspension of his appearance as a 'performing artist' and at the same time within the meticulous work of a new arrangement of the material in post-production – suspension and recomposition as the two sides of a line of flight. Whereas Gould rejected reproducing scores within the concert business, he attended all the more intensively to a potential new arrangement of the given material in an undefined score.

But this line of flight is no longer the exclusive competence of the virtuosic artist, today it also belongs to the contemporary everyday virtuosos Virno speaks of. The everyday flight from performativity as representation and the weapons of the new (social) arrangements are also implicit components of Expósito's description of Euromayday. If the factory spreads into the whole city, then 'the city is the new space of labour, the territory to be subverted and reorganised by the new antagonist forces'.[24] And this de- and reterritorialisation has also happened in many cities from the middle of this decade: Since 2004, like an accelerated variation of the practice of Reclaim the Streets, a stream of dancing, chanting, painting people rolls through many European city centres on May 1st. Reclaiming the city streets, the city walls and the social spaces occurs as a suspension of traditional protest forms and as a recomposition of bodies and signs in a territory where action and representation blur. In this way the diffusion of the virtuosic/artistic into the city of cognitive capitalism fights back: As the logos and displays of corporate capitalism, which differentially unify city centres, exist due to the creativity of a multiplicity of cognitive workers as virtuosos, the score of creativity – exercised within precarious jobs – now spreads as an opponent over the logos and displays of the urban zone of consumption: 'on the walls, the advertisements, the representations of the state, the banks or the big brands, appear the new signs that give visibility to the "precariato sociale" of the city as an emergent social subject'.[25]

Marcelo Expósito's video works actualise this twofold fleeing and invention (of searching/finding the weapon) movement to be found in different variations in Deleuze and Guattari, Negri and Virno, as well as in the artistic-political practices of the last ten years. The videos, however, cannot simply be understood as representation, but rather

3.2: Marcelo Expósito, video still from *First of May (the City-Factory)*, 62 min., 2004. Image courtesy of the artist.

empathically depict the interwoven currents of theory and practice. They draw a line of flight from conventional documentary practices (historiographic, artistic and activist), and at the same time they are interventions into those political practices that have abandoned the old figure of the opposition and separation of politics and aesthetics.

Translated by Anita Fricek and Stephen Zepke

References

Deleuze, G. (1994), *Difference and Repetition*, trans. P. Patton, New York: Columbia University Press.
Deleuze, G. (1995), *Negotiations*, trans. M. Joughin, New York: Columbia University Press.
Deleuze, G. and F. Guattari (1994), *What is Philosophy?*, trans. H. Tomlinson and G. Burchell, New York: Columbia University Press.
Deleuze, G. and F. Guattari (2004), *A Thousand Plateaus*, trans. B. Massumi, London: Continuum.
Deleuze, G. and C. Parnet (2002), *Dialogues II*, trans. H. Tomlinson and B. Habberjam, London: Continuum.

Hardt, M. and A. Negri (2000), *Empire*, Cambridge, MA: Harvard University Press.
Negri, A. (1998), *Ready-Mix: Vom richtigen Gebrauch der Erinnerung und des Vergessens*, trans. H. Teschke, Berlin: b_books.
Negri A. and F. Guattari (1990), *Communists Like Us*, trans. M. Ryan, New York: Semiotext(e).
Raunig, G. (2007), *Art and Revolution: Transversal Activism in the Long Twentieth Century*, trans. A. Derieg, New York: Semiotext(e).
Raunig, G. (2008), 'Fluchtlinie und Exodus: Zu einigen offensiven Figuren des Fliehens', in S. Nowotny and G. Raunig (eds), *Instituierende Praxen. Bruchlinien der Institutionskritik*, Vienna: Turia + Kant, pp. 209–18.
Raunig, G. (2009), *A Thousand Machines: A Concise Philosophy of the Machine as Social Movement*, trans. A. Derieg, New York: Semiotext(e).
Raunig, G. and G. Ray (eds) (2009), *Art and Contemporary Critical Practice: Reinventing Institutional Critique*, London: Mayflybooks.
Virno, P. (2002), *Esercizi di esodo: Linguaggio e azione politica*, Verona: ombre corte.
Virno, P. (2004), *A Grammar of the Multitude: For an Analysis of Contemporary Forms of Life*, trans. I. Bertoletti, J. Cascaito, A. Casso, New York: Semiotext(e).
Virno, P. (2005), *Motto di spirito e azione innovative: Per una logica del cambiamento*, Torino: Bollati Boringhieri.

Notes

1. I develop some of these figures in Raunig (2008).
2. I problematised this specific misunderstanding, mainly in terms of the art world, in 'Instituent Practices, Fleeing, Instituting, Transforming' (Raunig and Ray 2009: 3–11); also available at: http://eipcp.net/transversal/0106/raunig/en
3. 'I may be running, but I'm looking for a gun as I go' (Deleuze and Guattari 2004: 226).
4. See also Deleuze (1994: 37).
5. See also Deleuze (1995: 77).
6. The notion of the 'primacy of lines of flight' is explicitly developed in Deleuze and Parnet (2002: 102). On the primacy of resistance, see Raunig (2007: 44–54).
7. Marcelo Expósito has also expanded the notion of flight in a self-reflective text where he describes his double movement of entering into (art) institutions and escaping from them; see 'Inside and Outside the Art Institution: Self-Valorisation and Montage in Contemporary Art' (Raunig and Ray 2009: 141–53); also available at: http://eipcp.net/transversal/0407/exposito/en
8. Quoted from Marcelo Expósito, *The Year in Which the Future Ended (Began)*. The film can be seen at: http://www.hamacaonline.net/obra.php?id=592
9. Quoted from Expósito, *The Year in Which the Future Ended (Began)*.
10. See http://www.armhcuenca.org
11. Marcelo Expósito, in an email exchange with the author, 15 December 2008.
12. Translated as *Communists Like Us* (Negri and Guattari 1990).
13. For a critique of Negri and Hardt's exodus notion, see Katja Diefenbach, 'New Angels: On the Happiness of Being Communist: Multitude in Empire'; available at: http://eipcp.net/transversal/0303/diefenbach/en
14. See 'What Makes a Biopolitical Space? *A Discussion with Toni Negri*'; available at: http://www.eurozine.com/articles/2008-01-21-negri-en.html

15. The film can be seen at http://www.hamacaonline.net/obra.php?id=244
16. See Marion Hamm, 'Reclaim the Streets! Global Protests and Local Space'; available at: http://eipcp.net/transversal/0902/hamm/en; and John Jordan, 'Notes Whilst Walking on "How to Break the Heart of Empire"'; available at: http://eipcp.net/transversal/1007/jordan/en
17. Quoted from Marcelo Expósito's film, *Radical Imagination (Carnivals of Resistance)*.
18. John Jordan, quoted from Expósito's *Radical Imagination (Carnivals of Resistance)*.
19. Republished as 'Dell'Esodo', in Virno (2002: 179–84).
20. On critique as suspension and recomposition, see my 'What is Critique? Suspension and Recomposition in Textual and Social Machines' (Raunig and Ray 2009: 113–30); also available at http://eipcp.net/transversal/0808/raunig/en
21. Quoted from Marcelo Expósito's film, *First of May (the City-Factory)*; the film can be seen at http://www.hamacaonline.net/obra.php?id=240
22. See http://euromayday.org, as well as Raunig (2009).
23. Virno specifies the notion of performativity himself, mainly in relation to the contemporary social movement he therefore also calls 'performative'. See 'Un movimento performativo'; available at: http://eipcp.net/transversal/0704/virno/it. In this 2005 text Virno analyses the question of why the anti-globalisation movement 'did not sufficiently bundle those forms of struggle which are able to change the state of precarious, temporary and a-typical labour into subversive political potency'. For more on virtuosity, see Isabell Lorey, 'Virtuosos of Freedom'; available at: http://eipcp.net/transversal/0207/lorey/en
24. Quoted from Marcelo Expósito's film, *First of May (the City-Factory)*.
25. Quoted from Expósito, *First of May (the City-Factory)*.

Chapter 4

Anita Fricek: Contemporary Painting as Institutional Critique

Stephen Zepke

The strong always have to be defended against the weak.
Friedrich Nietzsche, *The Will to Power*

One place we might start a Deleuzian discussion of Contemporary art is with his definition of the 'contemporary'. For Deleuze the 'contemporary' is an ontological rather than chronological term, marking the emergence of something new as the construction and expression of being in becoming. As a result, 'contemporary' art produces sensations that exceed any pre-given conditions of possibility, in a genetic 'event' that constructs a new future. 'Contemporary' art is forever out of time, 'to come', an 'absolute deterritorialization' that *'summons forth a new people'* (Deleuze and Guattari 1994: 99). In this sense, Guattari suggests that instead of speaking of 'Contemporary art' we should speak of an *'Atemporal* art' (Guattari 1994: 64), one whose criteria are not history, medium, technique or content, but creativity. The 'contemporary' in art would therefore emerge, according to Deleuze, as part of a *tradition* of the 'new',[1] one which was not defined by the traditions of 'art', but neither was it denied to them. So although it is tempting to see the tradition of the new as equating with the avant-garde trajectory,[2] the 'contemporary' in art does not emerge simply through a critique of the present, or of its history, which both retain the 'before' as the condition of any conceivable 'after'.[3]

If the avant-garde sought to overcome the boundaries of 'art' in order to operate directly within, and as, 'life', it did so by defining these through a concept of 'art as institution' encompassing 'the productive and distributive apparatus and also to the reception of works'. According to this classic account by Peter Bürger: 'The avant-garde turns against both – the distribution apparatus on which the work of art depends, and the status of art in bourgeois society as defined by the concept of autonomy' (Bürger 1984: 22). For the avant-garde, even if only in a negative sense, the critique of the art institution was a condition of possibility to art being 'new'. While its adherents claimed, and still do, that this 'critical' relation to 'art' was political, it was, and is, a 'politics' that is primarily recognisable in the world of, and in fact *as*, art. For Deleuze and Guattari, on the contrary, art is already life, inasmuch as a sensation is a becoming. This immediately makes the question as to what constitutes 'contemporary' art an entirely practical one, it is a question of creating, as Guattari puts it, 'new modalities of subjectivity in the same way that an artist creates new forms from the palette'. The palette is a given tradition, but immersed in life this tradition is already 'contemporary' inasmuch as it is capable of what Guattari calls a 'realisation of autonomy' (Guattari 1995: 7). The autonomy of art, at least when it is realised, is not a bourgeois institutionalisation that must be rejected, but a radical alterity introduced into the social body as sensation. This sensation affirms a body uncontained by its institutions, a body that evades its negation in the critical 'consciousness' of the avant-garde and institutional critique.

As a result, the 'contemporary' does not spell 'the death of painting', which from an ontological perspective can produce the 'new' as well as anything else. Indeed, Deleuze argues, the tradition of painting is constituted by 'every painter [that] recapitulates the history of painting in his or her own way' (Deleuze 2003: 122). This 'recapitulation' not only reinvigorates the tradition of painting, but invents sensations that free subjectivity from its existing conditions, giving it a creative 'autonomy'. In Deleuze then, 'contemporary' art produces a new sensation as the becoming of life, while much 'Contemporary art' is concerned with defining itself against an existing 'art', so as to better embrace and utilise the 'life' of 'non-art'. A radical divergence seems to emerge here between 'contemporary' art as the production of new sensations (Deleuze), and the increasingly conceptual attempts by 'Contemporary art' to overcome itself and its institutions to live a life dedicated to 'politics'. The name of this divergence, indeed its condition of possibility, is Marcel Duchamp, and as a result perhaps Contemporary art should look elsewhere than Deleuze for its ontology.[4]

But Deleuze does more than simply affirm painting as one possible medium capable of producing a sensation, he provides us with a genealogy of painting that stretches from pre-historic cave art to the colour fields of American abstraction. Indeed at one point Deleuze tells us that his differences with Clement Greenberg and Michael Fried are merely 'a quarrel over words, an ambiguity of words' (Deleuze 2003: 107).

We shouldn't be surprised, considering how Deleuze emphasises the importance of colour and its production of a 'shallow depth' in painting's repeated breaks with his nemesis, representation. In this regard Deleuze's interest in how a painter 'recapitulates the history of painting' echoes Greenberg's account of modern painting as the immanent critique of its own transcendental conditions – colour and flatness – to produce abstract visual sensations. But although both Deleuze and Greenberg follow Kant in claiming that sensation constitutes the realm of the aesthetic, and both see Kant's concept of immanent critique as revealing its conditions, Deleuze's emphasis on producing the (ontological) new frees critique from simply revealing painting's transcendental and formal *conditions of possibility* (colour and 'flatness', or for the avant-garde its institutionalisation). Taking us beyond the Americans' affirmation of Abstract Expressionism, Deleuze's 'contemporary' sensation expresses art's *'real conditions'*; the becoming-active forces of 'Life'.

Like Greenberg, Deleuze's insistence on sensation as the realm of the aesthetic derives from Kant. Departing from the *Critique of Judgement*, however, Deleuze demonstrates how universal claims to aesthetic judgement (and the free play of the faculties that is their condition of possibility) find their limit and finally collapse into chaos in the experience of the sublime. Here, the transcendental synthesis of sensation in a perception breaks down into a rhythmical *perspective* expressing the genetic chaos of Nature. This sensation without conditions of possibility is an *individuation*, a *'form in itself* that does not refer to any external point of view' (Deleuze and Guattari 1994: 210). These immanent principles of individuation are sublime rhythms, *'material-forces'* (Deleuze and Guattari 1988: 342) acting as the transcendental and real conditions of sensation; they are unconditioned by consciousness and their 'transcendental materialism' (qua body of sensation) emerges beyond the all-too-Kantian Idealism of Greenberg's 'opticality'.[5]

This is not, of course, to say that artists have stopped painting; they have not. But painting after modernism has become contemporary by largely abandoning it's abstract singularities of colour and flatness, in favour of engaging with the world, and its discursive and 'readymade' modes of representation. Painting's historical trajectory is not, however, the problem of this essay; because of course it is not a problem at all. It happened, and often it was good. The problem is instead how we might be able to place Deleuze within this trajectory, a process that might allow us to reassess his relevance to Contemporary art. Rather than attempting some sort of synthesis, I would instead like to explore this relation as a disjunction. Indeed, it seems to me that it is only by understanding the disjunction between Deleuze and Contemporary art that we can possibly forge a path that retains a modicum of realism and respect in portraying both sides. Seen from the perspective of Deleuze or of Contemporary art the other often tends to become a convenient caricature rather than a divergence. As a result, I propose to explore this disjunction in what I take to be an imminently Deleuzian way, through the discussion of an example: some recent work by the Viennese painter Anita Fricek.[6] Fricek's work is on the one hand painting, and as such clearly falls within the logic of sensation Deleuze uses to define art, and on the other it offers an 'institutional critique' consistent with the 'political' ambitions of much Contemporary art. It is precisely this status as 'contemporary painting' (or as it is sometimes referred to, 'post-conceptual painting') that will allow us to move beyond the banal conflation or mutual exclusion of Deleuze and Contemporary art (to put the existing situation in its starkest terms).

Many of Fricek's paintings share a certain compositional structure with Bacon's work. They have an abstract background describing a shallow space in which various figures are in movement. This movement is both extensive, the figures launching themselves out of the picture frame, and intensive, as the figures seem to emerge from or fade into the canvas. We can see both movements in the main figures of *Bambule* (2005) (image 4.1) and *Butterfly Girl* (2002) (image 4.2).

The flat planes and the figures are often directly connected through a shared colour (the yellow vertical and shirt of the foreground figure in *Bambule*, or the blue vertical and habit of the Nun in *Butterfly Girl*). This conjunction operates like the contour in Bacon, either materialising the abstract ground in the body of the figure in a systolic spasm, or constructing an intense figure in a diastolic and dispersionary movement. In this way Fricek's figures manifest a series of differential relations – flat–volume, solid–sketchy, abstract–figurative, etc. – that produces a rhythmical vibration, as the figure is captured and escapes. This gives a strong torsion in the picture surface, a movement in place that is undetermined by optical space and produces a sensation, a feeling of force. Or rather it is the other way around, as Deleuze claims of Bacon's paintings: 'it is levels of sensation that explain what remains of movement. . . . it is a movement "in place," a spasm, which reveals . . . *the action of invisible forces on the body*' (Deleuze 2003: 41). In this sense then, Fricek's work clearly adheres to Deleuze's fundamental requirement: 'Painting must render invisible forces visible' (57).

What is also obvious however is that Fricek's paintings do not distort

4.1: Anita Fricek, *Day Room, The Girls' Dance (from a still from the TV film 'Bambule', Ulrike Meinhof/Eberhard Itzenplitz, BRD 1970)*, oil on canvas, 195 × 155 cm, 2005. Photo: Michael Nagl. Image courtesy of the artist.

the figure to the same extent as do Bacon's pools of flesh. Her figures are not so much deformed as de- and re-forming, and rather than registering force in a kind of aesthetic physics (like the paintings of Cezanne express gravitational or telluric forces), they express the vicissitudes of subjectivity – its capture and escape – within social institutions. The danger here, according to Deleuze, is that force is 'hidden' in narration, and so produces mere illustration and spectacle (Deleuze 2003: 62). Such figuration, Deleuze argues, passes through the brain, and rather than acting directly on the nervous system as sensation does, it becomes conscious (36). In this way figuration subordinates the manual aspects of the painting process, as well as its nervous reception as a sensation, to the readymade forms and clichés acting as our 'contemporary' conditions of possible experience. Fricek, however, employs a colour system based upon differential values (the mixing of complementarities that Deleuze calls 'broken tones') and constructs her figures from small modulated planes counteracting the effects of perspective (what Deleuze calls, in his discussion of Cezanne, 'patches'), but her paintings clearly do not reject all 'content'.[7] Fricek's paintings therefore ask an important question on behalf of contemporary painting, and indeed Contemporary art in its various expanded senses, as to whether the capturing of forces might not be able to achieve a 'critical' engagement with our social means of production.

To answer this question we first need to understand more precisely what the 'content' of Fricek's paintings are. For nearly ten years Fricek's work has had a single theme, to analyse various pedagogical theories and the institutions in which they are enacted through painting. The abstract fields making up the background of her paintings generally refer to the architecture of pedagogical institutions, as these exist not only in space but also as processes of subjection that she calls the institution's 'abstracting function' (Fricek 2007: 137). Fricek's work renders these forces in the children's home, the orphanage, or at school, but always places them in relation to another force that *resists*. Not in Bacon's sense of producing a 'hysterical presence' but, in the manner of Contemporary art, through a critical intervention in the social realm that transforms the oppressive forces of the institution into liberatory potentials. In this way Fricek opens up the intriguing possibility of using painting and the sensations it produces as a non-dialectical mechanism of institutional critique.

There are clear benefits to be gained from this approach. Fricek sidesteps the tendency within recent revivals of institutional critique to emphasise new technology and/or political activism as the proper mediums of its exercise, purged as they (apparently) are of any collaboration with the art institution or the parade of spectacle that fills it. As painting, Fricek's work refuses to subordinate 'art' to the 'political' criteria of 'non-art', a 'critical' move that cannot be understood outside the rarefied debates of the art world. On the other hand, Fricek's approach

4.2: Anita Fricek, *Butterfly Girl*, oil on canvas, 150 × 190 cm, 2002.
Photo: Michael Nagl. Image courtesy of the artist.

also enlarges the political horizon of painting beyond Deleuze's own obsession with the radical destruction of the human form (Bacon's ecstatic bodies without organs and the haptic vision that perceives/participates in them), to a critique of human institutions that allows us – perhaps even requires us – to transform their reactive 'sad' passions into active 'joyful' becomings.

In this way Fricek's approach enlarges Deleuze's discussion of the forces of sensation within Bacon's work by combining it with the critique of social forces Deleuze finds in Nietzsche. This allows Fricek to develop a painted sensation whose real conditions (qua individuation) extend the 'aesthetic' realm into the political. In this, Nietzsche is the source for Deleuze's response to Kant, because, as Deleuze puts it, 'Kant had not carried out a true critique because he was not able to pose the problem of critique in terms of values' (Deleuze 1983: 1). Nietzsche provides a form of immanent critique that brings Deleuze's vision of the sublime (real) conditions of sensation back from the 'beyond', to place them directly within the actual world of political conflict. In this way, Fricek 'paints with a hammer', she engages with (institutional) forces in a way that *creates* them anew through a critical evaluation. Here we enter into the realm of a *critical* sensation, one that determines a force's value as *high* or *low*, *noble* or *base* (see Deleuze 1983: 2). In the systolic and diastolic movements of Fricek's figures we see these reactive and active forces attempting to impose or escape the 'abstracting function' of the institution. Following Nietzsche, Fricek affirms and endeavours to protect – through paint and sensation – the strong (the active and noble force of the child we all are) from the weak (the servile and institutionalised adults we have become) (see Deleuze 1983: 53). Here contemporary 'content' is a conscious part of the sensation, but only as a 'symptom of a deeper transformation and of the activities of entirely nonspiritual forces' (39). In this sense consciousness is merely the symptom of a body (that is, an individuation) that is defined by the 'relation between dominant and dominated forces' (40).

Consciousness is integral to the functioning of the pedagogical institution, because the institution enforces a consciousness-of-servility, it 'is always the consciousness of an inferior in relation to a superior' (Deleuze 1983: 39). The institution produces a servile consciousness through series of mechanical *regulations* (see Deleuze 1983: 40–1) that 'subject' the child's body, detaching it from its active forces. It is precisely this aspect of the pedagogical institution that is examined in Fricek's work, in particular the areas for sleeping and washing where the body and its most instinctual functions are regulated and controlled (*Zéro de Conduite* [image 4.3], *Kindergarten* [image 4.4]). Fricek places these regulative institutional functions in a differential relation to the noble forces they seek to 'subject', exploring the ways the child embodies the insubordinate force-sensation of a becoming-active.[8] Here institutional critique becomes a revaluation of values.

This is precisely the meaning of the wonderful scene from Jean Vigo's film that Fricek uses in *Zéro de Conduite* (2005). On one side is the 'abstracting function' of the dormitory being checked and patrolled by the adult warden/teacher, while on the other the 'pagan procession' of the boys erupts in an anarchic autopoiesis that overcomes the architecture of the dormitory. This collective body of the 'procession' is a social individuation, a 'body without organs' to use the vocabulary of the Bacon book, expressing and constructing the 'constitutive difference of level' of the institution (Deleuze 2003: 37). Whereas the representation of the dormitory has an abstract regularity reflecting the way it homogenises and controls the boys' bodies, the scene of the procession is a fragmented and chaotic series of 'manual traits', a gestural abstraction that solidifies into the procession seen at the bottom edge. Although this

4.3: Anita Fricek, *Zéro de Conduite 1933 (Abstraction Machine – Re-entering the Abstraction)*, oil on canvas, 195 × 260 cm, 2005. Photo: Michael Nagl. Image courtesy of the artist.

final scene is clearly figurative, it is so only as a symptom of a broader 'body' that is constituted by the clash of active and reactive, manual and conscious, noble and base forces that constitute the painting (and institution) as a whole. The painting is, again to use the vocabulary of the Bacon book, an 'analogical expression' of the forces constituting the institution. Fricek is not interested in simply opposing these forces, good against bad, child against the institution, etc., but creates a diagram that revalues institutional forces so they are able to become-active, are able to overcome their confinement, transform servility into freedom, and finally through the painting give these active forces to us as a sensation.[9] There is, then, a 'feedback loop' within *Zéro de Conduite* that transforms the painting into an expression (rather than a representation/ regulation) of its constitutive clash of forces, a 'diagram of a revolution', as Fricek puts it, where the sensation unleashes a 'becoming-active' as the real condition of a 'contemporary' political intervention. Although Fricek utilises colour in constructing her 'haptic vision', its 'abstraction' is not modernist but seeks to engage the real forces at play in social institutions. In this way the Nietzschean institutional critique utilised by Fricek succeeds in using painting's haptic vision to intervene in the area of 'content'. Fricek's work incorporates the institution's figurative 'consciousness' as a reactive symptom of the battle of forces constituting the body, and explores how active forces can overcome these institutional boundaries. Critique in this sense is absolutely not figurative, or metaphorical; it is irreducibly real, embodied in the active force of the painting qua critical sensation.

This version of haptic vision, one that is directly transformational of the institution it escapes can be seen in the painting *Kindergarten* (2006). Here two pictorial systems of representation are mixed, an 'Egyptian' style seen in the flattened profiles of the figures, and the central point perspective of the mirrors and other bathroom fittings. It is the girls' vision that traverses and transforms these two systems, as they gaze into the mirrors, creating a kind of pictorial proliferation of forms that overflow both systems and create a new sensation. Fricek is clear about this: 'It is the girls' vision that uses the circular shapes as tools in order to spin into their own self-defined reality' (Fricek 2007: 137). This 'spiralling vision' creates remarkable deformations that are certainly worthy of Bacon. On the left the reflection of the foremost girl appears as if her head has been cut off and hung from the ceiling. Fricek's description is compelling: 'Within the context of the pedagogic institution she is Manet's Olympia, decapitated by Mondrian. It is the pumping force of the circle's arabesques that both reveals and revitalises the workings of

kindergarten 1978

Image source: http://imago.
onb.ac.at/Bildarchiv/baa/vga/1/mittel/VGA_B24_0628_0_m.jpg

4.4: Anita Fricek, *Kindergarten 1978 (The radical girlie perspective)*, oil on canvas, 200 × 200 cm, 2006. Photo: Michael Nagl. Image courtesy of the artist.

the scenario, just like an image medicine or a neutralising device' (137). In this way the painting not only operates critically, but also clinically. It has a medicinal element in the way it treats the symptoms of our conscious institutionalisation in order to free the active forces of the body and its desires. Fricek continues:

> The girls' answer is their singularised vision which overcomes self-reflexivity [in the mirrors] by producing desire . . . The radical girlie perspective is a spin-out machine that embraces conditions given in order to crystallise with all its elements. The girlie spin-out machine is a mechanism to face, neutralise and finally re-code memory. It is the seeing-machine of Olympia's powerful gaze, rebooting the system of her conditions. (Fricek 2007: 138)

This critical revaluation of the institution 'reboots' its memory by turning it towards the future. This is finally the active-force of a sensation, it is what turns consciousness to the body, and allows the body to escape its institutionalisation. This applies as much to painting itself as to its 'content', as Fricek's work also embodies a genealogical 'recapitulation' of the history of painting which answers all of Contemporary art's demands for political intervention!

The introduction of Nietzsche's genealogical critique allows Fricek's painting to engage with social forces more closely than either the abstract colourist realms of modern abstraction or the 'figures' of 'flesh' produced by Bacon. In the Bacon book Deleuze deals very peremptorily with such social forces, claiming their images are 'clichés' circulating within the 'infosphere', primarily in the form of photographs, which he then thoroughly rejects. The problem with photographs is that their representational narratives constitute our consciousness, they 'fill every room or every brain' (Deleuze 2003: 91). This requires the diagram, on Deleuze's account, to wipe the canvas clean of this photo-consciousness and its 'psychic clichés' (87). This process must be relentless and without exception, because today 'even the reactions against clichés are creating clichés' (89). This 'catastrophe' cannot simply be a deformation or manipulation of the cliché, which remain 'too intellectual' (i.e., reactive) and retain the cliché, even if only (or perhaps, in the case of Contemporary art, especially) as irony and parody (87, 89). Deleuze says something similar in relation to Nietzsche's method of critique: 'We cannot use the state of a system of forces as it in fact is, or the result of the struggle between forces, in order to decide which are active and which are reactive' (Deleuze 1983: 58). Instead, critique is achieved through an intervention *of another type of force*. This in fact suggests the path taken by Fricek's painterly institutional critique, which seeks to intervene within institutional architectures through the introduction (via evaluation) of an active force. This evaluation would produce an 'analogical expression', a resemblance (or diagram) of institutional forces produced from entirely different means (Deleuze 2003: 115). This would suggest an extension of the logic of sensation to Contemporary art that was both consistent with Deleuze's understanding of sensation, while nevertheless retaining a critical 'content'. The price to be paid for this, however, is a rejection of Deleuze's pronounced opposition to photography.

Photography, or more generally the photographic image, has become our dominant mode of visual communication, to the extent that Deleuze's rejection of it seems quixotic. To oppose painting to photography is no longer a 'contemporary' option, and painting as well as the other visual arts have in fact moved in the opposite direction.

Today photographic images and technology are increasingly integral to most forms of contemporary artistic practice, painting included. For Deleuze, on the other hand, photographs are posited as conditions of possibility (and will therefore be directly opposed to the random marks Deleuze calls 'possibilities of facts'). Photographs are 'pictorial givens' that invade vision *until finally one sees nothing else* (Deleuze 2003: 91). The photograph, Deleuze argues, 'creates' the person – 'in the sense that we say that the newspaper creates the event (and is not content to narrate it)' – by forcing upon them 'the "truth" of implausible and doctored images' (91). In this close association of photography and the mass media in contemporary forms of subjection Deleuze condemns photography as being 'information', quite opposed to the 'deformation' achieved by art.[10] But there is also perhaps some room to move in relation to Deleuze's animosity towards photography. Deleuze claims that Bacon denies the photograph's aesthetic value because it 'tends to reduce sensation to a single level, and is unable to include within the sensation the difference between constitutive levels' (91). Deleuze obligingly provides a footnote to this no doubt serious ontological objection to photography. But when we follow the footnote to its source we find that Bacon does not say this about photography but about abstract painting! (Sylvester 1999: 58–9). Ample evidence it seems, of Deleuze's famous claim: 'We don't listen closely enough to what painters have to say' (Deleuze 2003: 99).[11] The animosity against photography in the Bacon book is Deleuze's and not Bacon's, and this suggests that perhaps photography might, after all, have a role in a (or at least in Bacon's) logic of sensation. Furthermore, Deleuze's animosity is not unequivocal, and in another footnote Deleuze admits that 'the most interesting cases' of photography's relation to painting 'are those where the painter integrates the photograph, or the photograph's action, apart from any aesthetic value' (183). This remark not only redeems the French painter Gérard Fromanger, about whom Deleuze had written in 1973, and who projected photos onto canvas before painting them in bright, flat colours, but also describes the use of photography made by most contemporary painting.[12] Contemporary painting often projects photographic 'snap-shots' onto the canvas in a way similar to Fromanger, privileging their anti-art and democratised aesthetic as a way of reinvigorating painting's claim to being 'contemporary'.[13] While Fricek often uses snap-shots as sources, these are always found images, and are mostly institutional self-representations. This strategy is similar to what Deleuze sees in Fromanger's use of the photo (which is also taken by someone else), which establishes a 'vital circuit' (Deleuze 1999: 74) between the indifferent commodities and the abstract movements of the colours, of their cold and heat. 'This circuit of life feeds continually on the circuit of death, sweeps it away with itself to triumph over it' (73). Here Deleuze seems to chart a course that moves from photography to painting, from the cliché to sensation, which doesn't make the condition of painting the catastrophe of the photograph. Fromanger's work contains and critiques what the photograph embodies (the commodity, the artist's indifference), it endeavours to transform the reactive forces of the photograph into living sensations, *in painting*.

Fricek works exclusively from photographs, many of which have been 'harvested' (as she puts it) from the internet and so already exist in the public domain. Most are self-representations of institutions, often promotional images that seek to show the institution in a positive light. This makes their architecture, and its control and manipulation of force, all the more obvious and available to Fricek, who selects the most intense of these images and begins to work with it. She does not project the images onto the canvas, but re-paints the photograph in such a way as to revalue its forces. Fricek employs a German term to describe this process, *begreifen*, which means to both touch and to understand, to handle and to make sense of something. It is an understanding that is felt, a kind of *body intelligence*. In this sense, Fricek likens her painting process to dancing, she 'dances through an image' she says; she touches the images, handles them in order to understand them, and finally, through the dance of painting, liberates something in them which their abstract and reactive architectures had repressed. In this way Fricek expresses and constructs a circuit of life, an active power, a force going to the limit of what it can do before becoming something else. This critical 'method' begins from the photograph, but only in order to unleash a force that goes beyond it, a sensation able to 're-animate' the photo, but only by making it into a painting. This very contemporary form of immanent critique therefore begins in the world, with photographs embodying institutional forces, but in confronting these forces it also invents sensations by which active forces overcome their limits to create a new future. Here the figure of the child and the artist come together, and in a beautiful triptych Fricek turns her critical vision on herself within the institutional space of the museum. *White Cube Rush – Dancing the White Cube* (2005) (image 4.5) shows the de- and re-formations of the artist, as she dances through her own institutional conditions, producing a 'Figure' that is perhaps the closest she comes to a Bacon self-portrait. This figure of the dancing child-artist seems to be torn apart by the violence of the

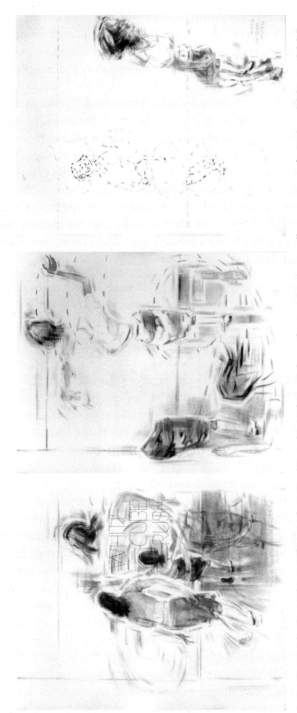

4.5: Anita Fricek, *White Cube Rush – Dancing the White Cube*, oil on canvas, woollen yarn, each 250 × 200 cm, 2005. Photo: Michael Nagl. Image courtesy of the artist.

confrontation, before re-forming in the white canvas where the walls have seemingly evaporated. This fragile and ambiguous power, this 'dancing star' as Nietzsche called it, must be protected – while at the same time being *projected* – against the weak 'consciousness' of the institution.

In Fricek's work the child or artist is always an active force that desires to overcome its limit and emerge transformed, as beautiful and free as the butterfly that is a recurring motif in her work. In this sense, Fricek tries to place a new future within the forced memory of the photograph, she tries to give a photographic 'treatment' or 'handling' to the image-memory, a treatment in the sense of *Behandlung*, the German word for medical assistance, but also a 'treatment' in the photographic sense. Fricek attempts to 're-flash' the photo, as she says, to make it undergo a 'shock' which removes it from its representational function and turns it active. As Fricek puts it:

> The artist searches and finds images that are screenshots of collective memory, scans them in the light of their potentials and deadlocks, throws them into the spin-out-machine and projects them back, until all the elements are set in motion and activate each other. In this way the original images undergo a revitalisation program. (Fricek 2007: 138)

This takes on a literal sense in the triptych '*Le Stelline*' (2006–7). The first panel (*1. The Image: 'Le Stelline', Orphanage, Milan, late '60s ('The Reward')*) shows a 'treated' photo of Le Stelline orphanage in Milan (the image was found on a website about the region and its history). One of the most cynical images Fricek has found, it shows the little girls standing around holding boxed dolls, gifts given to reward their ability to be dolls themselves, identically dressed and all with the same haunting empty gaze. This image is then 're-flashed' in the second panel (*2. The Flash (The Shock)*). Fragments from the image appear in luminous green, a bright fluorescent pigment that hurts the eyes to look at, creating purple hazes and irritation, similar to an actual flash. This is to go back to the moment the picture was taken, Fricek says, to release a new future within it. The final panel (*3. The Development Process (Die Entpuppung)*) is once more the same image but this time in white on white, and once more fragmentary and almost indiscernible. Here the image has returned to a stage of pure potential, a potential that inheres in the technologies of the original photo (in a kind of rewind back from 1) the photo, to 2) the flash, and finally 3) the (re)development), but can no longer be recognised within the institutions the original photo *represented*. This is finally the sense of '*Die Entpuppung*', taken literally it's a 'de-dolling', or more correctly an eclosion; the emergence of an adult from the pupa, like the butterfly.

Fricek's work expresses and constructs the vitality of 'content', it finds a way in which photographic representations and the regulation and equalisation of sensation they produce can be critically evaluated and transformed. Deleuze says 'Forces must not be compared abstractly' (Deleuze 1983: 59), which we might take literally in the terms of the Bacon book as meaning, on the one hand, that an institution's 'abstracting function' can only transform actual forces into a pre-given code, and so reduces their force rather than increasing it. But on the other hand, and against the radical abstraction of Bacon's sublime flows of flesh, Fricek compares real social forces, and produces social 'facts'. This is to acknowledge the difficulty of maintaining Deleuze-Bacon's 'path' in the face of the simple truth that Contemporary art has chosen another way, and suggests in a quite practical manner how we might dispense with some of Deleuze's principles. In this sense, Fricek's paintings map out a form of institutional critique that incorporates photography into its method and fulfils Contemporary art's interest in engagement with the world. But it is also consistent with a logic of sensation that attempts to express forces as pictorial 'facts'. This is where Fricek's work becomes so prescient, it utilises a Nietzschean form of critique that enables us to move beyond Deleuze's insistence on a modernist form of non-representational abstraction, that nevertheless remains consistent with his requirements of an immanent critique into transcendental conditions. These *real* conditions are active and reactive forces, and it is in this realm that Fricek's paintings revalue institutions in individuations that are strong enough to defend themselves. The strong must be protected against the weak.

References

Alliez E. and J.-C. Bonne (2007), 'Matisse-Thought and the Strict Quantitative Ordering of Fauvism', trans. R. Mackay, *Collapse*, Vol. III.
Badiou, A. (2008), 'Some Remarks Concerning Marcel Duchamp', in *The Symptom*, 9 (June); available at: www.lacan.com/symptom/?cat=7
Bürger, P. (1984), *Theory of the Avant-Garde*, trans. M. Shaw, Minneapolis: University of Minnesota Press.
Deleuze, G. (1983), *Nietzsche and Philosophy*, trans. H. Tomlinson, New York: Columbia University Press.
Deleuze, G. (1994), *Difference and Repetition*, trans. P. Patton, New York: Columbia University Press.
Deleuze, G. (1999), 'Cold and Heat', in *Photogenic Painting, Gerard Fromanger*, trans. D. Roberts, London: Black Dog Publishing.
Deleuze, G. (2003), *Francis Bacon: The Logic of Sensation*, trans. D. W. Smith, London and New York: Continuum.

Deleuze, G. (2006), 'What is the Creative Act?', in *Two Regimes of Madness, Texts and Interviews 1975–1995*, ed. D. Lapoujade, trans. A. Hodges and M. Taormina, New York: Semiotext(e).
Deleuze, G. and F. Guattari (1988), *A Thousand Plateaus*, trans. B. Massumi. London: Athlone.
Deleuze, G. and F. Guattari (1994), *What is Philosophy?*, trans. H. Tomlinson and G. Burchell, New York: Columbia University Press.
Fricek, A. (2007), 'The Radical Girlie Perspective', in *Multitudes*, 30 (Autumn).
Fricek, A. (2008), *Anita Fricek: Recent Paintings*, Vienna: Ange.
Guattari, F. (1994), 'Félix Guattari et l'art contemporain', *Chimères*, 23 (Summer).
Guattari, F. (1995), *Chaosmosis: An Ethico-aesthetic Paradigm*, trans. P. Bains and J. Pefanis, Sydney: Power Publications.
Guattari, F. (2000), *The Three Ecologies*, trans. I. Pinder and P. Sutton, London: Athlone Press.
Larsen, L. B., C. Ricupero and N. Schafhausen (eds) (2005), *The Populism Catalogue*, Berlin and New York: Lukas and Sternberg.
Sala Rekalde Erakustaretoa (2005), *The Invisible Insurrection of a Million Minds*, Frankfurt: Revolver Verlag.
Sylvester, D. (1999), *Interviews with Francis Bacon: The Brutality of Fact*, London: Thames and Hudson.
Toscano, A. (2006), *The Theatre of Production: Philosophy and Individuation Between Kant and Deleuze*, Basingstoke and New York: Palgrave Macmillan.

Notes

1. Deleuze is referring to what he calls the 'fine pages' of Harold Rosenberg's *The Tradition of the New* (Deleuze 1994: 91).
2. Guattari seems to have actively flirted with this idea when he writes: 'The incessant clash of the movement of art against established boundaries (already there in the Renaissance, but above all in the modern era), its propensity to renew its materials of expression and the ontological texture of the percepts and affects it promotes brings about if not a direct contamination of the other domains then at least a highlighting and a re-evaluation of the creative dimensions that traverse all of them' (Guattari 1995: 106).
3. As Guattari argues, in a comment applying as much to the avant-garde as to the traditional arts, the creation of new aesthetic futures must emerge 'without their authors having prior recourse to assured theoretical principles or to the authority of a group, a school or an academy' (Guattari 2000: 40).
4. Perhaps it should look to Alain Badiou, who argues that Duchamp's readymade is a process of thought that both introduces the 'contemporary' as such (a contemporary that is essentially conceptual), and is opposed to Deleuze's. The readymade, Badiou writes, 'is the visitation of the idea in its contemporary artistic form. Art is pure Idea. It is not, as in vitalism, corporeal energy establishing the embrace of percepts and affects.' This thought is in fact a 'discontinuity', an event in which not only a new 'art' but also a new 'truth' enters the world by marking what will have been missing from it. This is, perhaps, the Idea of Contemporary art (see Badiou 2008).
5. The term 'transcendental materialism' comes from Alberto Toscano's account of individuation, on which I have drawn here (see Toscano 2006, especially pages 193–201).

6. For recent catalogues of her work see Fricek (2008), Larsen et al. (2005), Sala Rekalde Erakustaretoa (2005). For Fricek's important statement regarding her own technique (in the context of 'Documenta 12') see Fricek (2007).

7. Deleuze's insistence on the rejection of content can seem exaggerated, such as when he upholds Bacon's rather unlikely claims that elements like a Nazi armband or a hypodermic needle play a purely compositional or abstract role, and should not be given any 'meaning' outside of their colour (the armband) or their ability to pin down the arm (the needle).

8. In the journal *Multitudes* Fricek writes regarding the work *Kindergarten*: 'The image of a bathroom was chosen because it is one of the sites that stages the most dramatic encounter between bodily functions/openings and the policies and rituals, thus ideologies of pedagogic institutions – like eating, washing, sleeping, defecating – the sites of dormitories, dining halls, shower rooms. It is where the institution inscribes itself most effectively and potentially violently into bodies, and can thus be a trigger place for the most transformative acts' (Fricek 2007: 136).

9. In relation to Nietzsche Deleuze develops the concept of 'constitutive difference' in terms of a force's quantity and quality, the difference between the quantities of active and reactive forces constituting the force's quality. 'Difference in quantity is . . . the irreducible element *of* quality' (Deleuze 1983: 44). Eric Alliez has developed this idea in relation to the colourism of Matisse (see Alliez and Bonne 2007).

10. 'Information is a set of imperatives, slogans, directions – order words. When you are informed, you are told what you are supposed to believe. . . . A work of art does not contain the least bit of information. In contrast, there is a fundamental affinity between a work of art and an act of resistance' (Deleuze 2006: 320, 322–3).

11. Many of Deleuze's stronger condemnations of photography that he attributes to Bacon are simply not present in the interviews collected in *The Brutality of Fact*. For example, Deleuze claims that 'Bacon has a radical hostility toward the photograph,' and that 'Bacon's whole attitude . . . is one that rejects the photograph' (Deleuze 2003: 92). But in *The Brutality of Fact* Bacon repeatedly states his fascination for photographs and explains the way he uses them in his practice. Indeed, this makes a mockery of Deleuze's claim that 'at no point does [Bacon] ever integrate the photograph into the creative process' (Deleuze 2003: 92). Even Deleuze's own description of Bacon's use of photographs, especially in his portraits, belies this statement.

12. In fact, Deleuze claims, in his essay on Fromanger, that by projecting a photo onto the canvas and painting on it, he 'reveals an eternal truth of painting: that the painter has never painted on the white surface of the canvas to reproduce an object that acts as a model, but has always painted on an image, a simulacrum, a shadow of the object, to produce a canvas whose very operation reverses the relationship of model and copy [to] produce a "heightened reality"' (Deleuze 1999: 65). This seems almost the opposite of claiming that all photography is a cliché, and instead claims that all painting starts with the photograph!

13. Deleuze and Guattari also mention the painter Florence Julien, who 'invented a procedure by which she extracts from photographs lines that are nearly abstract and formless' (Deleuze and Guattari 1988: 224).

THE AESTHETIC PARADIGM

Chapter 5

Capitalism and Schizophrenia and Consensus: Of Relational Aesthetics*

Eric Alliez

Populist Prologue

> And no doubt the combat appears as a combat *against* . . . But more profoundly, it is the combatant himself who is the combat: the combat is *between* his own parts, between the forces that either subjugate or are subjugated, and between the powers that express these relations of forces.
>
> Gilles Deleuze, *Essays Critical and Clinical* ·

There is an amusing article written some ten years ago by the French art critic Eric Troncy, entitled 'The Stockholm Syndrome'. Later revisited by Baudrillard, through Troncy, 'Stockholm syndrome' referred to the paradoxical relations linking socio-cultural consensus to the aesthetics of an avant-garde reduced to the most fashionable 'look' of the nineties. The fact that this was to end badly – today, Troncy writes quirky apologetics for reality TV as contemporary art's most radical readymade, by virtue of its renunciation of all claim to the elitist status of the artwork (the 'everyday' perfect crime!) – makes the article's opening lines all the more delectable: I quote, appropriating this ephemeral moment of lucidity: 'What is at stake is nothing less than the evacuation of revolutionary desire through the small door of communication, at the same time as the draining of alterity into the great pit of the same' (Troncy 1998: 49).

I could not think of a better introduction to the provocation that leads me to present a kind of critical and clinical treatment of relational aesthetics in the murky light of Populism, which we could envisage as signalling the dawn of a sleepless night, of the kind recently organised by Nicolas Bourriaud and Jérôme Sans in Paris, precisely under the heading

* Different versions of this paper, initially given at Tate Britain (14 October 2006), have been published in *Plato* (Istanbul), *Verksted* (Oslo), *Multitudes* (Paris), *Glenta* (Stockholm) and *Z/X* (Auckland). The initial translation was made by Tim Adams for *Z/X* #3, and the subsequent changes were revised by Robin MacKay.

Nuit blanche (or *White Night Event*). I'll be direct then, jumping with both feet straight into the factory of the 'populist' subject, the better to thrash out this question *for real* (or to be thrashed in turn): 'Is there a significant relation between aesthetics and politics to be studied today?' In order to do this, we shouldn't be afraid to introduce the Combat with Oneself and between ourselves, by making our own the cautionary note with which *The Populism Reader* opens: 'A project on populism should claim as a basic right the right to use the term in different ways. . . . It should enact difference. It should differ from itself' (Lesage 2005: 12).

Let us risk an initial and ostensibly controversial statement, which I will endeavour to articulate in its various dimensions:

(1) Contemporary populism is the ultimate (which is to say the complete and terminal) form of the expression of the People.

(2) Contemporary Populism is the post-historical/post-political expression of the People *after* the historical completion of its trajectory as a political subject, globally negotiated between real socialism and real social democracy; statist-proletarian incorporation and expanded reproduction of the people integrated into the co-management of the Welfare State. (The massive transfer of votes from the French Communist Party to the Front National in the 1980s, and from the Front National to Sarkozy very recently, or from the Austrian socialist SPÖ to Jorg Haider's extreme-right party in 2000, then to the conservative ÖVP party, and back to the former during the last elections, give flesh and body to the unprecedented floating Signifier that arises when the Name of the People is *deprived* of its transcendence as a political subject as well as of its reality as the economic agent of reformism. Is this a phenomenon of *afterimage?*)

(3) Contemporary Populism is the shadow cast by the *commodification of politics and life* when the 'people is lacking' and becomes, in its lack, the (most) 'dangerous Supplement' of parliamentary democracy in its reality as the production and media administration of consensus.

(4) Contemporary Populism is the dominant post-political form of globalised postmodernity inasmuch as it expresses in the most immediately 'binarised' manner the Rest of the World, when the Rest and the World (of the 'external' World there remains Nothing in the real subsumption of what I called, with Félix Guattari, *Integrated World Capitalism*)[1] are equally consigned to

the selective/participatory/interactive governmentality of *infotainment* (Market Populism *qua* Capitalistic Democracy).

(5) (In the guise of a riddle.) If the 'aestheticisation of politics' led to the State of Exception of populism in its modern form, what is the name for the (post-)aesthetic (neo-)populism which will necessarily 'make' its own the true hallucination of direct democracy in the contemporary age of the absolute market-form?

(6) (In the guise of an uncontrolled acceleration.) Does there exist a populism of the multitude, or more exactly a populism of which the multitude would be the (post-)aesthetic subject and the object of 're-aestheticisation'? Where the aestheticisation of dissensus would become the post-political form for the exhibition of a post-modernist consensus affirming its 'open' and 'relational' qualities, self-affirming the value of conviviality beyond antagonism and/or radicality. . .?

(7) ('Not nothingness, but powerlessness'. . .) – A relational aesthetics rather than art *and* multitude *qua* relational being?

(8) (. . . namely the power of capture of powerlessness) – Or in other words, it is the 'communism of capital' that will be called here 'formal communism', borrowing from post-Fordism its general regime of 'postproduction'.

I advance this 'between us', in order to achieve the un/doing of what Baudrillard, with that amazing reactionary ingenuity he displays when attending to such matters, called the 'Holy Cultural Alliance' – and offer it to the readers' wisdom as an impossible prologue for troubled times.

The Scenario of the Special Effect

> Techno is communism applied to the emotions.
> Nicolas Saunders, *E for Ecstasy*

I will limit myself to providing a quick sketch of the argument, leaving aside the artists, the works, their regime and places of exhibition (starting with the 'site of contemporary creation' at the Palais de Tokyo in Paris, founded and until recently co-directed by Nicolas Bourriaud and Jérôme Sans). Instead, I will dwell on the order of a discourse that, through its widespread dissemination, has become strangely familiar to us (and thus accounts for the 'symptomal' principle that governs my reading): *relational aesthetics*. We are all by now *all too familiar* with this discourse that focuses upon the art of the nineties, which claims that the 'misunderstandings' surrounding the latter are owing to a 'deficit of theoretical discourse' – namely, its failure to recognise the break with the critical art of the sixties. How familiar it seems, how 'resonant' with everything around us, that *this* art of the nineties *could* be nothing but the audiovisual archive of its commentary, a commentary invested in the *relational form* which supposedly animates a new partition of the art world (into what is *still* modern and what is *finally* contemporary). It is in this sense that we can reread Bourriaud's statement, located somewhere between the descriptive and prescriptive, according to which 'anyhow, the liveliest factor that is played out on the chessboard of art has to do with interactive, user-friendly and relational concepts' (Bourriaud 2002a: 8).[2]

This break, without which, if we follow Bourriaud's book-manifesto on the nineties, contemporary art would be incapable of entering into relations with the present – 'with society, with history, with culture', has a twofold and paradoxical characteristic: It can conform to the 'relational' perspective of an aesthetic marked by the category of *consensus* – restoring the lost meaning of a common world by repairing the fissures in the social bond, patiently weaving a 'relational fabric', revisiting the spaces of conviviality, groping about for forms of sustainable development and consumption, soft energies able to slip into the cracks of existing images, etc. – only by *divesting* the most innovative theoretical and artistic practices of the sixties and seventies of their forces, shunting them into humbler forms, the 'modest connections' of a *micropolitics of intersubjectivity*. . . This is all in the name of a new mental ecology of 'linkage' (*reliance*) (to borrow a term from Michel Maffesoli, who has long anticipated the overall features of this process of rupture with the 'revolutionism' of the 1960s),[3] a linkage put to work for the *reinvention of everyday life* (a theme 'bricolaged' by Michel de Certeau in his *The Practice of Everyday Life*, with respect to the principle of a 'user' *détournement* of consumer society).[4] Embracing this spontaneous hermeneutics that substitutes the cultural myths of network-economy liberalism for the critique of political economy and its sublation in the affirmation of a political economy of desire, Aesthetics becomes an 'alternative' training-ground for postmodern life (or a postmodernisation of life: 'learning to inhabit the world in a better way', says Bourriaud). Furthermore, this is to take place in the post-production of the *Blurring of Art and Life*, following a sequence that begins and ends in counter-effectuating the politics of the becoming-life of art (an art of *dispositive*), transforming it into a becoming-art of everyday life (an art of *attitude, where attitude becomes form*. . .) whose dialogical structure ('inter-human commerce') would constitute the ethical verification of a supposed community of feeling differentially nourishing 'everyday micro-utopias' (a romantic reconciliation with life, but a decidedly *local* one). Made 'ethical' by its desire for a 'social transparency' considered part and parcel of a 'democratic concern' for *immediacy* and *proximity*, this movement that appropriates the demand for a 'formal communism' (sic), and aims to promote 'lived time' as a 'new artistic continent',[5] derives its reality above all – as Jacques Rancière has put it very well – from 'its capacity to recode and invert the forms of thought and attitudes which just yesterday aimed at radical political or artistic change' (Rancière 2004: 172). In the age of communication and service capitalism, where 'marketing has preserved the idea of a certain relationship between the concept and the event' (as Deleuze and Guattari write in the Introduction to *What is Philosophy?* [Deleuze and Guattari 1994: 16]) only in order to become the laboratory for the 'society of control' where the culture of marketing governs the marketing of culture as lifestyle, we could put it as follows: *Schizophrenia and Consensus.*

And perhaps this parodic reversal of an earlier period's *Capitalism and Schizophrenia* might account for the obstinate *recuperation* of Deleuze and Guattari (but above all of Guattari) by the partisans of relational aesthetics. It partakes in fact of a *rear-view mirror effect* that makes the aesthetic rehumanisation of postmodernity dependent on the depotentialisation of art, and its consequential restyling, as the 'transversalist' political experience of the protest years. The *dissensual* transversality of new micropolitical and micro-social practices that focused artistic activity on 'the discovery of a negentropy at the heart of the banality of the environment' (Guattari 1995: 131) is here reduced to a consensual storytelling post-produced for this trans-media theatre of the *little form*, accommodated by the relationally revisited space of the exhibition. Whence the fact that the break announced at the start will be reformulated in terms of the need to reconstitute 'bridges between the 1960s and '70s and our own time' (Bourriaud 2005: 12–13). This proposition – what we might justly call a historico-transcendental monstrosity – represented by a *micropolitics of intersubjectivity*, gives voice to a short-circuit in which what is really at stake is to bring back into the intersubjective practice of an 'artistically' revisited communicative action the micropolitics that had in fact pre-emptively undermined the foundations of any such intersubjectivity by opposing *molecular revolution* to the 'recentering of economic activities on the production of subjectivity' (Guattari 1995: 122).[6] A process in which, essentially, the 'institutional framing' and 'the universe of valorisation' ('including economic valorisation', Guattari insists) of contemporary art today is participating.[7]

Whence the schizophrenia of relational aesthetics, as it seeks to confer upon its *surfing* on the new universals of communication some function of alternative democratisation. Far from liberating 'the inter-human exchange' from its economic reification 'in the cracks of existing social forms' (as relational aesthetics claims – but without ever losing sight of the trajectory leading from the gallery/art fair system to the museum-laboratories of the new economy of art, *and the accelerated return* through the succession of Biennales, Triennales, Documentas, Manifestas, and their integration into the new 'capitalism of cities', in Braudel's words. . .[8]), it instead tests out new criteria of commodification and the participatory management of life by means of these exhibition-*dispositifs* that stage the driving role of the 'culture of interactivity' (relation as *transaction*). The art commissioners (curators–advisors, museum directors–managers) are overjoyed, since they thereby gain, at a bargain price, a social function of 'proximity', testifying to the manner in which the postmodern democratisation of art has broken away from the dangerous avant-garde and 'revolutionist' practice of trans-forming art-forms *in situ* into life-forces *in socius*. (Liberating the forces of life from the forms that imprison them, so as to create, yes, something *new*, as the heterogenetic element of real experience positing difference in its reality-condition – this radical novelty which we are told is 'no longer a criterion' but merely outdated avant-garde rhetoric, now that the hour has come for '*métissage*' and a 'crossing of cultures', according to the strapline for the Parisian *White Night*, of which Bourriaud and Sans were the 'artistic directors' in 2006). The critics (who in this case are also the curators–museum directors, in answer to the post-Fordist call for mobility and flexibility) are equally delighted, as are the other 'media-tors' (when they have not been short-circuited by the curator-as-artist), because they find in intersubjectivity a 'theory of form' as the representa-tive or '*delegate [délégué]* of desire in the image', as the image's horizon of meaning, 'pointing to a desired world, which the beholder thus becomes capable of discussing, and based on which his own desire can rebound' (Bourriaud 2002a: 23). (Objection: has Form not always been, rather, the *relegation* of desire in the Image addressed to the spectator participat-ing in Re-presentation? And has the formal regime of the Image not been *undone* in this respect in the *longue durée* of modern art,[9] of its avant-gardist radicalisation, and in the diagrammatic regime of contemporary art — when it follows this 'hard line'? [10]) So that Duchamp's proposition, according to which *it is the viewers who make the pictures*, will be appro-priated in terms of social relations contra art-objects (against the 'trap of reification'[11]), and projected quite consensually by these brokers of desire onto the performative origin of the process of artistic constitution of which the *readymade* would then be the post-historic truth – cut off from any real negativity, except for its postmodern form directed against the new, against 'the reduction of being to novum' (following Vatimo's definition of modernity). And – *Worstward ho!* – to cap it all, judgement then becomes the lexicon of a participative practice that no longer cares to distinguish between the creative use-value of art and a personalised tourist circuit for the use of the *tenants of culture*: 'sensation depends on the simple "opinion" of a spectator who determines whether or not to "materialise" the sensation, that is to say, decides whether or not it is art' (Deleuze and Guattari 1994: 198). (I quote Deleuze and Guattari here, although the phrase, but for the difference in accent – deprecatory as opposed to laudatory – could be Bourriaud's.)

To this Duchampian *readymade* of the social 'infrathin', this human, all-too human Duchamp, customised as *Little Democracy* and recycled in the 'transactional' translation of the *new aesthetic paradigm* developed by Guattari (the political ontology of desire here finds itself inevitably redirected towards a 'policy of forms', or *an imaginary politics of forms*, which believes that the eradication of the 'objectivity' of the artwork eradicates capitalist exchange), one is tempted to oppose the hard truth of a *constructivism of the signifier* through which the Contemporary broke into the field of artistic Modernity – or more precisely, into the modern idea of art.

But before following this line in my argument, we must quickly return to the Guattari/soft Duchamp interface, because it is from this perspective that Bourriaud, in the last part of his book (Bourriaud 2002a: 86–104), appropriates Félix Guattari's 'new aesthetic paradigm' (the title of the penultimate chapter of *Chaosmosis*; the subsection 'Félix Guattari and Art' is included in the section of *Relational Aesthetics* entitled 'Towards a Policy of Forms').[12] In the conclusion of his long, filmed interview with James Johnson Sweeney, from 1955, Duchamp declares: 'I believe that art is the only form of activity through which man as such can manifest himself as a veritable individual. Only through art can he overcome the animal stage, because art is an opening onto regions that neither time nor space dominate.' This is the passage that Guattari quotes in *Chaosmosis*, reframing Duchamp's declaration in terms of those regions that do not sustain time and space *because* (and it is obviously Guattari who is speaking here) 'the finitude of the sensible material becomes the support for a production of affects and percepts which will tend more and more to become eccentric in relation to the preformed frames and coordinates' (Guattari 1995: 101). Killing two birds with one stone, he thus definitively takes 'out of the frame' the methodological individual-ism of a chess player little inclined to becoming-animal and to the cha-osmic plunge into the materials of sensation. . .[13]

I do not object here to the *new aesthetic paradigm* proposed by Guattari. *I object to the attribution of this proto-aesthetic ontology to Marcel Duchamp*. For the 'pictorial nominalism' of the latter is – liter-ally – *de-ontological*. 'I do not believe in the word "being"', Duchamp confides to Pierre Cabanne; a declaration to which one will oppose Deleuzo-Guattarian 'schizo-ontology' defined as a *'politics of being'*, a *'machinics of being'*, etc., whose proto-aesthetic heart beats, according to Guattari, in the process of non-discursive, or *'a-signifying'* semiotisa-tion belonging to the intensive domain of Affects ('comparable, in this respect, to Bergsonian duration', Guattari insists [Guattari 1996: 159]) – so that, in this absolute violation of the ontological tradition (to borrow Negri's re-presentation of Spinoza's ontology), Affect is 'the deterritori-alised matter of enunciation' = proto-energy (Guattari 1996: 168, and 1989: 231). On the contrary, Duchamp's 'strategic' radicalisation con-sists in *reducing* the Art-Form to language-games about art, and these in turn to a signifying iteration which cuts out its subject in order to turn the plasticity of language against the imagistic/imaginary regime of the so-called plastic arts (*cosa mentale*, grey matter, art is *first and foremost* what language unwittingly realises). In this way Duchamp signifies the abolition of any image-making, of any sign-making of the world, as the literalised signifier severs the link between expression and construction ('Phallus' or 'Art' come down to the same thing, from *Fountain* to *Dart-Object* [*Objet-Dard*], from *The Bride* to *The Given*). The cutting(-out) of Painting by the 'invisible colour' of title-words is thus negotiated in accordance with a logic of the event that reduces art to the Bachelor Machine[14] of a 'floating' Signifier whose 'expressions' no longer sym-bolise anything but the 'Tautology in acts' of construction *'without any resonance in the physical world'*, as Duchamp says. Its ultimate Reality is ex-posed in the guise of its image fetishised as object: *Given* [*étant donné*] the absence of sensible donation in the in-aesthetic state, art outside art is what *realises* and *de-realises* its own signifying-image. This is Duchamp's unique position in contemporary thought: To translate the real impossibility of Romanticism into a nihilistic irony that takes pos-session of the 'presentation of the unpresentable' traditionally reserved for aesthetics – no longer the Invisible of/in [*de/dans*] the Image, nor the Intersubjectivity of/in Form, but the Signifying-Image, the proliferating voiding of the Image out/of [*de/hors*] art as the in-aesthetic foundation of postmodernity *that is de-monstrated for the first time and, if not dismantled, exhausted as such in art, in art* qua *antiart = anart*. In the guise of the *Possible*, as Duchamp explains, and against its chaosmic Guattarian appropriation, the '*hypophysic*' of the letter '*has burnt any possible aesthetics*'. Michel de Certeau explains it fairly well: Its

> productions are fantastic not in the indefiniteness of the reality that they make appear at the frontier of language [this is the Guattarian vision], *but in the relationship between the mechanisms that produce simulacra and the absence of anything else*. . . . The machine producing language is wiped clean of history, isolated from the obscenities of reality, ab-solute and without relation to the 'celibate' other. (de Certeau 1984: 150–2)

It is in this sense that 'Celibacy is scriptural' and that the letter obeys 'the logic of a celibate narcissism', a logic whose rigorous protocol will be produced by Lacan ('*lalangue* is the place of the impossibility of the sexual relationship') and where 'is deployed the ironic and meticulous work of mourning' (de Certeau 1984: 150–2) – Of aesthetics' mourning, in its relational being.

It is this anti-aesthetic that will have determined the level of intervention of a conceptual art which is *simultaneously* 'exclusive' and 'inclusive',[15] in its 'informative' endeavour to neutralise the aesthetic plane of composition, so that – following Deleuze and Guattari – 'everything takes on a value of sensation reproducible to infinity' (Deleuze and Guattari 1994: 198) (this is the *primary information* of a materialist function initially articulated as Language Art after Analytical Philosophy); as well as the radicality of the alternatives required to make the machination of being that has been named Post/modern (with the bar expressing the phenomenon in terms of forces) pass through logics of sensation likely to disorganise or *affect* its course with their capacity for inventing mutant subjective coordinates of re-singularisation, in which experimentation implicates, explicates and complicates in a determinant fashion the physical as well as the social 'environment', *the boundaries of which no longer coincide with the participant individuals*. It *engages* what Guattari calls – we remember – 'the discovery of a negentropy at the heart of the banality of the environment' (Guattari 1995: 131), the better to project the re-making of the readymade he counter-produces into a constructivist bio-*aesthetics*.

As a weak thought (the new *Pensiero debole*), which reprocesses (and de-processes) this double movement, this movement *à double entente et détente*, into zero-sum cultural protocols of institutional re-aestheticisation (from the aestheticisation of the conceptualist neutralisation and the institutionalisation of environmentalist experimentation), relational aesthetics is the *postproduction brand* (*marque*) corresponding to that moment, diagnosed and denounced by Deleuze and Guattari, when 'the only events are exhibitions, and the only concepts are products that can be sold' (Deleuze and Guattari 1994: 10) – sold to the user-consumer of forms who will have forsaken any attack on cultural capital in order to adapt it to his or her desires, in an open conviviality opposed, with minimum expense, to consumer-driven uniformisation of past times. A managerial model for Art in our 'capitalogical' present.

Dans le texte, in Bourriaud's *Postproduction*: '*Artists today practice postproduction as a neutral, a zero-sum process, whereas the Situationists aimed to corrupt the value of the diverted work, i.e., to attack cultural capital itself. . . . Production is a form of capital by which consumers carry out a set of procedures that makes them renters of culture*' (Bourriaud 2002b: 37). However, it is not to Michel de Certeau, cited here, and to his creative alterconsumer, that Bourriaud ascribed the 'philosophical foundations' of his essay – but to Marx, according to an 'aesthetic' as well as an 'economic' gesture that will by now be familiar: '*for Marx, the only element capable of defining "human nature" is nothing other than the relational system established by humans themselves, that is to say the commerce of all individuals with one another*' (Bourriaud 2006: 50). The circle is in a certain sense complete when the humanist Marx's 'Total Man', severed from the analysis of fetishism that incorporates the social relations into the order of reification, becomes the last signifier of a cultural democracy rendering itself adequate to a world art market in the process of inventing a new consumerist model for counter-culture. And this circle may even take on the aspect of an infernal spiral when we encounter 'Deleuzo-Guattarians' identifying the situation of contemporary art practices with the field of relational aesthetics under the rubric of rhizomatics.[16] It is fortunate that Bourriaud, albeit in a confused way (but rightly centred on the question of the subject), has taken to recently mark the difference, from the point of view of a post-Romantic dynamic of the Subject-Form he will henceforth call *radicant*. . .[17] The radicant subject.

Altermodern Epilogue

> Never believe that a smooth space will suffice to save us.
> Deleuze and Guattari, *A Thousand Plateaus*

In the current era of (alter)globalisation, (self-)critically radicalised by the collapse of the world financial system, Nicolas Bourriaud now calls for 'ethical responsibility' in a 'global dialogue' enacting the diaspora of forms in motion and the formal transcoding of the worldwide culture we live in (a 'viatorisation' of forms that inevitably echoes the 'migration of forms' foregrounded by Roger Bruegel on the occasion of Documenta 12).[18] Consequently, he rearticulates relational aesthetics as/within a declared geopolitical *altermodernism* conceived as 'a synthesis between modernism and post-colonialism' (Documenta 12 is actively hybrid-ised with the Documenta 11 – led by Okwui Enwezor – from which it comes),[19] where the heterochronic 'journey-form' of the nomad-artist (the polyglot wanderer) emerges from the *death of postmodernism* to give rise to a 'networked "archipelago" form of modernity' (Bourriaud 2009b: n.p.). Beyond the fashionable celebration of nomadism as a self-sufficient *interform* of artistic identity in the age of trans-national smooth capitalism (as diplomatically pointed out by T. J. Demos in the Tate Triennial Catalogue) and the market-celebration of ex-eccentric artists (from China, India, the Middle East, Eastern Europe. . .) that structures so-called 'International Contemporary Art', we appreciate the opportunity to retain, at least, Bourriaud's symptomatic statement about the end of postmodernism (with the critique of hybridisation he is now developing in parallel with the critique of a multiculturalist essentialism – what Hal Foster called the 'hegelianism of the other' [Foster 1996: 179]). Even if we suspect that in this new storytelling of the ethnographic turn in contemporary art and criticism, it will appear that *the modern has always already been altermodern* (the Lyotardian refrain taken up by Simon Critchley) because the dialogical or intersubjective narrative that unfolds the critique of the (classic-modern) subject 'is still centred on the subject' (the travel-practice of a narcissistic self-refurbishing) (Foster 1996: 179–80);[20] while *the altermodern will always already be 'en retard'* (a delay in plexiglass) with regard to the political radicality of the real forces the post-relational narrative needs to recycle (formal communism of the Exodus) and 'translate' (aesthetic precariousness), with a perfect strategic professionalism, into the *geocustomisation* of the (art) world. . . It reads, with a certain formulaic air (perhaps because it no longer cares to hide its *après-coup* character): 'The altermodern is to culture what altermondialisation is to geopolitics' (Bourriaud 2009a: 185).

Translated by Tim Adams, revised by Robin Mackay

References

Alliez, E. (2007a), *L'Œil-Cerveau: Nouvelles Histoires de la peinture moderne*, Paris: Vrin.

Alliez, E. (2007b), 'Défaire l'image', *Multitudes*, 28 (expanded English version forthcoming in A. Avanessian and L. Skrebowski [eds], *Aesthetics and Contemporary Art*).

Alliez, E. (2008), 'Contemporary Matisse', in S. O'Sullivan and S. Zepke (eds), *Deleuze, Guattari and the Production of the New*, London and New York: Continuum.

Alliez, E. (2009), 'How to Make It a Body Without Image: Ernesto Neto's Anti-Leviathan', *Radical Philosophy*, 156 (July/August).

Alliez, E. and F. Guattari (1984), 'Capitalistic Systems, Structures and Processes', in F. Guattari, *Molecular Revolution*, trans. R. Sheed, London: Penguin Books.

Alliez, E. and G. Zapperi (2007), 'Multitudes Icônes *versus* Documenta Magazine', *Multitudes*, 30 (Autumn).

Alliez, E. and J.-C. Bonne (2005), *La Pensée-Matisse*, Paris: Edition du Passage.

Bishop, C. (2004), 'Antagonism and Relational Aesthetics', *October*, 110 (Fall).

Bourriaud, N. (2002a), *Relational Aesthetics*, trans. S. Pleasance and F. Woods, with M. Copeland, Dijon: Les Presses du réel.

Bourriaud, N. (2002b), *Postproduction*, trans. J. Herman, Dijon: Les Presses du réel.

Bourriaud, N. (2003), *Formes de vie: L'art moderne et l'invention de soi*, Paris: Denoël.

Bourriaud, N. (2005), *Expérience de la durée (Histoire d'une exposition)*, Lyon: Biennale de Lyon.

Bourriaud, N. (2006), 'Le scénario et l'effet spécial', *Art Press*, 2 ('La scène française').

Bourriaud, N. (2009a), *The Radicant*, New York: Lukas & Sternberg.

Bourriaud, N. (2009b), 'Altermodern', in *Tate Triennial*, London: Tate Publishing.

de Certeau, M. (1984), *The Practice of Everyday Life*, trans. S. Rendall, Berkeley: University of California Press.

Deleuze, G. and F. Guattari (1984), *Anti-Oedipus*, trans. R. Hurley, M. Seem and H. R. Lane, London: Athlone Press.

Deleuze, G. and F. Guattari (1988), *A Thousand Plateaus*, trans. B. Massumi, Minneapolis: University of Minnesota Press.

Deleuze, G. and F. Guattari (1994), *What is Philosophy?*, trans. H. Tomlinson and G. Burchell, London: Verso.

Doharty, C. (2004), *Contemporary Art from Studio to Situation*, London: Black Dog.

Foster, H. (1996), *The Return of the Real*, Cambridge, MA: MIT Press.

Gillick, L. (2006), 'Contingent Factors: A Response to Claire Bishop's "Antagonism and Relational Aesthetics"', in *October*, 115 (Winter).

Guattari, F. (1989), 'La récursion énonciative', in *Cartographies schizoanalytiques*, Paris: Galilée.

Guattari, F. (1995), *Chaosmosis: An Ethico-aesthetic Paradigm*, trans. P. Bains and J. Pefanis, Bloomington: Indiana University Press.

Guattari, F. (1996), 'Ritornellos and Existential Affects', in G. Genosko (ed.), *The Guattari Reader*, Oxford: Blackwell.

Lesage, D. (2005), 'Populism and Democracy', in C. Ricupero, L. B. Larsen, N. Schafhausen (eds), *The Populism Reader*, Berlin and New York: Sternberg Press.

Martin, S. (2006), 'Critique of Relational Aesthetics', in *Verksted*, 8.

Osborne, P. (1999), 'Conceptual Art and/as Philosophy', in M. Newman and J. Bird (eds), *Rewriting Conceptual Art*, London: Reaktion Books.

O'Sullivan, S. (2006), *Art Encounters Deleuze and Guattari: Thought Beyond Representation*, London: Palgrave.

Rancière, J. (2004), *Malaise dans l'esthétique*, Paris: Galilée.
Troncy, E. (1998), *Le colonel Moutarde dans la bibliothèque avec le chandelier (textes 1988–1998)*, Paris: Les Presses du réel.

Notes

1. See Alliez and Guattari (1984: 273–87).
2. I say 'between the descriptive and prescriptive' because we should note from the very start, without needing to return to it later, that the isolation of the relational form-function entails the selection of artists supposed to represent this tendency (the 'liveliest') by *reducing* exemplary artworks to their single structure as collaborative 'open works', 'opened' by the participation – *pars pro toto*, according to Hans Ulrich Obrist – of the public experiencing a 'social interstice' removed from capitalistic commodification. Reading Nicolas Bourriaud's further arguments, it seems that Rirkrit Tiravanija, whose work introduces the series of art examples in *Relational Aesthetics* and who features prominently in the chapter on 'Art of the 1990s' (in the first section, entitled 'Participation and Transitivity'), is the most paradigmatic figure of 'relational art'. This should not stop us from remarking that *even* Tiravanija's installations, and *many other* works by artists mentioned by the curator-critic (Felix Gonzales-Torres, Gabriel Orozco, Patrice Hybert or Philippe Parreno, for example), can be seen to be far more complex *and perverse* in terms of the modes of sociality (i.e. the social dimension of participation) they imply. This in order to emphasise that (1) we refuse to inscribe the art of the nineties, *as such*, under the monotonous rubric of relational aesthetics (to which Santiago Sierra is a perfect counter-example); (2) a good criterion for the evaluation of works might indeed be their *excess* vis-à-vis repeated calls to 'modesty' and 'conviviality' as reality-condition for an art of social autonomy in a realised arty 'micro-utopia' (undone by Sierra in the exhibition of the commodification of labour that produces the 'relational' artwork). . . It is on the basis of such an excessive criterion, certainly, that one could *oppose* Gordon Matta-Clark's cooperative *Food* to Rirkrit Tiravanija's culinary aesthetic. (Cf. the 2007 show at the David Zwirner Gallery in NY that pretended to bring back *Food*, in absentia, by juxtaposing a double reconstitution of Gordon Matta-Clark's *Open House* [1972] – originally located in the street, and open to the homeless – and Rirkrit Tiravanija's *Untitled 1992 (Free)*, exhibited at the 303 Gallery where Thai curry was cooked and served to visitors. . .). As we know, Matta-Clark escapes from (art-gallery/institutional critique of the art-gallery) representation (and the purely formal redefinition of the exhibition-medium) by proposing, within the urban territory, 'environmental' agencies and interventions that consist in a social disarchitecturing of the Art-Form which interproblematises art and politics at the point of their highest tension. . . But let us return to our concern in this text. In his response to Claire Bishop's article 'Antagonism and Relational Aesthetics' (Bishop 2004), Liam Gillick explains: '*Relational Aesthetics* was the result of informal argument and disagreement among Bourriaud and some of the artists referred to in his text. . . . The book does contain major contradictions and serious problems of incompatibility with regard to the artists repeatedly listed together as exemplars of certain tendencies' (Gillick 2006: 96). Take note.
3. See the interview with Michel Maffesoli in the catalogue of the 2005 Bienniale de Lyon, commissioned by Nicolas Bourriaud and Jérôme Sans (in Bourriaud 2005).

4. Bourriaud's reappropriation of Certeaudian thematics consummates the long-standing institutionalisation of the Everyday in the field of cultural studies, where de Certeau's theory loses the tactical horizon of its political semiotics ('a *polemological* analysis of culture' focused on the 'cultural activity of the non-producers of culture') in favour of an exclusively hermeneutical project (see de Certeau 1984).

5. Cf. Bourriaud (2002b, 2003 and 2005).

6. In his 'Berlin Letter about Relational Aesthetics' (2001) (republished in Doharty, 2004: 44–9), Bourriaud insists on the 'trans-individual' dimension of Relational Aesthetics. But the *collective transductivity* on the basis of which Simondon defined the very notion of the 'trans-individual' (as an alternative to any inter-individually shared form) is missing (and can't be added *a posteriori*).

7. See O. Zahm's interview with Guattari in *Chimères* 23 (Summer 1994), from which Guattari has concluded: 'It might also be better here to speak of a proto-aesthetic paradigm, to emphasise that we are not referring to institutionalised art, to its works manifested in the social field, but to a dimension of creativity in a nascent state' (Guattari 1995: 101–2).

8. Stimulated by the designation of European cultural capitals, in the early nineties 'global cities' developed the translation of site-specific projects into touristic-site specificity. Gordon Matta-Clark was inevitably co-opted into this project of translation obeying the 'global' method of rereading an oeuvre.

9. See my book entitled *L'Œil-Cerveau* (Alliez 2007a).

10. What Jean-Claude Bonne and I have called '*La Pensée-Matisse*' (Alliez and Bonne 2005) produced a true alternative to this relegation of desire into the form of the image (see also Alliez 2007b and 2009).

11. 'But to say this' – as Stewart Martin argues – 'is to be already trapped. . . . To think that the source of value is in the object-commodity is precisely the error that Marx calls fetishism. . . . If we avoid this fetishism we are stripped of any delusions that the simple affirmation of the social within capitalist society is critical of capitalist exchange; it simply draws attention to the social constitution of capitalist exchange, exposing it directly' (Martin 2006: 113).

12. This section has its origins in an article published in *Chimères* 21 (Winter 1994), and therefore finds itself reinscribed after the fact into an institutional field to which it was, to begin with, foreign.

13. Let's remember that, against the ambient Bergsonism of the beginning of the twentieth century, Duchamp continually declared and sought to demonstrate that art 'has no biological excuse'. . . The settling of accounts with Bergson (with Bergsonian vitalism) is played out between the *Nude Descending a Staircase* and the 'nominal' invention of the *readymade* against the illusion (*always* romantic according to Duchamp) of the *in-the-making*. See also the particularly transversal – auratic and 'affective'! – usage that Guattari makes of the *Bottle rack* in 'Ritornellos and Existential Affects' (Guattari 1996: 164). This will have (been) nourished (by) the final *détournement* of the notion of *readymade* in *A Thousand Plateaus* (Deleuze and Guattari 1988) and *What is Philosophy?* (Deleuze and Guattari 1994), where the *readymade* is associated with the *sensibilia* of the bird constructing a territory-scene.

14. We should remember here that the Deleuzo-Guattarian appropriation of Duchamp appears in *Anti-Oedipus* (Deleuze and Guattari 1984), where the question of the 'celibate machine' qua desiring machine is overdetermined by a quite *perverse* relationship to Lacan ('to schizophrenize Lacan'). Beyond *Anti-Oedipus*, Guattari will always recognise that Lacan had the merit of deterritorialising desire, in so far as his *objet a* was defined as 'non specularisable,

thus escaping the coordinates of time and space' (Guattari 1995: 94, emphasis added). I dealt briefly with this question in Alliez (2008: 144).

15. Which does not contravene the distinction – more phenomenal and historical – proposed by Peter Osborne between '*inclusive* or *weak* Conceptualists' and '*exclusive* or *strong* Conceptualists' (see Osborne 1999: 49).

16. Cf. O'Sullivan (2006: 14, 17). An 'identification' which, in fact, does not come about without a certain unease on the author's part: 'where are the becomings?'; how does this differ from 'the practices offered by consumer culture'? (177–8, n. 55). Nonetheless, to appeal to a supposedly Deleuzian definition of art as the '*expression* of an independent and private symbolic space' (181, n. 20) does not seem to us the best way of responding to the question.

17. 'Above all, unlike the rhizome, which is defined as a multiplicity that brackets out the question of the subject from the beginning, the radicant takes the form of a trajectory or path; the advance of a singular subject' (Bourriaud 2009a: 55). (Spot the difference between this 'path' and Guattari's process of subjectivation that proceeded through the rhizome he elaborated with Deleuze. . .)

18. For a deconstruction of the dispositive of Documenta 12, see Alliez and Zapperi (2007) and also the website http://multitudes-icones.samizdat.net

19. Of the many 'platforms' for discussion scattered around the world, let's mention 'Créolité and Creolization' and 'Four African Cities.'

20. And more specifically: 'In this light the othering of the self . . . is only a partial challenge to the modern subject, for this othering also buttresses the self through romantic opposition, conserves the self through dialectical appropriation, extends the self through surrealist exploration, prolongs the self through post-structuralist troubling, and so on' (Foster 1996: 180).

Chapter 6

The Practice and Anti-Dialectical Thought of an 'Anartist'

Maurizio Lazzarato

In Jacques Rancière's 'aesthetic regime of art', art is conceived of as a specific activity that suspends the ordinary spatiotemporal coordinates and connections of sensory experience and their dualisms of activity and passivity, form and matter, and sensibility and understanding. These dualisms, which Rancière claims constitute the 'distribution of the sensible', are political in the sense that they determine social hierarchies according to relationships of domination between those of 'refined culture' (the active) and those of a 'simple nature' (the passive), the power of people of leisure (liberty) over those who work (necessity), and the power of the intellectual working class (autonomous) over the class of manual labour (subordination).

This notion of art as a heterogeneous 'specific *sensorium*', opposed to the conception of work as domination, carries with it the promise of the abolition of the separation between 'play' and 'work', between activity and passivity, and between autonomy and subordination. These two different modalities, which in reality are two different politics of aesthetics, continue, according to Rancière, to inform the politics of art. In the first case (art becoming life), art is political in the sense that it abolishes the distinction between art and life by doing away with the notion of art as a separate activity. In the second case (resistant art), art is political in the sense that it carefully maintains this very separation, as a guarantee of autonomy from the world of merchandise, markets and capitalist valorisation.

In my opinion, however, we have been moving away from this model of the 'distribution of the sensible' since the end of the Second World War. In the societies of security the problem is less that of the disciplinary partition between activity and passivity than that of the directive to become active and assume responsibility for one's actions. It has become less a question of the partition between the mastery of 'speech' [*parole*] on the part of the bourgeoisie and the inarticulate 'cry' of the workers and the proletariat, than a kind of general incitement to expression. It is less a question of a separation between those of culture and those of nature, than of a continual process of education and acculturation throughout our entire lives. The dualisms of class (Marx), like the distribution of the sensible (Rancière), continue to exist, and both, although representing different perspectives, revolve around the same type of disciplinary capitalism. But these coexist with other modes of subjection and subjectivation that traverse the entire ensemble of differentiations of class.

Under the new conditions of contemporary capitalism, these dialectical oppositions no longer represent alternative positions but have simply become some of the many options for capital. But the notion of 'play', which, following Schiller, Rancière makes out to be a fundamental characteristic of humanity, represents an unremunerated and open-ended activity that both forms the basis for 'autonomy as the proper domain of art and the construction of forms of a new collective life' (Ranciére 2004) and no longer constitutes an alternative to labour as domination. The dialectical opposition between play and work has been transformed into a continuum within which work and play constitute the extremes. Between the two ends of the spectrum there are countless different coefficients of play and work, autonomy and subordination, activity and passivity, and intellectual labour and manual labour that capitalist valorisation lives from.

Marcel Duchamp invites us to insert a third term into these dialectical oppositions, which, however, would not function as a mediation or as an agent of overcoming, but rather as an operator of disjunction that disperses the oppositions that not only structure our ethical standards and our aesthetic tastes, but also, in a more general sense, our manners of speaking and of doing things. The result of these operations would be a new distribution of the sensible that would disperse dialectical oppositions, involving a new use of artistic techniques beyond the realm of art that would open up new modalities of action and subjectivation.

The sphere of influence of this artistic practice and of this way of thinking, which to a large extent was formed during the end of the extraordinary process of 'globalisation' that took place before the First World War, is expressly linked to the growth and the consolidation of power of those governments that further expanded after the Second World War and increased their power into the 1960s. And at the same time, it very precisely describes the conditions of the production of subjectivity, the conversion of the self, not only for the artist, but for everybody.

Duchamp inserts his most well-known invention, the readymade, into the interval between the work of art and the industrial object, and by doing this both reconsiders the use-value of the industrial object (its utility and functionality) and that of the work of art (its functional non-utility, a non-finality that nonetheless has its place in society and within capitalist valorisation). The readymade calls both the production of the worker and the talent and virtuosity of the artist into question. The readymade does not involve any particular form of virtuosity, technique, or know-how, and in this way it 'de-sacralises' and de-professionalises the function of the artist, and thus 'reduces his standing in society'.[1]

By introducing the readymade into the production of art, Duchamp reassesses the notion of professional craftsmanship in art through opening up the possibility of a hybridisation of the different realms of the artist and the technician. He places fine art and applied art on the same plane in defining himself as a 'benevolent technician', 'domestic *bricoleur*' or an 'engineer of lost time'. In contemporary capitalism, the 'profession' of the artist is more determined by 'action' than by 'production'. This does not signify the disappearance of hand-work or physical labour, but the constitution of another assemblage in which manual labour and intellectual labour, 'material' labour and 'immaterial' labour, are caught up in a 'machinic' process, which can be found not only in the 'actions' of the broader 'public', but also in artistic institutions, the state, business, local collectives, criticism and the media.

In this interval between play and work, we can introduce choice. The readymade was not made, but rather chosen. 'For me the difficulty is to choose.' And yet, for Duchamp, this choice is not intentional or conscious. It does not express any kind of interiority or the artist's taste. The artist chooses to choose instead of creating with his own hands. Duchamp even goes so far as to say, 'one does not choose a readymade, one is chosen by it', and in this sense choice is not opposed to determinism or free will. In the interval between activity and passivity, we can introduce the possibility of 'doing nothing', which is the refusal to accomplish what is expected of you, whether this be the passivity of the worker or the activity of the artist (or of the immaterial or cognitive worker). 'Acting to the minimum' rather than getting caught up in the alternative between artistic creation or wage labour. For Duchamp, both are functions or occupations that are assigned to us. For it seems that 'nowadays artists are integrated, they are commercialized, all too commercialized', and that ever since painting has had its own market, 'painters no longer make paintings, they paint cheques'. But at the same time, 'being forced to work in order to survive is a kind of infamy'. As a result, 'to do nothing', 'acting to the minimum', means being able to escape the distribution of competencies in contemporary capitalism.

Duchamp is quite explicit about the false heterogeneity represented by the couples of dialectical opposition. In fact, if two things are opposed to each other, it is because of their homogeneity: 'I am against the word "anti", because it is something like the 'atheist' compared to a 'believer'. An atheist is more or less just as religious as a theist, while the anti-artist is more or less as much an artist as an artist. . . . "Anartist" would be much better. If I could change the word, it would be "anartist"'.[2]

With his typical humour, Duchamp uses the readymade to disrupt the dialectical logic of the exclusive disjunction 'either/or' in order to allow the logic of the inclusive disjunction 'and' to function.

> In Paris, I was living in a tiny apartment. In order to make the best of this meager space, I imagined using a single swinging door that could alternatively close on two frames placed together at a right angle. I showed this to my friends, telling them that the proverb *'a door must either be open or closed'* was a flagrant act of inexactitude.

Porte, 11 Rue Larrey (1927), which is open *and* closed at the same time, is a good example of the 'co-intelligence of contraries' whose closest counterpart, in philosophical terms, would be the notion of the disjunctive synthesis.

In the age of mechanical reproduction, Duchamp deploys a theory and practice of the infinitesimal, the smallest possible difference of the 'hypophysical' which he light-heartedly referred to as the *'infrathin'*. Through being open to the new possibilities of production and diffusion, the readymade examines serial production through the logic of difference and repetition, the original and the copy. Grasping the different in the same, finding the *infrathin* interval in the identical, re-singularising mass production, creating a break within the age of the reproduction of the same, implies an entire methodology of difference and repetition that would distance us from the illusions of language. 'It would be better to pass through the *infrathin* interval separating two "identical things" than to simply accept the verbal generalisation that would make two twins resemble two drops of water.'

The *infrathin* is first of all not a spatial but rather a temporal dimension. 'In time, an object is not the same thing in a second interval.' Time is the *infrathin* that differentiates and alters, that hollows out a gap, even if two objects are absolutely identical. Identity is impossible, moreover, because it only operates on the macro level. There is only identity at the level of the verbal generalisation. Thus we can say that the readymade is not a testimony of the dialectical passage from the prosaic world of commodities to the unique world of art, nor is it a blurring of the borders between art and non-art, nor does it constitute a simple mixture (or collision) of heterogeneous variations.

According to Rancière's dialectical logic, modern and contemporary art is this passage, this blurring, this collision.

The readymade as an industrial, manufactured, mass-produced object, on the contrary, introduces us to a 'domain that is completely empty, if you will, entirely empty, empty to such an extent that I have spoken about a complete anesthesia'. This emptiness, this realm 'which is not ruled by time nor space' (Duchamp 1973: 137), is the place where it is possible to both problematise and experiment at the same time with the modes of constitution of the work of art (and the artist) and with the commodity (and the labourer) by examining the forces, principles and *dispositifs* which institute and consolidate them as values.

Art does not represent a promise of overcoming domination as it does in Rancière's aesthetic regime of art, since Duchamp's gesture not only suspends the conditions of this regime, but also suspends aesthetic taste, values and the artistic 'function'. What interests Duchamp in the 'creative act' is not the artistic work itself, but rather 'the subjective mechanism that produces art' (Duchamp 1973: 139), that is, the process of social production that establishes what is art, the artist, the work and the public. Duchamp's techniques are not exclusively artistic techniques, but rather much closer to 'mental techniques' (Jean Philippe Antoine[3]), 'techniques of subjectivation' (Félix Guattari), or technologies of the self (Foucault). These techniques invent a method for disentangling oneself from established values, including aesthetic values. Given a thing, a word and the relationship between them, how is it possible to defeat the social clichés that make this relationship possible?

'We are bewildered by an accumulation of principles or anti-principles that generally confuse our mind with their terminology.' This emptiness, this 'freedom of indifference' or this complete anesthesia are not the incarnations of some kind of postmodern nihilism, but rather techniques for suspending all ready-made sensations, habits, judgements (prejudices) that are crystallised in tastes as much as they are in words. 'To be shocking was one of the main characteristics of modern art, its material.' But with Duchamp, the shock does not merely serve a 'critical' function of unmasking the world of commodities and it does not represent a simple instance of a possible raising of consciousness. In effect, the suspension of established values that the 'shock' is capable of producing is the condition for mobilising the 'creative act'. This includes not only the consciousness of the author and of the public, but also their affects (in the way a medium or shaman might access), non-verbal semiotics (inert materials that become expressive), various forms of non-sense that set off a process that will produce meaning, the discursive, significations and the social. The shock is the precondition for opening up the process of transformation or reconversion of subjectivity.

Duchamp's puns and plays on words that accompany all of his works express modes of rupturing with the imperialism of signifying semiotics, and reveal pre-linguistic and pre-discursive forces. In order to express oneself in societies of security, artistically or in any other way, it is necessary to interrupt communication, to neutralise the signifying power of language. Words are used as weapons for opening a breach in consensus and the semiotic pollution in which we bathe.

Through disrupting dialectical oppositions Duchamp opens up an 'undecidable' process leading to 'possible ambiguities'. The propositions of Duchamp's artistic practices are undecidable because, to translate one of Deleuze and Guattari's notions into Rancière's dialectical categories, autonomy and heteronomy, activity and passivity, liberation and domination are not already assigned to different and specific *sensoria* (one part being art and the other labour), but are rather distributed along a continuum where the coefficients of liberty and domination, activity and passivity are as much a part of labour as they are of art. For Duchamp, the shock opens towards these undecidable propositions, because their destiny is solely dependent on their immanent becoming, because there is no model, neither positive (the 'play' in art), nor negative (domination and exploitation in labour), that could be realised or used as a point of reference in the fight. These undecidable propositions, these techniques and practices, which only with great difficulty could we define as exclusively aesthetic, have the production of subjectivity as their aim, the production of an *ethos* and *modus vivendi*. They are ethico-politico-aesthetic techniques similar to those described in Guattari's aesthetic paradigm or in Foucault's production of subjectivity.

Subjectivity and Belief

The theory and practice of the 'anartist' allows us to critically assess what we have already described as a process of subjectivation from a new and specific point of view, that of 'belief'. With the opposition between the sensible and the intelligible that Rancière uses to define the distribution of the sensible, we are able to introduce a 'belief' that calls into question (and in fact escapes) the limits of this division. Duchamp is more interested in the 'grey matter' than in the 'retinal' sensation, but ultimately grey matter does not lead us back to the 'intellect' – 'too dry a word, too inexpressive' – it leads to belief, that is the mental or spiritual dimension of subjectivity. 'I like the word "belief." I think in general when people say "I know" they don't know, they believe. . . . To live is to believe; that's my belief, at any rate' (Duchamp 1973: 137). Duchamp introduces into art the same passage that had come to operate within modern philosophy, between the system of belief and the system of knowledge. For Duchamp, the intellect is not a good means by which to understand art, because art is 'sensed as an emotion that is analogous to religious belief or sexual attraction'. Duchamp introduces a distinction between the affect (the emotion-belief, the aesthetic echo) understood as a genetic and constitutive force of subjectivity, and affections (tastes) understood as forces that limit and repeat 'aesthetic' habits and the authority that they convey.

> Taste creates a sensuous opinion, not an aesthetic emotion. Taste presupposes an authoritative viewer who imposes what he likes or dislikes, and translates it into 'beautiful' and 'ugly' or what he senses to be pleasant or unpleasant. In a completely different sense, the 'victim' of the aesthetic echo is in a position comparable to a man in love or a believer who spontaneously rejects the demands of his ego, and from then on, deprived of his support, submits himself to a pleasurable and mysterious constraint. By exercising his taste, he adopts an attitude of authority; while touched by an aesthetic revelation, the same man, in an almost ecstatic mode, becomes receptive and humble. (Duchamp, quoted in Marcadé 2007)

The dissociation of art and taste makes it possible for us to mobilise the force of the 'emotion-belief', which is a force that is not exclusively limited to the artist, but rather something that is common to everybody. The nature of the aesthetic emotion assimilable to belief is expressed both in the openness and confidence of the idiot who falls in love, as well as in the innocence of the idiot who believes in God – of which the Dada idiot is but one incarnation. By suspending tastes and constituted sensations, the readymade makes it possible to return to the 'point of emergence of the production of subjectivity', which is, for Guattari, the specific task of the artist. This task calls for techniques, forces and methods that come back to Guattari's 'aesthetic paradigm' or to Duchamp's expanded notion of art, where belief plays a role that is both genetic and constitutive.

During the nineteenth and twentieth centuries there were numerous profound theoretical elaborations, both in Europe and in America, of

the notion of belief that aimed at defining the conditions of its pragmatic conversion to immanence (I cite only William James and Gabriel
Tarde). If, as Duchamp did, we consider the creative process of art as
a subjective production that implies and transforms both the artist and
the public, then belief constitutes a force, both genetic and constitutive, that mobilises our 'active inclinations'. The two large 'mines' or
'reserves' that feed and make this 'driving force'[4] function, this 'disposition to act',[5] this power of affirmation and of subjective investment
referred to as 'belief', are religion and politics. According to William
James, in religious phenomena our experience is not limited to the
'visible' and 'tangible' world, but also incorporates an 'invisible' world
animated by forces (soul, spirit, etc.) whose perception and knowledge
eludes us and which at the same time make the visible world 'incomplete' and not entirely determined. The indeterminate and incomplete
nature of the visible world makes an appeal to belief, whose principle
and measure consists in action. The essence of faith lies in believing in
and affirming the invisible world, and betting our power to act on this
possibility.

Religion addresses our 'most intimate forces' that by nature are both
'emotional and enthusiastic' (James) or affective (Deleuze and Guattari).
This has less to do with personal or psychological forces than with what
we would today refer to as the pre-individual, subconscious or intensive.
Rather than belonging to us, these forces traverse and constitute what
Duchamp calls the 'mysterious and pleasurable constraint' and ecstasy
to which the believer or lover has abandoned herself. These forces bring
about a change and expansion of the state of 'consciousness' as well as
an expansion of our 'power to act'.

The Duchampian 'emotion' (the aesthetic echo) is the encounter-
shock of the forces that place us outside of ourselves, outside the 'ego'
and thus also outside of our 'tastes' and in a codified and institutional
sense, outside of the aesthetic habits and prejudices, and the social and
political prejudices, that constitute our customary modes of life. These
forces make us both 'humble', because *belief surpasses knowledge*,[6] and
'perceptive', because the contours of the ego and its modalities of perception limited by imperatives and routines are burst apart.

Belief (the 'disposition to act') is both a genetic and an expansive force,
a 'generous power' that believes in the future and its 'possible ambiguities', and an ethical force since it believes in the possibilities residing in
our relationship to the world and our relationship with others. It engages
and risks the subject in an action whose success is not assured. It is thus
the condition for every transformation and every creation. It establishes

a link to the world and a link between individuals that cannot be created by *knowledge* or *sensations*, because knowledge and the senses always present to us a closed world, without true 'exteriority'.

In the moral order, this force is described as courage or generosity, virtues that risk the unknown, making a wager about the future in taking charge of destiny. The secularisation of religious belief in the invisible world and in its forces could be described with Gabriel Tarde as follows: 'The real is only intelligible as an instance of the possible', 'the actual is but an infinitesimal portion of the real'. The real is not entirely actualised and our action only has an effect 'on the possibilities and not on the "raw and actual" facts'. Our knowledge of the 'invisible' world eludes us 'since the elements of the world conceal the unknown and profoundly unrecognizable virtualities, even to an infinite intelligence'. But this invisible world no longer constitutes a world beyond but rather an immanent and real 'outside'. It is a world much like Duchamp's notion of art that is not 'governed by space and time',[7] but by the logic of the event which is immanent and heterogeneous to chronological time, breaking with linear progress and in so doing creating a new chronology, energising the world with possibilities by making an appeal to our capacity to act. Based on this leap into the indeterminate, experience is transformed into experimentation, a risk or gamble driven by the will to put oneself, others and the world to the test.

But if the principle of belief is equated to action with respect to the religious phenomenon, if belief is to be measured according to the power to act that it inspires, what kind of 'action' are we referring to here? And this power or capacity to act – what form of subjectivity does it engage? The tradition of thought that moves from James to Tarde and continues to Deleuze and Guattari explains that these forces and their action are neither psychological, social nor organic. In this tradition, these actions are non-organic and the energy that animates them is 'non-energetic and non-informational'. For Guattari, it is a world that, while being immanent to reality, is situated 'outside of spatiotemporal coordinates', with an energy that 'does not engage a quantity of movement' and that operates according to 'infinite speeds'. Non-organic action, in contrast to organic or sensory-motor action that acts upon facts, brings about 'a particular matter: an optional matter'. These objects, according to Guattari, are the 'rhizomes of choice'. From this perspective, to act, much like in Duchamp's 'production' of readymades, means to choose.[8] Deleuze and Guattari make a distinction between action and the act, where (sensory-motor) action applies to the given 'raw facts', whereas the act applies to what is possible. With the act, we effect a jump in place. 'We have passed . . . from physical space to spiritual space which restores a physics (or a metaphysics) to us' (Deleuze 1986: 117).

Belief is an affective force that founds, supports and qualifies the act. It can be compared to Guattari's notion of the 'existential function' because it too represents an intensive, intentional,[9] force that affirms, marks and shows the emergence of an existential territory, and thus a force of existential auto-positioning, a taking of position with respect to the world and with respect to others. And at the same time, belief is a force that offers and recharges the world with possibilities, constituting an 'opening towards the future' (James). It is in this sense that belief-confidence [*la croyance-confiance*] establishes an 'ethical' link between the world and others. In this new 'mental or spiritual' dimension, into which belief enables us to enter, subjectivity takes on a new significance and is 'no longer motor or material, but temporal or spiritual' (Deleuze 1989: 47).[10] The relationship between sensory-motor action and non-organic action, between material subjectivity and spiritual subjectivity, is given by the dynamic of the event. Temporal or spiritual subjectivity and the anorganic intervene in the social, psychological and organic by means of 'incorporeal' affects.

When Duchamp speaks, in his polemic with 'retinal painting', of the 'grey matter', he is referring to this 'mental' or 'temporal' universe, and to what he wants to achieve through a new form of production of works that are not art. These are the forces that found and make perception possible, the forces that found and make enunciations possible, and that constitute their implicit and inexplicable preconditions.[11] With this in mind, it becomes easier to understand the reasons why Duchamp spoke of the 'medium-like role' of the artist who brings about a 'transference' of subjectivation to the public through acting 'with' its impersonal forces. Beuys would follow this logic in playing the role of the 'shaman', in the pagan and animist sense of acting 'with' non-organic forces and subjectivity. Deleuze, who brilliantly developed the differences between the organic and the anorganic in his two books on cinema, spoke in turn about 'actor-mediums' and 'visionary' spectators (Deleuze 1989: 20).

With postwar cinema, a 'spiritual or temporal' dimension is attained without having to pass through religious techniques and beliefs. Our usual perception always grasps less of what there is to be seen in an image, in an object, in a relationship, in a situation. We do not see anything but what we are interested in, that is to say that we see as a function of our economic interests, ideological beliefs or psychological demands. We perceive the world through clichés, habits of meaning and tastes that allow us to act in a world entirely pre-given and established by routines. Under these conditions, vision is nothing but mere remembering and thought nothing but simple recognition. When the force (belief) of habit that makes it possible for us to recognise things, roles and functions breaks down, when the spatiotemporal coordinates of the present (visible) world have been suspended by the aberrant movements of cinematographic images, what Deleuze calls the time-image emerges, an image that is both actual and virtual. We see both 'the state of things itself and the possibility, the virtuality which goes beyond it' (Deleuze 1986: 112).

Deleuze makes a diagnosis about the present that we must return to again: we see the 'invisible' and its forces, but our capacity to see beyond the actual does not correspond to an increase in our power to act, because we lack a belief in the 'possible ambiguities' that this world envelops. Why then should we, following Duchamp, introduce belief between the intelligible and the sensible, between knowledge and the affections? Because neither knowledge nor meaning provides us with an existential and ethical link to the world or to other people. Neither knowledge nor sensations give us the force to act from emptiness, something which the operation of the readymade demands. The emptiness operating in the choice of the readymade brings us back to the radicality of Guattari's a-signifying ruptures, in which, when there is a change of referent, a new meaning emerges, a new process of subjectivation is set into motion, and there is 'almost by definition, this kind of emptiness, this a-signifying point, or blind point'. And it is from this empty point,[12] from this point of non-sense that neutralises both taste and meaning, 'that one no longer sees the same thing, that one no longer understands the same thing'.

Guattari's emptiness, like Duchamp's anesthesia, represents a neutralisation of all 'tastes' and 'meanings' that have already been classified, organised or instituted. But this is an emptiness that is full of transindividual and pre-discursive forces that 'impassion and activate'. It is in fact a fullness of genetic forces that provides the means to take risks and to come to terms with an undetermined world in a 'new work' and in new possibilities. For this reason, the readymade must first bring about a rupture (polemic) with what already exists through neutralising the use and the meaning of the object, through suspending the belief-habits (tastes) and the belief-prejudices (meaning) that make us act and think in a predetermined world where everything is always already given. In this case, the belief that adheres to or focuses on an object or a relationship is what Duchamp with good reason would refer to as 'authority'. One of the main problems of the *dispositifs* of power has been to capture and control this 'disposition to action' and to fix it as an 'authority'. Even though neo-liberalism 'fabricates' belief in the same way that it produces 'freedom', it is not at all certain that belief would be able to guarantee an individual's investment in neo-liberal values.[13]

> Today, it is no longer enough to manipulate, transport, and refine belief; its composition must be analyzed because people want to produce it artificially; commercial and political marketing studies are still making partial efforts in this direction. . . . Shell Oil produces the Credo of 'values' that 'inspire' its top administrators and that its managers and employees must adopt as well. . . . It cannot be so easily directed back to administrations or businesses that have become 'incredulous.' . . . The sophistication of the discipline does not compensate for the fact that subjects no longer invest and commit themselves in believing. (de Certeau 1988: 179–80)

Subjection is not only a question of disciplinary *dispositifs* or of financial, legislative, or security-based incentives and demands. Subjection involves first and foremost 'belief', which the contemporary economy with its demand for autonomy, responsibility and risk-taking finds more than enticing. Subjection to the logic of self-enterprise as the production of subjectivity requires the institution or the displacement of the power to believe. Cynicism is a specific moral force in contemporary capitalism, as it produces 'beliefs without believers', which has resulted more and more in politicians resorting to all kinds of neo-archaisms (as imaginary reservoirs of belief and of believers), and notably to religious neo-archaism, for fixing belief.

Once the break has been made with belief-habits or with belief-authority, the readymade must disengage and re-organise the conditions of action in an undetermined, unknown world. Here, what is possible is not 'already there', is not yet crystallised into tastes that sustain authority, into habits and meanings that guide our actions. Instead, in an unknown world, what is possible presents itself as an occasion ('the points') of unpredictable bifurcations. On the edge of the void and anesthesia, belief is called *confidence*, because it no longer entails adhering to an idea or a given meaning, or of conforming to the force of habit, but rather implies creating a new idea or direction.

Most of our ways of behaving, as Duchamp anticipated, are not based on making something, on fabrication, but rather on 'action'. Our conduct and our modes of life can be described as a pile of choices in which the alternatives are predetermined, where the risks that they expose us to have nothing 'tragic' about them because the alternatives consist in the choice between different brands of yogurt, different politicians, different television channels, different outfits, different places to go on vacation, etc. Marketing, in both economics and politics, has but one real goal: to produce 'alternatives' where one exercises the 'freedom of action' of democratic man. The rupture with this situation, the flight of these modalities of subjection, is not only accomplished by forms of classical 'politics', but also and especially by methods that are related to the techniques of rupture and of Duchampian composition, and to Guattari's 'aesthetic paradigm'. According to Guattari, the force of this kind of artistic practice 'lies in its capacity to promote active, processual ruptures within semiotically structured, significational and denotative networks, where it will put emergent subjectivity to work' (Guattari 1995: 19). The kind of art that Duchamp practices, demands a conversion of subjectivity, that in turn supposes a suspension (or the displacement) of 'belief-habit' and the mobilisation of 'belief-confidence', of its availability, generosity, and will to put the world and others to the test, to experiment both with respect to the artist and with the public. What interested Duchamp more than the object or the work, are the 'incorporeal' transformations brought about by the artist (the transubstantiations of inert materials – 'color, piano' – into meaning) that simultaneously affect the subjectivity of the artist and the public. Duchamp's art promotes and works with the process of emergence and the constitution of the relation artist/work/public, which with its creation produces its own spatiotemporal coordinates, its own rules and its own 'tastes'. Whether or not the work is good, bad or indifferent is of little importance because the principle and the measure of Duchampian art is not the 'beautiful', but rather the 'disposition to action' for the transformation of subjectivity. Art is one of the techniques that favour the act, the conduct, the *ethos*, not of the subjectivity of the artist or the public of art, but rather of any subjectivity whatsoever.

> After all, the word 'art' etymologically means 'to act' not 'to make' but 'to act'. Any moment that you act, you are an artist. Of course, you are not really an artist, you haven't sold a work, but you have completed an action. In other words, art signifies action and activities of all different kinds. For each and everybody. But in our society we have decided to distinguish between a group of people called 'artists', a group called 'doctors', etc., which in the end represents a purely artificial distinction. . . . Art, instead of being a singularized entity in a little box such as this one, with a certain number of artists per square meter, it would be universal, the human factor in one's life, everybody would be an artist although unrecognized as an artist. Do you see what I mean? (Duchamp, quoted in Naumann 1999: 306)

Duchamp strictly followed the principles of using artistic techniques to produce a singular and partial subjectivation. Art does not completely turn into life, and neither does it maintain its own exceptional position of autonomy, as the avant-gardes dreamed. Between art and life there is always a gap that cannot possibly be filled. Duchamp maintained a difficult stance through his life towards art and artists. He placed himself in a position that was 'neither inside, nor outside'.[14] Instead, he placed himself on the limits, on the boundaries established by the history of art, between art and non-art, between the applied arts and the fine arts, between making and acting. But it is only with the gap between art and life, in placing oneself within this interval, that the production of subjectivity is possible.

> I wanted to make use of painting, make use of art as a way of establishing a *modus vivendi*, a way of understanding life, which is probably to try and make my life itself into an artwork, instead of spending my life making artworks in the form of paintings. . . . The important thing is to have a certain conduct [*comportement*] in life. This conduct governs my painting, my plays on words and everything I've made, at least from the public's point of view. (Duchamp, quoted in Marcadé 2007)

Making a work of art out of one's life, as Foucault sought to, implies the ability to grasp time and its intensity as an event and its capacity to affect subjectivity. Directly grasping time means living in the present moment where 'all of the future and anterior fractions coexist' 'reproducing themselves' and opening up to 'a certain kind of present with an expanse of multiples'.

In Robert Lebel's biography of Duchamp, he speaks of 'a taking charge of time where Marcel sought to unite the before, the during and the after'. The art of time, the art of the present with an expanse of different multiples is what, in another dimension, is at the heart of political and social battles. It is here that contingencies can be produced. To reduce these techniques of subjectivation to the individualism of Stirner, whom Duchamp read assiduously, would be as reductive as equating Foucault's practical and theoretical ethos with dandyism. It is more interesting to see in this *modus vivendi* a political problem: the impossibility of separating political revolution from a revolution of the sensible, macropolitical revolution from micropolitical revolution, the question of politics from that of ethics.

Translated by David Quigley

References

Antoine, J.-P. (2002), *Six rhapsodies froides sur le lieu, l'image et le souvenir*, Paris: Desclée de Brouwer.

de Certeau, M. (1980), *L'Invention du quotidien. Vol. 1, Arts de faire*, Paris: UGE, coll. 10/18.

de Certeau, M. (1981), 'Une pratique de la différence: croire', in *Actes de la table ronde organisée par l'école française de Rome*, Rome: École française de Rome.

de Certeau, M. (1988), *The Practice of Everyday Life*, trans. S. Rendall, Berkeley: University of California Press.

Deleuze, G. (1986), *Cinema 1: The Movement-Image*, trans. H. Tomlinson and B. Habberjam, Minneapolis: University of Minnesota Press.

Deleuze, G. (1989), *Cinema 2: The Time-Image*, trans. H. Tomlinson and R. Galeta, Minneapolis: University of Minnesota Press.

Duchamp, M. (1973), *The Writings of Marcel Duchamp*, ed. M. Sanouillet and E. Peterson, New York: Da Capo Press.

Guattari, F. (1984), 'La Machine – Discussion', Seminar 06.02.1984, available at the *Chimères* site: www.revue-chimeres.fr/drupal_chimeres/files/840206b.pdf

Guattari, F. (1994), 'Félix Guattari et l'art contemporain', *Chiméres*, 23 (Summer).

Guattari, F. (1995), *Chaosmosis: An Ethico-Aesthetic Paradigm*, trans. P. Bains and J. Pefanis, Sydney: Power Publications.

Guattari, F. (1996), 'Ritornellos and Existential Affects', in G. Genosko (ed.), *The Guattari Reader*, Oxford: Blackwell.

James, W. (2005), *La volonté de croire*, trans. L. Moulin, Paris: Les empêcheurs de penser en rond.

Marcadé, B. (2007), *Marcel Duchamp, la vie à crédit*, Paris: Flammarion.

Naumann, F. M. (1999), *Marcel Duchamp: L'art à l'ère de la reproduction mécan-isée*, Paris: Hazan.

Rancière, J. (2004), *Malaise dans l'esthétique*, Paris: Galilée.

Schwarz, A. (1969), *The Complete Works of Marcel Duchamp*, London: Thames and Hudson.

Tomkins, C. (1996), *Duchamp, A Biography*, New York: Henry Holt.

Notes

1. All quotations from Marcel Duchamp are from the Marcadé biography. Where possible, references to English translations have been given.
2. 'Marcel Duchamp speaks', interview with George Heard Hamilton and Richard Hamilton, BBC Third Programme broadcast, 1959. English translation quoted in Schwarz (1969: 33).
3. See Antoine (2002).
4. See de Certeau (1980; 1981).
5. See James (2005).
6. 'We believe and it is only because we know how and why.' And 'our principles are ridiculously out of proportion to the vast bulk of our feelings, but these suffice to make us act without hesitation' (James 2005: 117). 'In our universities, we learn to believe in molecules and the conservation of energy, in democracy and the necessity of progress . . . and all of these beliefs are not based on anything that would dignify them being called a principle' (James 2005: 45).
7. 'The event comes about like a rupture with respect to the coordinates of time and space. And Marcel Duchamp pushes the point of accommodation in order to

demonstrate that there is always a possible index at the point of the crystallisation of the event beyond time in the background of the relations of temporal discursivity that traverses time, transversal to any measurement of time' (Guattari 1994: 63).

8. Nevertheless, Guattari is suspicious of the notion of the act (and the choice), because it 'introduces a cut between the field of the act and the non-act, an undifferenciated field which the act will animate, overcode, organize, command'. Guattari's doubts are directed towards decisionism (for example, Badiou's idealist decisionism) which sees the act 'as something that occurs and one doesn't know where it came from, creating a link, in a certain way, between the mind and biological and material domains. . . . An act *ex nihilo* accorded to divine power, the word that becomes act . . . and from this an entire theology of notions of liberty, choice, an entire philosophy follow in this sense. Opposed to such conceptions that avoid the problem of the act, I propose the idea that there is no such thing as an act in itself, but rather degrees of consistence in the existence of the act – existential thresholds relative to the act. In other words, there are numerous *degrees of passage to the act. An act is always a passage between heterogeneous dimensions*. It is not a passage from "everything to nothing", based on a binary or dialectical logic' (Guattari 1984).

9. 'Assimilable in this regard to the Bergsonian concept of duration, an affect does not arise from existential categories, which are able to be numbered, but from intense and intentional categories, which correspond to an existential self-positioning' (Guattari 1996: 159).

10. There is nothing of a vague kind of spiritualism or irrationality in these notions. This new dimension of subjectivity is time itself, not chronological time but rather the event, the dimension in which the present and future are co-present, constituting the extra-temporal dimension of time.

11. One of the tendencies of art inspired by Duchamp works precisely with the nature of non-organic affects: 'Conceptual art produces the most deterritorialized sensations that it could create. . . . It works with a material that is the concept. But it's not a concept made for creating concepts, it's a concept that creates sensations. . . . In addition, it is more within the sensation that it deconstructs redundant sensations, dominant sensations' (Guattari 1994: 53).

12. As is frequently the case, Guattari provides us with a political translation: 'There are a number here who recall the transition to emptiness of February–March 68' (Guattari 1984: 11).

13. 'There are more and more things to believe in but not enough credibility', as the narrator says in Kafka's novel *The Man Who Disappeared*.

14. A saying of the *Coordination des intermittents et précaires d'Île-de-France*.

Chapter 7

Ethologies of Software Art: What Can a Digital Body of Code Do?

Jussi Parikka

Art of the Imperceptible

In a Deleuzo-Guattarian sense, we can appreciate the idea of software art as the art of the imperceptible. Instead of representational visual identities, a politics of the art of the imperceptible can be elaborated in terms of affects, sensations, relations and forces (see Grosz 2008). Such notions are primarily nonhuman and exceed the modes of organisation and recognition of the human being, whilst addressing themselves to the element of becoming within the latter. Such notions, which involve both the incorporeal (the ephemeral nature of the event as a temporal unfolding instead of a stable spatial identity) and the material (as an intensive differentiation that stems from the virtual principle of the creativity of matter), incorporate 'the imperceptible' as a futurity that escapes recognition. In terms of software, this reference to nonhuman forces and to imperceptibility is relevant on at least two levels. Software is not (solely) visual and representational, but works through a logic of translation. But what is translated (or transposed) is not content, but intensities, information that individuates and in-forms agency; software is a translation between the (potentially) visual interface, the source code and the machinic processes at the core of any computer. Secondly, software art is often not even recognised as 'art' but is defined more by the difficulty of pinning it down as a social and cultural practice. To put it bluntly, quite often what could be called software art is reduced to processes such as sabotage, illegal software actions, crime or pure vandalism. It is instructive in this respect that in the archives of the Runme.org software art repository the categories contain fewer references to the traditional terms of aesthetics than to, for example, 'appropriation and plagiarism', 'dysfunctionality', 'illicit software' and 'denial of service'. One subcategory, 'obfuscation', seems to sum up many of the wider implications of software art's resistance to identification.[1]

However, this variety of terms doesn't stem from a merely decon-structionist desire to unravel the political logic of software expression, or from the archivists nightmare à la Foucault/Borges, but from a poetics of potentiality, as Matthew Fuller has called it (Fuller 2003: 61). This is evident in projects like the I/O/D Webstalker browser and other soft-ware art projects. Such a summoning of potentiality refers to the way experimental software is a creation of the world in an ontogenetic sense. Art becomes 'not-just-art' in its wild (but rigorously methodological) dispersal across a whole media-ecology. Indeed, it partly gathers its strength from the imperceptibility so crucial for a post-representational logic of resistance. As writers such as Florian Cramer and Inke Arns have noted, software art can be seen as a tactical move through which to highlight political contexts, or subtexts, of 'seemingly neutral technical commands' (Arns 2005: 3).

Arns' text highlights the politics of software and its experimental and non-pragmatic nature, and resonates with what I outline here. Nevertheless, I want to transport these art practices into another philo-sophical context, more closely tuned with Deleuze, and others able to contribute to thinking the intensive relations and dimensions of tech-nology such as Simondon, Spinoza and von Uexküll. To this end I will contextualise some Deleuzian notions in the practices and projects of software and net art through thinking code not only as the stratification of reality and of its molecular tendencies but as an ethological experi-mentation with the order-words that execute and command.

The Google-Will-Eat-Itself project (released 2005) is exemplary of such creative dimensions of software art. Authored by Ubermorgen.com (featuring Alessandro Ludovico vs. Paolo Cirio), the project is a para-sitic tapping into the logic of Google and especially its Adsense program. By setting up spoof Adsense-accounts the project is able to collect micropayments from the Google corporation and use that money to buy Google shares – a cannibalistic eating of Google by itself. At the time of writing, the project estimated that it will take 202,345,117 years until GWEI fully owns Google. The project works as a bizarre intervention into the logic of software advertisements and the new media economy. It resides somewhere on the border of sabotage and illegal action – or what Google in their letter to the artists called 'invalid clicks'. Imperceptibility is the general requirement for the success of the project as it tries to use the software and business logic of the corporation through piggy-backing on the latter's *modus operandi*.

What is interesting here is that in addition to being a tactic in some software art projects, the culture of software in current network society can be characterised by a logic of imperceptibility. Although this logic has been cynically described as 'what you don't see is what you get', it is an important characteristic identified by writers such as Friedrich Kittler. Code is imperceptible in the phenomenological sense of evading the human sensorium, but also in the political and economic sense of being guarded against the end user (even though this has been changing with the move towards more supposedly open systems). Large and pervasive software systems like Google are imperceptible in their code but also in the complexity of the relations it establishes (and what GWEI aims to tap into). Furthermore, as the logic of identification becomes a more pervasive strategy contributing to this diagram of control, imperceptibility can be seen as one crucial mode of experimental and tactical projects. Indeed, resistance works immanently to the diagram of power and instead of refusing its strategies, it adopts them as part of its tactics. Here, the imperceptibility of artistic projects can be seen resonating with the micropolitical mode of disappearance and what Galloway and Thacker call 'tactics of non-existence' (Galloway and Thacker 2007: 135–6). Not being identified as a stable object or an institutional practice is one way of creating vacuoles of non-communication though a camouflage of sorts. Escaping detection and surveillance becomes the necessary prerequisite for various guerrilla-like actions that stay 'off the radar'.

The disruption of perceptions has been evident in such projects as Jodi's tactical computer 'crashes'. Glitches are part of the standard repertoire of software art and perhaps one example of a micropolitics of dysfunctionality, along with closer ties with malicious software as in the Biennale.py net art virus that was released in 2001.[2] Even though released at the 49th International Art Biennale of Venice, which fixed it to established art contexts, the workings and technical nature of the virus defied stratification by one institutional context. As a weird, intensive object in its own right, the virus written by two net art groups, 0100101110101101.ORG and *epidemiC* was distributed as a consumer object of a kind – sold with a high price to investors on a CD-ROM but also distributed through T-shirts on which the code was printed. Now again we could (too easily) make the connections to virality and parasitism as modes of resistance, but the interesting aspect for a Deleuzian approach lie in a wider articulation of ecologies.

The Biennale virus was clearly not intended as malicious software in the usual sense of the term, it was not a piece of destructive software that spreads and executes without the user being aware of its presence. Instead, it was widespread as an *invisible* piece of code, and yet described in an interview with Cornelia Sollfrank as embedded in absolute *transparency*. Their 'names and domains were written on the code', and the anti-virus software houses were notified; the virus was designed only to survive without harming its host (Sollfrank 2001: n.p.). 'So, it sucks energy, but tries to stay invisible as much as possible. . . . "Biennale.py" is completely invisible. It just installs itself in the background' (Sollfrank 2001: n.p.).

This technical invisibility can be understood as part of the imperceptibility of net.art and software art to which I referred. These examples of software remain in excess of their definition merely as 'art'. Such projects occupy a transinstitutional status characteristic of the network society, involving art, law, the economy of digital production, the politics of software, and so on, as their constituting forces. In other words, executable codes are exemplified through terms that take into account their nature as processes. This explains the emergence of Deleuzian notions surrounding software and media art, such as 'media ecologies' (Fuller 2005), 'processuality' (Rossiter 2006) and in general assemblages (see Wise 2005: 77–87).

Imperceptibility should not be understood solely in terms of the representational logic of what is seen and what is not. It refers as much to the powers of virtuality as well. In terms of approaching the virtual element of reality as one of potentiality not exhaustible by any (already) realised and extended actualities, we can appreciate the idea of this core of creativity as inherent to both a Deleuzian ontology and a digital ethology. Perhaps 'digital' as an ontology of binary coding into 0s and 1s is not a regime of creative differences, but at the same time the 'digital' is too broad a category for any specific understanding of the weird materialities of network culture; software is increasingly more about relationality within its code world but also in its relations to the outsides in which it is embedded (from the abstract machines of capitalism to concrete assemblages such as games, browsers or, for example, mobile phone interfaces). In this sense, software art utilises a virtual dimension that, as Keith Ansell-Pearson has said, 'stipulates the dynamic and inventive conditions of possibility of evolution as a creative process, as the open system *par excellence*' (Ansell-Pearson 1999: 28).

The emergence of network culture was characterised by the hype word of virtuality but in a very different sense to that of Deleuze's rigorous take that stems from pairing it with the real. The virtual has a different relation to the real than the actual, being an element of creative difference that is seen as a dynamic field of unravelling tendencies, so to speak. Boundas describes the virtual as consisting of incorporeal events and singularities, and this perhaps is a new way of thinking software art as well: they summon such singularities both as embedded in the nonhuman materiality of computers, and in the incorporeal events acting as experimentations (Boundas 2005: 296–7). Software is not an immaterial virtual in the sense that the 1980s and '90s hype suggested, but incorporeal-material in the Deleuzian sense. Experimental art projects are imperceptible in a political way: the imperceptible is the singular not perceived by coding mechanisms, it is the surplus of code and its potentiality for new connections. Staying imperceptible allows software art to both frame the political economic ontology of our culture of commercial software, but also to use its imperceptibility as a tactic to tap into that logic, and to work according to its characteristics.

To draw on the powers of the imperceptible, then, involves looking beyond the representational. Massumi explains the politics of camouflage that is continuously immanent to the actual world and works through its vacuoles and 'derelict spaces' (Massumi 1992: 104–5). New actual–virtual circuits can open up political imaginations, Massumi argues, the art of camouflage passes to the inside, but while doing so releases transmutational forces, producing resistance as friction in the molar machine, and the stuttering of language. As Matthew Fuller notes, software uses as its raw material subjectivities that are templated according to the 'actions, schemas and decisions performed by software' but as such produce further 'sequences of seeing, knowing and doing' (Fuller 2003: 54). Software is then not only a black box for input, but a process of modulation in itself, an example of the aforementioned 'poetics of potentiality'. This means looking at projects such as the Web Stalker alternative browser as 'not-just-art', but as a production of new social relationships, relations with data as well as relationships with art (Fuller 2003: 61).

Relationality: Ethology

What emerges from this discussion of the potentiality of software art is the conceptualising of software as a process of individuation and relationality. In order to extend from potentiality into relationality, software art projects need to involve themselves with other modalities of expression. Software is a relay between a plethora of cultural practices, and hence the most interesting points are those connections that software is able to establish. Imperceptibility and structural misperception evident in software art projects can in this sense serve as indexes for a wider media ecology of digital culture.

Assemblages of software act as *agencements*: agencies, vectors of transmission, always in the midst of becoming something else (or having the potentiality to do so). Assemblages are much more than functional elements as they carry with them affects (potentials to relate to other assemblages) as well as points of deterritorialisation and change. Assemblages do things, and this points to their ethological context. This potential for change relates to the point about imperceptibility – the element of difference and potentiality not already recognised, a future to come incorporated in assemblages as a virtuality. What is interesting is that in the context of software, these potentials for change are a crucial feature of software by definition. Software is a plug-in, in a way, that is defined by its capacities to connect or deny contact, to enable or disable, to afford or block. Software objects are constituted in wider assemblages of enunciation and the constellations that Deleuze and Guattari call abstract machines. Those assemblages work through other digital elements such as software objects, but also protocols, etc. Similarly, software extends to other realms of expression, as with cash-machines, digital games and the oyster card interfaces of the London underground that connect with the eye and the hand of the human user. In various cases and especially as a function of commercial digital culture, software has been 'hidden' under various layers and hence remains imperceptible. However, despite this, its crucial position as an interfacing of various regimes of expression and a crucial node in the abstract machines of capitalist digital culture demands careful scrutiny.

For sure, Deleuze himself remained very critical of the notion of code as a formalisation and standardisation of the relationality of the analogue. In the Bacon book, Deleuze writes about analogue language as one of relations, breaths and screams – a conception of expressive modalities that always work with their constitutive outside and materiality. Digital code, on the other hand, is relegated to the pattern of resemblance that functions to reproduce the Same (Deleuze 2005: 78–81). In this context, code becomes something resembling an image of thought, as suggested in *Difference and Repetition*, or Molarity in the jargon of *A Thousand Plateaus*; a mode of stasis and a closed system of binary coding that erases the intensive differences and creative relationality of analogue singularity (Massumi 1995: 106–7). Despite the Bacon book discussing various modalities of sensation and materiality, the specificity or even possibility of digital art remains, in its terms, problematic. Yet, it is exactly in this context that we need to bypass the cliché of reducing new media to a binary mode of coding and understand the potential relationality and processuality inherent in software environments. It's a cliché because such a view dismisses the more specific contexts in which digital code functions. In this sense Deleuze is more careful in *A Thousand Plateaus* and in his writing about the control society where he makes connections between politics and code as variation. Here it is not a case of seeing digital code as reducing all intensive differences to 0s and 1s, or of setting ethology against that kind of view – instead I suggest we bracket the question of binary codes as secondary to the more specific and important role software plays as part of cultural assemblages. Indeed, despite the obvious objection that Deleuze was concerned with what comes before any code, language or medium (see Rajchman 2000: 118) – the sense of being as elaborated in *The Logic of Sense* – I want to argue that *executable* code is not reducible to code as representational thought (society gridded through the codes of gender, race and other differences; digital code as a gridding of the fluctuating and differing world, etc.). This is not what Deleuze had in mind either: in *A Thousand Plateaus*, for example, we are reminded of how codes always have a surplus value that is not reducible to their function of coding and recoding values. Instead:

> Every code is affected by a margin of decoding due to these supplements and surplus values – supplements in the order of a rhizome. Forms in the parastrata, the parastrata themselves, far from lying immobile and frozen upon the strata, are part of a machinic interlock: they relate to populations, populations imply codes, and codes fundamentally include all phenomena of relative decoding that are all the more usable, composable, and addable by virtue of being relative, always 'beside'. (Deleuze and Guattari 1987: 53)

This 'machinic interlock' refers to software code as it is used and composed in a much wider ethology of relations and dimensions constituting network culture. Executable code is also relayed as part of non-technological dimensions triggering within them an increasing amount of actions and relations that one could describe as non-technological in nature.

What characterises several contemporary software art projects as well as what Rossiter calls the 'processual aesthetics of new media' is a willingness to dig deeper into the relationality of digital culture, beyond the screen. Rossiter writes how such aesthetics 'seeks to identify how online practices are always conditioned by and articulated with seemingly invisible forces, institutional desires and regimes of practice' (Rossiter 2006: 174). This becomes evident in software and net art projects' continuous interest in translations and transmutations – for example in alternative browser projects such as the Web Stalker and Peter Luining's ZNC browser[3] – and also in the ecological projects such as Google-Will-Eat-Itself that examine the continuum stretching from code to political economy and networks of agencies (in the sense of *agencements*) involved in search engines.

Rossiter extends his excavation of processuality towards a radical empiricism of digital culture, where the primacy of movement is posited as characteristic of new media, meaning what has emerged retains further potentialities that remain inherent in the durational ontology of the world (Rossiter 2006: 176–8). As a transmutational ethos, radical empiricism becomes a notion with which to account for the process of networks and software as defined by a temporality irreducible to predefined categories of identification. On a concrete level, this reference to the radical creative temporality in code becomes evident when we understand its executability. Code exists only in its execution – a theme made evident in the mock 'execution' of code through T-shirts (Biennale.py distribution) and oral performance (Bifo 'executing' the source code of the Loveletter-virus in 2001 in the 'Digital is not Analog-art' conference).[4] Code is by definition a process that unfolds in time and hence it is prone to the accidents inherent in any process defined by its duration. In this durational quality lies the virtuality of code as well as a poetics of the potential, it is an art of the imperceptible, one mapped by the software art that has emerged since the 1990s.

In an ethological context our task is to develop concepts resonating with computational culture through the notions of body, affect and ethology that Deleuze developed through Spinoza and von Uexküll. I would like to extend the idea of bodies – that Deleuze does not explicitly restrict to human or visible bodies – to algorithmic events, and so develop the notion of a software ethology. For Deleuze Spinozian ethology begins with the idea that bodies are composed of the relations of motion and rest between their particles as well as through the affects (affecting and being affected) produced through relations with other bodies. This kinetic-dynamic notion of a body allows for an approach to living things (and we are expanding that notion to such technological agencies as software) as defined not by their form, but 'a complex relation between differential velocities, between deceleration and acceleration of particles' (Deleuze 1988: 123). Deleuze's own example is music, which is quite fitting for an art of temporality. However, as briefly noted above, computational and executable media could also be seen as working through similar principles of temporality.

But what then defines (the body of) software? As an ethological process, we could say that software is defined by its motion and rest, speeds and slownesses, but also its affects, i.e. its relations with the other bodies involved in its unfolding in time. Deleuze and Guattari's famous example of the tick could be then reformulated: what defines a virus program? Its three affects: 1) Infection: the various ways a virus can distribute itself through other software and protocols. 2) Payload: what a virus 'does', from erasing the hard drive to playing a harmless tune. 3) Trigger: the routine that triggers the virus (Harvey, Slade and Gattiker 2001: 5). More specifically, 'affects' can be seen as a crucial way to understand specific types of programming and programs. Such 'affects' are evident in the emergence of object-orientated programming since the 1970s – what Casey Alt calls in a Deleuzian manner the abstract machine of contemporary culture. Object-oriented programming evidences the relationality, polymorphism and contexuality that characterises software culture on various scales. As Alt explains, software objects are polymorphic (open to various meanings, or affects, depending on their context) and defined by 'shifting topological surfaces' of clusters of objects that are in this sense virtual – open to emergent unfoldings. Also Alt uses the concept of affect from Deleuze, quoting affections as the occupying of the interval. Interval is what resides between the nodes, it is the relation that is often ignored as 'blank' but is actually the invisible that structures how things connect and don't connect. It is the moment of indetermination. Software objects can also be characterised as residing at this event of indetermination: they are grounded in durations and temporal unfoldings and are not purely prescribed structures.

Indeed, in an ethological manner these are not so much structural features of software as temporal tendencies, or potentials that allow certain relations and interactions with program environments, which then work in wider abstract environments such as the economy, politics, etc. For the virus, to modulate von Uexküll's idea, the milieu is opened only through its affects even though the wider environment expands much further. Software inhabits a specific universe only, and milieus are always defined by their relations (Bogue 2003: 68–72). The relationality of ethological assemblages provides a potentiality that several software art projects aim to tap into. They do so in order to map lines of becoming by injecting themselves into a logic of networks, software and the wider media ecology of contemporary culture. By functioning according to the same logic utilised by consumer software in control society, software art aims to find the cracks in the majoritarian language operating as the cultural relay of power and control. The question of joyful and sad software can then only be answered from the inside, and from the

assemblages in which software either helps to establish new connections and sensations, or closes them up in a technologically and legally
guarded proprietary system. The question continuously (and implicitly)
posed by critical experimental software is: how to find the defining singularities of current abstract machines of digitality, and how to take into
account the complexity of the ecological ties of software culture?

Mutationality, or :(){ :l:& };:

We can use the Deleuzian-Spinozian analysis of the dynamics of bodies-
in-relations to come up with cartographies of heterogeneous bodies in
concert. Ethology as conceived by Deleuze and Guattari necessarily dips
into the virtual in the sense of potentiality where the 'goodness' and
'badness' of encounters is fixed only in and through the unfolding of
their affective relations. Ethology is in this sense artistic by definition, or,
as Moira Gatens writes: 'Ethology does not impose a plane of organiza-
tion but rather posits a plane of experimentation, a mapping of extensive
relations and intensive capacities that are mobile and dynamic' (Gatens
1996: 169). This will necessarily involve 'a micropolitics concerned with
the "in-between" of subjects' open to a range of becomings (167).

Ethological cartographies look for experimentations and mutations.
Mutations take place through intervals, and express the potentiality in
any living system. For Simondon, potentiality, or metastability, is practically a definition of a living system. Life here does not have to be thought
according to the biological paradigm where 'living' is a characteristic
stratified according to the mode of organisation of animals, plants, etc.
Instead, we can talk of the non-organic life of various systems – or life
as individuation and intensity inherent in matter. Practices in software
art and related fields are exemplary social and critical interventions that
tap into this logic of the non-organic and function as (re)modulations of
what is real. Far from communication, or interpretation, such projects
tap into the very logics of power that are increasingly asignifying: algo-
rithms, computational processes, protocols and diagrams of how bodies,
social practices and codes are connected.

The ethology that seems to increasingly define software's topological spaces has to be connected to wider media ecologies, which is why
projects such as Google-Will-Eat-Itself gain their momentum from the
transdisciplinary zone between economy, politics and code – and hence
highlight the intimate and immanent connection with wider mechanisms
of biopower. In this sense of a continuous transdisciplinarity of its
assemblages, it is more akin to the ecological modes of the production of

subjectivity that Guattari and also Deleuze were interested in. In an eco-logical manner, the project is an exercise of immanent critique that acts as a modulation rather than simply reacting to the already given. The utopian nature of the project translates easily into a cartography of the various overlapping stratas on which assemblages are being contested.

In a Spinozist vein, ethologies deal with goodness and badness in terms of potentiality (ethics instead of norms as the micropolitical credo). The tactical irresponsibility that seems to characterise various software related art projects stems from an experimentation with such categories of the good and bad, and with the fuzzy borders of legality and illegality of network culture. The point about imperceptibility is easiest to make with examples that moved on this fuzzy border. In addition to the GWEI project, The Amazon Noir ('The Big Book Crime') is another example of such transdisciplinary projects. These projects emphasise the critical undecidability of software – understood as a cultural practice of transla-tion and processuality that ties together so many spheres as part of its diagrammatics. Perhaps this is the reason why the projects GWEI and The Amazon Noir are so interested in diagrammatics – turning their experimental software into tools of relationality of a kind that parodies control society's obsession with stratified flows.

The diagrams are in fact much more than representations of the projects. They are more akin to experimentation with the links and rela-tions inherent in the corporate software systems connected to various key sectors of the creative industries and information society. Diagrams (as abstract machines) are cartographies of the constitutive forces of the organisations of power, but they are as much, for Deleuze, distributions of singularities – and thus contain the potentials for deterritorialisation.[5] The Amazon Noir project is in itself an example of software tapping into the proprietary system – but only in order to subvert the logic of intellectual property, and liberating points in that system. Its software automated the process of copying books from Amazon.com and was left unnoticed and unannounced until it was finally settled with Amazon.com. As Michael Dieter points out, it worked through a diagrammatics of ambiguity that was 'heightened by the abstractions of software enti-ties' (Dieter 2007: 18), and established an ethology of software that did not work through morals but through ethics: what is software capable of and how can it experiment with the boundaries of the commercial system and its rules of accountability?

Through mapping relations that they then rework in their work of mutation (a parasite logic of a kind), these net art projects also produce a diagram-to-come.[6] In this, they are pushing the logics of those

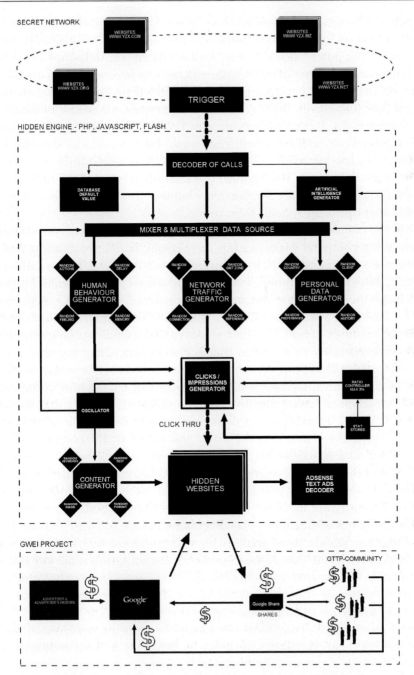

7.1: GWEI Diagram. Online at: http://gwei.org/pages/diagram/
diagram.html
Reproduced courtesy of Paolo Cirio.

diagrams to their limits and work as 'minor art'. The deterritorialisation of the logic is followed by a mock reterritorialisation. O'Sullivan points towards the potential humour in minor art deterritorialisations of language and underlines in a Deleuzian manner the need to see this humour as affirmative and removed from postmodern irony, or from signifying practices (O'Sullivan 2006: 73). Humour in itself is a vector of escape, a line of flight, most clearly evident in GWEI's utopian ideal of buying Google several million years from now. Humour works completely within the law but by pushing it to its limits by an over-obedient following of its commands. This changes our relation to law and the context in which such relations are illuminated – humour as a tactical accident of a kind that opens up systems from inside.[7]

In the diagrammatics of network society, which connects software as executing computer processes but increasingly social processes as well, order-words are embedded in the materiality of networks. To put it differently, software is continuously related and connected to different bodies through incorporeal transformations. Incorporeal events are executions of a kind (not always necessarily algorithmic or computer-bound) that fix the relations of bodies. Order-words can be seen as working through the incorporeality of the event that is always articulated together with the substance of expression – the materiality inherent in computer media or other technical media.[8] What is curious is of course how computer culture seems to have come up with a modality of language that works exactly through this logic of ordering and transforming reality. Software is an *agencement* that cuts the flows and pulses of the computational machine, and functions as a language of incorporeal events. It is the limit and the syntax of a language of digital culture that orders, organises and assembles. As part of wider abstract machines or diagrams, the language-software functions as order-words to place bodies in positions and carry out obligations. The diagrammatics of software culture try to organise standardised settings for such software acts that organise bodies, such as the user at the interface. Standardisation is the key strategy for a functionally and commercially viable context for the production of software. Yet, such relations of software in wider diagrams of society are prone to mutations from within that diagram.

As assemblages, code works not only through the order-word performativity that fixes states of things by executing its own message but also through a potentiality of the order-word to pass into something else – a password as much as a code that executes what it says. Deleuze and Guattari demand that we must elaborate on the powers of escape inherent in order-words, and in that way find the passwords beneath order-words (Deleuze and Guattari 1987: 110). In other words, if major language fixes constants, the minor languages of stuttering are pass-words, or modulations and variations that trigger transmutations.

For software artists such as Jaromil, this realisation of the updated language of digital code can be expressed through its powers of stuttering. Stuttering is the language of a people to come, a language not yet formed and recognised and perceived. Jaromil writes how

> In considering a source code as literature, I am depicting viruses as though they were the sort of poems written by Verlaine, Rimbaud, et al., against those selling the net as a safe area for straight society. The relations, forces and laws governing the digital domain differ from those in the natural . . . viruses are spontaneous compositions which are like lyrical poems in causing imperfections in machines 'made to work' and in representing the rebellion of our digital serfs. (Jaromil 2003: n.p.)

Indeed, I would add that this stuttering also refers to a wider potential of software art – or software that is experimental in the Deleuzian sense of mapping and probing potentials. The idea of experimental ethologies has a precursor in the methodological demand of experimentation in *Difference and Repetition*, it is a way to tap into the ontology of difference (instead of just repeating a recognition of the same) (see Williams 2003: 90). In software art contexts, and in the methodology of art practices, Fuller's point about interrogability is one way to frame this experimentality in terms of mapping differences in the layers of imperceptibility: Fuller writes:

> The quality of interrogability in software arises instead at those moments when perception as a media inherent to software becomes aware of and active in the multi-scalar terms and dynamics of its composition. It occurs when morphogenetic and experimental demands are made on, and recognized as occurring in, the expressive capacities of all elements in a composition. (Fuller 2006: 65)

In this context, experimentality extends towards a-signifying dimensions of executable language. However this executable language does not fix constants, but looks for variations and stutterings. For example Jaromil's poetics of code relates to a more condensed and effective piece of writing in the form of ':(){ :|:& };:' which is a piece of UNIX code that when entered into the machines command line causes an abrupt crash. It is described as a chain reaction that overstrains the system, and through that crash it exhibits the performative power of software as an active work, instead of just interpretation in the hermeneutical sense. Despite Jaromil framing his digital poetic language in terms of Saussure's langue/

parole, I would consider it more apt to place the idea of order-words and their ethological relationality in a wider context of control society at the core of the question. What Jaromil and the many software art projects addressed in this chapter work with is a more a-signifying concept of language that both looks for the stammering and stuttering of language in Deleuze and Guattari's sense and for the relationality of that language in a diagrammatics of political economy. The poetics of experimental software is a tapping into the existing ethological relations of software and the abstract machines of capitalism and digitality in which they are framed, but also a search for the singularities and mutations within those systems of relations. It is within those systems of coding and relationality that one finds politics as a mode of experimentation geared towards the unexpected, the imperceptible, that can be turned into a tactical methodology. Here the micropolitics of variation turns out to be an apt way to understand the immanent ways software art projects trigger and execute not only code, but ecological repercussions within the wider digital and capitalist system.

References

Alt, C. (2010), 'Objects of Our Affection. How Object-Orientation Made Computation a Medium', in E. Huhtamo and J. Parikka (eds), *Media Archaeologies*, Berkeley: University of California Press.

Ansell-Pearson, K. (1999), *Germinal Life: The Difference and Repetition of Deleuze*, London and New York: Routledge.

Arns, I. (2005), 'Code as Performative Speech Act', *Artnodes* (July).

Arns, I. and F. Hunger (2005), 'The Clean Rooms' Dirty Secret. Temporary Software Art Factory: Readme 100 in Dortmund, Germany, 2005', in O. Goriunova (ed.), *Readme 100: Temporary Software Factory*, Norderstedt.

Bogue, R. (2003), *Deleuze on Music, Painting and the Arts*, New York and London: Routledge.

Boundas, C. V. (2005), 'Virtual/Virtuality', in A. Parr (ed.), *The Deleuze Dictionary*, Edinburgh: Edinburgh University Press.

Chun, W. H. K. (2008), 'The Enduring Ephemeral, or the Future is a Memory', *Critical Inquiry*, 35: 1 (Autumn).

Deleuze, G. (1988), *Spinoza: Practical Philosophy*, trans. R. Hurley, San Francisco: City Light Books.

Deleuze, G. (2005), *Francis Bacon: The Logic of Sensation*, trans. D. W. Smith, London and New York: Continuum.

Deleuze, G. and F. Guattari (1987), *A Thousand Plateaus*, trans. B. Massumi, Minneapolis: University of Minnesota Press.

Dieter, M. (2007), 'Amazon Noir: Piracy, Distribution, Control', *M/C Journal*, 10: 5 (October); available at: http://journal.media-culture.org.au/0710/07-dieter.php

Fuller, M. (2003), *Behind the Blip: Essays on the Culture of Software*, New York: Autonomedia.

Fuller, M. (2005), *Media Ecologies: Materialist Energies in Art and Technoculture*, Cambridge, MA: MIT Press.

Fuller, M. (2006), *Softness: Interrogability; General Intellect; Art Methodologies in Software*, Huddersfield: Digital Research Unit at Huddersfield University; available at: http://www.interfacekultur.au.dk/enhed/aktiviteter/fuller/fuller_softness

Galloway, A. R. (2004), *Protocol: How Control Exists After Decentralization*, Cambridge, MA: MIT Press.

Galloway, A. R. and E. Thacker (2007), *The Exploit: A Theory of Networks*, Minneapolis: University of Minnesota Press.

Gatens, M. (1996), 'Through a Spinozist Lens: Ethology, Difference, Power', in P. Patton (ed.), *Deleuze: A Critical Reader*, Oxford: Blackwell.

Goriunova, O. and A. Shulgin (2008), 'Glitch', in M. Fuller (ed.), *Software Studies: A Lexicon*, Cambridge, MA: MIT Press.

Grosz, E. (2008), *Chaos, Territory, Art: Deleuze and the Framing of the Earth*, New York: Columbia University Press.

Harley, D., R. Slade and U. E. Gattiker (2001), *Viruses Revealed! Understand and Counter Malicious Software*, New York: Osborne/McGraw Hill.

Jaromil (2003), ':(){ :l:& };:'; Digitalcraft catalogue for the I Love You Exhibition, 2003; available at: http://www.digitalcraft.org/?artikel_id=292

Kittler, F. (1995), 'There is No Software', *Ctheory* (18 October).

Massumi, B. (1992), *A User's Guide to Capitalism and Schizophrenia: Deviations from Deleuze and Guattari*, Cambridge, MA: Swerve/MIT Press.

O'Sullivan, S. (2006), *Art Encounters Deleuze and Guattari: Thought Beyond Representation*, London: Palgrave Macmillan.

Rajchman, J. (2000), *The Deleuze Connections*, Cambridge, MA: MIT Press.

Rossiter, N. (2006), *Organized Networks: Media Theory, Creative Labour, New Institutions*, Rotterdam: NAI Publishers.

Simondon, G. (2007), *L'individuation psychique et collective*, Paris: Aubier.

Sollfrank, C. (2001), 'Biennale.py – The Return of The Media Hype', *Telepolis*, 7: 7; available at: http://www.heise.de/tp/r4/artikel/3/3642/1.html

Williams, J. (2003), *Gilles Deleuze's Difference and Repetition: A Critical Introduction and Guide*, Edinburgh: Edinburgh University Press.

Wise, J. M. (2005), 'Assemblage', in C. J. Stivale (ed.), *Gilles Deleuze: Key Concepts*, Chesham: Acumen.

Notes

1. The software art archive at http://www.runme.org demonstrates the multiplicity of projects – and the ensuing difficulty of general definitions which in itself feeds into finding much more open-ended and experimental definitions that grasp software art in terms of potentiality.
2. On glitch and software (art), see Goriunova and Shulgin (2008: 110–19). For Jodi projects, see for example http://wwwwwwwww.jodi.org and http://404.jodi.org
3. See http://znc.ctrlaltdel.org
4. On temporality, see the recent Jaromil and Jodi collaboration TBT: Time Based Text-project and software. The software allows a user to tap into the actual process of writing on the computer keyboard and frame that in its sheer materiality and unfolding temporality. See http://tbt.dyne.org. On the fundamental temporality of computing, see Chun (2008).
5. Alex Galloway produces a novel approach to the diagram in the context of the internet in his book *Protocol* (Galloway 2004). There he shows the multi-layered and multi-scaled ontology of the internet and how it can be understood as a diagrammatic distribution of relations and nodes which govern and distribute agencies.

6. Or, as Arns and Hunger write: 'By addressing the ubiquitous presence of program code, software art points to the fact that software is an invisible performative layer that increasingly structures our everyday life' (Arns and Hunger 2005: 10). They continue by pointing towards the possibility of new differentiations that software art frames through what different writers have characterised as its experimental, speculative and, for example, non-pragmatic aims.
7. On the point of humour in Deleuze's *Difference and Repetition*, see Williams (2003: 36–7).
8. On language, order-words and incorporeal transformations, see Massumi (1995: 27–32).

Chapter 8

Fractal Philosophy (And the Small Matter of Learning How to Listen): Attunement as the Task of Art

Johnny Golding

> What terror haunts Van Gogh's head, caught in a becoming-sunflower?
> Deleuze and Guattari, *What is Philosophy?*

8.1: Van Gogh, *Self-Portrait Dedicated to Paul Gauguin,* 1888, oil on canvas, 60.5 × 49.4 cm. Fogg Art Museum, Harvard University, Cambridge, MA.

8.2: Van Gogh, *Self-Portrait with Bandaged Ear, Arles,* January 1889; oil on canvas, 60 × 49 cm. Courtauld Institute Galleries.

8.3: Van Gogh, (Self-Portrait?) *The Sunflowers* (detail), 1888; replica (also by Van Gogh), January 1889, oil on canvas, 21 × 73 cm. National Portrait Gallery.

B-side Philosophy (The Transformation of Van Gogh's Right Ear)

Deleuze and Guattari offer three playful but coded journeys onto the broad arena they call 'the task of art'– where task, not to mention art, is meant to spill into, reconfigure and/or destroy the varying pragmatic-spatiotemporal intensities one might otherwise call 'life'. These three

journeys can be listed thus: that of an immanent 'becoming-x'; that of
the ever-sporing 'rhizome'; and that of the a-radical, surface-structured,
non-rooted 'refrain'.

Par-boiled into a manifesto-style primer, the first of these journeys is
shaded and toned by the concept-process-phrasings of a 'becoming', be
that as a 'becoming-intense', a 'becoming-animal', a 'becoming-woman',
a 'becoming-sunflower', a 'becoming-imperceptible' or a becoming-
n+1-combination-of-that-which-lies-to-hand-or-may-be-or-already-
has-been-becoming.[1] It all might seem a bit 'method acting' or indeed
'running towards' without ever really 'getting there'. Nevertheless,
Deleuze and Guattari proclaim:

> We are not in the world; we become with the world; we become by contem-
> plating it. Everything is vision, becoming. We become universes. Becoming
> animal, plant, molecular, becoming zero. This is true of all the arts. . . . Art
> does not have opinions. Art undoes the triple organisation of perceptions,
> affections, and opinions in order to substitute a monument composed of
> percepts, affects, and blocs of sensations that takes the place of language.
> It is about listening . . . This is precisely the task of all art. (Deleuze and
> Guattari 1994: 170–7)

These 'becoming-' journey-bandwidths mark the first stage of art's
work. But it is a 'first' not in a hierarchical, privileging sense, but rather
in a logical sense; that is, by taking as a given that one 'begins' precisely where one 'is' – a pragmatic 'start' that can only ever happen by
accounting for the constitutive reality of the present-tense 'is'; that is to
say, of the 'here and now'.[2] This is a very different accounting of the
'constitutive realities of the present-tense "is"' offered either by Hegel
on the one hand or Heidegger on the other.[3] A brief potted-review of
both on the question of what is 'the is' will serve to clarify what is at
stake for Deleuze and Guattari – what they steal and what they leave
behind from both treasure troves – and why.

Perhaps the clearest exposition of the constitutive 'is' for Hegelian
logic can be found in the *Phenomenology of Spirit* where, for our pur-
poses, three crucial distinctions are established: first, in terms of what
a 'Universal Concept' is (as distinct from any other kind of concept);
second, in terms of what the 'This' is; and third, in terms of what
'Negation' is.[4] At its most simple point, the Universal Concept names
the full or totalised expression of any object – no matter where or when
– without leaving anything to chance, opinion, perception or whim. To
do otherwise is to fall prey to the usual fault of confusing an 'abstraction' (or 'model') with a Concept.[5] The only way in which one can be
absolutely certain that the entirety of the picture has indeed been drawn

– that nothing has been left out or can be added at will – is thus to follow the dialectical formulation that Universality will always already consist of (a) an abstract version of 'all that there is (thesis)', plus (b) the point-for-point (but still abstract version) of 'all that there is not (antithesis)', whose (c) sublation of the one into the other (thesis into antithesis or vice versa) produces a synthesis, which (d) comes 'back around' to form the 'concrete-ground' (essence, basis) of the Absolute/Pure (Universality) of the Concept, itself now also 'grounding' (that is, giving meaning to) the aforementioned and previously abstract thesis/antithesis.[6] In short, this dialectically encased resolution of the thesis/antithesis from pure abstraction into its highest, fully synthesised, 'concrete' and purest form of Spirit-Knowledge – with no extraneous bits hanging outside of the 'whole picture' (Totality) – 'comes back around' to form the basis/ground of all meaning, truth, interpretation and reason. It is a tidy, self-satisfying, teleological move. As Hegel summarises:

§20. The True is the whole. But the whole is nothing other than the essence consummating itself through its development. Of the Absolute, it must be said that it is essentially a *result*, that only in the *end* is it what it truly is; and that precisely in this consists its nature, viz. To be actual, subject, the spontaneous becoming of itself. (Hegel 1977: 11)

The niggling problem of which Hegel was of course fully aware, was that Reality managed always to be greater than the sum of its parts; indeed, if this were not the case then by simple arithmetic, thesis + its point-for-point contradictory antithesis would always equal 'zero' or at best would simply establish a tautology ($A \Leftrightarrow not\text{-}A$). One could say, ⤳ names the synthesis ☞ : ☜ for no other reason than that I say it is so, a position that might be fine with Humpty Dumpty, but was far more problematic for Hegel.[7] And yet it was not possible to 'add' anything extra to the logic of the Concept in order to make it 'make' (as in produce, express, disclose) 'sense' (meaning, sensuousness, life). This is because at its most profound point, Idealism – and certainly Hegel's version of it – was attempting to press the argument that no 'outside' set of logics or omnipotent points of observation should be required to explain any given phenomenon. The logic had to hold, in and of itself; and more than that, it had to do so by simultaneously encompassing 'change', 'movement' and 'progress' as integral to any concept, and therewith, as integral to (i.e. 'within') the Totality.[8]

The question, then, of how systematically to add a 'something' to the immanent movement without raising the entire edifice of Totality to an unworthy, arbitrary ground – or, worse, to reducing it to mere tautology or opinion, perception or whim – was resolved in part by Hegel's neat reformulation of the 'This'. It was a curious kind of architectural move; one that not only led to one of Hegel's greatest achievements – that of 'Negation' and with it the notion of (a teleological unfolding) of the Universal 'becoming-a-something', be it through self-certainty, perception, consciousness, identity politics, mastery, bondage, etc. – but it ironically heralded his ultimate failure, at least from the vantage point of the politically committed scholar, artist, person-in-the-street, not the least of whom included Deleuze and Guattari, despite their obviously sticky fingers when it came to pinching a concept.

Hegel played his cards by problematising the whereabouts of the 'This', as well as the 'Here' and 'Now' which taken together constituted the dialectically informed manifestation of 'This'. He problematised their whereabouts in the following way: At the very moment one might point to or attempt to grasp (both intellectually and practically) the present-tense Real in all its glorious manifestations, this 'Now' will always already disappear into a Before or an After or a Somewhere Else. This is because the present – as present, i.e. as a 'not-mediated' entity, can never itself become embodied or 'fully realised', precisely because *ipso facto* it is 'im-mediate'. Or, to put this slightly differently, it is to say that this 'impossible' non-representational moment of the 'This' is both the expression and presencing of an abstract 'otherness' whilst, simultaneously, also expressing/presencing a radical fluidity of movement. A rhetorically demanding Hegel explains it thus:

> §95. What is the *This*? If we take the 'This' in the twofold shape of its being, as 'Now' and as 'Here', the dialectic it has in it will receive a form as intelligible as the 'This' itself is. To the question: 'What is Now?' let us answer, e.g. 'Now is Night.' In order to test the truth of this sense-certainty, a simple experiment will suffice. We write down this truth; a truth cannot lose anything by being written down, any more than it can lose anything through our preserving it. If *now, this noon*, we look again at the written truth we shall have to say that it has become stale. . . .
>
> §106. The Now that is pointed to, *this* Now: 'Now'; it has already ceased to be in the act of pointing to it. The Now that *is*, is another Now than the one pointed to, and we see that the Now is just this: to be no more, just when it is. The Now, as it is pointed out to us, is Now that *has been*, and this is its truth; it has not the truth of *being*. Yet this much is true, that it has been. But what essentially *has been* [*gewesen ist*] is, in fact, not an essence that is [*kein Wesen*]; [rather] *it is a 'not'*. (Hegel 1977: 59–60, 63; emphasis in original)

Or, to put it yet another way: the 'This', the 'Here', the 'Now' – in short, the 'is' of Hegelian Idealism – is nothing other than the *abstract surface structure* of any given Universality. And as with any surface (say, for example, the surface of a table) not only can the 'surface-is' not exist without the actuality of the structure to which it is attached acting as 'ground' to the said surface, but that the surface acts also as the 'expression' of the point-for-point structure to which it is attached. In the case of the 'This', the 'Here', the 'Now', and so on, each is 'surface' to the Totality, attached to and expressing in this case, the dialectical fluid structure of movement itself. And as that surface can never be larger nor smaller than the structure to which it is attached, nor for that matter, remain 'inside' or 'outside' any Totality, this 'surface' neither embodies weight nor substance nor essence nor space. Nevertheless, and as a surface expressing a (transcendental/immanent) movement-structure, it still names an eternally unfolding 'otherness' without which meaning cannot be sutured or made 'manifest', i.e. made present. Removed from its ground (synthesis), that is, taking the 'surface' to be 'in and of itself', the 'This' of the 'Here' and 'Now' simply cannot be 'grasped'. But as we will see momentarily, it is precisely the surface-immanent movement-structure called 'This' that Deleuze and Guattari wish to liberate from the shackles of a Universalised Totality. As we will see, this immanent-movement-structure will morph into many things: sometimes the 'refrain'; sometimes a 'viral assemblage'; sometimes 'logic of sense'; sometimes 'simulacrum'. (We might even wish to call it 'Van Gogh's right ear', but I am getting ahead of the argument).[9]

To the question, then, of what can be added in order to avoid tautology, whim, outside direction or authorial opinion, Hegel's answer is quite clear; he names it the Negative – the immanent teleological 'surface' unfolding of dialectical synthesis itself.[10] This may seem surprising, but this move to situate the 'is' as a Negative surface structure was quite an advance from the original zero-sum position of thesis + antithesis = the whole of the Universe. For not only did establishing 'the Negative' as an immanent and 'unnameable-something-other' allow for the breaking up and adding to an otherwise deadlocked and tautological A⇔not-A identity formation. It also meant that the so-called deep cut ('/') between thesis/antithesis could now no longer be envisioned as a logical no-man's land, i.e., as the 'excluded middle', often wrongly subsumed by political/creative identity inventors to be the 'in between space' of Otherness, and therewith of liberation, itself. If one were to stay within the confines of Universality, there could never be an 'in between' moment bracketing the past and the future, just an abstract, negative surface structure of 'a plurality' of Nows, which vanish at the very moment of their debut, though not without holding the door open so that 'meaning' can take (its) place.

§108. [What gives the Here its *gravitas*?]. The *Here pointed out*, to which I hold fast, is similarly a *This*. Here which, in fact, is *not* this Here, but a Before and Behind, an Above and Below, a Right and a Left. The Above is itself similarly this manifold otherness of above, below, etc. The Here, which was supposed to have been pointed out, vanishes in other Heres, but these likewise vanish. What is pointed out, held fast, and abides is a *negative*. This, which *is* negative only when the Heres are taken as they should be, but in being so taken they dispersed themselves; what abides is a simple complex of many Heres. The Here that is *meant* would be the point; but *is* not; on the contrary, when it is pointed out as something that *is*, the pointing-out shows itself to be not an immediate knowing [of the point], but a movement from the Here that is *meant* through many Heres into the universal Here which is a simple plurality of Heres, just as the day is a simply plurality of Nows. (Hegel 1977: 64)

Of course Deleuze, as well as Guattari, reject – and for good reason – the Hegelian dialectic, often demanding to rid philosophy, politics, science and art of, as Foucault so eloquently put it, 'the old categories of the Negative (law, limit, castration, lack, lacuna), which Western thought has so long held sacred as a form of power and an access to reality'.[11] But it was also no less the case that the Hegelian dialectic, and particularly the way in which the Concept itself had been formulated was, and remains to this day, a tough act to beat. For to rid Philosophy of the metaphysical 'is' seemed to imply a good riddance to some of its more eloquent fares – plurality, surface-synthesis, movement, the instant – not to mention 'pure immanence' and with it, the possibility of destroying the otherwise inventive categories of, say, 'becoming-woman' or 'becoming-animal' or 'becoming-sunflower' or 'becoming-ear', etc. It often seemed (and in some quarters, still does), that the price of fighting to create a wholly different set of anti-Oedipal identities and, with it, a wholly new set of social order(s) might just be worth the price of enduring, just for a moment or two, all the rotting bad smells of the Hegelian identi-kit corpse.[12]

And yet, this is precisely what Deleuze and Guattari set out to accomplish: a way to hold one's nose against Hegel and all forms of Metaphysical thought in order to conceptualise, materialise and endure the very act of 'becoming-x' without being penetrated by 'arboreal philosophy', even if 'just for a moment or two'. The dangers of allowing otherwise were too grave. For arboreal philosophy was their euphemistic way to identify the by now well-entrenched planters-wart logic of continuity, goals, processes and closed systems, thoroughly embedded in all flat-footed State philosophies and common-sense pronouncements – of

which 2000-plus years of Metaphysics, contemporary Warfare, instrumental Science, Literature, Art and Religion had done little to uproot.

In its most simple form, arboreal philosophy could be understood
in this manner: Take as a given a seed, for example, an acorn. Now,
no matter what one does (assuming it is gardened properly and not set
alight or mashed), it will only ever unfold/manifest itself as an Oak Tree.
The Tree is thus the 'goal' to which all little acorn seeds aspire. This
'aspiration', as it were, is continuous, linear (even if the path appears
convoluted, spiralled, hysterical, nasty or relaxed). This is because all
change, no matter how often or in what manner it occurs, does so in
relation to an always already 'unfolding' trajectory of that growth.
The Oak, as the 'outcome' of the acorn, names thus the very purpose
(ground) of the said seed. It is only the elemental processes to which that
seed might be subjected (wind, sun, rain, [unemployment, bullying,]
etc.) that determines 'how' the Oak might turn out (big, small, gnarly,
[demented, covered in law suits]). Thus is revealed the 'true purpose'
of one's Being; or, as eugenics might proclaim: it's all already coded in
one's basic DNA (Deleuze and Guattari 2004: 15).

Most crucially, then, and no matter what the seed might do, be it
wishing, hoping, praying (or even becoming a political militant), it
would only ever keep unfolding towards its proverbial goal (The Old
Oak Tree). The Oak-Tree-goal thus gives meaning, purpose, destiny
to our little seed, who in times of drought or strife or just hanging out
with Feminists, might otherwise be *tempted* to fall off the so-called True
path (though, in the cold light of day would 'come to its senses' and
realise, one way or another, that this kind of dreaming could/should/
would never do, as it was considered impossible to fall outside an always
already given 'nature'). To be sure, then, under this logic one could never
leave the family; one could never attempt the dream of becoming-x, if
that 'becoming-x' was something other than the already prescribed path.
One could never morph into, say, a butterfly or Maserati car, no matter
how dedicated to becoming 'butterfly' or 'car' that seed might wish to
be. This might be very well and good if one happens to be an acorn; but
if one happens to be a slave, woman, racial-Other, gay, transgender,
etc., if one happens to 'think outside the box' or grow 'bigger than one's
britches' or try to 'rise above one's station', etc., it becomes clear where
this grounded and continuously unfolding logic can go wrong. Mob-
lynching, stoning, raping, murder, ethnic cleansing, Sharia law, torture
all gain an ethical toe-hold in the culture as 'rightful' punishments
against those attempting to become a-something-other-than-what-they-
were-always-meant-to-be. 'We're tired of trees,' sigh Deleuze and

Guattari. 'We should stop believing in trees, roots, and radicles. They've made us suffer too much. All of arborescent culture is founded on them, from biology to linguistics' (Deleuze and Guattari 2004: 17).[13]

But the question remained: whether one *could* account, both epistemologically and analytically, for the 'constitutive is' as a something that 'made sense' – in the fullest use of the terms 'to make' (create, enable, force) and 'sense' (sensuousness, intelligence, the senses), without reintroducing the tetra-headed trap of Universal Totality, the Negative, and the teleological methods of Dialectic unfolding. If this could be done, argued Deleuze and Guattari, then the political and aesthetic yields would be substantial. Because, for the first time in a rather long time, not only would philosophy have caught up with the very reality it had been seeking to inhabit – i.e., one steeped in discontinuous logics, fractal codes, non-representational art, multiversal genders, non-national sovereignties – it would also mean bearing witness to our contemporary age in an active, participant manner, rather than as mere drones, couch potatoes or passers-by. Accounting both epistemologically and analytically for the 'constitutive is' in terms of this 'age' called 'technology' meant taking seriously the combinatory logics of 'techne' itself. It meant taking seriously that in our epoch/age a different way of systematising was virulently underway: one that foregrounded 'the art of grasping the "out-there"'; one that worked off of and around patterns and poeisis, simulacrum, circulation, assemblage and exchange. An epoch whereby wholly different end-games-as-mid-games become networked orders of the day, producing, expressing and demanding quite different politics, ethics, science and art – not to mention timings and spatialities – than those encountered by our Ancient, Modernist (and postmodernist) cousins, barely visible with a Metaphysical lens.

Not to be daunted, it seemed that the only way – or at least the main experimental way – to eliminate Hegelian substance, and with it, arboreal philosophy, was at first to commit to what would later be called the 'outside of thought'.[14] Here 'outside of thought' meant something quite different than a kind of anti-intellectual run toward 'Practice' (the usual partner-in-crime rallied against 'Theory'). Getting away from, or getting 'outside' of, thought was meant to take distance from metaphysical Contemplation rather than getting away from being conceptual. It meant trying to get away from the conflation of language with 'metaphor', 'semiotics', 'signifier,' and therewith, representation.[15]

In short, it meant trying to figure out how to 'picture' – without the visuals – the becoming-sunflower of Van Gogh's right ear.

A-side the B-side: Learning How to Listen (Attunement as the Task of Art)

But to give the 'outside of thought' a kind of coherence so that it too would not be indebted to the arboreal authority-voice of its makers required yet another subtle move. Speaking as they often did with 'a single tongue', Deleuze and Guattari thus dined out in several parallel universes at the same time. Pocketing ingredients from around the philosophical galaxy – from the worlds of expressionism (Spinoza), pure immanence, artifice and a-radical genealogies (Hume, Nietzsche), folds and monadology (Leibniz); élan vital, simultaneity and duration (Bergson); pattern, difference, repetition and time (Heidegger), sense and sensation (the Stoics, Lewis Carroll, Bacon) and the cartographically discursive, diagrammatically challenged regimes of power, ethics, aesthetics and existence (Foucault) – they began to build their counter-trans-immanent-logic. Long spoons were at the ready. For dangers lurked at every turn at this oddly Bacchanalian banquet: mix-matching such a heady crowd whose epistemological, not to mention political, allegiances were often suspect, or at best 'complicated'.[16] The seating arrangements themselves must have given grave cause for alarm.

And yet, despite being on such a wildly provocative intra-species guest-list, those invited did seem to have at least one thing in common (however differently each in their own distinctive way might have approached it). What they had in common was an analytic accounting for cultural reinvention beyond the usual binaries of good and evil; or to put this slightly differently, what they had or tried to have was a way to account for the truth of culture as that which must emerge from ungrounded 'difference', a 'difference' that was something to be grasped, invented – that is to say, *inhabited* – in all its inglorious manifestations, productions, changes without recourse to a totalising picture of reality. The Other, impossible, uninhabitable, excluded-middle, of the 'is' – dialectically formed or otherwise – was dead. And in its place, another kind of 'is', one that could not only acknowledge and express difference, but was the source of it. Foucault would name it as a 'stylistics' or 'art of existence', the multiple practice of gathering many selves – slices of selves, pleasures of selves – to the self. Nothing discovered, nothing revealed, just a sensitive/sensuous kind of whoring, a discursive whoring, along the lines 'share all reveal nothing'.[17]

> '[I]f I was interested in Antiquity,' Foucault remarked two months before his death, 'it was because, for a whole scenario of reasons, the idea of a morality as obedience to a code of rules is now disappearing, has already disappeared. And to this absence of morality corresponds, must correspond, the search for an art of existence.'[18]

The becoming-gay, the becoming-butterfly, the becoming-the-colour-purple, would instead be constituted by the very journey on which that 'becoming' had embarked. It would be re-envisioned by Deleuze and Guattari as a 'surface' journey, a pollinating, ruminating, sporing, folding and re-folding kind of journey, a journey of joining a 'this' with a 'that' for no other reason than that it could be (and in many cases, had to be) done; where nothing is 'True' (in the sense of being Universal, Totalised, Rooted); where the Ground that lies before us as 'ground' is nothing but the discursive structure of those sporing/pollinating movements, quite divorced from a given 'picture', 'representation', 'semiotic' or 'goal'. Where the political, ethical and aesthetic task, should one rise to it, would be to undertake this stylistics of existence, a mingling with free-fall experimentation and groundless-Grounds in order to make the assemblage of a becoming-x 'real', coherent, *sticky*. The issue, a wise Foucault thus tabled, 'is not: if there is no God, everything is permitted. Its formula is rather the question: if I must confront myself with "nothing is true", how am I to live?' (Foucault 2002: 174).

This, and not an 'im-mediate' Now-time is the 'where', the so-called 'de-territorialised plane' of one's 'beginning'. Or to say it with more force: the '*This*' of the Foucauldian question 'if I must confront myself with "nothing new", how am I to live?' is precisely the 'plane' upon which these disconnected (or not continuously connected) inventive journeys are mapped, a kind of web or discursive cloud networked cartography, neither virtual nor grounded, but tangible nevertheless. Entailing no end-points or goal or ground, Deleuze and Guattari would later refine this 'this' as precisely 'the plane of immanence', the critical dwelling 'plateau' upon which invention could and always did take place, however fleeting and oddly dimensional this constitutive 'spatiality' might be or become, without recourse to a prescribed Truth, Ethics, Spirit, Destiny.[19] As we know from their work, there are at least 'a thousand' of these plateaus.

This diagrammatic mapping 'plane of immanence' not only ventured beyond the good and evil limits of a constituted 'truth', now itself folded and in/formed by the seemingly endless vagrancies of free-fall experimentation and art. It was also a cartography that ventured beyond the concrete walls of the Universal Concept itself.

For the concepts Deleuze and Guattari started to invoke were curiously beginning to take on the atmosphere of not quite being concepts at all, at least not in the sense that Hegel would have understood. But neither were they non-concepts, that is, descriptions or markers which might tend to hark back to some kind of pre-existing rule, resemblance, metaphor or code, or not hark back to anything all, preferring to remain at some arbitrary level of a shopping-mall mentality. Instead it could be said that they ushered in, along with some of their guests, a serious break with the Universal and the Teleological, and flitted, instead, towards the 'multiversal' and the 'morphological' or 'teleonomic' surface-structure cohesions, clusters or assemblages with no 'other-side', no antithesis or thesis, no abstraction, concretion or synthesis, but which could nevertheless 'jump' or 'spore' to an 'elsewhere' in the same manner that grass and other rhizomatic entities took flight. A non-rooted (a-radical), ana-logical, slice-point 'singularity'– neither part of a whole (as in fragment, thesis, antithesis, synthesis) nor held hostage to the 'ground' for its breadcrumbs of meaning.[20]

The fractal points of resistance, curiosity, anger, boredom, etc. – otherwise called rhizomes – instead enframed the very journey of their de-territorialising map-making with whole series of mutant relativities and viral assemblages.[21] Each sporing move meant to pollinate or gather (or both or something else altogether) the nano-wave particles of life, death, grease, break-down, slice-of-ear into some kind of constitutive, becoming-x environ, a constitutive-now-time-space thus made present, coherent – A LIFE, to shout out with Deleuze – in the very event of its appropriation (Deleuze 2001: 27; see n. 16). A non-stratified, 'piece of immanence', to paraphrase the Deleuze and Guattari of November 28, 1947, to be constructed 'flow by flow and segment by segment lines of experimentation, becoming-animal, becoming-molecular, etc.' (Deleuze and Guattari 2004: 179).[22]

This appropriation – led, countered, laughed at – by the ana-human be-ing of rhizomatic fame, was given many nicknames: planes of consistency, a collectivity of desiring machines, intensities, deterritorialising 'bodies without organs', and was based on many kinds of ana-logics which, into the bargain, gave sustenance to an otherwise relentless onslaught of right-wing political, aesthetic, ethical and epistemological toxicities. A deterritorialisation that helped stave off organisation, stratification, sedimentation, all the sine qua non for fascist massification.

> People ask: So what is this BwO? But you are already on it, scurrying like a vermin, groping like a blind person, or running like a lunatic: desert traveller and nomad of the steppes . . . Experimentation: not only radiophonic but also biological and political, incurring censorship and repression. Corpus and Socius, politics and experimentation. They will not let you experiment in peace. . . . A BwO is made in such a way that it can be occupied populated only by intensities. Only intensities pass and circulate. Still, the BwO is not a scene, a place or even a support upon which something comes to pass. . . . It is not a space, nor is it in space . . . It is nonstratified, unformed, intense matter, the matrix of intensity, intensity = 0; but there is nothing negative about that zero, there are no negative or opposite intensities. Matter equals energy. . . . [It is] the tantric egg. (Deleuze and Guattari 2004: 169–70)

> The BwO is what remains when you take everything away. (Deleuze and Guattari 2004: 168)

There was only one, very tiny, somewhat off-putting, difficulty with their line of flight from the Negative, especially via the rhizomatically imbued bodies without organs: these ana-concepts still seemed closer to metaphor and description than a tool with which to combat the binaries and all associated restrictions. Or to put it somewhat harshly: It didn't seem to work.

It might not have worked because, quite frankly, maybe their 'mouth-breast', as they might say, was never meant to work. Maybe it was just a blood-curdling plea to get the hell out of Metaphysics, right here and right now, and like many a giant before them, rather than becoming-like-a-butterfly-and-stinging-like-a-bee, their becoming-x just kept amounting to the eternally returning nightmare of becoming-Descriptive or becoming-Metaphysics.[23] Because despite their arguments, supplications, tantrums, demands, sweet jokes, political commitment, intense rigour, hilarious drawings and sometimes indecipherable, insufferable wanderings, they were still saddled with the initial problem confronting Hegel and, indeed, all of philosophy, all those many years ago: how to present a logic that would accommodate reality (and not the other way around) without resorting to whim, opinion or might over right, especially if that whim, opinion or might over right just happened to be unquestionably 'molar', fascistic, oppressive.

Heidegger's move, with which Deleuze and Guattari were quite familiar, was to revisit the problem of the elusive presence by relocating Metaphysics, and with it, representation (i.e., the standing in for an 'x', by resembling or copying) as, also, and perhaps more importantly, a re-presenting (repeatedly presenting, 'bringing forth' [*stellen*]) of the relation of being (entity) to Being (*Da-Sein*).[24] For Heidegger, this 'bringing forth' could be retranslated as 'putting man [*sic*] in the picture'. But it also would mean to 'understand' or, more colloquially still, 'to get the picture'. To 'conceive' (understand) and 'get the picture' (grasp), when taken together, underscore the specificity of a time period – our time period, the 'Modern World' or 'Age of Technology' – when the ability both to 'hear' and 'do' (i.e., put oneself in the picture) and at the same time, be taken into this picture by one's relation to the 'There' of science and of life, become the binding feature of this epoch. It is, as Heidegger notes in 'The Question Concerning Technology', an age bound together by the logic of techne – the ability to 'grasp' the 'out There' and, simultaneously, be grasped by it, where, as he puts it, 'the essence of technology is by no means anything technological'.[25] This relation, the relation of b⇔B, enframes our world, and forms 'our picture' of it – a picture that is not particularly 'visual', and not at all anthropocentric. Its method is 'poiesis' and its path is nothing other than the sensuous logics initiated and 'brought forth' through the artistry of the grasp. This is the 'essence' of technology – having nothing to do with the usual understanding of technology as domination, machinery and computer, but instead, a 'This-world' constituted by the logic of its techne. Heidegger thus writes:

> This prospect strikes us as strange. Indeed, it should do so, should do so as persistently as possible and with so much urgency that we will finally take seriously the simple question of what the name 'technology' means. The word stems from the Greek. *Technikon* means that which belongs to *technë*. We must observe two things with respect to the meaning of this word. One is that *technë* is the name not only for the activities and skills of the craftsman, but also for the arts of the mind and the fine arts. *Technë* belongs to bringing-forth, to poiesis; it is something poietic. (Heidegger 1977: 11–12)

Accordingly, the constituted surface-structure 'This', the present-tense 'is', for Heidegger, is a surface-structure relation 'in-formed' by technology, by the logic of its technique/grasp/art. This sets apart our age from any other age, not because the age of technology is 'best' or 'new' or even *'our age'* and therefore particularly appealing to *us*. It is because the age itself is characterised by a particular combination of regimes of knowledge – an *ars scientifica* and an *ars erotica*, as Foucault would say – which taken together form the 'ground' of our truth. Heidegger would call it a 'gathering together', a becoming-*hypokeimenon* (subject) by grasping the that-which-lies-before as ground, a 'grasp' that – if it works (i.e., if it *can* bring-forth) – will not only re-make the very meaning of what is 'man' and what is 'the There', but will make that meaning 'stick' together (Heidegger 1977: 127).[26] Heidegger summarises:

> 'To get the picture' throbs with being acquainted with something, with being equipped and prepared for it. Where the world becomes picture, what is, in its entirety, is juxtaposed as that for which man is prepared and which, correspondingly, he therefore intends to bring before himself and have before himself, and consequently intends in a decisive sense to set in place before himself. Hence world picture, when understood essentially, does not mean a picture of the world but the world conceived and grasped as picture. What is, in its entirety, is now taken in such a way that it first is in being and only is in being to the extent that it is set up by man, who represents and sets forth. . . .
>
> However, everywhere that whatever is, is not interpreted in this way, the world also cannot enter into a picture; there can be no world picture. The fact that whatever is comes into being in and through representedness transforms the age in which this occurs into a new age in contrast with the preceding one. The expressions 'world picture of the modern age' and 'modern world picture' both mean the same thing and both assume something that never could have been before, namely, a medieval and an ancient world picture. The world picture does not change from an earlier medieval one into a modern one, but rather the fact that the world becomes picture at all is what distinguishes the essence of the modern age. . . .

Wherever this happens, man 'gets into the picture' in precedence over whatever is. But in that man puts himself into the picture in this way, he puts himself into the scene, i.e., into the open sphere of that which is generally and publicly represented. Therewith man sets himself up as the setting in which whatever is must henceforth set itself forth, must present itself [*sich. . . präsentieren*], i.e., be picture. (Heidegger 1977: 128–9; 130)

The move to 'picture' the logic of techne as the basis of an age that, for a variety of reasons, *could* grasp/gather 'the that which lies before us as ground' at once tore the 'present' away from the impossible inhabitation of the Hegelian dialectic. Indeed, with the Heideggerian move, the 'present' that the This thus named was precisely the interlocking tango of identity and difference, and, more than that, it was the poetics of the move which made it flourish, become 'real' and 'make' history. That history was called 'the age of Technology', and its primary loci was the art of making it so. In this sense, Aesthetics overtook Economics in the grounding of our contemporary modes of production.

However, it still managed to do this by keeping one large boot in the camp of Metaphysics.

Deleuze and Guattari presented a solution to this last problem. It made sense to import Heidegger's logic when it came to the role of techne and the 'gathering' into an inhabitable present the 'This' of that which lay to hand. The 'picture' worked, made cohesion 'real' and 'sticky', but in its present Metaphysical form had to be redrawn. To this end, they exchanged the visual for an 'aural' presencing-bringing-forth-gathering – recasting the material presencing of a 'world as picture' to the (im)material presencing of a 'world as refrain'. Everything, from power to poetics, from colour to shade, could (and would) be recast and called forth via the sonorous movements of rhythm, beat, improv, pacing. Father-Time became the more fleeting 'timing', or, at its most authoritarian, a 'sometime'. Space was simply the 'territory' that all refrains represented, that is, the segmented, slice of history-presents, which, in and of itself, had no limits (edges) and admitted no 'outside' or 'inside' modalities.

> I. A child in the dark, gripped with fear, comforts himself by singing under his breath. . . The song is like a rough sketch of a calming and stabilising, calm and stable, centre in the heart of chaos. . . . II. Now we are at home. But home does not pre-exist: it was necessary to draw a circle around that uncertain and fragile centre, to organise a limited space. . . This involves an activity of selection, elimination and extraction. . . Sonorous or vocal components are very important: a wall of sound, or at least a wall with some sonic bricks in it. . . . A mistake in speed, rhythm, or harmony would be catastrophic because it would bring back the forces of chaos, destroying both creator and creation. . . . III. Finally, one opens the circle a crack, opens it all the way, lets someone in, calls someone, or else goes out oneself, launches forth. This time, it is in order to join with the forces of the future, cosmic forces. One launches forth, hazards an improvisation. . . . along sonorous, gestural, motor lines that mark the customary path of a child and graft themselves onto or begin to bud 'lines of drift', with different loops, knots, speeds, movement, gestures, and sonorities. These are not here successive moments in an evolution. They are three aspects of a single thing, the Refrain (*ritournelle*). . .
>
> The role of the refrain . . . is territorial, it is . . . a territorial assemblage. (Deleuze and Guattari 2004: 343–4)[27]

The role of the Refrain then, is both territorial and improvisational. It calls forth a reality segment we could name: '1'. This '1' emerges from some place other than the traditional zero-sum binaric Totalities of a modern/liberal-arts world. It denotes, not to mention occupies, a critical spatiality whilst simultaneously dissipating into air. It has no weight, no volume, no 'other' to its name, but it still 'makes' sense. It names the segment, not statically, but in the beat, beat, beatings, pace, speeds of the launching forth. It is a '1' that marks out plurality as the multiple listening-gathering gestures which produce in their attunement, the 'here', right 'now'.

Deleuze and Deleuze and Guattari thus present a peculiar – but utterly profound – reconditioning of 'the becoming-x', of philosophy itself: it is the algorithmic encodings of the zeros and ones, torn from the usual binaric either/or casings, and cast instead as, on the one hand the rhizomatic bodies without organs, and on the other, the refrain. We might wish to call this fractal philosophy: an algorithmic hearing, a learning how to 'take note'. Deleuze simply calls it 'the task of art'.

Listen! Can you hear what is being written? It is the becoming-sunflower of Vincent's lost ear.

References

Adorno, T. W. (1990), *Negative Dialectics*, trans. E. B. Ashton, London: Routledge.
Blanchot, M. and M. Foucault (1989), *The Thought from Outside/Michel Foucault as I Imagine Him*, trans. J. Mehlman and B. Massumi, London: Zone Books.
Carroll, L. (2006), *Alice Through the Looking Glass* [1862], London: Random House.
Croce, B. (1909), *Philosophy of the Spirit*, trans. D. Ainslee, London: Allen and Unwin.
Croce, B. (1915), *What is Living and What is Dead of the Philosophy of Hegel*, trans. D. Ainslie, London: Allen and Unwin.
Deleuze, G. (2006), *Nietzsche and Philosophy*, trans. H. Tomlinson, London: Continuum.

Deleuze, G. (1988), *Foucault*, trans. S. Hand, Minneapolis: University of Minnesota Press.

Deleuze, G. (1990), *The Logic of Sense*, ed. C. V. Boundas, trans. M. Lester with C. Stivale, New York: Columbia University Press.

Deleuze, G. (2001), *Pure Immanence: Essays on A Life*, trans. A. Boyman, New York: Zone Books.

Deleuze, G. and F. Guattari (1984), *Anti-Oedipus*, trans. R. Hurley, M. Seem and H. R. Lane, London: Athlone.

Deleuze, G. and F. Guattari (1987), *A Thousand Plateaus*, trans. B. Massumi, Minneapolis: University of Minneapolis Press.

Deleuze, G. and F. Guattari (1994), *What is Philosophy?*, trans. H. Tomlinson and G. Burchell, London: Verso.

Derrida, J. (1995), *The Gift of Death*, trans. D. Wills, Chicago: University of Chicago Press.

Foucault, M. (1982/1988), 'Technologies of the Self', in L. H. Martin, H. Gutman, and P. H. Hutton (eds), *Technologies of the Self: A Seminar with Michel Foucault*, Amherst: University of Massachusetts Press.

Foucault, M. (1983), 'On the Genealogy of Ethics: An Overview of Work in Progress', trans. B. Wing, in P. Rabinow (ed.), *The Foucault Reader*, London: Penguin Books.

Foucault, M. (1984), 'Preface: Introduction to the Non-Fascist Life', in G. Deleuze and F. Guattari, *Anti-Oedipus*, London: Athlone Press.

Foucault, M. (2002), *Le Courage De La Vérité*, Paris: Presses Universitaires de France.

Fynsk, C. (1993), *Thought and Historicity*, New York: Cornell University Press.

Golding, S. (johnny de philo) (2003), *Games of Truth: A Blood Poetic in 7-Part Harmony*, London: University of Greenwich Press.

Halperin, D. (1997), *Saint Foucault: Toward a Gay Hagiography*, Oxford: Oxford University Press.

Hegel, G. W. F. (1977), *The Phenomenology of Spirit* [1807], trans. A. V. Miller, Oxford: Oxford University Press.

Heidegger, M. (1969), *Identity and Difference* [1957], trans. J. Stambaugh, New York: Harper Torchbooks.

Heidegger, M. (1976), *What Is Called Thinking?*, trans. F. D. Wieck and J. G. Gray, New York: Harper & Row.

Heidegger, M. (1977), *The Question Concerning Technology and Other Essays*, trans. W. Lovitt, New York: Harper Torchbooks.

Heidegger, M. (1979), *Introduction to Metaphysics*, trans. R. Manheim, Yale University Press.

Marx, K. (1971), *The German Ideology*, Moscow: Progress Publishers.

Mountain, H. (2007), 'Evacuating the Body: The Abyssal Logic of a Philosophy of Desire', *The Pornographical: An Ethics of Mimetic Bodies*, PhD Thesis, London: University of Greenwich.

Nancy, J.-L. (2000), *Being Singular Plural*, trans. R. Richardson and A. O'Byrne, Stanford: Stanford University Press.

Notes

1. A position articulated in much of their work, but see in particular '1730: Becoming-Intense, Becoming-Animal, Becoming-Imperceptible. . .' (Deleuze and Guattari 2004: 256–351).

2. Recall Glinda, the resplendent Good Witch in the populist US film version of *The Wizard of Oz* (1939), who, when giving advice to a very confused and lost Dorothy, suggests she begin her journey by starting precisely where she is already standing. The Yellow Brick Road eventually comes to a four directional impasse and Dorothy, along with her new friend The Scarecrow and her sacred buddy, Toto, decide to go North – for no other reason than that they just decide to do so.

3. The question of identity runs through the whole of their respective work, but for an overall reference to each consult Hegel (1977) and Heidegger (1969).

4. See in particular: 'Preface: On Scientific Cognition', and 'Introduction: A. Consciousness: I. Sense-Certainty: or the "This" and "Meaning"; II. Perception: or the Thing and Deception; III. Force and the Understanding: Appearance and the Supersensible World' (Hegel 1977: 1–45, 46–66, 67–78; 79–103, respectively).

5. See in particular: 'The Principle of Science is not the Completion of Science: Objections to Formalism' (Hegel 1977: §7–11, 26–7, 29, 36–7, 49, 70–1); 'Preface on Scientific Cognition' (Hegel 1977: 4–7, 14–17, 21, 29, 43–5).

6. Objecting to the abstract Idealist-speculative reformulation, Marx would have of course pronounced it thus: take 'all that there is' (in this case, the Bourgeoisie) and its 'point-for-point-Other' (in this case, the Proletariat), sublate one to the other (say, the Proletariat swallowed into – but not annihilated by – the Bourgeoisie) to produce the Capitalist Mode of Production, which 'comes back around' to give meaning (ground, substance, political context and revolutionary potential) to the two (heretofore) contradictorily abstract (but now 'impurely' concrete universals) Bourgeoisie and Proletariat. But see in particular Marx (1971), 'Part I: Feuerbach. Opposition of the Materialist and Idealist Outlook: B. The Illusion of the Epoch, Sections I.7 Summary of the Materialist Conception of History, and II. 1. Preconditions of the Real Liberation of Man', from where the following is taken: 'This [dialectical historical materialist] conception of history depends on our ability to expound the real process of production, starting out from the material production of life itself, and to comprehend the form of intercourse connected with this and created by this mode of production.'

7. As Deleuze spends some time on this particular aspect of the logic in his *The Logic of Sense*, especially Chapters 1–5 (Deleuze 1990: 1–35), we will return to these remarks later in the exposition. But it's worth taking a look-in on Humpty D and his conversation with Alice:

> There's glory for you!' [said Humpty] 'I don't know what you mean by "glory",' Alice said. Humpty Dumpty smiled contemptuously. 'Of course you don't – till I tell you. I meant 'there's a nice knock-down argument for you!' 'But "glory" doesn't mean "a nice knock-down argument",' Alice objected. 'When I use a word,' Humpty Dumpty said, in rather a scornful tone, 'it means just what I choose it to mean – neither more nor less.' 'The question is,' said Alice, 'whether you *can* make words mean so many different things.' 'The question is,' said Humpty Dumpty, 'which is to be master – that's all.' (Carroll 2006)

8. There is not sufficient room to develop the delicate intricacies of the Hegelian turn here. Suffice it to say that Hegel starts the dialectical move with an unmediated (abstract) 'now' (called now-time or now-thing or simply just 'the now') which can only be grasped in its im-mediacy (as in not-mediated and thus utterly present) by pitting it with/against its 'point-for-point' contradiction – in this case: abstract intuition (gut feeling or 'hunch'). This is then sublated, one to the other and

synthesised with the result that the now + intuition {hunch} produces (expresses) the Universal Concept: Intuition. But don't picture in your mind a linear train of thought linking one to the other; picture instead the rings of a tree, where each ring is itself this intricate, dialectical process, incapable of being removed from the trunk of a tree. Now, this Intuition happily includes both the 'now-time' and 'hunch', and, in so doing, is immanently returned to become the basis for a higher synthesis, in this case, the fully formed concept Intuition. This 'higher' synthesis (i.e. Intuition {(now-time/intuition)}) – again, picture tree-rings and not a ladder – is thus linked point for point to its antithesis: the as-yet-still-abstract 'sense-certainty', which continues apace, now sublated the one to the other and synthesised to form the Universal Concept: Sense-Certainty. Sense-Certainty as the highest form (thus far) of the sublated antithesis (constituted thus: {now+Intuition+Sense-Certainty} is immanently returned to provide a fresh base for the 'next' dialectical move: the sublation of the whole formulation {now+Intuition+Sense-Certainty} pitted, at this juncture, with and against an abstract perception; now taken together after sublation/synthesis to produce the Universal Concept: Perception. The whole process continues to progress (again, as 'tree-ring' rather than ladder), which results in the whole {now+Intuition+Sense-Certainty+Perception} being pitted against an abstract notion of understanding. Once again, and through the dialectical sublation/synthesis/immanent procedure Understanding is returned to form the Universal Concept called Understanding and thus also forms the basis for the next (and last) move, counter-poised with (against) abstract knowledge. And again this is sublated+synthesised+immanently returned to form both the 'ground' and 'goal' of Knowledge itself, a dialectically processed end-game (middle and start) for all meaning, beyond which nothing else exists. See 'Introduction, Section §80' of *The Phenomenology of Spirit* where Hegel summarises:

> But the *goal* is as necessarily fixed for knowledge as the serial progression; it is the point where knowledge no longer needs to go beyond itself, where knowledge finds itself, where the Notion corresponds to object and object to Notion. Hence the process towards this goal is also unhalting and, short of it [attaining this goal] no satisfaction is to be found at any of the stations on the way. (Hegel 1977: 51)

As strange as this may seem, and despite valiant attempts to the contrary, most current political militants, a strong handful of contemporary philosophers (including continental, structuralist and postmodern), quite a few sociologists, and most cultural theorists and artists have yet to break from these intractable Hegelian roots. For a fuller exposition, see Hegel's 'Preface: On Scientific Cognition,' and 'Introduction' (Hegel 1977: §1–12, §16–20, §73–85; §148; §159–63, pp. 5–7, 9–11, 46–54, 89–90, 97–100, respectively).

9. This is not to suggest that all these appellations are made equivalent one to the other; it is rather to suggest that 'sometimes' they can be. The question is, said Alice, whether you *can* make the plane of immanence mean so many different things. The question is, said Humpty, which is to be master, that's all. See note 7 above, but also Deleuze (1990: 217–23, 224–33, 234–8, 253–79).

10. Of course, Hegel comes in for tremendous attack from all quarters. For those wielding the knife but still remaining within the confines of dialectics, especially via the development and use of the 'negation of negation'; see for example, Croce (1915) as well as his voluminous *Philosophy of the Spirit* (1909). The most sustained – and yet to be equalled – attack which still employs dialectical logic, has been carried out by members of the Frankfurt School, most notably by Adorno in his *Negative Dialectics*, where 'The Logic of Disintegration', 'Dialectics Not A Standpoint', and 'The Indissoluble Something' boldly resituate the materiality

of the object as something always greater than the sum of its concept; where that which is 'left over' or 'excessive' is never 'other', but precisely a negative dialectic (Adorno 1990: 4–6, 135–6). But Deleuze hits the mark hardest:

> Universal and singular, changeless and particular, infinite and finite – what are these? Nothing but symptoms. What is this particular, this single, this infinite? And what is this universal, this changeless, this infinite? . . . The dialectic does not even skim the surface of interpretation, it never goes beyond the domain of symptoms. It confuses interpretation with the development of the uninterrupted symbol. That is why, in questions of change and development, it conceives of nothing deeper than an abstract permutation where the subject becomes predicated and the predicate, subject. . . . It is not surprising that the dialectic proceeds by opposition, development of the opposition or contradiction and solution of the contradiction. It is unaware of the real element from which forces, their qualities and their relations derive. (Deleuze 2006: 148)

11. See Foucault (1984: xiii). 'During the years 1945–1965 (I am referring to Europe),' says Foucault, 'there was a certain way of thinking correctly, a certain style of political discourse, a certain ethics of the intellectual. One had to be on familiar terms with Marx, not let one's dreams stray too far from Freud. And one had to treat sign-systems – the signifier – with the greatest respect. These were the three requirements that made the strange occupation of writing and speaking a measure of truth about oneself and one's time acceptable' (Foucault 1984: xi).

12. Most obvious: that all radical political movements, be they on the right or left, have often required the totalisation of an identity-Other to forge the basis of the movement. Whether it be the Women's Movement, the Black Panthers Movement, the Nazi Movement, etc., all groups must follow the first law of political science: Divide into Friend vs. Enemy, and proceed accordingly. This is not to suggest, necessarily, a better alternative path; it is simply to underscore how difficult it is to 'get out of' Hegelian Metaphysics. On a less obvious note: that a 'Pure' concept unfolding throughout history could not distinguish between slavery, misogyny, homophobia and the invention of space travel, except to say all were part and parcel of this immanent unfolding of Spirit. Even Deleuze's crucial reconstruction of 'Pure Immanence' via Hume and Nietzsche has, at first glance, this peculiar feature. Here he writes at a rather ecstatic pitch: 'We will say of pure immanence that it is A LIFE, and nothing else. It is not immanence to life, but the immanent that is in nothing is itself a life. A life is the immanence of immanence, absolute immanence: it is complete power, complete bliss' (Deleuze 2001: 27, emphasis in original). We will return to Deleuze's 'pure immanence' later in the text to see how he disengages from the criticism.

13. Hence the search for the 'smart gene', the 'gay gene', the 'Jewish-gene', with the not so surprising political outcome that these 'genes' can be modified and, more to the point, bred out.

14. The clearest discussion of this point can be found in the well-known discussion between Foucault and Blanchot (Blanchot and Foucault 1989). But see also the myriad of blogs and pop lyrics that have sprouted on the topic, including from 'Spurious' (http://spurious.typepad.com/spurious/2007/09/with-supreme-el.html) or from bands like Yattering (Inflow: Thought from Outside): http://www.metrolyrics.com/yattering

15. Indeed, much of the work in Conceptual Art, by the YBA, or works by, for example, Annette Messager, Barbara Gallagher, Manfred Kroboth, not to mention soundscapes by Eric Satie, Miles Davies, John Cage, or Art Clay, simply

make 'no sense' when filtered through the conceptual lens of a totalising, representational pineal eye, whose overarching glare tends to obscure the discursive aurality inherent in any visual art and visual culture.

16. The 'problem' of authenticity – which of course is not Heidegger's only problem – runs throughout his work and tends to support his (probable, supposedly 'unproven') links with National Socialism and the Nazis. His 'chequered' private life is not stellar, having outed his Professor (Husserl) to the Nazis, who then subsequently forcibly removed him from his post. Heidegger was Husserl's replacement, the salt in the wound which Husserl never forgot or forgave. Spinoza's 'difficulties' seem to pale in comparison. I mention this not only to underscore the profound differences, political, aesthetic, ethical, etc., between Heidegger and Spinoza, but to underscore the Trojan Horse Problem, i.e., the problem of the Gift – be that gift given in kindness or stolen outright, it always carries 'a-something-extra' for which one must remain alert (see Derrida 1995). On Heidegger's Nazism and its importance (or not) to his work, see in particular Fynsk (1993).

17. Developed in Golding (2003).

18. Quoted in Halperin (1997: 68). In a concise albeit at times romanticised précis of Foucault, he continues: 'What Foucault understood by an "art of existence," then, was an ethical practice that consisted in freely imposing the form of one's life into a distinctive shape and individual style, and thereby transforming oneself in accordance with one's own conception of beauty or value' (69–70). But see also Foucault (1982/1988 and 1983).

19. On Foucault as a cartographer, see in particular Deleuze (1988: 21–38 and 59–102).

20. The first use of 'ana-' as an attachable prefix denoting the fractal integrity of the aesthetic was coined by H. Mountain in her 'Evacuating the Body: The Abyssal Logic of a Philosophy of Desire' (Mountain 2007). The first uses of 'the multiversal' and 'teleonomy' as a 'goal-less' logic entered the fray as early as the mid-1850s with Darwin's cyclonic *On the Origins of the Species*.

21. Cf. Deleuze and Guattari's 'Introduction: The Rhizome' in *A Thousand Plateaus*, especially on the six characteristics of the rhizome, which include: the principles of connection, heterogenity, multiplicity, asignifying rupture, cartography and decalcomania (Deleuze and Guattari 2004: 7–13). See also their celebrated *Anti-Oedipus*, especially Chapter 1, 'The Desiring Machines', sections 2, 5 and 6 (Deleuze and Guattari 1984: 9–15, 36–41 and 42–50, respectively). On the question of multi-singularities and politics, see in particular (but from an entirely different angle), Nancy, especially 'Of Being Singular Plural', and 'The Surprise of the Event' (Nancy 2000: 1–100 and 159–77).

22. Cf. Deleuze and Guattari's 'November 28, 1947: How Do You Make Yourself A Body Without Organs', in *A Thousand Plateaus* (Deleuze and Guattari 2004: 177–9). But see also their subsequent chapter, 'Year Zero: Faciality', especially, the section 'Theorems of Deterritorialisation or Machinic Propositions' (193–211).

23. Think particularly of the weary Heidegger, whose fall-back position, after painstakingly demolishing the paucity of Hegel's 'Negative' (and in its place re-staging 'identity' as precisely the sight of 'difference' – as perdurance and as an event of appropriation, replete with the mental athletics of leaps forward and springs backward) still brought him right smack into the lion's den of an onto-theo-logic Metaphysics.

No one can know whether and when and where and how this step of thinking will develop into a proper (needed in appropriation) path and way and road-building. Instead, the rule of metaphysics may rather entrench itself, in the shape of modern technology with its developments rushing along boundlessly. Or, everything that results by way of the step back may merely be exploited and absorbed by metaphysics in its own way, as the result of representational thinking. (Heidegger 1969: 72–3)

Of course it is entirely debatable – though for some, not debatable at all – as to whether Heidegger wished to 'get out of' Metaphysics or, as seemed more the case, make Metaphysics do his bidding for him. See in particular Heidegger (1979), but also 'The World as Picture' (Heidegger 1977: 115–54), to which we will return momentarily.

24. There is space here to give only a superficial nod to Heidegger's complex set of arguments concerning the layering of meanings, particularly with the verb to represent (*stellen*; *Vor-stellen*, *Ges-stellen*, etc.), or the nouns 'truth' (*aletheia*, subjectivity, *subiecum*, *hypokeimenon*), and indeed, 'man', 'world', being⇔Being. At this juncture, the move is to point to the way in which a 'picture' becomes 'voice'.

25. Heidegger goes on to say in his *Question Concerning Technology*: 'We shall never experience our relationship to the essence of technology so long as we merely conceive and push forward the technological, put up with it, or evade it. Everywhere we remain unfree and chained to technology, whether we passionately affirm or deny it. But we are delivered over to it in the worst possible way when we regard it as something neutral; for this conception of it, to which today we particularly like to do homage, makes us utterly blind to the essence of technology' (Heidegger 1977: 3).

26. In his 'The World as Picture', he amplifies thus: 'What is decisive is not that man frees himself to himself from previous obligations, but that the very essence of man itself changes, in that man becomes subject. We must understand this word *subiectum*, however, as the translation of the Greek *hypokeimenon*. The word names that-which-lies-before, which, as ground, gathers everything onto itself. This metaphysical meaning of the concept of subject has first of all no special relationship to man and none at all to the I' (Heidegger 1977: 127).

27. See '1837: Of the Refrain' (Deleuze and Guattari 2004: 343–4).

SCENES AND ENCOUNTERS

Chapter 9

An Art Scene as Big as the Ritz: The Logic of Scenes

David Burrows

Introduction: Art + Life = Scene

How did it happen? How did the problem of the separation of art and life, essential to the development of avant-garde art, come to be overshadowed by concerns for criticality and taste? No doubt critical postmodernism – the drive to emphasise the place of art within cultural, socio-economic and institutional frameworks – and the heady cocktail of creativity and celebrity promoted by the art market in the 1980s both played a part in eclipsing the problem of the sublation of art and life. Perhaps too, the critique of avant-garde groups – the dismissal of their Popes and claims for originality – cast a shadow over practices that sought a basis for life in art. Most likely, it was the collapse of avant-garde politics that rendered this problem a *vanishing mediator* for many.

The sublation of art and life – art 'transferred to the praxis of life', thus transforming both – was identified as the primary theme of the historical European avant-garde by Peter Bürger (1989: 49). Bürger argued that the advent of avant-garde art marked a rejection of *art for art's sake*. This rejection was twofold: not only a refusal of everyday life produced by capitalism but a refusal too of the separation of art and life that characterised bourgeois art. To this end, comments Bürger, the avant-garde addressed an essential element of aestheticism: the presentation of art's distance from the praxis of life *as* the content of art (Bürger 1989: 49). For Bürger though, this venture fails when avant-garde artefacts end up in the museum as curiosities for the bourgeoisie (58). Nevertheless, and as Denis Hollier argues, the avant-garde was significant not just for producing new forms of art but for developing practices through group experimentation; a pluralising of speech and writing – and one could infer production too – that the writer regards as anonymous enunciation; something that, as Hollier notes, Bürger is silent on (Hollier 1988: xiv). From Hollier's perspective, Bürger's criticism of the avant-garde is unfair; it is the European avant-garde's focus on communal experimentation – requiring a group to live 'unproductive' lives (which artworks cannot capture) – that is important.

However, despite Hollier's rebuttal of Bürger's thesis, both view the negation of existing society as the alibi of avant-garde art, an interpretation that muddies an understanding of the affirmative aspects of avant-garde practice. For the European avant-garde opened up the potential of matter, bodies and groups. In this sense, avant-garde artworks might be thought of as elements within new *arrangements* of life and, indeed, that those artworks called forth new arrangements of life and practice. It is this legacy that *a logic of scenes* addresses. In contrast to arguments that privilege either artefacts (that endure) or enunciations (that are transitory but shape the sensible), *a logic of scenes* asserts that artworks, writing, performances and the enunciations and actions of individuals and groups are all important for producing arrangements with the potential of registering new orientations.

In this sense, art both emerges out of a scene and produces a scene. This plurality is found in the word scene itself, which can refer to a performance *and* the setting of that performance, as well as a stormy or emotional encounter between two or more people and the milieu of a specific group or activity. *A logic of scenes* addresses two aspects of art then: that which captures our attention within an environment (content) and the responses, actions, articulations and statements (expression) which register and shape the sensible (and present specific encounters as art). At no point can either aspect of this equation be privileged as the genetic material of art scenes, indeed *art as scene* is defined through the relation of the two.

There is a *time of the scene* which might be the time of spectacle or theatre, but certain scenes have a *durational quality* that might be that of an affective (emotional or stormy) encounter or the playtime of practices engaged with experimentation and nonsense. Here we might distinguish between practices or aspects of art scenes that contribute nothing but spectacle (art produced for existing fashions or discursive regimes) and practices or aspects of art scenes that call forth a people-yet-to-come.

An art scene is not produced by the labour or imagination of an individual; it is the murmur of collective or rather anonymous enunciation. This does not mean that a logic of art scenes privileges collaboration over individual practice, as this would be to confuse multiplicity with the many. An art scene can be defined as a distribution of presentations:

a field of activity marked by affective and intensive encounters but also articulations. In this definition then, an art scene is not a professional network of individuals and institutions but an informal presentation of events *in and as their affects*, and therefore different to the formal (physical or semiotic) organisations of art. However, these strata give a specific and local 'shape' to an art scene, just as a specific terrain gives shape to the flow of spilt water.

The size of a scene is of no importance; only the different durations produced by a scene matter. For scenes can have a *(virtual) scale* that bears no relation to the *actual size* of any group or environment, or to the degree of visibility achieved by practices or a group. In this sense, art scenes can be thought of as a distribution of loops (and as loops within loops), each possessing different durational qualities. Just as with a Möbius strip so it is with some art scenes: while possessing specific spatial qualities it is the duration of travelling along a Möbius strip – a movement that is an eternal return – that is compelling, impossible and beyond comprehension. The durational qualities of these impossible loops cannot be measured; they can only be explored.

This notion of an art scene as a distribution of events draws upon the concept of the *diagram* thoroughly developed by Gilles Deleuze in two books, *Francis Bacon: The Logic of Sensation* and *Foucault*. The former is concerned with art and the latter with discursive regimes and expression. While Deleuze's *logic of sensation* proposes art as a diagram that localises and captures random traits, it is the notion of the *diagram* and the *statement* expounded by Deleuze in *Foucault* that I draw upon to develop *the logic of art scenes*. In both books the diagram is defined as a distribution of points of resistance that arrest signification or distort existing formations. Within art scenes, it is the practices that present these points of resistance (rather than address existing problems and relations) that register multiplicity and new means of expression.

It might be said today that art circulates as spectacle. While the professionalisation of art often leaves artists and audiences outmanoeuvred, many are as concerned with *making a scene* as they are with *making it*. Furthermore, practices that achieve visibility emerge from the anonymous murmur of a scene of some kind,[1] and while regimes might capture scenes so might scenes transform regimes. This essay, though, does not chart the shift in the fortunes of different scenes; it is specifically concerned with how art and art scenes function diagrammatically. To this end, five examples of scenes in London from the last twenty years are cited that, in various ways, developed *diagrammatic practices*. In exploring such ventures, the essay proposes that only those practices that make a scene (of affective encounters *and* mutating statements) produce something new.

The Diagram in Painting

Before exploring art scenes as diagrams a summation of the processes identified by Deleuze in *Francis Bacon: The Logic of Sensation* is needed, for it is in this book that the philosopher addresses art and the concept of the diagram in detail. One criticism that could be levelled at Deleuze is that he almost exclusively addresses art through painting, and this is true of the philosopher's writing on Bacon. However, Deleuze's logic of sensation has much relevance for *a logic of scenes*. Deleuze argues for an encounter with art that involves neither judgement or critique but the *utilisation* of points of resistance to signification. In this, Deleuze outlines a practice for producing *and* encountering the diagrammatic, a practice directed towards the production of new worlds and forms of expression – something that is sketched out in *Foucault* too but with a different focus.

Deleuze develops his notion of the diagram and painting through interpreting Bacon's remarks about 'the graph' which refer to disturbances, or as Deleuze suggests 'catastrophes', that disrupt the figurative. Bacon's comments aid Deleuze in developing a notion of painting as random marks that produce a deterritorialisation (a desert zone inserted into the head), in which the figurative is replaced by the cosmic (Deleuze 2004a: 99–100). It is through such catastrophes that another world opens up; it is through marks that are asignfying that something new emerges.

Importantly, the diagram is indiscernible and therefore never an optical effect; it is an unbridled manual power (Deleuze 2004a: 138). This gives the eye a different function to that given by figurative or optically ordered passages of painting. When encountering the diagram the eye has a *haptic* function, the eye feels rather than sees.

For Deleuze, the diagram as the operative set of asignifying lines and zones should be abstract but 'suggestive' of something, of new relations of forms. He argues that the diagram is not sufficient on its own to be a successful painting: the diagrammatic marks must be utilised in some way to disrupt figuration. In this, Deleuze argues for the diagram in painting as a localisation of random traits or events.

Drawing once more upon Bacon's comments to explain how the diagram registers multiplicity, Deleuze cites a description of the painter marking out a form only to find that the marks suggest something else – a bird suggests an umbrella or a carcass: the painter finds organic resemblances. Deleuze asks whether the diagram allows the painter to pass between one form and another and concludes that this is not the case in Bacon's portraits, which present only a single form, that of the head, where passing between forms is not evident or possible. Rather, the heads painted by Bacon seem to turn inside out as a multiplicity of head-like forms surface in a single portrait. Change then, is not produced through a process in which one form replaces another but through a deformation of form: as a form becomes scrambled something new is suggested and a number of (formless) forces, presented by the diagram, surface in one place (Deleuze 2004a: 158–9).

In this way, the diagram is untimely; it is an objective zone of the indiscernible that lies between two other zones, one that no longer exists and one that is 'not yet'. While Deleuze states that the diagram destroys the figuration of the first zone – it erases what exists – he writes that the figuration of the second zone is neutralised by the diagram, so that a new figure (the figure in its original relations) emerges between the two zones: duration interrupts the flow of time and other figures or worlds are suggested (Deleuze 2004a: 156–7).

Performing the Diagram

A first response to this conception of the diagram might be that it is tied to figuration (and to early modern painting). Equally, a response might be that the diagram can be related to artists working with an expanded art practice[2] concerned with producing *haptic* encounters or disruptions of sense. Such practices present *art as a scene*, in which different orientations or worlds are registered or articulated through the scrambling of an environment or existing formations. Here we might think of the intensive encounters produced by the reflections or repetitions found in the mirror displacements of Robert Smithson or the fields of polka dots that cover environments and people created by Yoyoi Kusama.

To encounter the work of these artists is to be *within* the temporal and spatial dimensions of their art *as* a component of the work. As critics of minimalism and post-minimalism have suggested, this can be thought of as a theatrical space, and as the time and space of performance. Deleuze writes about art as a composition and, for the most part, privileges the eye. This eye registers the infinite by seizing upon points that resist signification within a composition. What differentiates this logic of sensation from a Kantian analysis of aesthetics and the sublime is Deleuze's call for the utilisation of a-signifying traits. In the case of painting, this utilisation arrests figuration. But what if compositions are produced in which the body within an environment (and everything that is performed and expressed within that scene) is counted as an element of the composition? And furthermore, what if that body transforms the relations between forms within an arrangement, through actions and articulations that utilise asignifying traits presented in a composition? In such a case, it is not figuration that is disrupted but existing formations and functions that some count as reality. And this does not lead to the integration of art with everyday life and opinion; rather, the formations encountered in everyday life are destroyed or neutralised.

In the 1960s Kusama practised *self-obliteration* by covering herself, other people and things with dots. The effect of Kusama's polka-dot universe was to arrest the identification of material qualities and the boundaries between bodies and things; a practice that produced a disruption of the optical – an anti-vision of a kind – designed to release individuals and forms from roles and identities, so that new creative formations and relations might be realised. As Félix Guattari wrote: 'Kusama destroys materials, forms, colours and meanings in order to acquire the vector of creativity far freer than that from which she departed . . . through the process of undifferentiated and modulated proliferation', a process, he notes, that uses the materials through which 'consumer society secretes its miserable and disenchanted universe' (Guattari, quoted in Matusi 2000: 96). As Kusama herself said: 'the polka dot has the form of the Sun . . . and also the form of the moon, which is calm. Round, soft, senseless and unknowing. Polka dots can't stay alone like the communicative life of the people, two or three and more polka dots become a movement' (Matusi 2000: 95).

As well as the haptic characteristics of the diagram, other functions of the diagram identified by Deleuze are pertinent to Kusama's art. Her performances and installations produce scenes in which multiplicity surfaces in bodies and formations, through a disruption of hierarchies, scale and boundaries – only a different emphasis is placed on the functions of the body by such expanded practices compared to that of painting. These practices have a biopolitical dimension, in that the body is the territory through which new political, social and aesthetic orientations are explored. Such practices can produce a body without hierarchies (a body-without-organs[3]) open to different durations and functions. The body, then, becomes a diagram through 'catastrophes' (points of intensity) that disrupt or disturb the body's organisation and relations to other formations (organisations of forces).

To present the body as a diagram is to propose that the body is not just a point of intensity within a scene but also a scene *in and of* itself.

In recent years, it was Leigh Bowery who, perhaps more than any other figure, experimented with the body – and its functions and relations – for the most inhuman and fantastic ends.

Scene One: A Body (Without Hierarchies) – Leigh Bowery (1980–94, London). Leigh Bowery (fashion designer, performance artist and club organiser) adopted many names and manifested a number of 'looks', *Black Angel*, *Piggy Leigh* and *Anne Versary* among them. And it was through these different 'looks' that deformed or re-shaped his body that Bowery performed as a body-without-hierarchies (and a body-without-shame), within art events and clubs, and in pop videos and dance performances. Bowery's engagement with London's club scene in the 1980s produced multiple collaborations and led to him establishing his own club, Taboo – a production of scenes for others to experiment with. But more than this, his body was a scene too – a diagram registering a multiplicity of forms. Bowery's art developed through getting dressed up to go out – a dressing-up that made sense within certain scenes exploring different styles of life. He said of the body, 'its kind of like the imagination – I mean its endless, there is so much you can do' (Jaeger 1994: 153). He claimed that fashion had addressed all the zones of the body except the belly, which he celebrated in a number of 'looks' including *Session IV, Look 20*, a headless brown-skirted form with a beach-ball of a swelling for a mid-riff. This 'look', like all his others, is a parody – of fashion? behaviour? the body? – that has been taken too far: an acceleration, to hysterical and absurd ends, that leaves behind any source of parody as hilarious new relations between forms surface.

Bowery's 'looks' exhibit a key process of the diagram outlined in Deleuze's logic of sensation: in that the diagram is a deformation of existing forms presenting multiple forces, a process or distribution in which forces are localised. Deleuze's insight concerning the diagram and the localisation of forces is mirrored by an observation in *Foucault*: although the diagram is defined by its informality (in contrast to the formality or concrete forms of the strata of society), the diagram is a 'map' that is coextensive with existing strata. This observation provides an insight as to why art scenes produce encounters that are *untimely* but that also appear *of their time*, in that art scenes can only utilise what exists to register what is yet-to-come. Furthermore, any such untimely disruption or deformation produces a *minor art*,[4] through play or laughter that warps or makes strange the functions and relations of existing forms, so as to produce new formations. An example of a scene that produced such minor formations, contemporary with Bowery's experiments, is the collaboration between Sarah Lucas and Tracey Emin entitled *Shop*.

Scene Two: (Minor) Formations – Shop by Sarah Lucas and Tracey Emin (1993, London). *Shop*, made by two artists – two friends – in a disused shop, sold a variety of hand-made goods (art? junk? jokes?) such as T-shirts with joyful slogans – COMPLETE ARSEHOLE, SPERM COUNTS, FUCKING USELESS – and a vase of what? Flowers? Or a vase at least, containing wire stems budding with black-and-white photographs of Sarah Lucas. And on the top floor of the shop, there was a small space with a worktop covered in ink; a dirty roller, perhaps the residue of an interrupted printmaking session, lay on its side. In the moment of Neo-Conceptualism, a *Technique Anglaise* (see Gillick and Renton 1991) pitched as a cool and cerebral zeitgeist, why would anyone make expressionist-looking monoprints? Another question: was the roller and ink part of the exhibition? Was *Shop* an exhibition of works, an artwork in itself or a place to hang out, make stuff or bargain hunt for one-liners? Perhaps this untimely scene, that was of its time too, was produced by economic recession – so many empty shops, so much unused (useless) space. But (economic) context alone did not produce *Shop*: a sense of humour and an attitude to making were explored there.

Art Scenes as Battlefields

Shop had fun with the conventional in various ways, not least through transforming objects and materials into humorous artefacts in a milieu that combined the functions of a gallery, retail space, studio and meeting place. This brief collaboration produced attitudes and approaches different to those exhibited by contemporaries of Lucas and Emin concerned with more formal modes of production and dissemination, in that life (the lives of the artists and their friends) became the material through which Emin and Lucas played with the relationship between content and expression.

To fully develop this idea that art scenes produce new orientations or worlds through utilising the play (or disruption) of relations between the sensible and the articulated, a more in-depth examination of *Foucault* is required. In the book, Deleuze states that Foucault defines the diagram as a display produced through forces affecting other forces: a mixing of non-formal functions and informal matter. In contrast to the *Logic of Sensation*, in which the diagram is explored through the utilisation of abstract marks of paint, in *Foucault* the diagram is explored as the distribution, organisation or utilisation of forces in the realm of the social – as forces that affect other forces or that deform existing formations. If an *art scene* is to be considered as diagrammatic then it will be defined as a display of the relations of power and resistance: that is, the art scene as a diagram is, first and foremost, a distribution of points – of practices, works, performances and articulations – that resist signification or run counter to the formal organisation of art. This distribution of points emerges out of a scene as the latter mutates.

Deleuze notes that Foucault's exploration of the diagram is undertaken through an analysis of disciplinarian societies and of the panoptican in particular, which Deleuze presents as a breakthrough for Foucault. Deleuze observes that in *The Archaeology of Knowledge*, Foucault is unable to find a relation between the 'visible' and the 'articulated'. The problem is resolved through the invention of the diagram as *abstract machine*: a battleground – not as a condition that contains specific elements but as a field of distribution – in which what is seen and said attempt to capture each other (Deleuze 2004b: 34).

In *Foucault*, Deleuze places a different emphasis on the diagram than when writing about painting where the desert is evoked: in *Foucault* the diagram is presented as a continuous folding and unfolding of informal matter and functions – it is a *battlefield* of expression and content (expression having priority through spontaneity). This concept of the diagram as a battlefield engenders an understanding of how an art scene can be thought of as a non-unifying cause for new relations of forces, and as the cause of new concrete arrangements. To explore art scenes through Deleuze's insights concerning the diagram in *Foucault* – to view art scenes as battlegrounds in which practices organise forces or take flight from organisation – is to open up the relations of art beyond that of a body standing in front of a canvas or artwork.

The problem of moving beyond Deleuze's privileging of the canvas without rejecting the philosopher's insights has been addressed by others, most notably by Eric Alliez and Jean-Claude Bonne with the concept of 'Matisse Thought' (Alliez and Bonne 2007). In discussion, Alliez argues that Matisse's late work exceeds the form of the canvas, offering the possibility of a practice 'beyond painting' that is less a problem of the spatial expansion of painting than an investment in the problem of space itself (Alliez and Osborne 2008: 59–60). Alliez states that the problem for contemporary artists, now that the space of art is no longer given as 'neutral', is to produce, 'in the socially charged time of a (performative) construction', a local event from 'a-signifying interstices' that 'reintroduce life at the very level of the most deterritorialised space' (60). In thinking through this insightful statement I would wish to accent 'the socially charged time of a (performative) construction' as the problem that many artists are addressing. A slight shift in emphasis then – barely a shift at all – but one that moves away from Alliez's own perspective which, whilst developing Deleuze's conception of art within a contemporary framework, still privileges painting (colour and composition) and the eye. For art today is more than just a concern with the problem of space and its lack of neutrality. There are problems addressed by art other than that of the deterritorialisations of space – problems of the body and the functions and relations between bodies, of memory, of signification and language, and of play-time and work-time. Art today is a whisper, a flood of tears, a joke, a ritual, a word or sentence written or spoken, a change in the weather, the crack of a whip, a sweet in the mouth, a silver chain drawn from an anus; all of which, while having spatial attributes, might be thought of as artworks less concerned with the problem of space than with exploring different durations, forms of expression and relations between forms.[5]

The key 'local event' in art then, is an encounter that produces durations different to the time of the everyday and of administered society. In this sense, art is not only concerned with registering sensation and new *percepts* but with what bodies and minds can do when encountering scrambled forms and formations. Deleuze comes close to suggesting something similar when he asks whether minimalism 'seeks to attain a unity of art as "performance", and draw the spectator into this very performance. . . Folding and unfolding, wrapping and unwrapping are the constants of this operation, as much now as in the periods of the Baroque' (Deleuze 2001: 122–3).

This question is developed through proposing modern art as a venture concerned with the extension of one art form into another – painting extending into sculpture extending into architecture extending into the design of cities: a looping of a kind, but one that is spatial rather than untimely. By utilising the diagram defined in *Foucault*, a logic for art can be outlined as the untimely scene or fray of the sensible and expression. This is not to oppose object and performance, or to dismiss the problem of 'the deterritorialisation of space' for art; instead it is to emphasise that the primary registers of the new in art are the performances and orientations engendered through encounters with the untimely. And art scenes accelerate towards such encounters by scrambling relations between forms and gambling on the outcome. Such are the experiments of the group Bughouse, a bloc of impossible loops and layers of time.

Scene Three: (Vacuole of) Chance – Bughouse (circa 2000–present, London, Vancouver and elsewhere). Bughouse is a secret world, a group of friends (the friends of good chance) invisible to most, travelling in time and through the channels of analogue and digital audio and visual technology. These friends of good chance are barely a group of artists except when they decide to present themselves as such, and then only with some reservations. The Bughouse scene was formed through an interest in the sci-fi of Phillip K. Dick – and the near sci-fi of William Burroughs – and in their modes of operation: Bughouse employ the cut-up, games of chance and the paranoid-critical method (paranoia as collective enunciation). Through such methods the friends of good chance trace out a diagram of worlds past and yet-to-come. One of their projects, *Control Script*, begins with a talking head that is filmed-edited-screened/re-filmed/edited and then screened/re-filmed/edited. . . over and over, over years and years. . . each new version a scrambling of time through loopy durations. The friends of good chance are always looking for interference, coincidence, malfunctions (messages from the outside) – to aid travel out of (everyday) time. And then sometimes the world of Bughouse leaks into everyday time. Or suddenly something in the world of Bughouse makes perfect sense – Tom Cruise the actor, projected or mixed into a Bughouse performance, suddenly makes sense (to the friends of good chance). Cruise has a message – the acting, the hysteria, his performance in the film *Magnolia*; he is trying to communicate with us – it is important that he says 'realities' and never 'reality'. Beware. Cruise has access to other realities! And he is trying to ensnare us. Tell the world, or just the friends of chance who want to touch the outside.

A Diamond as Big as the Ritz

In relation to the processes of the cut-up and paranoid-critical method employed by Bughouse, one more response to Deleuze's logic of sensation might be to address how the diagram opens onto new worlds. In painting, a new world is opened up by an encounter with the 'Sahara', but this desert must be explored through processes – through involuntary memory, through the tracing of rhythms within compositions or through giving oneself up to the duration of a 'monochromatic eternity' – or there is a risk that an artwork remains simply an encounter (with non-sense), or merely sensations produced by an arrangement of colour, tone and form. This exploration, like the practices of Bughouse, would have to be a singular performance of a kind – *a becoming* or utilisation as Deleuze might say – that produces new orientations.

In *Foucault*, the production of the new is similarly described but in different terms. For Deleuze, it is Foucault's concept of the *statement* that produces a major contribution to the theory of multiplicity. Deleuze defines the statement in *Foucault* as communicating the particular arrangement of elements in a corresponding space (our places and functions within specific regimes) (Deleuze 2004b: 3–4). Statements operate in a realm of rarity, in that only a few roles can be enunciated – there are a limited number of roles within any regime, such as doctor-nurse-patient-cleaner-porter in a hospital ward or artist-critic-curator-dealer-public in a gallery. What counts in any regime is the *regularity* of statements; that is, what is important is the repetition of enunciations that mark functions within specific regimes. However, if statements mark the relation of elements in a specific space, Deleuze, following Foucault, argues that statements are durational, in that they operate transversally, across different localised spaces or regimes, that is, through *variable* relations. Each statement is a multiplicity and not a structure or system (5–6). Deleuze describes statements as multiplicities of the kind that Bergson attempted to define as durational in contrast to spatial multiplicities (13).

Each statement refers not to a 'unique subject of enunciation' but to intrinsic and variable positions or points within a discursive formation. Deleuze compares Foucault to Blanchot who denies linguistic 'personology', arguing that the speaking subject emerges from an 'impersonal murmur' (Deleuze 2004b: 7). The same is true for the objects and concepts of the statement, in that they stem from the statement itself. The intentionality of the statement (what is said or communicated) is not important. Neither does it matter whether the statement is derived from existing conditions or is fictional or absurd. What matters is the affect of the statement (what is captured or shaped by the statement). In *Foucault*, Deleuze offers the example of Scott Fitzgerald's strange and disturbing short story, *A Diamond as a Big as the Ritz*, as a fictional world traversed by statements. The story narrates the downfall of a family who possess unimaginable wealth and power and who live on a mountain that is one enormous diamond. Deleuze suggests that *A Diamond as a Big as the Ritz* is a discursive object without an actual referent, and one that does not relate to fiction in general but to the world that is created by and surrounds the fictions of Fitzgerald. Again, it is the rarity of what is stated and the regularity or repetition of statements that not only create the 'world of Fitzgerald' but that link this world to other statements found in other worlds.

This observation is pertinent to art scenes that do not refer to art in general, or just art in general, but to the realms produced by those scenes, as in the example of Bughouse or the collaboration *Shop*. As with the fictions of Fitzgerald, the repetition of statements not only creates the world of the scene, but links this world to other statements found in other worlds. It is this variability or multiplicity, this diagonal movement, which marks out the potential for statements to change or mutate over time: such events are produced through a repetition that introduces difference or that generates an alteration in the relationship between statements.[6] In *Foucault*, Deleuze asks,

> what is the conclusion to Foucault's 'Archaeology' if not an appeal to a general theory of production which must merge with revolutionary praxis, and where acting 'discourse' is formed with an 'outside' that remains indifferent to my life and death? For discursive formations are real practices, and far from being a universal logos their languages are transient and tend to promote and sometimes even to express mutation. (Deleuze 2004b: 13)

It is the diagram, as developed in Foucault's later work, that Deleuze cites as producing new statements: that is, by utilising the diagram and localising forces (the outside), acting discourse deforms existing relations. One potential function of an art scene (as a distribution of practices that includes re-presenting, repeating, twisting and re-shaping the nonsensical as well as the sensible and the conventional) is to promote and express mutation; a potential best explored through the example of BANK.

Scene Four: (Mutant) Statements – BANK (1990–2002, London). BANK were called BANK because the artists' group had their first exhibition in a disused bank. One day Britain's leading collector arrived at the space of BANK to purchase something, a BANK work. He couldn't do it, the collector, he went away empty handed. He wanted something from BANK, he liked BANK, but he couldn't bring himself to buy a work. What was he after then, this collector? It must have been something from the BANK scene – something of their objects, installations *and* enunciations – that certain something that flowed through and around the trashy, nonsensical, rude artefacts of the group. For the BANK scene was a series of mutating statements, mutating out of necessity, or out of a view that everything could be BANK: this was the mutation of artist-curator-publicist-technician-designer-cleaner-invigilator-barperson-fundraiser-zombie. The latter role emerged when the group played a starring role in the exhibition *Zombie Golf*, a presentation of zombies – modelled on BANK and friends in wax – playing golf with an eyeball amidst work

9.1: BANK, *Dog-U-Mental VIII (Goffick, Go-Orphic)*, 1996, installation view. Photo credit: BANK/Simon Bedwell.

9.2: BANK, *Zombie Golf*, installation view. Photo credit: BANK/Simon Bedwell.

by Martin Creed, John Stezaker and Peter Doig. And this unruly scene expanded to reach a critical mass with the curation of BANK TV, an exhibition that featured a cast of hundreds (of artists) all making art/TV programmes. BANK were a bad-mannered group of mutant statements – now split and mostly forgotten.

An Art Scene as Big as the Ritz

The name adopted by the artist's group BANK always seemed, and still seems, to make little sense, and this is important. For the group had to be called something but the moniker BANK did not bind the group to a particular idea or tradition.

In *A Thousand Plateaus*, Deleuze and Guattari state that abstract machines have proper names and dates, such as the names of paintings and styles of art (Deleuze and Guattari 1987: 142). This observation relates not only to how a diagram is coextensive with strata, but also how deterritorialisations (of the diagrammatic component of a regime of signs) are in a circular relation with reterritorialisations (of machinic components) effectuating new concrete assemblages and relations that can be named and dated. Such is the logic of art scenes, in that they can be named and dated as well, and then catalogued and exhibited too: that is, scenes become history. A problem then, is how to ensure that a scene remains open, that a scene continues to breathe even after its demise.

A name that makes too much sense may limit a scene, in that what can be enacted or created within a scene can become defined or captured by the name. The mutation of statements requires a certain literalness or dumbness then, or a name that is opaque or absurd, or at least a name that suggests nothing too serious or does not elicit any clear identities. For names can weigh heavily on scenes, like a branding tool, and take the edges off a scene, as happened with *Young British Art* (YBA). It is important then that a name engenders *an art scene as big as the Ritz* or as multi-faceted as a crystal mountain. A name should engender a plurality of different performances and expressions: such is the name 'The Children of !WOWOW!'

Scene Five: Performance (Swarm) – The Children of !WOWOW! (2003–present, London). The Children of !WOWOW! presented a multitude of performances for 'Late at the Tate' in January 2008, and as with Kafka's *Nature Theatre of Oklahoma* (Kafka 1985: 246) it seemed anything could be performed: a circus of singing stones, a nudist chased and beaten by cops, a human traffic light, a glam rock god, a torch song terrorist, death by glitter. . . Who or what is !WOWOW!? It is a name (or perhaps a verb?) associated with art, performances or parties. The name gives nothing away and perhaps means nothing at all. But then !WOWOW! can mean anything too. And what is in a name? A name can be limiting if it happens to be *The Photographers Gallery*. But !WOWOW! has no referent, it refers to nothing. !WOWOW! can only be performed. Yes, the name has a history and an on-line presence. But that is the history of The Children of !WOWOW! And yes, the name !WOWOW! can be repeated but each time it is articulated it is performed a little differently, or it might not be !WOWOW!. The Children embody this multi-faceted quality. They are a performance swarm, sometimes seen, sometimes only heard fleetingly in the distance as they run past at great speed: a swarm of mutant statements too chaotic, too multiple to be viewed in their entirety.

Diagrammatic Practices

The performances presented by The Children of !WOWOW! appear to be from any-point-whatever, in that the group presents a scene of playful and nonsensical encounters with multiple references and registers: !WOWOW! could be anything. Such a scene might be described as a lottery – *a throw of the dice* – each 'draw' operating only under the rules or results of the last draw. In this sense, a scene (as diagram) utilises something 'outside' or unregistered by knowledge or existing formations. As Deleuze states, the diagram is always a mixture of the aleatory and the dependent (Deleuze 2004b: 86). In relation to this last point, Deleuze states that it is important to distinguish between *exteriority* and the *outside*. The exterior can be thought of as historical forms that surround us, whereas the outside concerns forces operating in a different dimension (duration rather than time). Importantly, the diagram does not merge with these forces (the outside), which continue to draw new diagrams (and therefore continually mark the scene of art) (86). And Deleuze concurs with Foucault that the diagram does not bring change to the strata (to historical forms) but to the composing of forces (the relations within compositions) (89).

A question might be posed here, as to why Deleuze's writing (and Deleuze's *Foucault*), rather than Foucault's writing, is proposed as the key to developing a logic of scenes. The answer is that there is a notable difference between Deleuze and Foucault over the term desire, a term Foucault understood as *lack*. Deleuze argues that desire circulates in (is one with) any assemblage of heterogeneities. This idea forms the basis of Deleuze's assertion that society is defined through lines of flight (that which flees social organisation). In contrast, Deleuze suggests that Foucault defines society as an organisation that contradicts itself (Deleuze 1977: n.p.). This difference might be further characterised in the following way: Foucault is concerned with truth, whereas Deleuze (conceding that there is a truth of power but uncertain that there is a power of truth) is concerned with what the body can become by constituting a field of immanence defined as 'zones of intensity, thresholds, gradients, flux'. Deleuze, in unpublished notes written for Foucault, states:

> This body is as biological as it is collective and political; it is on this body that assemblages make and unmake themselves, it is this body which bears the points of deterritorialisation of the assemblages or lines of flight . . . If I call it body without organs, it is because it is opposed to all the strata of organisation, that of the organism, but just as much the organisations of power. (Deleuze 1977: n.p.)

It is Deleuze's impersonal, biopolitical orientation that illuminates the potential art scenes; insights that explore the technology of the body or, why not, a technology of bodies that like Kusama's polka dots cannot help but become a *movement* producing mutant statements and a basis for a praxis of art and life.

References

Alliez, E. and J.-C. Bonne (2007), 'Matisse Thought', in *Collapse*, III, Falmouth: Urbanomic.

Alliez, E. and P. Osborne (2008), 'Philosophy and Contemporary Art after Deleuze and Adorno: An Exchange', in R. Garnett and A. Hunt (eds), *Gest: Laboratory of Synthesis*, London: Book Works.

Bürger, P. (1989), *Theory of the Avant Garde*, trans. M. Shaw, Minneapolis: University of Minnesota Press.

Deleuze, G. (1977), 'Desire and Pleasure', trans. M. McMahon, available at: http://info.interactivist.net/node/1406

Deleuze, G. (2001), *The Fold*, trans. T. Conley, London: Continuum.

Deleuze, G. (2004a), *Francis Bacon: Logic of Sensation*, trans. D. W. Smith, London: Continuum.

Deleuze, G. (2004b), *Foucault*, trans. S. Hand, London: Continuum.

Deleuze, G. and F. Guattari (2003), *Kafka: Towards a Minor Literature*, trans. D. Polan, Minneapolis: University of Minnesota Press.

Deleuze, G. and F. Guattari (1987), *A Thousand Plateaus*, trans. B. Massumi, London: Athlone.

Gillick L. and A. Renton (eds) (1991), *Technique Anglaise*, London: Thames and Hudson.

Hollier, D. (ed.) (1988), 'Foreword: Collage', in *College of Sociology 1937–39*, trans. B. Wing, Minneapolis: University of Minnesota Press.

Jaeger, J. (1994), 'Interview with Leigh Bowery', in V. Webb (ed.), *Take a Bowery*, Sydney: Museum of Contemporary Art, 2003.

Kafka, F. (1985), *America*, Harmondsworth: Penguin Books.

Matusi, M. (2000), 'Beyond Oedipus: Desiring Production of Yayoi Kusama', *Parkett*, 59.

Spinoza, B. (1998), *Principles of Cartesian Philosophy*, trans. S. Barbone, Indianapolis: Hackett.

Notes

1. For example, the celebrity-laden YBA scene emerged out of artist-run spaces in London and Glasgow.
2. Expanded art practice might be best understood as practices that followed in the wake of minimalism's exploration of temporality through the relation of artwork-body-space.
3. Deleuze and Guattari (1987:149–66). The body without organs can be understood as a body 'populated only by intensities' (153).
4. The notion of a minor art is derived from the concept of a *minor literature*, developed in Deleuze and Guattari (2003). The pair suggested that Franz Kafka's writing stutters and stammers the major language of German to make the familiar strange.
5. Duration, as Baruch Spinoza defined it, 'is the attribute under which we conceive the existence of created things, in that they persevere in their actuality' (Spinoza 1998: 104). As Steven Barbone suggests, for Spinoza, time is the measure of duration, the metric field imposed on duration.
6. In this, Deleuze's and Foucault's interest in the vectors traversed by statements are more helpful than Alain Badiou's negative ontology based on set theory, which cannot account for the new except as a rare accidental encounter.

Chapter 10

Abstract Humour, Humorous Abstraction

Robert Garnett

Abstract Humour

About ten years ago I was taking part in a graduate seminar held in a room at a gallery that was showing a retrospective of the work of the American artist Haim Steinbach. We were all sat in a circle around the artist who was responding to questions from the students. It wasn't going too well, the atmosphere was a bit stiff and the questions weren't really that interesting. Most of the students were quite familiar with the work, it being a paradigmatic, almost textbook example of the kind of art we used to call 'postmodern' back then. Most of them were familiar with the critical discourse around the work and how it was seen to critically reflect upon the contemporary 'economy of the object', 'exhibition value' and how it partook of the critique of 'autonomy', 'transcendence' and 'originality'.

Suddenly, a student got up and walked towards one of the works – a typical Steinbach consisting of a quasi-Donald Judd shelf unit upon which were placed shop-bought commodities. He then started to move some of the carefully arranged objects; he placed one on its side, one upside-down and placed another half over the edge of the shelf. He then asked, 'how does this change the work?' Everyone was palpably nonplussed, including the artist. After a while an embarrassed silence gave way to a stilted laughter. A lecturer apologised on behalf of the student and the artist nonetheless went on to answer his question by saying that the altered work would not in any real sense have been transformed; it would just be mis-installed and would therefore not properly represent his intentions. After a few more questions the discussion ended.

On the coach on the way back to London much of the conversation inevitably concerned the student's intervention earlier in the day.

We realised that he'd raised some quite interesting questions. Had the work been transformed? Well, in one sense no, because it was technically still the same in terms of its material constituents and the critical claims that could ostensibly be made for it. In another sense, though, it was transformed in that it looked completely different, looked rather 'funny' in comparison with its previous state. The impeccably 'cool' 'ironic' comportment of the work had been completely undermined by the student's gesture. We realised he'd made a very good joke. It maybe wasn't a work of art but it was a joke that reminded one of the similarities between art and the joke.

The student conceded, however, that his action had been quite involuntary. But this only served to remind me of how Freud, when discussing the 'authorship' of jokes similarly claimed that they simply 'occur' to their author. And this joke lingered in my memory for some time after – unlike a verbal joke that you 'get' and then invariably forget until it involuntarily re-occurs to you at a later date. It lingered because it seemed to encapsulate for me a number of the questions and problems presented to me by some of the new art practices that had emerged in the 1990s, particularly in London. One of these was a problem of 'attitude'; much of this latter work seemed vivid in terms of its demeanour or posture but it was also confounding because one couldn't precisely work out its critical 'pre-text' in the same way in which one could before a piece of 'discourse-specific' work from the 1980s, like Steinbach's was or eventually became. It confounded my sense of what constituted artistic intelligence and at the same time elucidated or uncovered a blind spot in the discussions around art since the '80s. It showed maybe how superficial we had been in disregarding the sur-face appearance of a work in favour of its ostensible status as 'text'.

I was later reminded of this joke when I came across Deleuze's distinction between irony and humour in his book Proust and Signs. *Here Deleuze contrasted the way in which 'irony is always prepared in advance for the encounter' with the sense-Event, whereas humour is the act of being open to the encounter. In humour 'the intelligence comes after' the event, the bloc of material affects and percepts, the 'non-sense' that constitute the very 'food for thought' (Deleuze 2004: 30). This is not necessarily a laughing matter, it is more like being placed in a 'funny' or 'preposterous' situation, like that of the critic encountering a work of art that seems to disable one's prior criteria for determining the success or failure of a work of art, a work that might only be amenable to sense. This might be a kind of work that is humorous in an 'abstract' sense; 'abstract' in the way in which Warhol used the term as a studio litmus test for the success or failure of a new work. If a work didn't add up, didn't make sense, if it was 'abstract', then 'it might be art', he used to say.*

Humour Noir is the New Black

References to humour currently abound in contemporary art discourse, and it appears that a widespread outbreak of laughter has been underway in recent years that would ostensibly seem to drown out the chorus of melancholy that has prevailed since the gradual demise of the postmodern. This would not be unwelcome were it not for the fact that much of what passes for humour within these discussions functions, I wish to argue, as little more than a perpetual pathos of a refrain of resignation. In Deleuzian terms, I wish to argue, this amounts to irony, rather than a genuinely affirmative humour. A crucial theoretical task is to deconflate irony and humour, in order to foreground the specificity and, indeed, 'autonomy' of humour and the distinct ethics and politics of its aesthetic modality. Almost all mainstream artworld and philosophical conceptions of humour are psychoanalytically based, variants of what Deleuze specifically refers to as 'Oedipus-irony' (Deleuze and Parnet 1987: 68). 'Irony rises and subverts, humour descends and perverts', wrote Foucault of Deleuze (Foucault 1977: 165). Irony rises to a transcendent Law or Idea and then descends in order to demonstrate its inadequacy to any worldly determinant context. Psychoanalytical (de)sublimation is similarly situated on a vertical, transcendent axis, an ascent to the 'dignity of das Ding', the 'impossible' Real Thing, that precedes a sublime descent to the abjection of the body and of sexuality. As one mainstream paradigmatic account of our contemporary tragi-comedy goes:

> The very fact that the comic hero evokes not life's triumph, but its slipping away, also entails that we are not adequate to the Thing that comedy presents to us. Even as we laugh at and with the comic Thing, it laughs at us, making us look ridiculous. Comedy is the relief that permits no escape . . . from the limited condition of our finitude, the shabby and degenerating state of our upper and lower bodily strata, and it is here that the comic allows the windows to fly open onto our tragic condition. (Critchley 1999: 234–5).[1]

That 'Humour Noir' is very much the 'New Black' is evidenced by the proliferation of art practices that are seen to partake in just such a carnivalesque cartoon Batailleism of the body as abject object – from Mike Kelley to the Chapman Brothers, from Paul McCarthy to Maurizio Cattelan. When read 'literally', as they almost always are, these practices display a contemporary obsession with what Deleuze, contra Bataille, referred to as the 'dirty little secret of sexuality' that is always, already known in advance (Deleuze and Parnet 1987: 47). Armed with this fore-knowledge, contemporary 'post-postmodern' irony always subordinates the saying to the said, always misses the event of the joke, never really gets *it*, remains detached from the *gesture*, the qualitative difference that the joke-work produces on and in the utterly superficial depths of its sur-face. What made the above work vivid, at least to me and my peer group, was not its pre-text but its energising, affective and contagious attitude. Attitude can be seen to be an operative mode of not taking seriously clichéd images of art and the artist, of 'de-facing' them. Long before theory, a humorous art 'senses' when a problem has become a 'false problem', when it has become a 'critical' or academic problem. When a first-order 'critical' content can be read straight off the surface a work, it is time to go elsewhere, to create new problems.

The ironist, says Deleuze:

> is someone who discusses principles; he is seeking a first principle, a prin-ciple which comes even before the one that was thought to be first. He finds a course even more primary, then he rises. He constantly goes up and down. This is why he proceeds by questioning, he is a man of conversation, of dialogue, he has a particular tone, always of the signifier. (Deleuze and Parnet 1987: 68)

Humour is 'completely the opposite', it is 'completely atonal, absolutely imperceptible, it makes something shoot off. It never goes up or down, it is on the surface: surface effects. Humour is an art of pure events.' Humour takes one to the Outside of signification; it aims to stop the 'good conversation' in its tracks, to confound it in favour of producing new questions: 'the art of constructing a problem. None of this happens in an interview, a conversation, a discussion', states Deleuze (Deleuze and Parnet 1987: 69). Humour is treachery; its agent is the traitor as opposed to the trickster. The trickster plays on words, practices the ironic *positionality*, of 'discourse specificity'. The traitor makes gestures, proceeds through *Posture* as opposed to positionality.

One prominent instance of an irony of positionality is that of the British artist Liam Gillick. He is usually associated with 'Relational Aesthetics', the most successful curatorial marketing phenomenon of the 1990s. Gillick's art and parallel writing practice consists of an ongoing process of the referencing of an unproblematically readable series of current critical-curatorial concerns. In his own words, he describes his work as being part of a 'discursive tendency' in contemporary art, 'the key strategy employed by the most dynamic contemporary artists'. This, as he puts it, 'is an offspring of critical theory and improvised, self-organised structures'. It is 'self-conscious' and 'critical', is concerned with the 'movement between subjects without or beyond order', and constitutes 'a set of discussions marked by their adherence to one or more models of analytical reason' (Gillick 2009: 1). Gillick is without doubt a 'man of conversation', and his ubiquitous presence on the international circuit of panels and symposia is second to none. And, 'his tone is definitely that of the signifier', indeed the constructions he produces are deliberately aesthetically neutered, functioning, as he puts it, as 'backdrops' to putatively discursive 'movement between subjects'. Clement Greenberg once used the term 'Scene Art' to refer to a kind of practice that deliberately aligns itself with the prevailing doxa, a kind of art that consists of 'playing the scene', that directly appeals to an existing discursive formation, that perfectly ticks all the right curatorial boxes. We might consider Liam Gillick's work to amount to just such a contemporary Biennale academicism, an always timely art-world profes-sionalism perfectly reconciled with its epoch.

'Art is One Big Running Joke' (Martin Kippenberger)

The antithesis of an art that 'works' an existing discursive formation is an art that creates its own scene or 'formation of immanence'. One artist who created a scene wherever he went was Martin Kippenberger. Kippenberger was no more and no less than an attitude, an ongoing series of humorous postures and gestures. His friend and fellow artist Christopher Wool has described his humour as an 'abstract humour', that was 'endless' and 'senseless' (Wool 2003: 89). Kippenberger's work never arrived at some dissipative and cathartic punchline, was never aligned on a vertical axis, rising and critically subverting. Rather, his whole oeuvre consisted of a 'perverse' and infinite practice of synthetic combination. Take *Disco Bomb*, of 1989, for example (image 10.1). A spot-lit dancefloor disco ball simply juxtaposed with a fluorescent nylon party wig, the work does no more and no less than harness a surface effect that nonetheless affectively energises the entire space of the gallery, wherever it might be. Like much of his work, it revels in its utter superficiality, while nonetheless creating a spatial-temporal breach in and *out of* the centre of the art space.

Made out of readymade elements, these are not, however, conceived as 'fragments' or 'ruins'; here there is no allegory to decipher. Contrary to the one-dimensional critical appropriation of Steinbach and his '80s

10.1: Martin Kippenberger, *Disco Bomb*, 1989, mirrored disco ball with synthetic orange wig, 12 in. diam., ed. 4/9, The Museum of Contemporary Art, Los Angeles, gift of Christopher Wool, Copyright: Estate Martin Kippenberger, Galerie Gisela Capitain, Cologne.

peers, this work partakes in what Deleuze called 'double theft' – a stealing and a 'stealing away' which produces an excess, an elsewhere in the here and now (Deleuze and Parnet 1987: 40). It does not partake in the postmodern critique of transcendence; rather Kippenberger's practice was at all times a future-orientated and affirmative work of 'un-mourning'. Here, to quote Deleuze, 'there is nothing to understand; there are only varying levels of humour' (Deleuze 1995: 142). And this was precisely what made Kippenberger such an untimely figure at the height of '80s 'discourse fever'. What occurs within his work, to quote Deleuze again, is that 'we are led back to the surface, where there is no longer anything to denote or even to signify. This is the place where pure sense is produced. It is produced in its essential relation to a third element, this time the nonsense of surface.' 'Once again', he continues, 'what matters here is to act quickly, what matters is speed' (Deleuze 1990: 154). 'Witz ist ein Blitz!', as some of Kippenberger's German philosophical predecessors used to say.

Kippenberger worked at a relentless pace, as evinced by one of his most important works, *the Hotel Drawings*, the ongoing series of collages and drawings on hotel paper he collected when constantly on the move. Here again there is nothing critically to reconstruct; all one can do, if so disposed, is to go with the flow of absurd and nonsensical juxtapositions of recurring motifs and phrases. Like Deleuze and Guattari's 'Russian Idiot', however, Kippenberger can be seen to 'raise the absurd to the highest level of thought', which, 'in other words' they continue, 'is to create' (Deleuze and Guattari 1994: 65). Such an affirmative gesture amounts to a kind of extra-rapid thinking that is a kind of thinking, a kind of intelligence, nonetheless. Art Theorist Thierry de Duve has suggested that such gesture-presentations are a means through which 'art responds to questions yet to be asked' (De Duve 2000: 181). Art, as in Deleuze, is the process of creating new problems, new questions; it is the task of a differently paced theory to extract the new concepts implied in art's extra-rapid thought.

However, there are still no really satisfactory art-theoretical readings of Kippenberger's work simply because theory doesn't get that there's nothing in the first instance to theorise, that, initially, the work might only be amenable to sense, to one's 'sense of humour'. But this is precisely what Art Theory still lacks, and is largely the cause of the much-discussed 'crisis in criticism'. It is my argument here that Deleuze's humorous aesthetics can help us to account for the singular intelligence of not only Kippenberger, but a large part of a generation of artists who have fallen under the radar of the dominant *October* journal-style 'serious' art theory since the 1990s. One could mention artists such as Kippenberger's colleague and collaborator, Albert Oehlen, other major figures such as Franz West, Pipilotti Rist, Jeff Koons, and not least the YBA phenomenon in London. But I wish to further suggest that there remain obstacles to this, and some of these exist in Deleuze's own writing, particularly his writing on art. Also problematic is Deleuze and Guattari's singular, but now rather dated philosophical rhetoric that is reiterated in the secondary literature. The Francis Bacon book is a main case in point here, and one could argue that this more than anything else has prevented or at least stymied the proper deployment of Deleuzian ideas in relation to contemporary art. The vital fact here is that we cannot in the twenty-first century believe in art in the same way that Bacon did. We cannot believe in Bacon's 'cry' anymore – and after the joke-Event of Duchamp and Dada it is arguable as to whether it was believable in the first place. Art can't shock and traumatise us in the same way anymore; art's affectivity and effectivity is today of a different and more 'pre-posterously' humorous order.

Bringing the Event Down to Earth

And this is where the joke comes in. A Deleuzian rethinking of the joke, or of art as a joke, offers, I wish to suggest, a means of bringing Deleuze's conception of the humorous art of the Event-encounter a bit more down to earth, so to speak; it offers a way of bringing his thought a bit closer to the art of today. According to Paolo Virno, 'there exists no attempt as significant as Freud's to distill a detailed taxonomy, *botanical*, so to speak, of the various kinds of jokes' (Virno 2008: 72). Freud sharply distinguishes between the joke-work and the species of the comic on the basis that the joke is a counter-repressive, counter-narcissistic operation that opens onto the radical alterity, the radical otherness or nonsense of the unconscious; comedy is a function of pre-conscious thought, or thought that can be represented to consciousness. Both modalities, however, are 'methods', writes Freud, 'of obtaining a yield of pleasure through an economy in psychic expenditure', a principle that forms the basis of Freud's 'relief theory' of humour (Freud 1960: 42). They are processes through which one economises on an anticipated expenditure of psychic energy which is interrupted in its nascent state by the effect of humour, the comic object or the joke; energy which is then rendered surplus and expelled in the form of pleasurable laughter-discharge.

A key distinction, however, remains the fact that the comic requires only two protagonists at most, whereas the joke is a collective process.

Comedy requires only the witness and comic object to complete its course; humour, or humour-noir, is conducted at the expense of the bodily self as abject object; and the prerequisite of the process of irony is the addressee of the sarcastic remark. The joke, however, has a quite different structure. Freud states, 'jokes are the most social of all psychical processes that aim at producing a yield of pleasure' (Freud 1960: 222). Whereas comedy is produced at the expense of another – hence its 'superiority' and 'exclusivity' – the joke is a product of a pact.

'Laughter is among the highly infectious expressions of psychical states', Freud states, and 'when I make the other person laugh by telling him my joke, I am actually making use of him to arouse my own laughter' (Freud 1960: 100). Freud is implying that one cannot tell a joke to oneself; the joke is always directed towards an addressee. This third listener then functions, firstly, to 'provide objective proof of the joke's success'; secondly, to complete my own pleasure by a reaction of the other person upon myself; and thirdly – where it is a question of repeating a joke that one has not produced oneself – to make up for the loss of pleasure owing to the joke's lack of novelty. In turn, 'the third listener invariably feels compelled to repeat the joke to another person', thus creating a collective-comic chain of reaction – a kind of 'existential refrain' (100). These distinctions, along with Freud's insistence upon the 'recentness' of the joke that is essential to its operation – the fact that it has to be new to be successful – are precisely those dimensions of the joke-work that, after they have been subjected to a 'Schizoanalytic remodelisation', seem to me to be strikingly suggestive in the ways in which they might be considered within the context of contemporary art.

Freud deploys the metaphor of a seduction scene to describe the structure of the joke-work. It is initially a failed seduction attempt. An exhibitionistically inclined boy spots a girl, and moves in by making a smutty remark in order to elicit her sexual arousal. In walks another man. Game over. For now. There's no chance of the seduction attempt continuing in the presence of the rival, who stands in the position of the Paternal bar, the Law or Father's 'No', who is Freud's 'third listener'. A joke 'occurs' to the first boy, the teller, and what happens now is that the rival begins to assume the position of the second person, the 'You', and finds himself the addressee of the joke, seduced in turn and lured into being a protagonist in a joke scene. This is potentially a very risky situation because the teller puts himself on the line, the joker risks total humiliation, or as comedians put it, risks 'dying on stage' before every performance. This is, of course, completely absent from a knowing irony. If the joke comes off, however, the addressee laughs at the punch line, and in the process of getting 'it' the Father is disarmed, displaced, and the Law becomes not transgressed or subverted but literally perverted or 'Pere-verted'. With this switch of position, the Law is in effect suspended, as is the desired object. As in Deleuze's conception of the masochistic scenario, here is a situation suspended between the ideal and the reality principle. And the game is still not over, because the listener is immediately compelled to repeat the joke to another, 'fourth' party – he, in effect, then takes the place of the teller. Freud however, could not build upon the politicality of the joke aesthetic; he ironises it away by tying it to the logos and telos of repression and pleasure-discharge. Nevertheless, we can productively reclaim the joke-work from psychoanalysis in order to conceive of a specific kind of slow-release art joke as a perversely intensive movement of becoming – a kind of abstract humour.

What Freud, in effect, creates here is a perfect instance of an affective formation-encounter as collective individuation. The ego of each participant in the joke-scene-event is undone, is dissolved by its intensive suspense-affect; the inter-subjective 'abstract machine' breaks down as a residual line of flight is opened onto an Outside. This constitutes a becoming-Other, that, as Deleuze puts it, 'spills over and beyond whoever lives through it (thereby becoming someone else)' (Deleuze 1995: 137). This 'someone else' is an instance par excellence of what Deleuze referred to as the '4th-Personal', the singularity of 'free-indirect discourse' (Deleuze 1990: 160). When the joke 'passes through' via the 'repetition compulsion' of the Third-listener, it creates a bifurcation, it contagiously spreads out to form an affective or 'magnetic' force field, map, diagram or phylum. What passes through is the continuous, infinite flow, the material flux of the joke-affect. As Martin Kippenberger put it: art is precisely like 'one big running joke' (Kippenberger 1991: 1).

All this takes place in the here and now, or the 'erewhon'. And we can also think of this in more down-to-earth terms as constituting the kind of virtual–actual 'buzz' or 'vibe', that 'something in the air-ness', which is constitutive of the energetic intensity of a 'scene' in its becoming. The performative 'making' of a scene provides a distinctive way of thinking Guattari's 'existential refrain', and this whole repetitive movement of the 'ritornello' is of course nothing like Freud's 'Fort-Da' repetition of (de-) sublimation, the perpetual ascent and descent on a vertical, transcendent axis. 'What counts in desire', writes Deleuze, 'is not the false alternative between Law and spontaneity, it is the respective play of territorialities, reterritorialisations and movements of deterritorialisation'

(Deleuze and Parnet 1987: 99). Crucially, he further argues, 'this has nothing to do with pleasure and its festivals', and it is here that Deleuze enables us to deconflate humour from another oft-cited theoretical resource within current discussions of comedy: the irony of the spontaneous pleasure-discharge of Bakhtin's Carnivalesque conception of the comic. Deleuze argues that desire pertains to joy, which is 'the immanent process of desire which fills itself up, the continuum of intensities, which replace both the law-authority and the pleasure discharge' (Deleuze and Parnet 1987: 95). Becoming-Child is forestalled by the momentary discharge, after which we all grow up and resign ourselves to the Oedipal Law; similarly; when the carnival is over we all soon find ourselves back in our places within the prevailing social hierarchy. It is precisely 'the relief that permits no escape' mentioned earlier (Critchley 1999: 234). The same writer contends that 'the comic opens onto the It, the es, id', which is the impossible Real Thing (Critchley 1999: 236). To Deleuze, however, *It* is positivised; *It* has no logos or telos, It is precisely the *going for It*, that is prior to any Law and its negation-transgression. *'Let's go for It, It'll be a laugh.'* This is not the momentary dissipative discharge of laughter-pleasure, but the sustained intensity of the making of a scene that is nothing like a Law-sanctioned carnival.

What makes a scene is attitude as an affirmation of possibility, which is 'the production of an unconscious as a social and political space to be conquered', 'the construction of a collective machine assemblage as well as an expressive cause of utterance' (Deleuze and Parnet 1987: 78). *It* happens, the joke occurs to its mechanic-author as a kind of 'quasi-causal' auto-production of desire that directly penetrates the social field. *It* is an event made *out of* the here and now that trans-forms the here and now.

It is un-written right across the sur-face of a work; 'humour is the art of the surface' (Deleuze 1990: 159). Humour is inclusive, 'superior irony' is exclusive. The joke is empathetically addressed to a 'you'. Detached irony is addressed to a 'them'. You can't tell a joke to a 'them'. The 'third' as touchstone is un-done by the 'subjectless action' of the joke-work that constitutes a relationality without relation, that exceeds the oxymoron that is a 'Relational Aesthetics'.

Humorous Abstraction

Sometime during the mid-'90s I was standing in the middle of a gallery in front of a painting entitled Gorgeous Beautiful Kiss My Fucking Ass Painting. *I was with a friend, and we both looked at each other as if to*

say, 'You can't argue with this, this just works.' It was an abstract paint-
ing made by Damien Hirst – just before his burnout and descent into
super-lucrative self-parody – one of his Spin Paintings. It was made by
pouring paint onto a rapidly revolving turntable; a simple method that
nonetheless produced what was for us a rather incredible effect. It was,
as its title more than suggests, brazenly affirmative. This was odd, was
very funny at the time, because it was doing everything that intelligent
art was not supposed to do. But this was also what seemed to make it
work. It had a right kind of wrongness. Serious painting was supposed to
be about painting; one was supposed to proceed at one critical remove.
This, though, was empathetic in its mode of address – to say the least.
It was addressed to a you; in other words it was not ironic. But it did
not at all seem to hark back to any kind of authenticity either; it did not
seem to be the expression of the interiority of a sovereign 'I'. But neither
did it seem to be like previous kinds of expressive modern abstract art; it
did not seem sublime in the sense of Barnett Newman's 'One'; it did not
seem to purport to open onto or elevate onto some transcendent void. It
was none of these things.

It was around this time that similar kinds of abstract art, such as
Albert Oehlen's 'Post-Non-Figurative painting', as he calls it, began to
make sense. Then there was work like Mary Heilmann's abstraction,
Wolfgang Tillmans' abstract photographs, Ugo Rondinone's Target
Paintings. They all seemed of now, and curiously expressive or render-
ings visible of very similar sensations that good popular music renders
sonic. The painting seemed to be expressive in a quite impersonal way
of the kind of intensive energy that one sensed was 'happening', was
'in the air' in London at the time. A kind of energetic intensity similar
maybe to what Georg Simmel used to call the Geist *of the City, that does*
not however, precede or exist outside of its expression in art, in music.
What gradually became palpable was that this intensity is humour, the
electricity that generates and sustains the assemblage. Assemblages, as
Deleuze insisted, are constructions of desire on a plane that makes them
possible; and all assemblages are collective, 'every desire is the affair of a
people, an affair of the masses, a molecular affair' (Deleuze and Parnet
1987: 96). Ultimately, 'the construction of a plane is a politics' (91). Art
as politics? *One big joke. . .*

References

Critchley, S. (1999), *Ethics, Politics, Subjectivity*, London and New York: Verso.
De Duve, T. (2000), 'Interview', *Parkett*, 40.

Deleuze G. (1989), *Masochism: Coldness and Cruelty*, trans. J. McNeil, New York: Zone Books.

Deleuze, G. (1990), *The Logic of Sense*, ed. C. Boundas, trans. M. Lester with C. Stivale, New York: Columbia University Press.

Deleuze, G. (1995), *Negotiations 1972–1990*, trans. M. Joughin, New York: Columbia University Press.

Deleuze, G. (2004), *Proust and Signs*, trans. R. Howard, Minneapolis: University of Minnesota Press.

Deleuze, G. and Guattari, F. (1994), *What is Philosophy?*, trans. H. Tomlinson and G. Burchell, New York: Columbia University Press.

Deleuze, G. and C. Parnet (1987), *Dialogues*, trans. H. Tomlinson and B. Habberjam, New York: Columbia University Press.

Foucault, M. (1977), 'Theatrum Philosophicum', in *Language, Counter-Memory, Practice: Selected Essays and Interviews*, edited by D. Bouchard and I. Simon, Ithaca: Cornell University Press.

Freud, S. (1960), *Jokes and Their Relation to the Unconscious*, trans. J. Strachey, Harmondsworth: Penguin Freud Library.

Gillick, L. (2009), 'Maybe it would be better if we worked in groups of 3 (Part 1 of 2: The Discursive)', available at: http://www.e-flux.com/journal/view/35

International Necronautical Society (2009), 'Manifesto on Inauthenticity', in N. Bourriaud (ed.), *Altermodern*, London: Tate Publishing.

Kippenberger, M. (1991), *I Had A Vision*, San Francisco: Museum of Modern Art.

Virno, P. (2008), *Multitude: Between Innovation and Negation*, trans. I. Bertoletti, J. Cascaito and A. Casson, Los Angeles: Semiotext(e).

Wool, C. (2003), 'Blue Streak', *Artforum* (February).

Note

1. Critchley, writing under the guise of The International Necronautical Society (2009), makes identical claims in the catalogue of the recent survey exhibition of contemporary art, 'Altermodern', at Tate Britian. Curated by prominent curator and author of *Relational Aesthetics*, Nicolas Bourriaud, the show explicitly positioned itself in opposition to postmodernism, indeed the promotional material was emblazoned with the slogan 'POSTMODERNISM IS DEAD!' It was curious, then, to encounter a featured text espousing what was largely a kind of inverted postmodern irony, only this time an irony of infinite deconstruction was replaced by that of an infinite resignation.

Chapter 11

From Aesthetics to the Abstract Machine: Deleuze, Guattari and Contemporary Art Practice

Simon O'Sullivan

The following essay is in three inter-related parts. The first section introduces and attempts to think through a certain kind of contemporary art practice utilising what might loosely be called a Deleuzian framework (and via an argument that is in part made against Craig Owens and Nicolas Bourriaud). This section begins with an account of my encounter with a particular object and an art scene that contributed to my own rethinking about what the contemporary is and what it does. The second section revisits some of the points made in the first but is more explicit (and abstract) in its mobilisation of Deleuze's thought in that it takes concepts from across Deleuze and Deleuze and Guattari's corpus of work and brings them to bear on the field of contemporary art practice in general. The third brief and concluding section homes in on one particular concept and also turns to Guattari's solo writings in order to think a little more about what I take to be one of contemporary art's most important characteristics: its future orientation (and it is in this sense, ultimately, that contemporary art names not just a type of art, but art's very diagrammatic function).

Aesthetics and Art Practice

It seems to me that a new style – or attitude – has emerged in some of the contemporary art that has recently been exhibited in London and indeed elsewhere in Britain. A style that, I want to claim, has a certain resonance with Deleuze's philosophy, and, as such, I want to use it as a personal and somewhat idiosyncratic 'way in' to think about the conjunction Deleuze *and* contemporary art. It is a style at odds with the more conceptual and post-conceptual work of the 1980s and early '90s; that work, we might say, involved attention to the signifier and indeed an emphasis on art as sign (albeit one often in crisis). One of the characteristics of this new attitude, if there is one, is a turn towards more object-based practices and more specifically towards the production of new 'assemblages' (I am thinking here, for example, of artists such as Jim Lambie and Eva Rothschild). It also seems to involve a re-engagement with painting, a painting that oscillates between figuration and abstraction and is characterised by its own idiosyncratic, we might even say specifically *subjective*, subject matter (examples here would be the painting practices of Rachel Morton and Hayley Tompkins).[1]

In this context I want to mention Cathy Wilkes' work, which involves both the kind of painting and assemblages I mentioned above, as an example of this 'new' style of art practice. I remember the first time I saw Wilkes' work in the late 1990s. The particular object I have in mind is *Beautiful Human Body*, an assemblage of different parts and pieces in a careful, and seemingly precarious construction that was somehow figurative and yet non-figurative at the same time (see image 11.1). Quite frankly I found this particular assemblage unfathomable, impossible to place. It seemed to stymie any interpretive strategies at my disposal (signifier enthusiast as I was myself back then). Although I knew something was going on with the work – it had a certain complexity and a definite intentionality – I found I had very few reference points with which to approach it. In fact, Wilkes' art was not alone in eliciting this response from me. The artists mentioned above were, with Wilkes, part of a particular scene in Glasgow that was producing work that just seemed, at that time, *different*. Looking back, this art did not seem to fit in with the 'political' practices being carried out elsewhere and that in general characterised what for many, including myself, was the more interesting and important art being produced at the time. Put even more bluntly it did not fit my own interpretive frameworks and although this was bothersome, I also found it interesting, in fact, ultimately, compelling.

This turn, within some of these practices, away from straightforward signifying strategies and away from a certain kind of politics of art might be characterised as a turn (back) to what I would call the aesthetic potential of art. This is not necessarily to reinstate a transcendent space for art, to position it in an 'elsewhere' or to suggest that it transports us to an 'elsewhere', but it is to say that art is more than just an object to be read. Another way of saying this is that art is ultimately irreducible to signification and indeed to any discursive account given of it (something always remains – an excess – after any written/spoken report). As a first moment then, the aesthetic, as I am using the term, names art's specificity *as* art – its operation up and beyond signification. Such art, we might say, is not just 'meaningful', or, not only an object of knowledge

11.1: Cathy Wilkes, *Beautiful Human Body*, 1999; mixed media, dimensions variable. Installation view from *Fantasy Heckler* (curated by Padraig Timoney), Trace, Liverpool Biennial, Liverpool, 1999, image courtesy of The Modern Institute.

(although it is that too). It goes without saying that art has always had this character, however a certain kind of conceptualism, allied with a particular attitude within art history and theory (we might call it simply the prevalence of 'ideological critique'), has for a long time stymied this aesthetic character of art in an over investment of the idea of art as sign (albeit, again, one that is often in crisis).

Of course, aesthetics also names a response to the world and specifically to certain objects in that world. Following Kant, at least on this point, aesthetics names a specifically disinterested response, or, we might say, a response that is not 'of' the self as already constituted. This amounts to saying that it is not enough for new assemblages and combinations to exist, after all, anything can be *read*, that is to say, can be referred back to previous knowledges and frames of reference. There will always be those 'maintenance crews for the big explanatory machines', as Jean-François Lyotard once called them (Lyotard 1989:

182). At stake in this 'new' work, if it really is new, is then also a new spectator or participant and his or her own particular 'production of subjectivity'. Put simply, the change in attitude – if there is one – is one which these artists and their public share (even if the latter is often only a limited scene). To return to my encounter with Wilkes, we might say that I was somehow ready, open perhaps, to being challenged (or, at least, to having my ideas about art tested).

These art practices (and here I am thinking of Wilkes, but also Rothschild and Lambie for example) do not however just involve this aesthetic impulse as I am calling it. Indeed, paradoxically, they also often involve the utilisation of signifying material, previous art for example, and indeed other aspects of popular and mainstream culture. Here the production of new assemblages involves a recombination of already existing elements in and of the world. In general however, at least at first glance, this latter strategy (if we can call it one) of reappropriation/ recasting does not appear to be that new. Certainly 'postmodern' practices, as characterised by Craig Owens amongst others, self-consciously utilised previous forms (this was the so-called allegorical turn tracked by *October* and its writers). Owens' seminal essay mapped out this 'allegorical impulse' that was also a particular mode of reading objects ('one is text *read through* another' [Owens 1998: 317]). It is here that we encounter that specifically deconstructive attitude – the solicitation and deferral of meaning – that characterised much of the art (and art theory) of the 1980s (see, for example, Owens discussion of Brauntuch [Owens 1998: 317–18]). Another name for this attitude towards art is the aforementioned crisis in representation.

It might be instructive to move forward here from Owens' postmodernism to Nicolas Bourriaud's *Postproduction*. In that book Bourriaud makes the argument that contemporary art today – post-postmodernism as it were – likewise utilises previous artistic and other cultural forms (often more popular cultures) in its practice. Hence the 'twin figures of the DJ and the programmer' are seen by Bourriaud as being characteristic of our age, 'both of whom have the task of selecting cultural objects and inserting them into new contexts' (Bourriaud 2002: 7). Bourriaud names these 'new' art practitioners, 'semionauts', characterised as they are by a 'willingness to inscribe the work of art within a network of signs and significations, instead of considering it an autonomous or original form' (7, 10). In a sense then, Bourriaud is proffering a kind of intertextuality for art practice, although he does make the point that such practices are linked to other non-discursive regimes, other circuits of production, and, as such, we might say he has moved, at least a little, away from the restricted textual economy of Craig Owens and the other *October* writers.

We can certainly agree to an extent with Bourriaud that contemporary art does indeed involve the recasting of signifying material from elsewhere. Indeed, in one sense at least, it is the specific character of this manipulation that distinguishes art from other aspects of culture. It is this that constitutes an artist's archive as it were, an archive that is then worked over by the artist in question (I am thinking here particularly of the manner in which art utilises/references previous art). Again, this is not to return to Craig Owens et al. and to identify a general postmodern allegorical impulse within art, but it is to note that contemporary art is involved in multiple regimes of signs. We might say then, taking this point and what I have already said about the aesthetic above, that art – and specifically the work I introduced at the beginning of this section – is both asignifying *and* signifying, or, that it is both simple *and* complex. I will return to this point towards the end of my essay.

But is such art also involved in the crisis, or critique, of representation that Owens saw as characteristic of the allegorical impulse? Are these recastings that we see today deconstructions? Or, is there something different in these newer practices? Well, I would claim (in addition to the points made above) that there is indeed a different attitude at stake here. Whereas the *re*presentation of modern forms in the 1980s often operated as an ironic critique of the tenets of modernism, what we have with some of these other practices is a *repetition* of the modern. A repetition that repeats the energy, the force, of the latter. We might say then that rather than a critique of originality and authenticity these practices repeat and celebrate the modern impulse, which we might characterise generally as the desire for, and production of, the new (these practices cannot be understood as parodies or pastiches in this sense). Again, for myself, this is what is at stake in what I have been calling the aesthetic: an impulse towards the new, towards something *different* to that which is already here.

We might ask ourselves what this means in terms of the politics of art practice? What indeed constitutes contemporary art's political effectivity? For, I would argue, political art does not always look political and art that looks political ('speaks' its message as it were) does not always operate politically. In fact art is not politics in the typical – or molar and signifying – sense. It operates under a different logic. Such a politics, if we can still call it this, comes from this play with matter and with this production of difference. Returning to Wilkes' work, we might say that it is this, the production of something different – often a construction as in image 11.1 but also sometimes the arrangement of found objects and materials (some worked on, others left as found) in a very specific, but unfamiliar and surprising composition (for example the work *1/4 Moon* [image 11.2]) – that gives the work its singular and forceful character. Put simply, it is a new thing, a new assemblage in the world that has a definite intentionality albeit one that is difficult to read (it is not just more of the same however this might be dressed up as innovation). Much more might be said about Wilkes' work – especially in relation to the maternal and to our present-day commodity culture – but it is this *strangeness* and what I would call *newness* that, for me, is most compelling.[2] Contemporary art might indeed involve itself in critique, the critique of representation or of that apparatus of capture that feeds off creativity (deconstructive strategies/ideological critique), but it can also plug into the creativity and fundamental productivity in and of the world that is ontologically prior to this capture. It is this second move that I think characterises a practice like that of Wilkes.

I want to end this first introductory section of my essay, then, by foregrounding a notion of difference and repetition. Perhaps what is at stake with contemporary art is the repetition of previous art forms, and indeed non art forms of life from elsewhere, but a repetition with difference. A new dice throw, as perhaps Deleuze would say. This production of difference in itself involves the deployment of different temporalities, for example, a general slowing down, even a stillness, or, in other cases, an absolute acceleration (when thought leaps or pounces at a speed irreducible to the regulative movements and rhythms of the market). Indeed, time, as well as matter, becomes a material of sorts to play with in these practices. I will be returning to this point below, but we might note here the different temporal experiments at the cusp of modernity/ postmodernity where these different speeds were also at stake. Allan Kaprow's *Happenings* or Carolee Schneeman's performances, for example. In passing we might also point to the different temporalities at stake in other media, for example film, which, as Deleuze argues in the *Cinema* books, involves precisely the exploration of different space-times. And then, following Spinoza, there is the possible deployment of the eternal *against* temporality, when art offers us an experience (though perhaps it is not an unaltered 'us' that experiences) that takes place 'beyond' time (again, I will return to this). Suffice to say, in a time of total capitalism (when lived time is increasingly colonised), the time of art becomes crucial.[3]

None of this, I think, is really new. Modern art certainly, in some of its instantiations, has always involved this logic of difference. Perhaps

11.2: Cathy Wilkes, ¼ Moon, 2004; drill, wood, paper, glass panels, fabric, candles, telephones, VHC, plastic, oil on canvas, mixed media on canvas, 167 × 465 × 430 cm. Installation view at '¼ Moon', Galerie Giti Nourbakhsch, Berlin, 2004, image courtesy of The Modern Institute.

what is new then, as I suggested above, is our attitude as participants with such art. Rather than mobilising pre-existing reading strategies and interpretive paradigms, capturing art within our already set up temporal frames and systems of reference, we have become attentive to art's own logic of invention and creation. This does not mean a simple turning away from critique, for the production of something new will always also involve the turning away from, or simply the refusal of, that which came before. It does, however, mean taking a more affirmative attitude towards contemporary art understood here as the production of new combinations in and of the world which suggest new ways and times of being and acting in that world.

Concepts and Components

So far I have been writing about my encounter with a particular kind of contemporary art practice from what might be called, again very loosely, a Deleuzian perspective. I want now to change tack and attempt to account for the effectivity of these new practices, and of certain aspects of contemporary art in general, by being a little more specific, but also more abstract. Below then, I assemble a number of concepts or components, seven in all, that I think are useful for thinking the expanded field of contemporary art. All of them have been extracted from Deleuze or certainly use the latter as their point of departure (although the last one, it seems to me, moves away somewhat from what we might call a strict Deleuzian take on art).

1. *Aesthetics*. As I have already mentioned, reinstating a notion of aesthetics within contemporary art discourse need not involve a wholesale turn to the Kantian heritage or indeed to (re)installing a transcendent operating space of, and for, art. Aesthetics might in fact be a name, on the one hand, for the rupturing quality of art: its power to break our habitual ways of being and acting in the world (our reactive selves); and on the other, for a concomitant second moment: the production of something new. We might say then that what is at stake with aesthetics is what Deleuze would call a genuine *encounter*. For Deleuze such an encounter is always with an object of sense that in itself involves the short-circuiting of sorts of our cognitive and conceptual capacities (see Deleuze 1994: 139). We might add to this, following some of my comments above, that such an object of encounter might also operate to rupture certain circuits of reception and consumption and other habits of 'spectatorship' (those that reinforce a certain 'knowledge' of art, or

even a given subjectivity) whilst opening us up to other perhaps more unfamiliar but more productive economies.

At stake then are two moments in what I am calling the aesthetics of contemporary art: one of dissent (a turn from, or refusal of, the typical) and one of affirmation (of something different). Two operations then: one of criticism, one of creativity. We might call the first parasitical (on an already existing body, for example an institution); the second, germinal (the birth of the new). Often it is only the former that is discussed in relation to contemporary art (as I indicated above, this was, it seems to me, the 'attitude' of the Academy in the 1980s and '90s: critical art practice was positioned as a form of expanded ideological [and institutional] critique). And certainly an untheorised celebration of the latter, particularly when it is pinned to a transcendent aesthetic, can be nothing more than an apology for the status quo (the critique of the latter being precisely the position of the former). We might say then that the more interesting examples of contemporary art today (and here I am thinking of those practices I introduced above) take the former – the critique – as their point of departure, but are not content with remaining with the critique, trapped as it can be by the very thing it critiques. These new practices have *worked through* the ruins of representation, hence, I think, their often 'knowing', or self-conscious character. One way of thinking this is that such practices are involved in the production of worlds rather than in the critique of the world as is. And at stake here, I think, is one's style of thought, as Deleuze might say: whether one is drawn to negation and critique or to affirmation and creativity.

2. *Affect*. Affect names the intensive quality of life. The risings and fallings, the movement from one state of being to another, the *becomings*. For Deleuze-Spinoza, ethics would be the organisation of one's life so as to increase specifically joyful affects, those that increase our capacity to act in the world (see Deleuze 1988a: esp. 48–51). This ethics will then involve certain kinds of encounter, for example when we come across an object with which we positively resonate, or when two or more individuals come together that essentially 'agree' (albeit this agreement might operate below that of apparent complicity in a register of *becoming*, as it were). This is to move the register from one of rupture to one of conjunction. In Spinoza's terms it is to form a 'common notion' that refers to an essence shared by two or more modes. It is in this sense that the concept of 'disinterest' I introduced above might be seen to involve the mobilisation of a 'common notion' in that it moves the dynamics of an

encounter away from purely subjective coordinates towards those of the longitudes and latitudes that determine the limits of wider assemblages.

Our encounter with art has the capacity to produce these kinds of common notions and transversal becomings (and this might be specifically the case with collaborative practices, or more generally with art scenes). We might say then that art practice can involve the production of specifically joyful affects as oppose to sad affects, for example that fear and paranoia produced by our encounter with more typical affective assemblages (I am thinking here of the mass media). Sad affects, of course, specifically decrease our capacity to act in the world. (It is as well to remind ourselves here that joy is not just an ego term, that is, having simply to do with 'getting what we want', but is something more impersonal, again, more 'disinterested'. Put starkly, sadness, in Spinozist terms, is a diminishment of life; joy its increase.)

Certainly the encounter with art can produce this kind of joy. Indeed, many of the practices I mentioned above have this joy-increasing effect; there is something fundamentally affirming of life and of creativity within them. However, the same work, as I suggested in my opening section (and indeed in point 1 above), also operates to undo, or to break with, typical ways of thinking and feeling. Indeed, the work's work is often about stymieing any agreement or simple 'understanding'. From a certain point of view we might say then that contemporary art can problematise the idea that we are purely rational beings, or that our experiences in the world can be the basis for a rational system of ethics. There will in fact always be moments of rupture – irrational points – within life that open us up to something different. However, from another perspective, we might understand these affective ruptures as ruptures in an already ruptured world, as it were. This then is a rupture of the already existing rupture between subject and object, which is to say the production of something 'common' that operates specifically *contra* alienation. The common notion overcomes the rupture between subject and object and it is this that allows Deleuze to use the former to examine the transcendental conditions of individuation as such, beyond the subject–object determination.

For Deleuze and Guattari, affects can also be thought of as self-supporting elements in the world and art itself figured as a 'bloc of affects' (see Deleuze and Guattari 1994: 163–99 and esp. 164). Art, we might say, is made of those becomings mentioned above frozen in time and space, waiting to be reactivated, waiting to be unleashed. It is an artist's style that coheres this assemblage together into a particular composition. Artists offer up new compositions of affect, new affective assemblages that are different to those we are more familiar with. It is this that differentiates art, as a specific form of thought, from mere opinion (a more habitual assemblage and one tied to a certain 'common sense'). Indeed, art practice does not necessarily communicate anything in this sense (and, as such, does not, I think, offer any knowledge of the world *as it is*). Art, when it really is art, operates at the very limit of our understanding, hence its always difficult (and often bothersome) character.

3. *The Production of Subjectivity*. It follows from the above that art is involved in a different kind of production of subjectivity from the typical. Indeed, the active production of subjectivity – our processual self-creation – is in general an aesthetic business. We can understand this in two ways: i) art objects and practices – specific combinations of affect – offer us models, or diagrams, for our own subjectivities (after all, we are also blocs of affect); ii) such practices might also operate to break a certain model of subjectivity and indeed other dominant modes of subjection. Again, this is the production of a kind of affective break within the typical (I will be returning once more to this point in my conclusion). Following on from my introductory remarks, this might involve a rethinking of the political functioning of art and an assessment of the role the latter might have in a programme of the production of subjectivity rather than in critiquing the existent or of being at the service of political regimes of signification (left-wing or otherwise).

Guattari's solo writings are particularly attentive to this question of how we might reconfigure – or resingularise – our own lives through interaction with one another, with groups, with different objects and practices and so forth. In Guattari's terminology, we access 'new universes of reference' through interacting and experimenting with new and different 'materials of expression' (Guattari 1995: 6–7). In passing it is worth noting the similarities with Spinoza here; both philosophers offer a kind of chemistry of subjectivity. In relation to the art cited in my introduction we might say that this kind of active mapping, what we may also call a realm of heteorogenetic encounter, constitutes a particular art *scene*. This, I think, is also to begin to bring the aesthetic and the therapeutic together, and, as such, points towards a notion of art practice as a form of schizoanalysis.

4. *The Minor*. Deleuze and Guattari's concept of a minor literature as it is developed in the *Kafka* book involves three components (see Deleuze and Guattari 1986: 16–18): i) The foregrounding of the affective – or

intensive – quality of language, or simply the latter's operation on an asignifying register. A minor literature stutters and stammers the major. It breaks with the operation of 'order-words', or simply stops making sense.[4] ii) The always already political nature of such literature (it is always connected to the wider social milieu and not fixated on the domestic/Oedipal). iii) Its collective nature. A minor literature is always a collective enunciation, in fact a minor literature works to pave the way for a community – sometimes a nation – yet to come. This is a minor literature's peculiar future orientation.

Each of these components of a minor literature seem pertinent to contemporary art practice. Indeed, the first has resonances with what I have been saying above – and will return to below – about asignification and rupture. The second also would allow us to move from the critique of sorts I made of notions of a political art above (for example, we might position contemporary art as a desiring-machine that is always connected to [and interferes with] larger social-machines). However it is the last point that seems to me especially relevant to many of the practices I mentioned in my first section. These practices are not made for an already existing audience as it were, but in order to call forth – to invoke – an audience. We might say, following point 3 above, to draw out a new subjectivity from within the old. Such practices do not offer a reassuring mirror reflection of a subjectivity already in place (they do not multiply the 'fantasies of realism' as Lyotard called them [1984: 74]). Indeed, with such art 'the people are missing'. We might say then that the operating field of these practices is the future, and that the artists operate here as kind of prophets, and specifically *traitor* prophets (traitors to a given affective/signifying regime). Traitor prophets offering up traitor objects perhaps? This gives art a utopian function of sorts, although it is a specifically *immanent* utopia intrinsically connected to the present, made out of the same materials, the same matter, as it were. I will be returning to this crucial point in my conclusion.

5. *The Virtual.* Although in his own writings Deleuze characterises philosophy itself as that form of thought that actualises the virtual (art being concerned with the possible) (see Deleuze 1988a: 96–7; 1994: 211–12), it might be useful to borrow his terminology and understand art as operating as a kind of 'actualising machine' (and, of course, there is the more obvious point to be made here that contemporary art today, post-Duchamp, might also operate through the concept). We might briefly remind ourselves of Deleuze's ontology here: a univocity of Being when the latter is understood *as* multiplicity. This is to foreground a

'fullness' or plenitude in and of the world. A superabundance of which only a fraction is ever actualised. Rather than looking to a transcendent horizon, or positioning art as taking us to 'another place' (or promising to take us there), we might then understand art practice as simply being involved in the actualisation of some of this potential that surrounds us here and now.

If with point 2 above we looked briefly at Deleuze's Spinozism, then the present point relates to his Bergsonism. The world, or rather space *and* time, are fractal in nature. We only ever access (perceive/remember) a part. For Deleuze technologies such as cinema – especially when it moves from the movement to the time image – continue Bergson's intuitive method of thinking beyond this human configuration. Put simply, and as I remarked at the end of the first section, the camera eye actualises different spatialities and different temporalities. It is in this sense that Deleuze's writings on cinema are so useful for thinking through the potentialities and operating logics of new media in contemporary art. However, I think we can also understand other art practices as actualisations; certainly Wilkes' work actualises a different sense of space, and, more importantly, opens us up to unfamiliar durations. For example, and as I also briefly mentioned above, it slows us down, and in this sense operates as what Deleuze might call a 'vacuole of non-communication' inasmuch as contemporary communication technologies – and the worlds they produce – specifically operate at a certain speed of contact and commerce (Deleuze 1995: 74). In Bergsonian terms we might say such art can further open that gap between stimulus and response from within which genuine creativity arises (I am thinking here of the celebrated virtual-cone of Bergson [see Bergson 1991: 150–5]). Again, this is the *time* of art, a time different to our more habitual clock-work-leisure time. I will be returning to this point in a moment.

6. *The Event.* The state machine increasingly utilises indeterminacy in its strategies of control and coercion. These strategies move from anticipatory 'pre-emptive strike' politics and military action through to 'softer' media strategies that utilise an affect of fear. In each case there is an attempt to colonise the virtual, or, we might say, to harness the strange temporality of the event, understood as a point of indeterminacy, a point of potentiality *before* bifurcation, *before* signification and action. This point operates on and at the very cusp between the virtual and the actual.

However, as I also implied above, we can see art as a kind of counter-technology to this nervous-system-machine. Put simply, indeterminacy is the very operating logic of certain objects and practices, and especially, I would argue, of performance. Indeed, if the current strategies of fear (and especially the production of a kind of ambient anxiety) are to be countered they need to be met with something operating with a similar logic and on a similar level, albeit for different ends. Performance art, and especially more absurdist performance that 'stops making sense', can incorporate these points of indeterminacy. Practices such as these mobilise the transformative power of the event – the way in which it holds the potential to open up new pathways, new possibilities of being for all participants (artists and spectators as it were). To stay with the Glasgow scene in particular, we might point to Sue Tompkin's spoken performances, which, in their use of breaks and pauses, slowness and speed, stutterings and stammerings, foreground these points of indeterminacy, these glitches.[5] In fact, I would say that it is a characteristic of much of the artwork cited earlier that it presents itself *as* event in terms of being a point of indetermination (and this logic is accentuated by the work in question being in a gallery, that is, isolated from typical regimes of circulation, set free from the burden of being useful, as it were).

It is also in this sense that chance is an important part of contemporary art practice. Chance understood as a specifically productive technology, a mechanism for escaping cliché and the habits of the self. We might say then that an art practice, as well as having a certain cohesiveness, also needs to be able to incorporate points of collapse. This is the mobilisation of indeterminacy through a determinate practice. This might involve accident or just the chance coming together of objects and/or other materials (and it is in this sense that art is always, ultimately, a thinking with and through materials) or it might involve a practice that deliberately moves between sense and nonsense (which is to say, deliberately scrambles existing codes and coding).

In passing we might remark that this time of the event is not only a key logic of art practice today, but also that a radical politics can learn much by following this aesthetic event-based technology. Indeed, if Antonio Negri is correct in his thesis in *Time for Revolution* (Negri 2003) that there has been a complete colonisation of time by capital, then the time of this affect-event becomes crucial. This is then to argue that both the state, and that which attempts to orientate itself against the state, increasingly operate in and as an aesthetic-temporal modality. All sorts of strange strategies might make themselves apparent here, for example, short circuiting the aesthetic-nervous system or producing random feedback and diverting flows into other stranger circuits.

7. *Mythopoiesis*. Mythopoiesis names the imaginative transformation of the world through fiction. This is the production of new and different myths for those who do not recognise themselves in the narratives and image clichés that surround them. The expanded field of contemporary art includes many explicit examples of the production of these new fictions, for example the *Cremaster* films of Matthew Barney, but, I would argue, we can also understand art practices like Wilkes' as mythopoietic inasmuch as they present us with a different narrative of sorts – a different arrangement of reality – albeit one that is difficult to read using our typical frames of reference. Such narratives need to be built up using a variety of techniques, objects and text, which is to say, echoing a point made in the opening section and in point 5 above, that mythopoiesis involves both signifying *and* asignifying components (again, it is complex *and* simple).

In fact so-called 'reality' is always already the result of myth-construction in the above sense. Events are made sense of through causal logic and other framing devices that dictate meaning and, indeed, the conditions of what might be considered 'meaningful'. Language, and especially the language of commodities (inasmuch as the latter are signs that give life 'meaning') produce our dominant sense of the world. When we grasp the world as fiction in this way we begin to 'see' the limits of what is seeable/sayable and are thus able to gesture beyond these very limits. Indeed, released from the political obligation to speak of the world *as it is*, contemporary art practice, in its mythopoietic character, is able to imagine another place in another space-time. We might say that art operates in two directions in this sense. It has a face turned to us and towards the world we inhabit, but it also has a face turned to that which is precisely otherworldly.

Finally, to return to point 5 above, mythopoiesis can also operate as a general slowing down so as to allow access to something beyond the world. In a contemporary world that celebrates contact and communication, ever-increasing accessibility and an ideal of always-being-switched-on, this slowing down has an important, if not crucial role to play in actually living a life. We might note here Bergson's ideas on fiction, or what he calls fabulation. The latter can, again, produce a gap, for those who choose to hear, between the fixed habits and rituals of society which in itself allows for what Deleuze calls 'creative emotion' to arise (see Deleuze 1988a: 111; Bergson 1935: 209–65). Fabulation involves the use of signifying material to access something specifically asignifying. More simply put, story-telling allows us to unplug and to enter a different duration. It functions as a catalyst for that idleness, which, as Nietzsche remarked, is the progenitor of any truly creative thought (Nietzsche 2001: 183–4). This is the productivity of anti-productivity; in fact the *super*-productivity of that which is, from a certain point of view, useless.

Ethico-Aesthetics and the Abstract Machine

In conclusion I want to look a little more closely at what might be called my eighth concept or component, the abstract machine, and link this briefly to Guattari's solo work on ethico-aesthetics. The abstract machine names something that is perhaps most characteristic of Deleuze's aesthetic, and something I touched upon earlier: the future orientation of art. Indeed, for Deleuze, the future holds a kind of potential that can be deployed in the present. Art especially draws its own audience forth, calls a people into being. Again, we might say that such art is not just made for an existing subject in the world, but to draw forth a new subject from within that which is already in place. This constitutes the very difficulty of art, we might even say its ontological difficulty. But if art's operating field is the future, how does this link with the production of subjectivity that must always begin in the present? Well, it might be said that art – and in particular the contemporary art practices mentioned above – operates as an intentional object, a point of subjectification as Guattari might call it, whilst at the same time functioning as a corrective to any simple assertion and affirmation of a 'new' people that is already here.

In one sense then, the sense of the present, art might be understood as always already incorporated within various systems and circuits of reception and consumption. But from another perspective this incorporation will always necessarily miss that which defines art: its future orientation (this orientation, I would argue, is not necessarily disabled even if such art is located within a gallery or other institution). The operating field of contemporary art might then be understood as a future field, which is to say the field of the abstract machine itself: 'The diagrammatic or abstract machine does not function to represent, even something real, but rather constructs a real that is yet to come, a new type of reality' (Deleuze and Guattari 1988: 142).

Indeed, the abstract machine is the cutting edge, the point of deterritorialisation, of any given assemblage. It is where everything happens. In order to understand the mechanism at work here we can look once more to Guattari's solo writings. For Guattari – following Jacques Lacan and Melanie Klein, but also Mikhail Bakhtin – in the art experience, there is a 'detachment of an ethico-aesthetic "partial object" from the field of dominant significations' that 'corresponds both to the promotion of a mutant desire and to the achievement of a certain disinterestedness' (Guattari 1995: 13). The partial object operates as a rupture but also a point around which a different subjectivity might crystallise; a point of entry into a different incorporeal universe. Importantly, and as Guattari remarks, this must involve a certain disinterestedness. As I remarked in the first section, art, in order to be activated, requires the prior preparation of the participant. One has to be open to the deterritorialising power of art, its molecularity, or affective power, operating 'beneath' its molar 'appearance'.

Our interaction with art then has the character of an event, as I discussed it in point 6 above; an event that must be seen, and responded to, as an event, 'as the potential bearer of new constellations of Universes of reference' (Guattari 1995: 18). This is to affirm an 'ethics and politics of the virtual that decorporealises and deterritorialises contingency, linear causality and the pressure of circumstances and significations which besiege us' (Guattari 1995: 29). Art ruptures dominant regimes and habitual formations and in so doing actualises other durations, other possibilities for life. It is within the field of contemporary art (and indeed with that which is contemporary in all art) that this future-orientation – this diagrammatic function – is particularly evident. Contemporary art then has what Deleuze, following Nietzsche, might call an 'untimely' character. It operates on the cusp between any given present and the future (and, in this sense, is always irreducible to any present it belongs to). Certainly, it is 'made' in the present, out of the materials at hand, as it were, but its 'content' calls for a something yet to come.

We might say then that contemporary art practice, as I am figuring it here, turns away from the habits and impasses of the present, offering up new assemblages – new refrains – to those that surround us on an everyday basis. I began this essay thinking about specific kinds of practice and indeed about specific artists, in particular Cathy Wilkes, but I want to end on a more general and expansive note that, I think, follows from the above. Everyone can break with habitual patterns at least to a certain extent. Everyone can experiment with the materials at hand and produce something new in the world or themselves anew in that world. Indeed, it is only with this creative participation in and with the world that the production of an 'auto-enriching' subjectivity can proceed (Guattari 1995: 21). Perhaps then, finally, we can think about two different kinds of contemporary art practice with Deleuze: the production of actual artworks or simply of composed things in the world, but also the practice of a life and of treating one's 'life as a work of art' (see Deleuze 1995:

95). In both cases such aesthetic production will involve working against the habitual and the normative, working at the very edge of our subjectivities as they are. In each case we might then also call such an aesthetics an ethics, inasmuch as we ask the question (following Deleuze) 'what am I capable of creating?' And further (following Deleuze and Guattari, following Spinoza) 'what am I capable of becoming?'

References

Bergson, H. (1935), *The Two Sources of Morality and Religion*, trans. R. A. Audra and C. Brereton with W. Horstall-Carter, New York: Doubleday Anchor Books.

Bergson, H. (1991), *Matter and Memory*, trans. N. M. Paul and W. S. Palmer, New York: Zone Books.

Bourriaud, N. (2002), *Postproduction*, ed. C. Schneider, trans. J. Herman, New York: Lukas and Steinberg.

Deleuze, G. (1988a), *Bergsonism*, trans. H. Tomlinson and B. Habberjam, New York: Zone Books.

Deleuze, G. (1988b), *Spinoza: Practical Philosophy*, trans. R. Hurley, San Francisco: City Lights Books.

Deleuze, G. (1990), *The Logic of Sense*, ed. C. V. Boundas, trans. M. Lester with C. Stivale, New York: Columbia University Press.

Deleuze, G. (1994), *Difference and Repetition*, trans. P. Patton, New York: Columbia University Press.

Deleuze, G. (1995), *Negotiations: 1972–1990*, trans. M. Joughin, New York: Columbia University Press.

Deleuze, G. and F. Guattari (1984), *Anti-Oedipus*, trans. R. Hurley, M. Seem and H. R. Lane, London: Athlone Press.

Deleuze, G. and F. Guattari (1986), *Kafka: Towards a Minor Literature*, trans. D. Polan, Minneapolis: University of Minnesota Press.

Deleuze, G. and F. Guattari (1988), *A Thousand Plateaus*, trans. B. Massumi, London: Athlone Press.

Deleuze, G. and F. Guattari (1994), *What is Philosophy?*, trans. H. Tomlinson and G. Burchell, London: Verso.

Guattari, F. (1995), *Chaosmosis: An Ethico-aesthetic Paradigm*, trans. P. Bains and J. Pefanis, Sydney: Power Publications.

Lyotard, J.-F. (1984), *The Postmodern Condition: A Report on Knowledge*, trans. G. Bennington and B. Massumi, Manchester: Manchester University Press.

Lyotard, J.-F. (1989), 'Philosophy and Painting in the Age of Their Experimentation: Contribution to an Idea of Postmodernity', trans. M. Minich Brewer and D. Brewer, in A. Benjamin (ed.), *The Lyotard Reader*, Oxford: Basil Blackwell.

Nietzsche, F. (2001), *The Gay Science*, trans. J. Nauckhoff, Cambridge: Cambridge University Press.

Negri, A. (2003), *Time for Revolution*, trans. M. Mandarini, London: Continuum.

O'Sullivan, S. (2005), 'Ten Concepts Following Cathy Wilkes' Practice', *Afterall*, 12: 65–70.

O'Sullivan, S. (2008), 'The Care of the Self and the Production of the New', in S. O'Sullivan and S. Zepke (eds), *Deleuze, Guattari and the Production of the New*, eds. London: Continuum.

O'Sullivan, S. (2009a), 'The Strange Temporality of the Subject: Badiou and Deleuze Between the Finite and the Infinite', *Subjectivity*, 27: 155–71.

O'Sullivan, S. (2009b), 'From Stuttering and Stammering to the Diagram: Deleuze, Bacon and Contemporary Art Practice', *Deleuze Studies*, 3(2): 247–58.

Owens, C. (1988), 'The Allegorical Impulse: Toward a Theory of Postmodernism', in D. Preziosi (ed.), *The Art of Art History: A Critical Anthology*, Oxford: Oxford University Press.

Notes

1. These four artists are represented by The Modern Institute in Glasgow. For representative images of each practice (and for further images of Cathy Wilkes' work) see www.themoderninstitute.com
2. I have attempted a more sustained engagement with Wilkes' practice that addresses some of these other aspects of the work in O'Sullivan (2005).
3. My article 'The Care of the Self and the Production of the New' (2008) explores this idea – via Spinoza, as well as Bergson and Foucault – of 'accessing' a time, or truth, beyond the finite, as it were. This is also the subject of my recent article, 'The Strange Temporality of the Subject: Badiou and Deleuze Between the Finite and the Infinite' (O'Sullivan 2009a), which thinks through the same themes in relation to Badiou and Deleuze. Both of these essays are work towards a future monograph on *The Production of Subjectivity*.
4. I have attended to this second component of a minor literature – in relation to contemporary art and what I call the 'glitch'– in my article 'From Stuttering and Stammering to the Diagram: Deleuze, Bacon and Contemporary Art Practice' (O'Sullivan 2009b). That article is a companion of sorts to the present one inasmuch as it mobilises a number of other Deleuzian concepts – specifically from the Bacon book – to think contemporary art.
5. For still images of these performances see www.themoderninstitute.com

Chapter 12

Traps Against Capture

Edgar Schmitz

> I cannot tell now whether escape was possible but I believe it must have been; for an ape it must always be possible.
>
> Kafka, 'A Report to an Academy'

Talking of traps solely in terms of capture is always too simple because it cuts out whatever else they might articulate. And it is too lazy because it avoids whatever else needs to be thought in order that capture can multiply and become plural, complicated and un-captured. Indeed, talking of capture as if it were finite means giving into it; it is to be captured by capture. Such a framing consolidates capture into a given state and condition, yet it is precisely the opposite that is needed: capture needs to be undone and re-configured to allow for the invention of new ways out.

Closure only happens, if it ever does, because it is brought to a situation. Immanent to the situation there is always more, so long as you refuse to give up on other possibilities, and the more capture seems complete, the more urgently this 'more' needs to be mobilised through a whole different set of attitudes. If 'an attitude of resignation is out of the question' (Nancy 2000: 54), one possible attitude against capture is that form of humour Deleuze describes as intrinsically lateral, which spreads milieus sideways and which he differentiates from irony operating as yet another stratifying regime of signification. Humour, by contrast, offers a topology of evasive moves and a continual slippage in which it seems implausible that capture could ever be finalised, and in which even extreme forms of closure are undone from within. Attitudes like these never cohere into models. They need to be played out rather than defined, and they need to animate rather than describe examples which in themselves do not illustrate anything but rather play alongside the fields they engage, '(like the German *Bei-Spiel*, that which plays alongside)' (Agamben 1993: 10). What these attitudes generate are clusters made up of works and situations and terms and concepts, and the very mobility that goes into generating them and that can in turn be recuperated from their assemblage. The nature and scope of this mobility is the possibility itself of re-configuring, no matter on what level. Its horizon is not redemption but operation. 'No, freedom was not what I wanted', says the ape when talking about how he invented his way out of the cage, 'only not to stay motionless with raised arms, crushed against a wooden wall' (Kafka 1999b: 253f.). There always needs to be a way out, or at least the possibility that one could be invented. The traps which are opened onto ways out here are Andreas Slominski's,[1] and the approach to what they set up, what (if anything) they enclose and what kind of mobilities they allow for, is assembled mainly from what Deleuze puts forward as humour. Bringing them together re-configures both beyond the frameworks within which they are generally negotiated and at the same time challenges some of the more redemptive claims made for either.

But first back to that other reading of the trap as capture: read in terms of its overall functional horizon, a trap rigidly frames a creature into immobility, one that is otherwise and originally unframed in its inhabitation of a given and normally shared environment (it is the sharing that is contested, and that the trap is set up to regulate). Waiting for the animal's movement and then body to complete the set-up, the trap's apparatus is a more or less elaborate device for bringing about closure, set in anticipation of an action and acting merely as a trigger to generate finite conclusions. Produced are tangible, even quantifiable results: once the trap snaps close, its success and degree of efficiency can be measured by what remains in the mechanical fangs, as it were. The intricacies of its arrangement, its making, placing and setting are purely preparatory in this scenario and important only as preliminaries to the outcome they facilitate.

All this is thought from the perspective of an end where the trap appears as point of closure for a movement it terminates and completes by cutting it off. Yet reading the trap as cut-off point is always reductively simple. First, because it simplifies what happens at this end and indeed beyond it. Not even the closed trap is necessarily definitive since the trap itself does not have to seal the fate of the prey. Rather, the basic principle and sole common denominator of traps is the (more or less drastic and more or less temporary) restriction of movement. The use then made of that condition is a separate issue – killing is only one such use, close examination or even simply transit and transport are others. All of these are arrangements of movement that overspill the idea of

210 Deleuze and Contemporary Art

even the closed trap as static by inscribing them into a scale of differing degrees (of constraint, of mobility), so that even the restrictions they produce need to be read in terms of the modifications of movement they produce, rather than being read in relation to the stasis they supposedly move towards.

Any reading premised on an apparent finality of the trap as endpoint overlooks the connections set up in preparation of the catch which are always on the edge of overspilling the trap. '[E]ven technology makes the mistake of considering tools in isolation: tools exist only in relation to the interminglings they make possible or that make them possible' (Deleuze and Guattari 1988: 90), so that what is ostensibly a dominating machine is always also (at least possibly) a connector that follows an operating logic that is at least as reliant on fusions as it is on separations. Even if one were to assume the finality of a full trap, up until that point the trap is necessarily an arrangement of attractions and interferences, not simply an outcome. It consists not so much in an action comple(men)ting a given setting, but rather in setting up (soliciting, facilitating and arranging) encounters as partial overlaps between territories that only ever seem to blend in the moment of their coming together when the trap snaps shut. Traps are always multiple set-ups because they involve at least two courses of events (one empirical and one potential, one habitual and one exceptional, one regular and one illegitimate) and fundamentally negotiate their interferences as interplay where inside and outside, movement and stillness, are simply indications of different states on a sliding scale of forms and motions. Capture then ceases to be a functional horizon and starts occurring instead in a whole series of attitudes, attractions and sympathies that prolong themselves right through to the inside of the trap, and out again.[2]

From the start and in the very nature of its make-up, any trap is primarily an insert premised on the implicit assumption that there already is a territory – normally that of the elusive and/or dangerous animal – that this territory is worth interfering with and that it is made up of patterns of movement (path) or of behaviour (habit) which can be known, at least vaguely, and translated into trajectories to be crossed. And rather than complementing this territory in the same way in which an action complements a setting by fulfilling it, a trap adds to this original milieu by doubling parts of it, and reaching out for a movement (it is movement that triggers off traps) that takes place in its own separate milieu, its own set of conditions, possibilities and arrangements. One milieu is a supposedly given habitual set of patterns carried out by the animal, the other is set up by the trap and synthetic; but their crossing is of the order of the encounter and dislodges both.

The trap is a mode of interfering that involves and requires smell to be copied and re-placed, directions to be deviated ever so slightly, and sets up the potential of tension in anticipation of a finalising impact. The hunt for food as way into the hole, the bite at the bait as the snap of the trap, operate first and foremost through replications. They replicate food as bait, jaws as steel and bite as snap, invert the bite at the bait into the snap of the trap and in doing so not only catch, but re-arrange elements that make up the animal's trajectory: its paths and preferences for certain spots over others, its most desired smells and tastes and forms of attention.

By appropriating bits of processes, sequences of movement and patterns of preference, a trap assemblage encompasses both the trap and the animal as diagrammatic configurations. Necessarily accounting for the animal 'less by its genus, its species, its organs, and its functions, than by the assemblages into which it enters' (Deleuze and Parnet 2002: 69),[3] the trap replicates and appropriates the animal by turning it into a complex of operations. This translation affects the animal as much as its territory. Caught in the same overlapping connectivity of operations, the existing territory and the trap's setting are likewise assemblages, neither spatial nor natural but operational. In the sense of what Deleuze and Parnet call the relays, echoes and working interactions of creative functions, traps too 'are not encounters between domains, for each domain is already made up of such encounters in itself' (28), but 'rather an encounter between two reigns, a short-circuit, the picking up of a code' (44). Setting a trap thus does not consist in the (re)creation of a complete environment to duplicate the supposedly natural habitat of the species at stake. On the contrary: for the trapper, a habitat, too, only ever exists as a functional arrangement made up of attractions and needs and patterns and all the provisions to accommodate these. Understanding the environment means being able to break it down into an (always approximate) understanding of its make-up and thus being able to interfere with it by multiplying and/or substituting attractors, movements and trajectories.

This is how, in a work by Slominski, an arrangement of plastic tubing can become a *Fox Trap* (1998) that replicates the den without copying it through the kind of operation Deleuze and Guattari define as a 'productive mapping' in contrast to a reproductive and representative 'tracing' (Deleuze and Guattari 1988: 12f.). Slominski's setting up of tubes and attractions is fox den as diagram and not as image (copy), and sets up movement as trajectory and condition within which a trapping can best take place. The narrow tube and its arrangement are an approach to the condition most suited for the particular capacities and preferences of the fox in movement. Rather than the replication of a natural given, coming close to the model here is an optimisation of conditions.[4] Those that seem most appropriate, promising and thus appealing for the fox are reconstituted in an attempt to appropriate and integrate its movements. The trap operates by what Deleuze calls stealing, in the context of a different kind of capture: a capture that does not produce closure (capture of the animal), but that 'takes hold of a form and a subject to extract from them variable speeds and floating affects' (Deleuze and Parnet 2002: 99). This is a way of interfacing through 'capture and thefts' (14), dislodging 'combinations of fluxes, emissions of particles at various speeds' (98) and re-arranging them in an assemblage 'the only unity [of which] is that of co-functioning' (69). Stealing or finding become operations of the encounter, and contrast with the normative operations of 'regulating, recognizing and judging' that rely on clear-cut entities and established relationships between these (8). The trap is set up as an interface to, not as the opposite of, the animal's habitual movements in an overall smooth space of solicited entanglements.

Features (bifurcations and zigzag) and conditions (narrow long spaces to be traversed) of the den are appropriated yet re-arranged so as to constitute a different sort of territory. They differ above all else in their directionality: whilst the den is an open-ended arrangement of entries and exits, the tubing is centred and one-way in character. Lured in by the scent of the bait, the fox is prevented from exiting. The trap aims at a convergence between the two movements that eliminates their distance in space and difference in character and interlocks them in a forced joint duration. That is the horizon of the trap as fulfilled potential where relationships are stable and lasting.

Yet whilst the den assembles a functional machine for engaging the world (survival), the trap consists in the reverse engineering of an approximating functional analogy for the purpose of closure (catching), and so relationships between den and trap have to be established before the trap can be imposed on the den. Any setting of the trap is firstly an attempt at setting up the sheer possibility of interference. The interception of the animal takes place in the collision between a movement on one side and a partial reconstitution of its setting on the other side. Any set-up is a trap only after having been a (partial) facilitator (the 'nature-artifice distinction is not at all relevant here' because both are synthetic if that term designates a composite of functional elements) (Deleuze and

Parnet 2002: 98). Once the given territory is understood as assemblage, it too is a 'nature which must be constructed' and always already is (98).

Setting it up is therefore to aim at contact between two assemblages that are different in nature as well as already heterogeneous in their respective make-ups. The difficult part is making all the elements of a non-homogeneous set, making them function together. Structures are linked to conditions of homogeneity, but assemblages are not. The 'assemblage is co-functioning, it is "sympathy", symbiosis' and as such happens in the (partial) overlap of operations (Deleuze and Parnet 2002: 52). The encounter between den and trap is an approximation along operational lines rather than mimetic ones and replaces the linear coming close of similarity with the multiple coming together of functional sub-sets and their short-circuited operations. The trap is not a copy but re-arranges these sets and operations in an approximating combination. Its working takes off from wherever contact is established because it consists much more centrally in interfering with and getting involved in the animal's movements, perceptions and operations, than it does in potentially catching it.[5] First and foremost (and certainly for the exhibition context), the trap adds to the existing animal assemblage, albeit in an attempt to subtract the very animal from that assemblage. And since the points of interference are multiple in terms of their elements, in terms of the way in which they encounter each other and in terms of the quality of their outcomes, the relationship between animal, environment and trap remains quintessentially unstable.[6] It is articulated through the very interrelationship between attitudes, forms and their mutual contaminations.

One place from which to revisit the trap in terms of such expanded connectivities is the difference between a mode of 'sympathy' on the one hand and patterns of 'seduction' on the other. *Seduction* as a dimension of the trap's overall projected horizon places the emphasis on strategic functionality and is fundamentally uni-directional. The *sympathetic* exchanges between trap and den that determine both its making and its processes of operation are, however, not only multiple but also multi-directional: attractors and their arrangements have to be configured with 'deepest sympathy', in a balance of variables that is always experimental (Deleuze and Parnet 2002: 52). A tentative solicitation of the encounter through the setting up of attractions as connective sympathising, enabling a co-functioning lateral to scripted procedures. Suspended in hopeful anticipation that an encounter will take place, this lure is the effective condition of the trap and stands in stark contrast to the finite character of the projected outcome. Against the implicit claim of a close fit that collapses both territories into one that is manageable and under control, the set-up opens onto a multiplicity of possible contacts before the decisive moment of the trap snapping to or not. It is in and from this moment of suspended outcome that this ambient proliferation of encounters can be played out, as a way of overspilling closure.

For the individual sample of a targeted species, this is mainly a question of the relation to bait or scent or the appeal of a fragment of environment. But for the trap as a device and an invention this interface is multiplied further because it always aims at a population, not just an individual specimen. This plural imposes its own approximating condition which distinguishes traps from weapons and improvisations. Weapons are applied in a specifically focused way, directly aimed as they are at a target; improvisations feed directly on the immediate conditions of a given situation. Both are ways of responding to a specific set of elements and simultaneously projecting them as targets and set horizons for their operations. A trap by contrast works on assumptions of a more general kind. It is premised on a notion of plausibility that comes out of the history of its use and its having been tested on the real. Embodying the knowledge of a trade, traps have a history of development and optimisation that constantly attempts to narrow the gap between their own workings and that of the territory preyed upon. But precisely because traps inevitably encompass this sum of experiences and failures and improvements, closure inevitably remains evasive. The width of encounters and the notion of the population itself defy it and as such undermine any finitude.

Instead of snapping shut, Slominski's *Mass Mousetrap* (1990), which literally hinges on a tube attracting mice to then tip them into a bucket and swing back into position immediately after, is a device for continual processing that groups multiples in one direction and organises their movement as an entry without exit. Often in traps, the re-setting is an implicitly acknowledged but well-disguised background of the trap's operations. Here, it is one of its most prominent dimensions and highlights the infinite populations it is set up to take on. Since the tube swings back into position each time a mouse has passed and tipped the tube into a slide, re-setting the device consists solely in emptying the bucket before the volume of mice inside reaches critical mass. The emptying has to be imagined as a repetitive gesture in a futile attempt to eliminate masses. And like the individual prey, these masses too have to be thought of as multiple. Additionally and always in the background lurk all those other animals that might not have responded to this

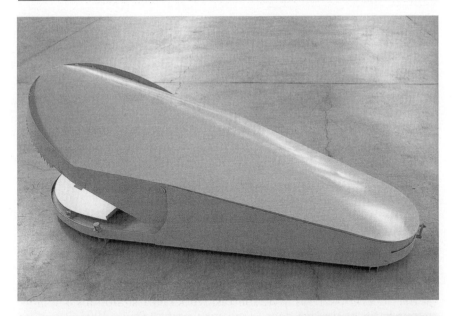

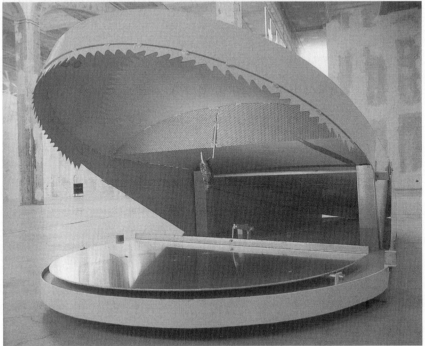

12.1 & 12.2: Andreas Slominski, *Leopard Trap*, 2002, aluminium, paint, 67 × 103 × 207 cm. Courtesy: Fondazione Prada, Milan. Photo: Attilio Maranzano.

set-up, that remain indifferent to the type of bait or are deterred by the construction itself, other active populations not reached by this machine that remain to be grasped by other machines, both existing ones and those yet to be invented. Plural in populations and multiple in attractions and modes of encounter, trap arrangements are never complete because there is no definitive trap and never just one register they have to answer to. Control is only ever containment (if that) and thus vague and only relative, constantly allowing for change and invention. This is why, in trapping, there is always a broad range of technically very different traps targeting the same species. And it is how a whole range of Slominski's traps targeting very different species can be juxtaposed in one and the same territory without this superimposition affecting their basic, always already multiple operations. Juxtaposing traps for different species and traps aiming at the same type of animal, some of them similar, some very different, in one and the same space, Slominski only highlights their mutual overlaps and necessary lack of overarching efficiency. Where a trap for leopards (*Leopard Trap*, 2002), a re-enforced container for aggressive dogs (*Trap for Combat Dogs*, 2001–2), and a housing suggestion for guinea pigs (*Guinea-Pig Trap*, 1997–8) come together and constitute an excessive overlap of solicited territories, they inevitably mark out more potential inhabitations than the one(s) they respectively target. One only ever multiplies the other in an always potentially expandable series. Setting them up remains a tentative activity on all levels – an elaborate staging that hijacks preferences to divert movements, to introduce altered trajectories by always only partially following lines of attraction. Against an ever-receding horizon of all-encompassing efficiency, the real activity of the trap arrangement lies in setting up a becoming possible of contact and in arranging the coming together of trap and prey as a sympathetic intertwining.

For the situation set-up by the trap, this establishes a new type of grid. 'A thing, an animal, a person are now only definable by movements and rests, speeds and slownesses (longitude) and by affects, intensities (latitude)' on a field of 'cinematic relations between unformed elements', as Deleuze outlines it, rather than being defined as or indeed definable by established sets of characteristic features (Deleuze and Parnet 2002: 93). The 'map of speeds and intensities' resulting from this kind of account can never account for results and closure and has to replace questions of particular characteristic qualities with an attention to modes of movement and their overlaps (93).[7]

Slominski's traps negotiate the crossovers of these multiple solicitations on a ground where trajectories are organised along lines of attraction and directed across the adjoining surfaces of the floor and the trap. In a proliferation of traps for mice, hamsters, guinea pigs, the prey operates on floor level. Their traps are set up as a continuation of this ground that directs movements by leading snails up a slope that continues the floor at a slight angle (*Ditch to Trap Slugs*, 1998), and by guiding mice up a ramp that takes off from the ground by continuing and diverting it in a whole variety of mouse traps. What matters here is that this floor is sometimes tilted, sometimes folded up but never pierced.[8] Rather than digging out a double ground as a challenge to the integrity of the given space, these traps project themselves onto it. Even where a weighed-down lid balances precariously above the bait to make up a *Trap to Throttle Small Vermin* (1992), the decisive gap is constituted between additional grounds that open only to then come down again. And *Birdstation* (1998/2002) folds up in the form of nets that become a container of three-dimensional space only when activated.[9] In all of these, depth and the puncture of a given ground are replaced with the modulations of a plane that translates one movement into another.[10]

Deleuze elaborates such smoothly lateral types of motion as a form of *ad-venture* in his reading of *Alice in Wonderland*: It is 'by sliding' that Carroll's Alice arrives at 'her climb to the surface, her disavowal of false depth and her discovery that everything happens at the border. This is why Carroll abandons the original title of the book: *Alice's Adventures Underground*' (Deleuze 1990: 9), why Deleuze himself reads Carroll, and why Slominski places his traps on the surface of the gallery floor and negotiates encounters by overlapping trajectories on top of it. 'Digging and hiding', which are the beginning of Alice's journey and conventionally prominent forms of making traps, here '[give] way to a lateral sliding' that stays at the surface: 'It suffices to follow it far enough, precisely enough and superficially enough in order to reverse sides' and get to the other side of the trap (9).[11]

In *The Logic of Sense*, this is played out, once more, as a logic of humour, or 'the art of the surface, which is opposed to the old irony, the art of depths and heights' (Deleuze 1990: 9). Whilst irony introduces different distinct levels and occurs in their clashes, in humour 'all height and depth [is] abolished' (141). The shift from irony to humour marks a change mainly of direction, 'one could say that the old depth having been spread out became width' (9).[12] Movement towards and into the ground spreads out into a continual lateral displacement that inaugurates an 'art of the surfaces and of the doubles, of nomad singularities and of the always displaced aleatory point' between juxtaposed milieus (141). No longer grounded, this art and the exposed trap[13] take up a

12.3: Andreas Slominski, *Snow-Grouse Trap*, 2002, wood, iron, wire mesh, paint, 57 × 159 × 258 cm. Courtesy: Fondazione Prada, Milan. Photo: Roberto Marossi.

random position on the floor, which becomes its sheer support rather than constituting its material. A sledge/container such as *Snow-Grouse Trap* (2002) does more than simply integrate the transportation of the prey into the make-up of the trap as an additional function. Rather it places the image of an environment on the surface of the floor on runners so that it skids and turns into an explicitly mobile occupation. The perspective of the quest and its focus of direction are replaced with a laterality that occupies a plane by moving sideways along it.[14]

In doing so, the trap opens up to a proliferation of encounters not only with its prey, but also with other occurrences taking place on the same plane. When a trap takes the form of a rocking horse (*Mouse Trap*, 2003), it challenges the supposed idyll of a child's playroom and incorporates it into the extended play of a becoming childish. Another one, from the same year and under the same title, fuses the exhibition space with the festival by appropriating the garish decor of the latter. In the same move, their visual appeal mirrors animal behaviourism into a play with aesthetic responses habitually codified along the stimulus-response lines of decoration and advertising. Next to the ornamental excesses of domesticity and the child's playroom, the advertising-led design of a brightly branded tin-drum, too, coexists then with a new set of appeals for a new set of audiences set up by using the drum for a bird trap (*Bird Trap*, 2000–1) which also exists under the conditions of an art piece. In all of these, the trap is the ungrounded and blatantly exposed *aleatory point* of more or less plausible encounters, and creates a level playing field for the different machines and milieus invoked. The diverse assemblages are grounded by the overarching condition of their supposed functionality, but grounded only ever as heterogeneous assemblages and in a mobile way, as an engagement with potential inhabitations. The trap serves as a working premise here and a particular operation of linkage, not as a metaphor for their motivation. Exceeding notions of and allusions to nature, these traps install a multiplicity of milieus that set up environments as well as formats and attitudes of interference. Way outside the parameters of reasonable efficiency, the impossible horizon of function is supplanted by an indifferent excess of theft that (re-)claims the cage, the trap, domesticity,[15] but also the readymade, craftsmanship and the attitude of the trapper.[16]

The obvious exposure of their workings on the hyper-visibility of the gallery floor forecloses the depth of analytic operations and undoes any detailed understanding and appreciation of the trap's making and mechanisms on the slippery surface of humour. Beyond the supposedly

12.4: Andreas Slominski, *Bird Trap*, 2000–1; tin, 60 × 23.5 × 37 cm
(left), *Bird Trap*, 2000–1, tin, 83.5 × 23.5 × 23.5 cm (right). Courtesy:
Fondazione Prada, Milan. Photo: Attilio Maranzano.

clear targets and prey, these traps cannot be 'closed on recognition,
but [are] open to encounters' (Deleuze and Parnet 2002: 24) that are in
themselves multiple. In and through the blur of the set-up, setting and
trap as well as background and action are fused as a complicated form
of mutual capture[17] that confuses supposedly discrete registers of the
assemblage and instead sets up potential sites of encounter as a series of
aleatory points.[18]

Encounters with the object now occur under unclear terms because
any possible critical distance makes way for an involvement for which
form is simply permeable: traps include smoothing out transitions, blurring the edges of different realms to such an extent that it becomes a
near-impossibility to designate an inside and an outside in relation to
them. Arranged on the flat surface of the exhibition space and articulat-
ing precisely this flatness as a milieu where attractions can be inserted,

played out and followed, the traps claim the ground for (and articulate the ground as) a smooth interplay of lateral attractions. Their simultaneously abstract and empirical morphology of humour evades capture precisely by playing into the trap.[19]

References

Agamben, G. (1993), *The Coming Community*, trans. M. Hardt, Minneapolis: University of Minnesota Press.

Deleuze, G. (1990), *The Logic of Sense*, ed. C. V. Boundas, trans. M. Lester with C. Stivale, London: Athlone Press.

Deleuze, G. and C. Parnet (2002), *Dialogues II*, trans. H. Tomlinson and B. Habberjam, London: Continuum.

Deleuze, G. and F. Guattari (1988), *A Thousand Plateaus*, trans. B. Massumi, London: Athlone Press.

Funcke, B. and J. Hoffman (1999), '"SlominSki" – A Conversation with Boris Groys', *Parkett*, 55: 99–102.

Haraway, D. (1991), 'A Cyborg Manifesto: Science, Technology, and Socialist-Feminism in the Late Twentieth Century', in *Simians, Cyborgs and Women: The Reinvention of Nature*, New York: Routledge.

Heynen, J. (1999), 'Wordless', *Parkett*, 55: 96–7.

Kafka, F. (1999a), 'The Burrow' [1924], in *Franz Kafka: The Complete Short Stories*, ed. N. N. Glotzer, trans. W. and E. Muir, London: Vintage.

Kafka, F. (1999b), 'A Report to an Academy' [1917], in *Franz Kafka: The Complete Short Stories*, ed. N. N. Glotzer, trans. W. and E. Muir, London: Vintage.

Nancy, J.-L. (2000), *Being Singular Plural*, trans. R. D. Richardson and A. E. O'Byrne, Stanford: Stanford University Press.

Spector, N. (1999a), 'Berlin Detours', *Parkett*, 55: 70–5.

Spector, N. (1999b), 'Of Traps, Tricks, and Other Riddles', in *Andreas Slominski* (exhibition catalogue), Berlin: Deutsche Guggenheim.

Wechsler, M. (1998), 'Kunst aus dem Hinterhalt: Ein Fall für Verblendung', in *Andreas Slominski*, Zürich: Kunsthalle.

Notes

1. The traps, in turn, appear in clusters. The cluster mobilised here was an installation at Fondazione Prada, Milan (*Andreas Slominski*, Fondazione Prada, Milan, 10 April–13 June 2003).

2. Unreading traps in particular through such ontological mobility not only challenges the very possibility of closure by playing out its undoing against its most explicit formation but it also mobilises this ontology against straight overall functionality, lifting its material from the (differently oriented) circulation it has for the trappers who use these machines in the first place. The appropriation of one form of knowledge for another usage needs to always be both indifferent and inappropriate, if it is to escape the condition of metaphor.

3. The assemblages are also constituted by different modes of attention that condition fundamentally different types of traps. Some are disguised and account for an ambient mode of perception, others functionalise a highly focused attention to the bait that necessarily excludes seemingly more marginal information. In

this model of the trap, its workings can be blatantly exposed because attention will not be brought to them.

4. Donna Haraway describes the transition from perfection to optimisation as one of the features of emerging 'informatics of domination' with 'biotic components' replacing the 'organism' (Haraway 1991: 167). In this reading, both fox and trap need to be understood as elements in a cyborg arrangement of feedback and control.

5. Boris Groys proposes this kind of sympathetic engagement as a central characteristic of Slominski's practice. He sees it as an attempt 'to say more with the fulfilment of expectations than with deviations from these expectations' (Groys, quoted in Funcke and Hoffman 1999: 100).

6. Shifting the focus towards the making and the processes invoked, solicited and triggered is not an art-effect, even though achieved through the art placement. It is rather at the very core also of the trade and craft of the trapper and constitutes the trapper's particular form of knowledge. In relation to the notion of the trapper and the complication of the readymade see also Spector (1999a and 1999b).

7. Even inside most traps, the animal is not still at all. Very often its movement is much more intense, because more contained. Movement is not arrested but organised in a different way. Although this could appear as a blatant illustration of the structural opposition between the planes of 'consistency' and 'organisation' (Deleuze and Parnet 2002: 91f.), to read it as such would reduce the trap to an outcome and foreclose an understanding of how its overall set-up aims at diverse (invisible) populations and potential inhabitations of space. The inverted mirror of this undoing lies in the den's potential for closure: in Kafka's 'The Burrow' (Kafka 1999a), the den/burrow can be a trap and vice-versa in a continual oscillation between protection and capture, and plays on the fundamental proximity between both types of assemblage. What is installed as a safeguard against intrusion is inevitably polyvalent and also potentially traps the inhabitant.

8. Even the fox's den in *Fox Trap* is arranged on the surface rather than underground.

9. Even birds are caught only at the moment when they approach the floor. In *Trap for Birds of Prey* (1997), they are (imagined as) impaled on its spiky extensions, in *Bird Trapping Compound* (1998–99) contained in its vicinity by the activated nets.

10. This flatness is not automatically a feature of all traps; see, for example, Carsten Höller's children's trap made by digging a hole on a beach and filling it with jellyfish before covering it with sand and baiting it with a toy (Carsten Höller, *Jenny*, 1992, 13 mins, colour, sound).

11. In Deleuze's reading of Carroll's Alice, sliding is primarily a movement between the two sides of the surface. Yet it is also a mode of engaging with material that oscillates ('slides') between registers of description and affirmation, analysis and claim, following the work and re-arranging it. A similar approach is adopted here for the engagement with Deleuze and Slominski: Alice's ad-venture is Deleuze's adventure with Carroll, their coming together with Slominski is mine.

12. Even though Slominski often interferes with the very fabric of the gallery setting, he digs no holes as traps that one might fall into. In a similar way to Alice's 'digging and hiding [giving] way to a lateral sliding' (Deleuze 1990: 9), Slominski's solicitations present an engagement with space that supplants the more metaphysical/ transcendental depths of, for example, Joseph Beuys' *Tramstop* in the German Pavillon of the Venice Biennale (1976) or Gordon

Matta-Clark's cuts, which are vertical as well as horizontal. In art historical references, Slominski's traps are closer to the anticipated effectivity of Marcel Duchamp's snow shovel set-up *In Advance of the Broken Arm* (1915) than they are to these only seemingly related excavations.

13. Slominski's traps are always exposed. In his actions/performances, the question of visibility is itself challenged; yet his ongoing series of traps exist and operate exclusively under the condition of the exhibition venue's hypervisibility. Max Wechsler argues that the exhibition space produces a visibility which contrasts with the trap's functionally inevitable invisibility to the animal (Wechsler 1998: 37f.). The problem is more complex however. Challenging precisely the visible as guarantor of either insight or safety, the traps stage the compossibility of their being set and being exposed. Looking at a trap does not stop it from operating since it is not automatically defused through recognition. Often, vision does not even come into the functionality of the trap, either because the gaze is simply not a dominant sensory regime, or because it is bypassed by other, stronger stimuli through which the visual becomes potentially irrelevant in spite of its explicit staging.

14. Institutional critique is intrinsically ironic in its claim for revelation because it relies on a crossing of separate layers of meaning production, through highlighting hidden layers underneath (a surface of appearances) or beyond (a veil of disguises). Its premise is necessarily transgressive and clearly directed even where it operates in contiguities/metonymies because the laterality of these moves gains its political, ideological and counter-institutional currency from the crossing of a supposedly given limit that normally blocks access. In the works under consideration here, *sliding* has to be understood as a different mode of movement that constitutes and operates in milieus, and is therefore aleatory rather than focused, and generates encounters rather than addressing organising structures.

15. *Guinea-Pig Trap* (1997–98) is a trap and a cage that looks like a house. It is probably the closest such fusion between habitat and domesticity that can be achieved – in the form of a trap that emulates the cage as given condition of the animal.

16. The level of their craftsmanship is only a further element in this arrangement; not the aim but the necessary condition of the trap and its functioning. Since they are either bought or reconstructed from existing models and functioning plans, craftsmanship is not the subject of perfection, but the embodiment of and response to processes. The traps incorporate and display a particular kind of knowledge rather than constructing it. Even the attitudes behind them are readymade parts of the assemblage. The work is not about the craft that has gone into their making and could be deciphered or appreciated in its product. On the contrary, the objects stand in as blatantly obvious embodiments of a skill base that does not have to hide behind the product but explicitly generates it as a particular form of knowledge; traps are machines, not objects. The craft of their making is invoked as a format that has its own tradition but then figures simply as a found attitude, a found history, a found charge in the overall set-up. All these elements and formats are 'captured', not 'produced', as is the formal vocabulary of sculpture (see also Wechsler 1998). The obvious pilfering of kitsch domesticity is just another level of this activity.

17. Function is set up only in order to challenge appropriateness. Even the exhibition as (intellectual and factual) 'minefield' (press release *Andreas Slominski*, Fondazione Prada, Milan, 10 April–13 June 2003) or 'landscape painting' (Heynen 1999: 96) viewers find themselves immersed in, is only ever a series of elements in an expanded 'geography of relations' (Deleuze and Parnet 2002: 56) set up by the works' multiple interferences.

18. That these cut across art and habitat, venue and situation is simply another register of its un-grounding confusions.
19. That this evasion needs to be played out rather than described, and that it involves a politics of dispersal across a whole series of inappropriate moves and oblique investments, is precisely one of the opportunistic luxuries of the example. Its singular ambiguity ('neither apathy nor promiscuity nor resignation') always makes it play up, 'just when one has decided to take it really seriously'; that 'the proper place of the example is always beside itself' may well be its strongest implicit promise (Agamben 1993: 10).

TECHNOLOGIES

Chapter 13

Sign and Information: On Anestis Logothetis' Graphical Notations

Claudia Mongini

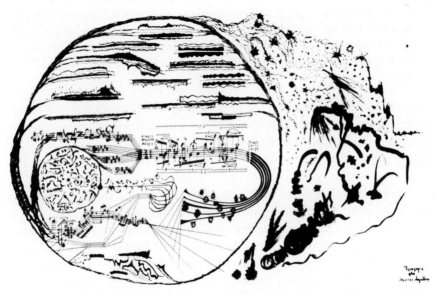

13.1: Anestis Logothetis, score for *Ichnologia*, 1964. From John Cage and Alison Knowles, *Notations*, 1969. Image courtesy of the Logothetis estate.

Signs for Polymorphic Compositions

'I construct my signs as an information source for sound', is a programmatic statement by the composer Anestis Logothetis.[1] In his 1974 text 'Signs as Aggregative State of Music' Logothetis relates the notion of sign as a musical notation to that of information, exploring the tension between his compositional directions and the performative freedom it leaves to the musicians.

Logothetis started to explore new methods of compositional notation in 1958, six years after Earle Brown first departed from standard

notation in his composition *December 52*,[2] and John Cage began exploring new acoustic territories by translating randomisation processes into
sounds.[3] Logothetis however, develops a different position from Brown
and Cage. He is not, as is Brown, interested in giving stimuli for improv-
isation, nor does he follow John Cage in making music into something
instantaneous and non-reproducible as a result of its randomised composition. He writes:

> The possibility of improvising – with all due respect to its liberating role –
> did not captivate my imagination. I had in mind, rather, to explore those
> limits where an object – in our case of an acoustical nature – offers itself
> in varied aspects, while it still radiates enough intrinsic features to be rec-
> ognized. This means creating something restrictive that takes into account
> the diverging reactions of the interpreters, from which, through feedback,
> the multiformity emerges of what is compulsorily read. (Logothetis 1975b:
> n.p.)

Logothetis thus emphasises the importance of the functional and informational aspects of the notation, which neither improvisational endeavours nor chance manipulations take into account. This theoretical
exploration of the relationship between written signs and played sounds
was a result of his extensive studies of musical history, which led him to
the conclusion that a new form of musical notation was necessary for
the development of a wider range of sound organisation.

On the other hand, Logothetis shares with Cage and Brown a dis-
satisfaction with music completely determined by the imagination and
authority of the 'composer-initiator' and the use of pentagrammatic
notation.[4] The traditional form of musical notation represses, according to Logothetis, a great number of 'gliding and vibrating' sounds –
tonalities that the composer clearly distinguishes from noise – because
they cannot be fixed within the five staffs of standard notation. These
sounds were thus kept outside of the 'musical' realm.[5]

Logothetis is determined to integrate these 'exterior' sounds into his
work, not through a prescriptive approach, but in a performative, generative way; his notation aims to activate processual sound flows that take
account of the situation in which they are played and the mood of the
interpreter. The result is not a fixed sound, completely predetermined
by the composer, but the active production of a rich variety of gliding
tonalities. An example of such a gliding tonality is the noise produced by
a fly caught under a glass cylinder, which the composer recorded for his
work *Daidalia* (1976–78). The composer developed a sensitivity to these
kind of tonalities through attempts to carefully and obsessively grasp

the most disparate noises deriving from natural sources as well as from technical devices, and translating them into both instrumental and vocal performance.[6] Furthermore, Logothetis sees the importance of assigning the same level of significance to qualitative aspects of sounds as to quantitative features; that is, elements like intensity, density, dispersion, timbre, etc., are treated in the same way as the pitch and the duration of a tonality, which is the key information that pentagrammatic notation provides. Logothetis describes the momentary and multiform nature of these gliding tones as 'polymorphy'. Whilst 'monomorphic' sounds represent a specific 'motif', a 'polymorphic' composition 'would show one of its many aspects at a time in every interpretation and would allow for the simultaneous performance of different interpretations' (Logothetis 1975b: n.p.).

In order to construct a notation able to produce this complex panorama of sounds, Logothetis drew on his previous education as a building engineer. He referred to the semantics of the word 'architecture', composed by the pairing of *arché*, meaning beginning or precept, and *tektoniké*, denoting giving birth (Logothetis 1998: 95).[7] An *architectural notation* would activate a process that evolves within the settings defined by each performance; the bodies of the musicians, the instruments, the technical and electronic devices used, as well as the audience and the physical space in which the performance takes place. Following the architectural analogy, many of the composer's works are contained within a single page, in contrast to John Cage, who often made use of dozens of notation sheets in order to express his musical thoughts (Henke 1996: 44). Furthermore, the signs and symbols of an architectural map allow the reader to establish a *unequivocal* relation with the object that is to be considered. Logothetis translates this relationship between signs and sounds to his 'plans', which are characterised by a variety of shapes that at first glance seem to have the aesthetic character of a drawing rather than the functional purpose of a sheet of music. Logothetis coins the term 'mandatory association' to specify the expressive content of his signs; the spatio-temporal dimensions of the composition have to be *precisely* discerned by its interpreters, and driven into sound through their affective states. The term 'mandatory' is not understood as leading to a pre-established interpretation, rather the accuracy it suggests produces diverging reactions amongst the interpreters, whose singular expressions are an integral part of the composition itself. It is the precision of the interpreters' approach to the notation that accounts for the development of the polymorphic tonality of the shapes.

The conceptual and theoretical tracks on which the scenario is formed lead to an expression of affective 'disruptions' and 'attacks' that, operating as a feedback process, reconfigure the initial 'architecture' out of which the music is generated (Logothetis 1998: 95). The notation thus not only has a semiotic character as a representation and preservation of sound events but can also be understood in terms of a diagram. Within this diagram the signs have three different roles: 'Symbols' give a specific tonality or pitch; 'association signs' give properties like intensity, duration, change of timbre, etc.; and 'signals' are long lines or curves of various intensity and thickness that give patterns to be simulated by the instrument. As in traditional notation, symbols define sounds in a structural way, while the other two signs have more of a transitional character, as they provide a means of sliding from one pitch to another, defining a dynamic of various speeds in between singular sounds.

Whilst in Logothetis' first attempts to escape pentagrammatic notation we can still perceive the difference between these three classes of signs, it soon becomes clear that the composer's ambition goes beyond this classification system. The lines of the associative signs and signals melt with the punctual symbols to generate a *becoming* from one tonality to another; a *deviation* from the punctual path drives an individual symbol into a dividual sign, which allows for an exploration of the tonalities between distinctive sounds and white noise.[8] Traditional, singular, isolated notes do not capture such a series of subtle tonalities; Papaioannou notes that Logothetis replaces – as do other contemporary avant-garde composers such as Cage, Ligeti, Christou and Xenaxis – the concept of singular isolated notes with patterns. In particular Logothetis translates a rich variety of visual patterns into a fine web of sound by the superimposition of

> the divergent interpretation of the same score at the same time by different members of the performing group: each one introduces his own personality by a different reading of the same sign (or group of signs) – and the corresponding variation can be quite an extensive one, while strictly respecting the basic nature of the sign(s); these different readings are superimposed without precise synchronisation. (Papaioannou 1975: n.p.)

The convergence and precision of the reading, implied by the term 'mandatory association', is given by the fact that everyone interprets the same signs that refer to the quantitative rules, symbols and signals, as outlined above. But the rigour required by Logothetis' compositions includes an extreme degree of variation, as the singular, momentary expressions of the players are taken into account. It is not the one-to-one relationship between a sign and a sound that produces the exactness intended by the

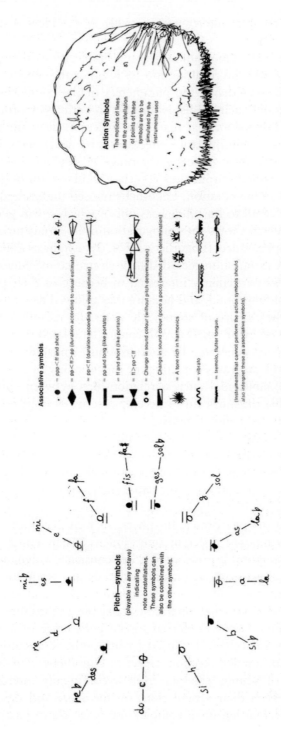

13.2: Anestis Logothetis, *Musical Signs*. From Anestis Logothetis, 'On Musical Notation', in *Anestes Logothetes: Concise Documentation on Anestis Logothetis*. Image courtesy of the Logothetis estate.

composer, but a complex intertwining between *assemblages* of signs and sound *events*.

This procedure has important conceptual implications that produce significant changes in the resulting music; it is not the precise pitch or a regular rhythm that define the parameters of the composition, but topological functions such as (dis)continuity, smoothness vs. roughness, and density vs. dispersion, that mark the structural lines along which the music evolves. A multiplicative effect arises by which the synergy of the musicians' interaction increases the range of available sounds to a vast degree. The sound output thus reflects a similar form of grouping to that observed in the notation. Logothetis himself understands sound as the '*synthesis* of all technical devices out of which it was generated, like a material which shows the configuration of its atoms through the structure of its appearance' (Logothetis 1974: 35, emphasis added). The technical devices in question included new electronic machines, which the composer was particularly interested in because of their potential for generating gliding sound, and because they allowed new conceptual approaches to the essence of sound. He notes, for example, that the sounds constructed by an oscillograph cannot be related to a punctual notation, as they are generated by a (continuous) sinusoidal curve. On the other hand, the diagrams depicting the functionality of these devices (electric circuits, sinusoidal curves, relationships between sound and impedance) enable the musician to develop a series of optical signs for sound shapes into the realm of music.

In Logothetis' notations the conception of time is of particular interest, as it is more complex than the one set by the traditional left–right axis of standard notation. In those of his scores characterised by a signature in each of the four corners of the paper such as *Osculationen* (1964) and *Linienmodulationen* (1965), Logothetis leaves the decision of the starting point to the interpreter. In others, such as *Dynapolis* (1963), Logothetis superimposed different time dimensions by constructing a multiplicity of temporal centres so as to re-construct a dynamic city.[9] These different dimensions of musical intervals are often constructed in order to lead to a succession of continuous sound formations (*Klanglichkeit*) with varying tonal colour; again architecture was an inspiration as the composer referred to the persistence of a building surviving the gradual changes caused by atmospheric conditions and time. There is also a mnemotechnic aspect to Logothetis' time-patterns. The formation of sounds emerges from a continually interchanging relationship between their articulations on the score and the musical performances, accounting for a complex interweaving of past, present and future. Music becomes memory, not through aesthetic analogy, but through the gradual accumulation of the materials (the particular notational plan, its translation into sound and the choice of the specific performative devices) out of which it is generated (Logothetis 1974: 34). Moreover, and as we have seen, his constructive methodology does not aim to drag the musicians or audience into a particular mood, but encourages the expression of their actual psychic caprices, as singular affective states and 'intellectual brainwork' are put into a state of mutual interaction. In this sense music is *played*. The interpreter is not put in front of an already fully existing composition, but enters into a process that on the one hand follows specific rules, but on the other is also open for polymorphic shaping, surprises and chance. The affective charge of the composition is not simply determined by the composer, but includes the momentary expressions of each performer that feed back into the process of the composition itself. For Logothetis music is thus understood as *dance*, inasmuch as it is the interweaving of these diverse but nonetheless immanent elements. This scenario also requires another form of participation by the public; the listeners do not become emotionally involved through their recollection of known tonalities, but by the effect of the instant and singular sound constellation to which they contribute, inasmuch as their presence might evoke particular reactions within the players. The pleasure of recognising already heard melodies, the motivation for much of the audience at classical music concerts, is replaced by the joy of discovering new sound experiences.

In this regard, thinking through an image that Deleuze and Guattari attribute to John Cage (Deleuze and Guattari 1987: 267), it is possible to say that Logothetis, like the American composer, frees the singular moment by detaching the expressive 'now' from a structure of duration. But the 'floating time' that he generates is not set 'against all structure and genesis' as is the case for Cage, but arises from the structural and generative moments of 'pulsed time or tempo' given by his three categories of signs. The acts of experimenting, of acting creatively in the bubble of the instant, and those of interpretation, which instead follow an already created structure, are not opposed, but intertwine within a space of mutual composition and reciprocal determination. In this way, Logothetis' precise distinction between different signs functions to decelerate the infinite speeds of chaos. It enables a *degree of consistency* to be constructed between heterogeneous elements; the molecular elements of the composition, the specific function of the technical devices, and the affective states of the interpreters. A 'calculated sobriety' enables a clear distinction between the singular compositional elements and allows the composition to 'open onto something cosmic, instead of lapsing into a statistical heap' (Deleuze and Guattari 1987: 344).

Information as Vital Dynamism

The development of cybernetic theory in the 1950s and '60s, with information as one of its key concepts, was a crucial influence on Logothetis' work. For example, the composer actively inserted the principle of feedback into his compositions; the flow of information in Logothetis' musical production is not directed solely from the composition to the players, as the recordings of single (unique) performances were often used to reshape the notation themselves. Furthermore, the public contributes in an active way to the momentary affective state defining the singularity of each performance; electronic recording and sound-processing devices also allow for an investigation into what has already been performed, which can then be translated into new sounds and graphic patterns.

Although Logothetis made use of cybernetic principles in order to construct his notation, it is questionable if a cybernetic 'strategy' could be used to analyse, a posteriori, the oeuvre of the composer.[10] The problem concerns the definition of information in relation to noise. In information theory, the two quantities have an inverse relationship to each other, the more noise enters into the system, the less information it contains (Wiener 1953: 33). As we have seen, this strict distinction between information and noise, between the 'usable' element on one side and the carrier of disruption on the other, is not consistent with Logothetis' intentions.

It is possible, however, to use another definition of the term 'information', one that is more suitable to Logothetis' compositions, by turning to the theory developed by the French philosopher Gilbert Simondon. Simondon's book *Du mode d'existence des objets techniques* was published in 1958, the same year in which Logothetis began to work on his graphical notation. Although there is no evidence that Logothetis and Simondon were aware of each other's work, they both conducted a careful study of cybernetic principles and actively introduced them into their work. On the other hand, both dismiss the reductionist aspects intrinsic to information theory, which retains an idealised system in which the main components of sender, receiver, channel, sent information and noise, can be clearly distinguished from each other and are able to be quantified mathematically. Simondon and Logothetis adopt a 'strategy' that Deleuze and Guattari would call *diagrammatic* (Deleuze and Guattari 1987: 145), and both extract the key concepts of the math-ematical theory of information and combine them with notions pertain-ing to other fields of knowledge; anthropology and sociology in the case of Simondon, and aesthetics for Logothetis. In both cases there is a higher form of abstraction involved, a sort of translational meta-theory, which is not to be understood as representative of scientific observations or artistic expressions, but as a tool allowing for the construction of new forms of composition.

In *Du mode d'existence des objets techniques* Simondon is interested in questions regarding the nature of machines, their mutual relationship and their relationship to humans. By considering the principles of cyber-netics in relation to more general physical laws such as thermodynamics, electrical principles and quantum mechanics, he elaborates a concept of information understood as a *metastable state* between completely unde-termined noise and the strictly fixed form. Similarly, Logothetis situates information in between the pure randomness of aleatory sound and music defined by fixed pentagrammatic notation. Information carries, according to its nature, determination to the system. On the other side, in the absence of any indetermination within the system, no new state can be brought to the system and information thus ceases to have any creative effect.

Information is by definition unforeseeable by the system it relates to, but its result is foreseeable because it leads to regularity and periodicity, that is, to form (Simondon 1958: 252–3). In accordance with gestalt theory, Simondon understands form as an upper limit to the acquisition of transmitted information (Moles 1987: 110). But what demarcates the difference between Simondon and the psychological theories of perception is the importance he assigns to dynamics. Form is not an entity necessarily defined a priori, as it is in Gestalt theory; it is shaped, destabilised and reshaped through the information flow itself. Another fundamental discrepancy between form and information is that the latter cannot be conceived as a single and enclosed term, but because of its metastable character it is necessarily bound to a difference between at least two energetic levels; heterogeneity is not a property that arises from a procedure of subsequent differentiation, but is intrinsic in the initial condition itself.

Due to this procedural character, information cannot be given an abstract ideal value – an informational correlate to the Gestalts of the square or the circle – but is always dependent on context, on the field of forces at play in the 'now'. More than being determined by pure – abstract and context independent – quantitative or qualitative values, the reality of information is better captured by a *measure of intensity*. This is not a measure of a predefined pattern of organisation, but quantifies a tendency towards organisation in relation to the general degree of entropy in the system. It is not the property of a specific point that is taken into account here, but the *general state of an area*, as is the case in the study of electric or magnetic fields. The systems in question are characterised by *states of disadaptation* that arise when information reaches a critical state. This means that at some crucial stage the general configuration of the system is affected, and it is reshaped towards a new state. Disadaptation is thus inherently different to the notion of degradation, which designates processes of decay.

Thus the onset of information does not produce a well-defined quantitative result, but generates processes of *internal resonance* within the receiving system.[11] It constitutes a *flow* of subtle communications between structures of different degrees, producing a continuous renewal of their organisational patterns.

This broader understanding of information allows Simondon to translate this concept from the realm of physics and to apply it to the affective life and social configurations of the subject. This is the general content of Simondon's subsequent books, *L'individu et sa genèse physico-biologique* and *L'individuation psychique et collective*, first published together in 1964 under the title *L'individuation à la lumière des notions de forme et d'information*. These books develop the possibility of a translation of concepts and laws pertaining to inert systems to the realm of macrophysical organic states, by supposing an intermediary state of genetic, chronological and topological processes. This intermediary state consists of a particular topology in which a relationship between a psychic and an external space is produced, a sort of 'topology of the living', a form of mutual metastable presence between inside and outside, past and future. This is a liminal stage in which space and time are tightly interrelated within the same dimension of the sensitivity of the evolving living system. This complex topology, allowing for an intertwining between exterior and interior dimensions and coordinates, is peculiar to the procedural creation of living beings, as Deleuze in his comments on Simondon's work points out (Deleuze 2004: 88).[12] When information enters the domain of life, it becomes *vital dynamism*.

Through an operation of *dephasing*, in which the dimension of space gets disentangled from the dimension of time, information acquired by perceptual and sensational states is transduced into emotional and affective life. This process leads to an operation of *individuation* that positions the subject within the world. But a certain dimension of *archetypical pre-individuality remains*, allowing for new processes of dephasing to continuously arise. The individual is both a result of individuation and a potential for further individuation. Becoming is bound to a complex interrelation between space and time, emerging between the coordinates continuously detached from each other during dephasing, and re-attached as the potential for new individuation processes is recreated. As Toscano states, information becomes 'both the plan and the motor' of a metastable generative process (Toscano 2005: 144). This process not only accounts for the enabling of the organisation and the becoming of the individual on a singular level, but also for the genesis of collectivity on a social level. Collectivity here is not understood as the grouping of an ensemble of individuals fully individuated in a previous moment, but as a process involving a fragmented multiplicity of pre-individual potentials. A common action, a coincidence of time, combines these hidden energies into a process of resonance on a larger scale, accounting for the arousal of *transindividual* relations (Simondon 1964: 248–50).

It is at the level of this complex web of collective relations that the abstract quantity of information becomes a *sign*. A sign is created in the moment in which the code *flashes*, that moment when it acquires a particular intensity. In order for this event to happen, preliminary conditions of reception within what Deleuze calls a *signal* are necessary. A signal is a system that 'is constituted or bounded by at least two heterogeneous series, two disparate orders capable of entering into communication' (Deleuze 1994: 222). The intensity of the flash demarks the onset of another process of individuation, which is not placed on the level of singularity, but involves the elaborate composition of a collective formation.

Becoming Expressive: The Early Development of Logothetis' Graphical Notation.

The first examples of graphical notation the composer discusses in 'Signs as Aggregative State of Music' are *Structure, Texture, Mirror, Game* and *Parallaxe* (image 13.3), composed between 1959 and 1961. Both reveal the composer constructing a compositional plan by a procedure of gradual detachment from pentagrammatic notation. In the first composition the still very slick signs might recall the musical symbols contained in Wassily Kandisky's, *Point and Line to Plane* (1926), a book that Logothetis was particularly fond of (Henke 1996: 43). The notations are presented on different sheets according to their function

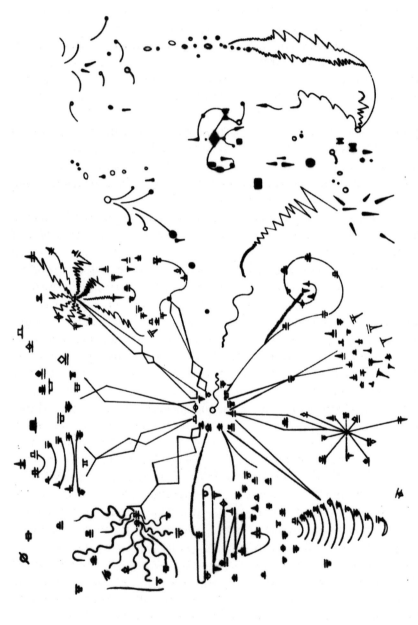

13.3: Anestis Logothetis, score for *Parallaxe*, 1961. From Krones (1998). Image courtesy of the Logothetis estate.

as symbols, association signs or signals. In *Parallaxe* they are integrated in order to form a single notation, which is the same for every musician involved in the piece. Both the titles suggest the active role of the players whilst performing the notations; they *play* the *structure* constructed by the composer in the sense that they optically acquire the signs and express them in sound according to their own affective states. Every performance allows for *parallaxes* – deviations, 'the shifts and the modifications of the [compositional] criteria' (Logothetis 1974: 51) in relation to the moods of the interpreters and the external conditions of the performance. If we follow the writings of the composer, we infer that *Parallaxe* also denotes the continuity between sound and noise, between the individuality of a single sign and a dividual assemblage; that is, the complex scenario accounting for *polymorphic* music, which is clearly distinguished from chaotic amorphousness inasmuch as the game's rules are precisely set (Logothetis 1998: 147).

Using Simondon's terminology, we might describe these early compositions as an information flow in which Logothetis' signs are *dephased* into the actual state of autonomous intensities, that is, the elaborate assemblage of performers, audience and technical devices that produce the singularity of the musical event. The original *form*, the predefined score, is expressed in Logothetis' work through an intertwining of different levels; flowing architecture, language, mathematical logic, expression of psychic states, and dance, all coexisting components of what he understands under the notion of 'music'. This aspect is further developed in his '*Musik-Hörspiele*' (musical dramas) where the music is extended by visual inputs that open up more means of expression. In the opera *Karmadharmadrama* for example – composed between 1961 and 1967[13] – the dancer draws the musical notation on the walls, according to specific directions given by the composer, which the musicians subsequently interpret (Logothetis 1972: 544–5). It is in this sense that one can conceive Logothetis' scores as *flows of metastable information*, as it is 'readable but not ritualisable, not literally repeatable' (Logothetis 1975a: 34). The scores carry specific and precise musical information without being impervious to the actual surprises of the here and now. In this opera in particular the role of change acquires particular importance; the different combinations deriving from the same signs make it possible to generate heterogeneous musical configurations that could even sound as if they were opposites of each other (for example a very dense sound pattern opposed to sporadic tonalities) (Logothetis 1980: 294).

In the mid '60s the composer departs further from the patterns of traditional notation by integrating the signs he had already developed into the formation of 'sculptural shapes'. These are found, for example, in the compositions *Ichnologia* (1964) (image 13.1) and *Labyrinthos* (1965), the former being included by John Cage in his famous collection *Notations* (Cage and Knowles 1969). The title *Ichnologia* refers to a branch of palaeontology studying the effects of biological life upon inorganic sediments through the traces left by living beings. In the composition recognisable and less recognisable pentagrammatic 'traces' are integrated into an organic whole, out of which, in a sort of cascade, signs peculiar to Logothetis' notations emerge. Here again, single notes are part of a series of subgroups. Prior to the performance, the sequence and the duration of each group is defined by the conductor or the players, whereas the acoustics of the single signs are left open to the interpreters. This work rotates around the problem of the membrane; a porous membrane standing between the singular scattered signs and those coupled into more organic assemblages. But also a membrane that constitutes a 'nondecomposable, nonsegmentary line', a resonance between inorganic strata, the emergence of biological life and the musical signs flashing into the expressive states of the players. This abstract machine connects 'a multiplicity of perfectly discontinuous states of metastability constituting so many hierarchical degrees' (Deleuze and Guattari 1987: 56) and generates what Simondon calls a *topology of the living*, the relation between heterogeneous milieus of interiority and exteriority as the necessary condition for the genesis of biological life (Simondon 1964: 258).

    Labyrinthos (image 13.4) is characterised by the convergence of two kinds of rhythms, the rhythm of the soloist or soloists is drawn within a self-contained section at the core of the notation, which is the same for every performer involved in the piece. The outer section is dedicated to the orchestra and, as the composer himself explains, it 'has two breaks which may be used either as beginning or end. When the section is repeated long rests are to be inserted within these points during which the solo-section continues to be played' (Logothetis 1967: n.p.). Furthermore, the structure of the whole composition is sustained by bold 'scissor-like' walls (the labyrinth walls) that have a dynamic function, denoting the rise and fall of the volume. The interplay between the expressions of the single player, the conductor and the composer himself also appears in the three possible readings that Logothetis left open for this piece: 1. each single sign can be read according to a predefined succession that is followed by all the players. 2. The signs can be interpolated into various groups, whose duration is determined by the conductor in advance or during the realisation. Within the group, the

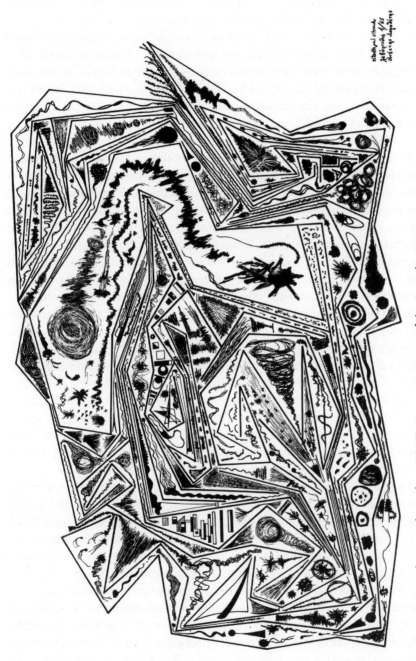

13.4: Anestis Logothetis, *Labyrinthos*, 1967. Image courtesy of the Logothetis estate.

order and the duration of each sign are left to the interpreter. 3. The succession of signs and their duration are entirely left over to how each single player processes the given information.

The piece therefore unfolds onto multiple levels through the resonances it establishes between singularities and assemblages. It thus reflects the concept of heterotopia, intrinsic to the notion of a labyrinth, whose complex structure, folding in and out in synchrony, generates a space in which the distinction between inside and outside becomes indeterminable. Only from a position of what Deleuze and Guattari, quoting Raymond Ruyer, call a 'survey without distance' – a sort of mythical 'third eye' present at all places of the surface at the same time – could one tell with certainty if a particular position is more out or in than another. This 'self survey that no chasm, fold or hiatus, escapes' (Deleuze and Guattari 1994: 210) corresponds to a primary conscience which synthesises any kind of spatio-temporal perceptions into an absolute a-dimensional state. From this position, the labyrinth walls get transformed into a dynamic tool for the definition of acoustic parameters, allowing for osmosis between the groups (the orchestra) and the individuals (the soloist[s]). An expressive landscape is produced by a relation of intense and affective 'exchanges', where reference points are not assigned by a predefined system, but are generated spontaneously through the formation of sound assemblages. In Simondon's terminology, a level of *transindividual* resonance is produced where groupings are not the sums of pre-existing individuals, but both the singularity and the multiplicity are shaped through a process of mutual individuation involving the common potential of the pre-individual state (Simondon 2007: 211). The singular, emotional and expressive faculties are integrated into a wider dimension where a common sensor combines and redistributes all sorts of analog and digital information.

The metastable moment demarking the flash in between the signs and the sound, the abstract and the expressive, accounts for a collapse of Logothetis' two-dimensional 'maps' into the multi-dimensional states of his music. In this instant of void, free-floating time emancipated from the 'hinges' of chronological succession opens the present up to action. Affective richness between heterogeneous materials is transferred by translational configurations which themselves actively contribute to the diversification and the enhancement of various registers of sensation. Because of the freedom left to the musicians, an intense form of communication and intersubjective action is necessary in order to push singular emotional states into the compositional plane of each performance. That is, the procedure of interpreting the notation is not only the task of the conductor, but becomes a much more democratic process involving all the parties; by means of their creative contribution the players become 'responsible musicians' (Logothetis 1998: 82; Krones 1998: 14).[14]

This democratisation process happening within the orchestra goes along with a broader social ideal that Logothetis pursues:

> I gladly indulge in the naivety that artistic creation is able to sharpen the criteria of the social and that it prepares thought and feeling for the acceptance of new social dimensions. I am convinced that social impotence in front of a war can be counteracted by a creative aesthetic consciousness that penetrates into the criminal conflictual power drives and enlightens them. (Logothetis 1980: 292)[15]

Logothetis 'virtuosity', his aesthetic and implicitly ethico-political engagement,[16] consists in the creation of *dividual* refrains: complex human and nonhuman assemblages defined not by the sum of the people, signs or devices involved, but by the simultaneous and successive interplay of affective forces able to individuate and form a *transient* multiplicity. It is exactly this ephemeral, improvisational character of the collective which cracks the labyrinth and allows it to meld with a wider dimension of collective compositions and their de- and re-territorialisation of cosmic speeds and sonorities.

References

Cage, J. and A. Knowles (1969), *Notations*, New York: Something Else Press.

Deleuze, G. (1994), *Difference and Repetition*, trans. P. Patton, New York: Columbia University Press.

Deleuze, G. (2004), *Desert Islands and Other Texts 1953–1974*, ed. D. Lapoujade, trans. M. Taormina, Cambridge, MA: Semiotext(e).

Deleuze, G. and F. Guattari (1987), *A Thousand Plateaus*, trans. B. Massumi, London: Continuum.

Deleuze, G. and F. Guattari (1994), *What is Philosophy?*, trans. H. Tomlinson and G. Burchell, New York: Columbia University Press.

Flotzinger, R. and G. Gruber (eds), (1995), *Musikgeschickte Österreichs. Band Drei: Von der Revolution 1848 zur Gegenwart*, Wien: Böhlau.

Henke, M. (1996), 'Anestis Logothetis entfesselte Klänge', *In Positionen*, XXVIII (August): 41–4.

Herfert, F.-J. (2004), 'Kybernetik als Analysemethode zeitgenössischer Musik', in L. Holtmeier (ed.), *Musiktheorie zwischen Historie und Systematik*, Augsburg: Wißner.

Hiller Lejaren, A. (1964), *Informationstheorie und Computermusik, Zwei Vorträge, gehalten auf den 'Internationalen Ferienkursen für Neue Musik'*, Darmstadt, Mainz: Schott.

Karkoschka, E. (1966), *Das Schriftbild der neuen Musik*, Celle: Moeck.

Krones, H. (1998), 'Komponieren für mündige Musiker', in H. Krones (ed.), *Anestis Logothetis: Klangbild und Bildklang*, Wien: Lafite.

Logothetis, A. (1960), *Zu Parallaxe*; written on the occasion of the debut perform-
ance of *Parallaxe* in Vienna. Reprinted in H. Krones (ed.), *Anestis Logothetis:
Klangbild und Bildklang*, Wien: Lafite, 1998.
Logothetis, A. (1967), *Labyrinthos*, Wien: Universal Edition nr: 14319. Unpaginated.
Logothetis, A. (1972), 'Karmadharmadrama – Oper in graphischer Notation',
Österreichische Musikzeitschrift ÖMZ, 27 (10): 541–6.
Logothetis, A. (1974), *Zeichen als Aggregatzustand der Musik*, Wien: Jugend und
Volk. Reprinted in H. Krones (ed.), *Anestis Logothetis Klangbild und Bildklang*,
Wien: Lafite, 1998.
Logothetis, A. (1975a), 'Komponieren für die Jugend', *Österreich Musikzeitschrift
ÖMZ*, 30 (1–2): 20–41.
Logothetis, A. (1975b), 'On Musical Notation', in J. G. Papaioannou (ed.), *Anestes
Logothetes: Concise Documentation on Anestis Logothetis = Anestis Logothetis*,
Athens: Ora. Unpaginated.
Logothetis, A. (1980), 'Von der Bedeutung der Dinge', *Österreich Musikzeitschrift
ÖMZ*, 35 (6): 292–5.
Logothetis, A. (1998), 'Die Geschenke meiner Ungebung anhand der Frage: "was
denn nun Musik sei"', in H. Krones (ed.), *Anestis Logothetis Klangbild und
Bildklang*, Wien: Lafite.
Moles, A. A. (1987), *Informationstheorie und ästhetische Wahrnehmung*, Köln: Du
Mont Schauberg.
Papaioannou, J. G. (ed.) (1975), *Anestes Logothetes: Concise Documentation on
Anestis Logothetis = Anestis Logothetis*, Athens: Ora. Unpaginated.
Simondon, G. (1958), *Du mode d'existence des objets techniques*, Paris: Aubier.
Simondon, G. (1964), *L'individu et sa genèse physico-biologique*, Paris: Presses
Universitaires de France.
Simondon, G. (2007), *L'individuation psychique et collective*, Paris: Aubier.
Toscano, A. (2005), *The Theatre of Production: Philosophy and Individuation
Between Kant and Deleuze*, Basingstoke: Palgrave Macmillan.
Virno, P. (2004), *A Grammar of the Multitude*, trans. I. Bertoletti, J. Cascaito and
A. Casson, New York: Semiotext(e).
Wiener, N. (1953), *Introduzione alla cibernetica*, trans. D. Persani, Turin: Einaudi.
Weibel, P. (1998), 'Musik / Spiel als kybernetisches Modell', in H. Krones (ed.),
Anestis Logothetis: Klangbild und Bildklang, Wien: Lafite.

Notes

1. Logothetis was born in 1921 on the Bulgarian coast of the Black Sea to Greek
   parents. He moved to Vienna in 1942 in order to start his university studies, and
   he lived there until his death in 1994.
2. According to Logothetis, Earle Brown's piece is the first example of graphical
   notation from which music could be played (Logothetis 1975a: 41). In this
   composition a series of tetragons are distributed in between lines of various
   length and intensity; the musicians being free to play the 'score' according to
   their inspiration.
3. In 1952 Cage performed his famous composition *4' 33"*. This piece does not
   contain any 'notes', its music is solely generated by the sounds that the listeners
   and the general environment produce.
4. The collection *Notations* (Cage and Knowles 1969) shows a rich panorama of
   artists exploring new domains of signs. Karkoschka (1966) provides a theoretical examination of their development and main criteria. Roman Raubenstock-
   Ramati (1919–94), another contemporary of Logothetis who also lived in

Vienna, composed works that unfolded within a structure defined by strict geometric forms (Flotzinger and Gruber 1995: 372).

5. Logothetis found evidence that particular forms of oriental and pre-Byzantine music allow for a wider spectrum of tonalities than pentagrammatic notation, as they are not composed in a linear structure (Logothetis 1974: 36).

6. Private communication from Julia Logothetis.

7. Logothetis shares this active transposition of architectural thinking into music with his Greek colleague Iannis Xenakis.

8. White noise is the technical term used to denote complete randomness. Its power spectrum, that is the representation in a Cartesian diagram of the intensity of the signal and its frequency is characterised by a flat behaviour, that is, the value of intensity remains the same whilst frequency increases. It thus has different properties from a specific and distinct sound whose power spectrum would be characterised by a single point (or a few points) around a certain frequency.

9. In this composition Logothetis recalled his 1958 stay in Rome on an Austrian Cultural Institute scholarship. This piece constitutes an attempt to transpose the architectural dynamics of the city into music (see Logothetis 1998: 94).

10. This approach has been explored by Hiller (1964) and Herfert (2004).

11. With a similar argument it is possible to demonstrate that processes of resonance also generate information.

12. Physical entities, on the contrary, develop within the borders of the body that determine the upper limit of their physical growth (Simondon 1964: 132).

13. The 'Chor der Puppen' (Chorus of the dolls) section of the drama was first performed in 1967 at the Vienna Konzerthaus under the direction of Herwig Reiter. Another significant performance of the play was held in 1971 in the Vienna Planetarium under the direction of Logothetis himself. Here the notations were projected on the ceiling and mixed up with the view of the stars. (Private communication from Julia Logothetis.)

14. The role of social responsibility constitutes a common denominator between the work of Logothetis and Cage, who understood his social contribution as an attack on general stupidity (Henke 1996: 44).

15. Logothetis carefully analysed in his writings the social and political role that music played historically (Logothetis 1975a: 32–4 and 1998: 78–89).

16. Virno defines the concept of virtuosity in relation to a work or an action which does not lead to a finished product (Virno 2004: 53). This idea fits with Logothetis as only very few recordings of his work exist, and only one CD is available on the market at present. The rest of the music has to be imagined from his notations. As the notations are immanent to the singular performative act, they cannot be conceived as a 'product' per se.

Chapter 14

Anti-Electra: Totemism and Schizogamy

Elisabeth von Samsonow

Which path leads back to the pre-Oedipal, back to the universe of the primal Mother, the mother *as the world*? Freud bracketed the continent of the pre-Oedipal out of psychoanalytical theory, considering it a sphere without words or concepts. Indeed, one is always already expatriated; one has already emigrated when one begins thinking about it. For this simple reason the pre-Oedipal rose to become the greatest field of projection for feminist psychoanalysis, onto which was pinned the hope that it could, as an ancestral and prior continent, be (re)conquered exclusively by means of a feminine logic.[1] Its mythical nature has lent itself to many interpretations: it is often projected as a Golden Age representing lost experiences of oneness and bliss; or, it serves as an ontological frame for the construction of a non-castrated, unpunished 'phallic' mother. But it's hard to accept this 'non-castrated mother' because in this super-dialectic she stands for a perverse logic of loss, that is, for the *loss of the Oedipal in the pre-Oedipal* as seen from the nostalgic standpoint of the Oedipalised. For the concept of the mother can only appear 'non-castrated' from the perspective of loss (from the perspective of an internalised castration) that looks back to a phantasmatic and original possession. Yet wouldn't a memory that can be *re-collected* or re-called in fact reconstitute a condition of non-castration where nothing was lost or fell off, and make the positive condition of completeness precisely this ability (or power) to remember? If anything gets lost it is not a sex organ, which is usually quite well attached, but the memory of that which organises the deepest layers of memory. The anxiety of losing sex organs covers the threat of a loss of memory related to the preconscious, the pre-Oedipal. The *sexual code* of amnesia conceals the fact that the origins of a person are lost in a darkness that is *itself* a cultural product. A 'non-castrated' mother becomes under these conditions someone who, as if by a miracle, one begins to remember. But she will appear as an *other* mother, a *strange* mother.[2]

For interpreting the figure of Electra all of these questions seem to me to be extraordinarily important. Electra's mediocre ability in acting out can be explained by her 'pre-real' status, by her general regression into primal femaleness. Indeed, the figure of Electra implies regression, and to understand this we must shake her in such a way that the pre-Oedipal world falls out of her. Electra and her sisters are 'the last girls' of the pre-Athenian, Cycladic, Mycenaean, or Minoan world. For this reason it is only as a misreading that Electra could qualify for the role of 'Athena', a daughter subservient to the father. In the end, and this constitutes the core of the tragedy, these daughters serve more as symptoms of an abdicating territorial queen. To derive a psychologically standardised father-love from the sadness and desperation that these daughters must have felt over the public offence and scandal of their mother is truly high art, ideological poiesis. In this way, a trail of deceit was laid out to legitimise the girl's orientation toward the father and her ideal 'masculinisation'. What made this even more convincing was that the girl-daughter, whose becoming-woman was not yet completed, had no right in her in-between-state to a sexual definition other than 'not-(yet)-woman', which might also be read as 'man'. This would be to confirm the official generative pole of the *Electra complex*: being-woman (which is also becoming-woman) is an explicit and obsessive partiality for a *certain man*. But even assuming that love is always a phenomenon of polarisation there remains another possible trajectory for becoming-woman – Deleuze's *becoming-woman* – that leads to the universal *girl*. The idea of a universal *devenir-femme* as the first stage in the recovery of an open existential potential is a sophisticated philosophical attempt by Deleuze and Guattari to account for repressed otherness as our structural super-motor. It is not by accident that what immediately follows it is the *devenir-animal*, becoming-animal. Woman and animal make up an amnesic complex, a matrimonium of regression, which navigates the descent to the plutonium of primary energy.

Becoming-woman develops in two directions. First it moves ahead, forward into an open future, as a virtual being that projects potentialities under unrestricted emergent conditions. The Electra complex could earn philosophical honour and attention as such a future-oriented project. In fact, however, there is a lack of definition in the Electra complex's 'becoming-woman' that *returns* the girl to a primal scene that celebrates in song an unknown but always taken for granted hardly-I and hardly-thou. This song, incanted and magically fixed with phonetic signs, carries the royal dada-esque title of MAMA. As a result, Electra's relationship with her mother is focused almost exclusively on her most

14.1: Elisabeth von Samsonow, *Xylosophy*, linden wood, wood marker, 2009. Photo: Tal Adler. Image courtesy of the artist.

interesting organs; she constantly imagines her productive and creative functions and her sexual activity. As if Clytemnestra were *in truth* a machine disguised by a mask of the Mycenean queen. Electra ignores the actual mother in front of her in order to get on the track of the *real* Clytemnestra. One senses that Electra is psychically fixated on a mother who has very little to do with both the very complex personality of her actual mother, and with Clytemnestra's dreadful tale of woe as it is presented in the myths and dramas. Electra directs at this mother representing a sort of pre-human being, the barely-thou, her primary love and its counterpart of unchecked primary hate, the desire to bash away at her, to bite into her and to destroy her with toxic pee and exploding poo. Why these extreme feelings? Because Clytemnestra let the king's daughter cry and didn't come at once, because she, for whatever reason, turned away from the consummate love relationship with her daughter and did something else while little Electra screamed for the eternal milk, similarly to how Melanie Klein imagines it. Because in accordance with Athenian propaganda, she must come to terms with the end of matrilinearity: there is nothing left to inherit. The girl who witnesses the disempowerment of her mother will function as a royal symptom of her suppressed state, appearing in the Electra complex as if in a distorting mirror. And when all she receives as consolation is the advice to be 'daughter of the noblest father of the world' (Sophocles 2001: 57, line 366), the outbreak of mother-hatred parallels the internalisation of the inescapable – which will later give material to the psychological sketches of the dramatists.

Constitutive Strangeness or Primary Exoticism?

The mother lineage defines itself through the kind of a priori foreignness we have seen in the pre-Oedipal; for how could a first mother have been produced from a mother? The Bible makes an attempt at an answer when it makes man into the 'mother' of the first mother, Adam as the first 'genetrix' who lends the first flesh. There are representations that depict a caesarean-section-like wound on the breast of Adam, from which Eve arises. This wound imitates the vulva, and becomes Christ's organ of blessing. But when a female child feels her way into the primitive layer of identification within her mother, she will discover that the mother-image does not transform into a 'hu-man', but rather changes anamorphically into a dragon-, snake-, or monster-image, which, like Dali's clocks, stands only half upright while the other half hangs down into an abyss where it loses its form and face. Womanhood is to be grounded in that female property from which one emerges, a 'mother-ness' (*Mutterheit*) that is hypothetically represented, for example, in the animal vitality of an elongated muscle that terminates in a mouth, exactly like that given by the appearance of the snake. Wherever the specific, particular mother gets caught up in the unending curvatures of 'motherness' – as always happens when memory provides only faded images – she is represented by an appropriate symbol that has a certain functional similarity.

Female identity that is produced in relation to the snake – namely, in a proto-Hegelian sense, in the passage through archaic otherness – will have to imbue social relations with this specific quality. First, the 'mother' symbolised in the form of a venerable animal is invoked as con-stitutive of harmonious ascendance, and then, in order to generalise this animal alienness, the exogamy rule is formulated. Exogamy is the proof of the fact that the mode in which the familiar (i.e., 'motherness') is welcomed is the alien. If matrilineal society attempted to set up the pre-Oedipal as permanent, then the logic of its relationships will not find its (Lacanian) condition in a breach of the original bond with the mother, which is assumed to be obligatory for the Electra complex. The exogamy rule expresses the quality of the first love that led to the theriomorphic symbolisation of the mother. The exogamous relationship therefore recalls and repeats the constellation of the first symbiosis, inasmuch as this is grounded in a 'mother' who manifests itself as an intimate alien. Clytemnestra's relationships are thereby constituted xenologically, and only allow the husband a place at the systemic location from where she derived her snake identity. Who then will be desired by a woman who isn't conditioned to reject the mother by the Electra complex? Will the desired be a *non-woman* (man?), and will he consequently have to acti-vate that dimension of 'mother' (as archetype of the pre-Oedipal erotic relationship) that is the 'not-woman' (animal) in her? If, as psychoanaly-sis never tires of claiming, the primordial relationship supplies the model for every relationship, then this must count for pre-Oedipal society as well. In the coupling of adults the relationship that an omnipotent child has established with its animal becomes dominant again.

The imperative to seek out the strange and unfamiliar (in exogamy) expresses a particular mode of human self-description that is both a modality of *eccentric* hominisation and a structure of sexual difference. The animal in this respect serves not only to present a certain dimension of the non-animal (human), but also – something so far neglected – serves the internal differentiation of humans into female and male. If the female is conflated with the animal it gives a primary gender constellation in the

14.2: Elisabeth von Samsonow, *Philosopher from Stella Centauri*, painted linden wood, 2007. Image courtesy of the artist.

form of 'motherness' becoming the origin and reference of both sexes. Unlike the symbolic order of the father, which introduces an authority like a transpersonal clamp enclosing the feminine and the masculine in his various avatars (justice, law, name, the state), the symbolic order of the mother implies both the difference between the sexes and the commerce betweens humans and nonhumans. The symbolic order of the mother therefore opens onto the trans-human, and pairs the human with the animal in a common socius. In this sense, totemism is the political expression of becoming, offering a model for collective ascendance with the animal as its patron. One recalls that 'man', before he became one, looked different, exotic. First he was an egg, then a cotyledon, then a kind of crocodile, finally a grand water being before he fell onto dry land as an infant – before, that is, he began to grow and finally became that which simply no longer grows: a grown up.

Schizogamy

We intend a descent, not into the cave of Trophonius where an 'intra-uterine' visionary culture had created its cultic space,[3] but rather into the basement of the Athenian Agora where trophies from the Cycladic, Mycenaean and Minoan cultures are displayed. This cellar corresponds to an older sediment in a literary stratigraphy. At this level it is true that the animal belongs essentially to the human, but in a way opposed to the argument that demands reconciliation with the animal. That is to say, *before* 'man' notices the animal, the animal – and this is the totemic thesis – has already noticed man. The animal is there first. It is already *there* when humans were not yet humans. To a consciousness that does not yet possess its humanity as a reflex, the level of the animal precedes identification. The animal does not mark the purely functional line of emergence (evolution) as the milieu of pristine nature that, as Schelling imagined it, is struck by the beam of consciousness. If consciousness searches for this emergence, behind and below itself, it despairs because it is always just the most luminous part of a history that loses itself in the dark. In its symbolic form pre-Oedipality gives a different solution to this problem. The level of emergence in the totemic model is as little unconscious as would be the mother goat for her kid. In contrast to the notion that we have simply forgotten our emergence, which can be regained in the pre-conscious, totemism achieves in its affective mood a relationship with the level of emergence that repairs the damage of primal amnesia. The level of origin is 'motherness', not yet recognised as human it has no face (because it is seen from inside), it is merely a stimulus-triggering schema. Would this be Mrs. Miller down at 1 Parish St? No, how could she be! Mrs. Miller is too civilised to have ever caused such a storm of primary desire. Then who? It is an animal mother who, once known so intimately, is the first intuition of being for those on their way to becoming human.

If we assume hypothetically that layers of identity are communicated from this first great mother-animal to *both* sexes, to male and female children, the modality of male and female gender identification nevertheless differs considerably on the one point that is of such encompassing significance it is overlooked: mothers are experienced both *from inside and from outside*. Woman is thus originally faceless (from the inside), a Container-Thou or inner-skin, before she turns herself 'inside out' and shows the child her sur-face. She is like a Möbius strip, while the father always appears outside, showing only his 'exterior' skin and surface. He never presents himself *from inside*. Whereas the mother is anthropomorphic in respect to one of her two modes, the father always has the human, the male form. The proof that the mother is human is, even today, still pending; fathers, on the other hand, are happily assured of their humanity or their absolutely human mode of appearance, which people call masculinity.

What memory will one have of this first Container-Thou, and in what symbolic form may it be *recovered*?[4] Which mask will be given to the vital inner skin, and what kind of image would be projected on it in remembering our first partner?

If little boys succumb to Oedipalisation and enter into identification with the father, then when it comes to their own sexual role they can at least build on the literal, really existing father or father-like figures, even if parting from their mother sets up a deep and abiding destabilisation.[5] If a father shows up on the horizon, he comes as human. The mother never shows up on the horizon like the father. First of all, she always looks different, and so – this is the most important point – doesn't look human. The conditions for falling into an Electra complex are obviously more difficult and radical than Oedipalisation, which describes a relation of power between three 'really' existing agents. Identification with the mother, the process of becoming-woman, points down into the psychic antiquity of a pre-human 'motherness'. If the girl succeeds in imagining herself in the place of the mother, she is immediately implicated by concurrent modulations of femininity. That is, if the little girl envies her mother, then she envies her for everything that she has, and most of all, what she fantasises about calling her own. This is the comprehensive conflation of, irrespective of rational objections, a great animal mother with a specific person. The lines of sexual identification part at exactly this point: in the contrast between a type of gaze that unites an interior and an exterior sur-face, and another one that arrives purely 'from the outside'. The girl who observes her mother feels that she must be hiding something from her, that she has concealed something constitutive, i.e.,

14.3: Elisabeth von Samsonow, *Asino Academico*, ink and oil pastel on paper, 2009. Image courtesy of the artist.

her inner skin, so that the mother seems double, a binome of pre-human and human. Freud would have done better to ground the fear of the hole along this trajectory rather than having the little girl become aware of her inferior sex (according to his theory) from an already punished and castrated mother whose penis is, clearly, missing. The girl who, ignoring reason and 'reality', tries to align a Great Animal Mother with her concrete mother becomes aware, in the 'fear of the hole', less of the lost penis than of the depth of the procreating Container-Thou and its remembrance.

Now the manner in which the animal helps in the determination of gender difference begins to become clear. With the assistance of the animal, the lines of identification are traceable in a double derivation and find corresponding titles: jaguar woman, dragon lady, toad woman, spider woman, wild buffalo, big bear, cat woman, sweet sly fox. And one begins to understand why contemporary feminism has taken such vehement shots at the hegemony of the exterior gaze, at the male gaze that makes woman an object.

Why are women so hypersensitive about this gaze that encounters them only on the 'outside', in *extimity*, that entire feminist libraries have been composed as war machines against its validity? The primordial layer, the human female-animal and animal-mother, is by definition missing in a society of the privileged male gaze, both symbolically and politically. This is why it is reflexively registered in all women as their deficient being, as insufficient beauty, insufficient intelligence, *insufficient humanity*. Women despair of this regime of the exterior gaze that doubts the complex folding of inner and outer truth where space and subjectivity coincide. The daughter therefore perceives that the mother inexplicably believes herself to be stuck in the pre-human – caught in the preliminaries of becoming-human. Deep inside, girls know that if they want to hold onto their mothers then they too are not-yet-human. In a world determined by human and man, girls cannot rid themselves of the suspicion that something is wrong with them, increasingly falling into panic as the time to bring about the realisation of their becoming-human-woman slips away. Baudelaire wondered why girls fall into the underworld at the age of 15 and remain there until the age of 50.

In the symbolisation that totemism proposes, this portion of the girl's primary capacity for a relationship that connects her to the 'Container-Mother' is invested in the personification of the mother as an animal. Inasmuch as it ascribes the intuition of the nourishing and caring quality of the Container-Thou to the animal, it truly earns the title of a *feminist humanism*. In this feminist humanism, the portion of diffuse

14.4: Elisabeth von Samsonow, left: *Shrine of the Beast*; middle: *Capatoline Wolf*; right: *The World*. Painted wood. Image courtesy of the artist.

pre-humanity is identified and defined as being-animal and integrated into a significant position within the social structure. It becomes the Archimedean point of ascendancy. In this way the animal embodies the *legacy of the mother*.

The interpretation of totemism as arising from the social fact of a matri-focal cultural type is only partially opposed to that of Freud. Inasmuch as we assume that the level of emergence is personified by the animal, in which we find not only our ancestor, but a being fully capable of love and other caring relationships, then (repudiating Freud) we will designate it as 'mother'. That the goddesses are represented either theriomorphically or accompanied by an animal has been understood by feminists such as Göttner-Abendroth to mean that the animal is the consort of the goddess. In fact the animality of the mother and her consort don't contradict each other, they necessarily belong together according to the principle of exogamy. This confirms, if by other means, Freud's assumption that female identification and erotic orientation do not come about by a change of object.[6] Freud definitely registers the ambivalence of feelings that the continuity of the mother bond make apparent: 'The woman's husband, who to begin with inherited from her father, becomes after a time her mother's heir as well' (Freud 1963: 597).

The patterns developed through the relationship with the first (animal) mother are reactivated by an intimus who, like the apersonal Mama, is animal-shaped (as in 'the beauty and the beast', or the frog prince). The bride vaguely remembers that great intimacy is to be felt close to animal warmth and animal instinct-automatism. The actual man, in this respect like the mother, will have to rise from exactly this level. From a distance he is nonhuman, other, a stranger. The exogamic model, which demands a bridegroom in the model of a stranger, is quite opposed to the general Platonism of things erotic, which are clearly based upon recognition. In feminist humanism or totemism the one to be married will not be the original one, finally recognised, but the unknown. The stranger becomes the alien intimus, sharing the hypothetical title of the living first *mater-ial*, the monumental intimate Mama. As a result of the fact that the animal Ur-mother as principle of imaginary and social cohesion must be split up so that the groom may be produced as her equivalent, we must speak of *schizogamy* (rather than of exogamy). In schizogamy a triangle is in fact inscribed – but it is a *pre-Oedipal* one: the split partner embraces the two modes of appearance of the Ur-mother, one part showing her as a trans-human (animal) that is transferred into the (re) cognitive pattern of strangeness, the other one being a pure symbiotic being (without any threat of Oedipalisation). The loving girl, and an element of pure strangeness that has the intriguing force of an eternal bond, therefore marks the pre-Oedipal triangle. The last two elements are to be composed in what will appear as the schizogamic bridegroom.

Schizogamy explains that the woman, in the orientation of her attachment, does not really change her object of love (as Freud suggests), while also showing how the permanency of the object is to be conceived. The constant object is grounded in a deeper layer that introduces a certain distance or haziness into the character of the attachment, through a mnemological difference ('antiquity of the soul') that establishes not a 'cool' relationship, but rather, *Eros as a modality of searching.*

Schizosomatic Art

The concept of *schizosoma* describes the affective and aesthetic quality of the mother/child pair, and casts light on the realm of the sculptural understood less as artistic academic discipline than as a form of experience and productive technology. As schizosoma the sculptural belongs to the girl as the phantasm essential to her desire related to her privilege of making men. Along with the fabrication of cult images and puppets, the production of mummies is part of the phantasmatic 'business of people-making', and shows how birth and death coincide once the girl puts her potential to work symbolically. Electra functions as a 'spare parts depot' for the older sister Iphigeneia who is already abandoned to sacrifice; Electra is always already a potential candidate for sacrifice, depending on the sacrificial king with whom she forms a couple (Agamemnon). The girl waiting for her sacrifice is closed up in a labyrinth, which is why the specific body- and space-constructions that are derived from the analysis of plasticity have to be examined again in relation to her. The girl in the underworld is archetypically Kore or Persephone, and Electra is her exemplar. The Electra complex has remained distinctively indistinct, an *almost complex*, a reminiscence of her fate of being sacrificed in an act to come (not *devenir fiancée*, but *devenir sacrificée*). Against this should be placed a *strong girl* who is destined to become queen (as Clytemnestra's successor, despite everything): *Anti-Electra*. For in the mega-measure of globalisation an Electra complex would mean that mother-hate affects the Earth. A system that is built upon the sacrifice of the girl inevitably presents an all-too dominant mother who then, in the next step, becomes the object of a general aggression. The vindication *of the Earth itself* is at stake here. The schizosoma that the girl forms with her mother is itself, however, characterised by death and imbalance, disturbed by the rage of Demeter who searches for the sacrificed daughter (and hangs a veil of grief over her feelings of guilt). But if the girl were to return, if she could conclude the story of her shadow existence, how would the schizosomatic relationship that humans have to Earth (which they call *mother*) take shape? Would the Earth be a 'mother' at all if the girl was given back her rightful place? The one who returned from out of the labyrinth was Ariadne, the daughter of Pasiphae. She had the red thread. Is she 'Anti-Electra'?

Much has been written about phallic objects. The story of Daedalus introduces us to the main objects that symbolise the maternal genitals around which pre-Oedipality circles. In place of the *schizoanalytical quadrant* that Deleuze and Guattari constructed with the phylum of machines, the flux of libido and capital, the immaterial constellations, and the territory, there is a *schizosomatic quadrant of pre-Oedipality*, containing necessarily, *objects* – sculptural things with the quality of living machines. There are four Daedalian objects: the labyrinth, the living statues,[7] the copulation apparatus of Pasiphae, and the satellite (Fontisi-Ducroux 1992/3: 98–100). The labyrinth and the automata appear together, the latter interpreting and at the same time forming a compliment to the former, living statues made by the engineer march back and forth in front of the labyrinth. These two objects – the labyrinth and the automata – constitute a set which presents *maternal genitality* in mirror mode: to the pre-human mother embodied in the labyrinth belong the walking and talking statues that issue from her and move around *in front of the entrance*. In the third primary object, Pasiphae's copulation apparatus, the totemistic logic of the pre-Oedipal imaginary becomes sculptural. In this apparatus appears the central operator (the thing with a genital function) that sets up parallels between humans and animals (copulation as a function, a 'copula'). This copula-tion apparatus will be especially important in our age of electrification and global networks. The fourth pre-Oedipal object unfolds the systemic quality of the labyrinth. It is Daedalus himself, who, as the story tells it, rises into the air from the centre of the labyrinth and flies away.[8] He embodies the 'external observer' as a *deus ex machina* compensating for disorientation by technical means, and as its engineer, he ensures the complexity of the labyrinth that he will have both stayed in and left. This fourth pre-Oedipal object has only recently developed into an actual apparatus, namely the satellite. Daedalus as interpreter of the pre-Oedipal horizon produces 'objectivities' in order to give a structure to affective moods, and therefore archives within these Daedalian objects significant scenes of 'inter-corporeal' communication, a communication for which the (child-)body is specialised.

The *girl* therefore represents both an imaginarium and a specific form of corporeal intelligence that are based on her 'interest' in birth, deriving from a birth expectation in a general sense. In other words, with

14.5: Elisabeth von Samsonow, *Enlightenment*, painted linden wood, 2006.
Foreground: *Heart of the Earth*, painted linden wood, 2008. Image courtesy of the artist.

regard to the corporeal being of the human the girl is the one and only true capitalist. She is a capitalist because of her exclusive possession of the means of production. The girl is the potency of birth. Thus a serious discussion of the (re)production of the human – as well as of the artistic – has to begin with the girl. It is doubtful that the interminable feminist discussions of birth privilege and birth envy have been successful in creating or acknowledging the laws for becoming mothers. The condition of possibility of this acknowledgment necessarily precedes birth and must be clarified normatively *before* birth, thereby constituting an *a priori* of the mother–child constellation in the mode of becoming, which is perfectly embodied in the girl. The girl represents the collective phantasm of a body able to produce a body, and accordingly the girl emerges as this body and so specified by this body. In so far as the girl *expects* the realisation of a body capable of giving birth and refers it directly back to herself, she is in possession of a logos of creation, whether we discuss the imaginary of birth or the potency of artistic production.

In order to be clear: If I speak of the one and only real and existing capitalist in relation to human-production, I refer of course to the real girl – but at the same time I don't mean the real girl. In my analysis the 'girl' appears as a *signifier*. This is surprising considering the undesignated position of the girl within the bourgeois family, which suggests the girl would never be capable of performing a career move on the level of the signifier. One of the few texts considering such a possibility can be found in Deleuze and Guattari's *A Thousand Plateaus*:

> The girl is the first victim, but she must also serve as an example and a trap. That is why, conversely, the reconstruction of the body as a Body without Organs, the anorganism of the body, is inseparable from a becoming-woman, or the production of a molecular woman. Doubtless, the girl becomes a woman in the molar or organic sense. But conversely, becoming-woman or the molecular woman is the girl herself. . . . She never ceases to roam upon a body without organs. She is an abstract line, or a line of flight. Thus girls do not belong to an age group, sex, order or kingdom: they slip in everywhere, between orders, acts, ages, sexes; they produce *n* molecular sexes on the line of flight in relation to the dualism machines they cross right through. (Deleuze and Guattari 1987: 272–3)

It is therefore indispensable to ask what the girl actually does to stage the impending birth, or rather to guarantee this act in accordance with a corporeal logic. It is indispensable to attentively observe the girl in this respect. Certainly the girl's acts are not restricted to girls but appear, as an image of Deleuze and Guattari's model of molecular becoming-woman, *everywhere*.

When the girl brings her physical ability of producing bodies into action, she *plays*. In this way she anticipates birth in play. She plays *production* with suitable means. Intimately feeling kinship in a theatrical way, she embraces objects that for her represent the born body as a *substitute*. The girl is the master of *doll play*, which is a *three-dimensional (plastisch) body play*, an artful play, an object play. She is the master of the living sculpture, a *first-class sculptress*. As a result, the problem of birth does *not* arise in the relationship between mother and child in a real dimension, but as an *aesthetic and technical* problem within the manufacture of *three-dimensional stuff*. The girl fantasises that 'children' soon to appear are within her. Therefore she simulates acts according to them already being with her. Within the so-called latency phase following puberty which represents a more or less culturally induced and difficult suspension of sexual and reproductive power in the prolongation of her 'girl status', the play modus intensifies towards bricolage, craft and the technical. The girl puts her potency into the work – this could be called the sublimation of a body-producing competence – within technology, where 'technology' means the general system of objects. Technology forms the level where the interest in the aesthetic and the functional thing is brought into a system. The semantic of sublimation, which is transferred to technology by the girl, becomes her 'sex appeal', to quote Benjamin's and Mario Perniola's description (Perniola 2004: 1). If doll play, where the girl plays at reproduction, anticipates, simulates and affectively modulates the real, the question of the suitable horizon for this 'play' should be investigated.[9] The matter related to the sculptures in which the girl renders her objects, the plastic art *forms*, could stand in for her 'object play'. This plastic form covers both the contemporary technical field and its *gadgets* as well as *artistic sculpture* – whose connection to the four Daedalian objects are obvious. As the four Daedalian objects interpret and cultivate the relation between the girl and the 'world', mobile phones, hand-helds, laptops and head-sets guarantee a form of 'being online' that reintroduces nothing other than the pre-Oedipal condition. In all these plastic forms – in so far as they are both simulation and function – new coding and transformations of the girl's logos can be read as *symptomatic transformations of meaning*. The plastic object in art therefore comes closest to the production logos of the girl. It is a hybrid of birth, action and production – in exact accordance to the ideal of contemporary art – and traverses what Hannah Arendt saw as the realms connected to 'giving birth-ness'. The *art object* – as plastic object, sculpture and installation – *expresses* symbolic characteristics of the object-like or the thing-state, making the re-arrangement of birth a mode of self-invention in art.

14.6: Elisabeth von Samsonow, *Electra*, performance/procession, 11 September 2009, near Vienna. Photo: Josef Kahofer.

Anti-Electra consistently backs her mother against the allegation of incest by her complete lack of suspicion. This could be called the privilege of being a witness, and it will raise her to the contemporary ideal of an artist. Anti-Electra not only knows but also playfully tests the technical functions bridging a (lost) I and the accompanying objects (world objects), and her ability to connect life and action is a guiding star in the twilight, allowing the boundaries of the human to become blurred.

Translated by Victor Faessel, revised by Stephen Zepke

References

Deleuze, G. and F. Guattari (1987), *A Thousand Plateaus*, trans. B. Massumi, Minneapolis: University of Minnesota Press.
Fischer, N. and G. Fischer (1996), *Museum von Menschen oder wo sich Kunst und Wissenschaft wieder finden*, Frankfurt/Main: Strömfeld Roter Stern.
Fontisi-Ducroux, F. (1975), *Dédale: Mythologie de l'artisan en grèce ancienne*, Paris: F. Maspero.
Fontisi-Ducroux, F. (1992/3), 'Die technische Intelligenz des griechischen Handwerkers', trans. W. Rappl, *HEPHAISTOS, Kritische Zeitschrift zu Theorie und Praxis der Archäologie und angrenzender Gebiete* 1 (12).
Frazer, J. (1910), *Totemism and Exogamy: A Treatise on the Early Forms of Superstition and Society*, Vol. III, London: Macmillan.
Freud, S. (1963), 'Femininity', in *New Introductory Lectures On Psychoanalysis*, trans. J. Strachey, London: Hogarth.
Göttner-Abendroth, H. (1997), *Die Göttin und ihr Heros, die matriarchalen Religionen in Mythos, Marchen und Dichtung* (11th edition), München: Frauenoffensive.
Perniola, M. (2004), *The Sex Appeal of the Inorganic*, trans. M. Verdicchio, London: Continuum.
Plutarch (1952), 'On the Daimon of Sokrates', in *Über Gott, Vorsehung, Dämonen und Weissagung*, ed. and trans. K. Ziegler, Zürich und Stuttgart.
Rohde-Dachser, C. (1991), *Expeditionen in den dunklen Kontinent: Weiblichkeit im Diskurs der Psychoanalyse*, Berlin: Springer.
Samsonow, E. (2007), *Anti-Elektra: Totemismus und Schizogamie*, Zürich-Berlin: Diaphanes.
Sophocles (2001), *Electra*, trans. J. March, Oxford: Aris & Phillips.
Zeul, M. (1995), 'Weiblichkeit, Bild und Wirklichkeit', in A. Szanya (ed.), *Elektra und Ödipus. Zwischen Penisneid und Kastrationsangst*, Vienna: Picus.

Notes

1. The problem of this reconquering was seen clearly, for example, by Rohde-Dachser, see especially Chapter 15.1, 'Abstiege: Auf der Suche nach der "anderen" Kultur' (Rohde-Dachser 1991: 270–73).
2. In primitive totemism it is expressly denied, according to Frazer, 'that children are the fruit of the commerce of the sexes. So astounding an ignorance cannot but date from a past immeasurably remote' (Frazer 1910: 158). Yet for this 'remote past' Frazer offers a rather practical explanation that is related to the interval between conception and birth. We would prefer to conceive of the 'remote past' in the sense of a weakness of memory or of a memory 'lost' in primary consciousness. The 'savage idea' of totemistic ascendancy would then not be an expression of 'ignorance', but a symbolically satisfactory solution to the impossibility of adequately remembering the 'remote past' within 'adult' consciousness.
3. Plutarch describes how Timarchos descends into the Trophonius cave where he comes across a scenario that one could characterise as 'being worldless'. He hears noises, sees colours, and witnesses the rotation of the spheres. Finally, he has the feeling of being 'violently compressed', before a 'violent blow to the head' brings him back to the world.
4. Christa Rohde-Dachser writes: 'This cave beyond the phallic discourse is a female space' (1991: 272). Rohde-Dachser, however, defines the feminine 'container' as

a 'site of the warded off (negative) self of the patriarchal, grandiose male subject' (277). I do not follow this interpretation.

5. 'Stoller, in *Sex and Gender*, postulates a symbiotic phase between the mother and the girl, like that with the boy, which ends around the end of the second year with the development of their core gender identity, expressed in the child's conviction that it is a girl or a boy. This gender identity derives, Stoller argues, directly from the primary identification with the mother. However, the boy has first to differentiate himself from his primary object, the mother, with the result that the core gender identity of the male child is less secure than that of the girl, because the boy is always exposed to the pull of falling back into symbiosis with the mother and the identification with her' (Zeul 1995: 105).

6. 'We will now turn our interest onto the single question of what it is that brings this powerful attachment of the girl to her mother to an end. This, as we know, is its usual fate: it is destined to make room for an attachment to her father. Here we come upon a fact which is a pointer to our further advance. This step in development does not involve only a simple change of object. The turning away from the mother is accompanied by hostility; the attachment to the mother ends in hate' (Freud 1963: 585).

7. See Fontisi-Ducroux (1975: 96–117).

8. In their Daedalus project, Nora and Gerhard Fischer have documented MIT's flight experiment (Fischer and Fischer 1996).

9. I discuss the technical objects upon which the girl casts her phantasy in Chapter 5 of *Anti-Elektra*, 'Die vier ödipalen Gegenstände" (Samsonow 2007: 209–30).

Chapter 15

Unimaginable Happenings: Material Movements in the Plane of Composition

Barbara Bolt

In 2005 W. J. T Mitchell published a book entitled *What Do Pictures Want? The Lives and Loves of Images*. It is a provocative title, one that raises the possibility that pictures might just be animated beings possessed of a vital life. In a coda to the second chapter, 'What Do Pictures Want?', Mitchell is asked by a number of respondents – including Charles Harrison, Lauren Berlant, Teresa de Lauretis, Terry Smith, Mary Kelly and others – to address the following 'troubling' questions: 'What constitutes "animation" or vitality? What defines a living organism as distinct from an inanimate object? Isn't the notion of the living image a mere conceit that has gotten out of control?' (Mitchell 2005: 50–1). It is questions such as these that have motivated the present essay. However, rather than ask what pictures want, it asks specifically what is it that pictures do? In fact, Mitchell suggests that, along with the inevitable question of what pictures mean or signify, we already ask the question of what they do. The focus of such questioning, he notes, is concerned with their power to effect our emotions and behaviour (Mitchell 2005: 28). Furthermore, such questions tend to be framed within the context of the artist's intentions or desires. In returning to the question of what pictures do, I propose to shift the locus of discussion from the picture as object to the event of picturing. In such an event, there is, according to Gilles Deleuze and Félix Guattari, a summoning forth in which 'invisible forces of gravity, heaviness, rotation, the vortex, explosion, expansion, germination and time . . . make perceptible the imperceptible forces that populate the world' (Deleuze and Guattari 1994: 181–2). These forces, they argue, are not just glimpsed, but actually affect our becoming.

If art is concerned with summoning forth the imperceptible forces of the universe, what then is the difference between chaos and what we have come to term art? In *What is Philosophy*, Deleuze and Guattari propose that art's role is to confront chaos, to throw a net over it and create a plane of composition.[1] What is not composed, they argue, is not a work of art (Deleuze and Guattari 1994: 191). This summoning forth produces a synthesis of forces constructed as a bloc of sensation. In creating this bloc, they tell us, 'the plane of material ascends irresistibly and invades the plane of composition of the sensations themselves to the point of being part of them or indiscernible from them' (166). This is a powerful image, one that may resonate with our own struggles to paint or draw if we are visual artists, to write if we are writers or compose if we are musicians.

Here, I take up the movement whereby the plane of material invades the plane of composition, in order to reconfigure the dynamics of practice and argue for a materialist performativity in the event of imaging. Through addressing the dynamism of material – in which colour vibrates and shimmers, texture rubs and bruises, lines quiver, and shapes push and shove and topple over – the essay aims to demonstrate the expansive force that undoes representation and creates something unimaginable yet precisely 'true-to-life'. By true-to-life, I do not mean our everyday experience in the world. True-to-life is the athleticism, the vital life forces under experience; the percept that precedes perception and the affect before affection.

The essay proceeds in three movements; first, it lays out a plane of composition; second, it draws out the dynamics as the plane of material invades the plane of composition, and finally it charts a confrontation with forces through which the image becomes an intensive reality.

Movement 1 – The Plane of Composition

In 1952 John Cage staged the first performance of his composition *4'33"* at Maverick Concert Hall in New York. The pianist David Tudor entered onto the stage armed with a stopwatch, sat down at the piano, placed the score on it and lowered the lid of the piano. During the next four minutes and thirty-three seconds Tudor lowered and raised the piano lid at prescribed intervals and turned the pages of the score to mark the three movements of the composition. At the conclusion of the performance he raised the piano lid and left the stage. Despite the opinions of the seated audience, this performance was not merely nothing nor was it just the chaos of the everyday. By creating a frame of four minutes and thirty-three seconds, Cage had thrown a net over the chaos of the world and laid out a plane of composition.

Composition is a term that is common to the arts. Musicians, writers,

painters, printmakers, drawers and digital artists all create compositions. Yet Deleuze and Guattari's understanding of a plane of composition cannot simply be conflated with our common sense or pre-existing
concept of composition. Within the visual arts (and it is to these that
I will confine my discussion), composition is figured as the relation
between form and content. Content is concerned with the 'subject
matter, story or information that the artwork seeks to communicate to
the viewer', whilst form is the result of the manipulation of the various
(visual) elements and principles of design. In other words, 'content is
what artists want to say' and 'form is how they say it' (Lauer and Pentak
1990: 2).

Deleuze and Guattari's conception of an aesthetic plane of composition is not one of technical composition, that is, of the relation between
content and form. They are adamant that the work of art is never produced by or for the sake of technique. Further, in contrast to much contemporary thinking on art that posits artworks as texts to be decoded
and read,[2] Deleuze and Guattari do not believe that art is concerned
with communication and, whilst it might be concerned with expression,
it is not the expression of an artist's intention (on this point contemporary thought would seem to be in agreement). In their thought, it is the
material that becomes expressive, not the artist (Deleuze and Guattari
1994: 196).

However we are getting ahead of ourselves here. First we need to
establish what Deleuze and Guattari mean when they invoke the call
to cast out a net over chaos and lay out a plane of composition. In the
visual arts, we are familiar with the notion of the picture plane, that
two-dimensional surface on which shapes, lines, marks and colour
patches are organised into a composition. For Deleuze and Guattari, the
plane (whether it be the plane of immanence in philosophy, the plane of
reference in science or the plane of composition in art) is not an actual
construction. It is always a virtual construction containing infinite possibilities from which we join series of frames and sections and create a
territory. Accordingly, as Cliff Stagoll notes, 'a plane does not precede
the connections and synthesis brought about between events' (Stagoll
2005: 205). Whilst the plane of composition is a virtual containing infinite possibility, we may understand 'composition' as a particular event
or an assemblage on the plane of composition. It is through the interconnection of events, occurring at different speeds, that an assemblage on
the plane of composition is constructed. Each performance is an event or
assemblage producing different connections and syntheses.

From Matisse we have learned how a composition is becoming

expressive: we may begin a painting by marking the surface, laying down patches of colour, rubbing back and remarking. As soon as a mark is made or a colour patch is laid down (even an accidental marking of the canvas), a tension is created between the colour and the space around, between the mark and the edge. A second mark or patch of colour creates a new dynamism, overtaking the first impulse and so on. Drawing from infinite possibility the work of art proceeds to make connections and build these connections into planes. However, as with Cage's *4'33"*, this process does not go on in a purely random manner. Matisse observes that:

> There is an impelling proportion of tones that may lead me to change the shape of a figure or to transform my composition. Until I have achieved this proportion in all the parts of a composition I strive towards it and keep on working. Then a moment comes when all the parts have found their definite relationships, and from then on it would be impossible for me to add a stroke to my picture without having to repaint it entirely. (Matisse 1995: 41)

Here, Matisse recognises the tenuousness of the event of painting; with one more stroke a painting may unravel and return to chaos.

The work *of* art is to create the finite (what we call the artwork) in a way that does not tie it to representation, but instead enables possibility and restores the infinite. According to Deleuze and Guattari, art 'lays out a plane of composition that, in turn, through the action of aesthetic figures, bears monuments or composite sensations' (Deleuze and Guattari 1994: 197). Aesthetic figures, they tell us:

> Take effect on a plane of composition as image of a Universe (phenomenon) The great aesthetic figures of thought and the novel but also of painting, sculpture, and music produce affects that surpass ordinary affections and perception. . . . Figures have nothing to do with resemblance or rhetoric but are the condition under which the arts produce affects of stone and metal, of strings and wind, of line and colour, on a plane of composition of a universe. (Deleuze and Guattari 1994: 65–6)

There is a demand here that requires us to encounter art quite differently than is our usual habit of being in and responding to the world. Where we see resemblance, for example, the two men talking in Hockney's *Picture Emphasising Stillness* (1962) (image 15.4), Deleuze and Guattari ask us to consider not what it is, but what are the conditions through which it works. It is a very difficult task for us to let go of our preconceptions and opinions about art. It is so easy to say that this is a picture of two men being attacked by a leaping leopard. Whilst an image is conceived as a representation of the world, we remain perfectly safe. What happens though, when art produces affects of line and colour that surpass ordinary affections and perceptions? What are the conditions that enable this?

Even within a postmodern worldview, we remain content to attribute the conditions of possibility to the 'genius' and skills of the artist and to our capacity to read the relation between form and content. Bernd Kuhnert describes precisely this dynamic in the production of John Heartfield's photomontages:

> To realize an idea for a picture, he had scissors, the tonal value of photographs, paint for retouching, and printing technology at his disposal. What resulted were original montages with an exciting, aggressive content and a technical mastery in the handling of the material means. He worked with the grey tones of a photograph just as a painter uses paint. Each tonal value is related to, and functionally depends on, the content. (Bernd Kuhnert, cited in Pachnicke and Honnef 1992: 81)

The word montage derives from the German word *montieren*, meaning to assemble or fit. The term photomontage, as a variation on the theme, was first used to describe the particular technique used by the Berlin Dadaists (artists such as John Heartfield and Hannah Höch) that involved using photographs and typography from printed mass media in the creation of compositions. On first impression it seems that Heartfield's approach to his work involves a technical composition. Technical composition, we will recall, operates on quite a different plane from the aesthetic figures that 'take effect on a plane of composition as image of a Universe' (Deleuze and Guattari 1994: 65). What then takes us beyond simple technique, beyond perceptions and affections, into what Arkady Plotnisky terms 'the intersection between the thought of art and the chaos of forms' (Plotnisky 2007: 181)?

Both Heartfield and Höch draw from the seemingly infinite image repository that the universe of publishing offers in order to construct their assemblages. Here Deleuze might argue that working with these 'figurative givens', Heartfield and Höch just offer us more 'ready-made perceptions, memories and phantasms' (Deleuze 2003: 87). Citing D. H. Lawrence's observation that 'once you have got photography it is a very, very difficult thing to get representation more true-to-life', Deleuze remarks that even when a photograph ceases to be merely figurative, it remains figurative as a given, as a 'perceived thing' rather than a vital life form (Deleuze 2003: 88, 92). Yet the photomontage, like the ready-made, is not a ready-made perception. It is an assemblage that produces new resemblances with non-resembling means.[3] Peter Boswell observes that working with the 'line, colour and texture' rather than the representational content, Höch 'sliced and shredded her source material to a degree that all but obliterates the original images' (Boswell et al. 1997: 20).[4] For example, in Höch's *Strange Beauty II* (1966) some tropical fish and coral are becoming strange, whilst a coiled shell and two legs take huge strides at great speed in the *Seven-League Boots* (1934). We recall that the plane of composition takes place through the interconnection of events that occur at different speeds. It is not just the legs that take great strides. In photomontage what were once photos of fish and coral or lions and tigers become indiscernible as they transform into shapes, marks, tones and coloured bits that have direction, weight, force and move with differential speeds.

The photomontage is constructed as the work progresses – the dismantling of readymade images, the opening and mixing around of visual fragments and the reassembling of the latter in new ways. The connections and syntheses produced in Höch's photomontages mark out a territory and produce a particular assemblage or compound that 'gives sensation the power to stand on its own within autonomous frames' (Deleuze and Guattari 1994: 179). Thus, from all the possible materials available to her, Höch filters and selects, and creates interlocking planes and frames that mark out a territory and construct a house. Deleuze and Guattari call this framing, the territory-house system.

The frame is the skeleton that holds things in place and acts as the sides of the bloc of sensation. The materials – the lines, textures, shapes and colours – each in their own way lend Höch a hand to create an aesthetic rather than merely a technical composition. Thus, with *much* more than scissors, the tonal value of photographs, paint for retouching, and printing technology at her disposal, Höch pieces together the shapes to define planes, and to join planes to mark out a territory and create a composite system. This is the house with its windows and doors that open onto a universe. It is this intersection on the plane of composition that provides the condition for the artist to compose what Proust called the 'art-monument' (Deleuze and Guattari 1994: 177). On the great infinite plane of composition, art composes its monuments. The art monument is not to be understood as an object. It is a bloc of sensation.

Drawing out this territory is no mere technical mastery of material means and the house is not a place to settle back and find comfort. The photomontage is simultaneously both homely (*Heimlich*) and unhomely

(*Unheimlich*). While framing marks out a territory, every framing also activates a force field, that carries out a 'kind of *deframing*' or deterritorialisation (Deleuze and Guattari 1994: 187). Rudolph Arnheim explains that while the frame is the foundation on which a composition can be constructed, it has its own dynamics. Taken by itself, he comments, 'the empty frame establishes its own centre simply through the dynamic interaction of the four sides' (Arnheim 1988: 66). In his discussion of the centric pull of the geometric centre, eccentric vectors, tensions created by the focus of energy in a picture (the 'rubberband effect'), animation of eccentric positions and the sensation evoked 'from standing in the wrong spot', Arnheim alerts us to the forces operating in the construction of the plane of composition (66–8). The frame or the picture's edge, Deleuze and Guattari explain, provides the 'external envelope of a series of frames or sections that join up by carrying out counterpoints of lines and colors, by determining compounds of sensations' (Deleuze and Guattari 1994: 187). This is also the frame provided by Cage's 4'33".[5] However, Deleuze and Guattari also insist that the picture is 'traversed by a deframing power that opens it onto a plane of composition or an infinite field of forces' (Deleuze and Guattari 1994: 188). While Arnheim worries that this deframing has the potential to disrupt the meaning and 'stimulate the viewer to embark on some shaping of his own' (Arnheim 1988: 66), Deleuze and Guattari believe that it is this power that takes us beyond perceptions, affections and opinions into percepts and affects. Here they see a spectator or an artist entering into an unholy alliance with the forces that populate the frame to create a new assemblage on the plane of composition.

The marking out of territory is a complex business. Thus while Deleuze and Guattari may agree with Kuhnert that an artist needs a method in order to cast a net over chaos, they do not hold that a method is the same thing as 'technical mastery in the handling of the material means' (Kuhnert, in Pachnicke and Honnef 1992: 81). They are adamant that the artist 'needs more than the skill of a draughtsman who notes resemblances between human and animal forms and gets us to witness their transformation' (Deleuze and Guattari 1994: 173). In their assessment, the artist must create the syntactical or plastic methods and engage the necessary materials to activate the 'power of a ground that can dissolve forms and impose the existence of a zone in which we no longer know which is animal and which is human' (Deleuze and Guattari 1994: 173–4). Thus whilst a method is needed and technical means are employed, the conditions under which an artist produces aesthetic figures requires that the material becomes expressive. Making a painting allows us to witness the creation of such conditions.

Movement 2 – Making a Painting: The Plane of Material

Deleuze and Guattari describe the ritual activity of the Australian bird *Scenopoetes dentirostris*:

> Every morning the *Scenopoetes dentirostris*, a bird in the Australian rain forests, cuts leaves, makes them fall to the ground, and turns them over so that the paler, internal side contrasts with the earth. In this way it constructs a stage for itself like a ready-made; and directly above, on a creeper or a branch, while fluffing out the feathers beneath its beak to reveal their yellow roots, it sings a complex song made up from its own notes and, at intervals, those of other birds that it imitates: it is a complete artist. (Deleuze and Guattari 1994: 184)

Deleuze and Guattari explain that this ritual performance is not synaesthesia, but rather consists in 'blocs of sensations in the territory – colors, posture, and sounds that sketch out a total work of art' (Deleuze and Guattari 1994: 184). In this ritual act, there is the marking out of territory, the preparation of the ground, the positioning above the stage and then the singular unique performance.

While *Scenopoetes dentirostris* cuts leaves and turns them over to show their paler side, I go out to Neil Wallace Printmaking Supplies. I feel the quality of the canvas, turn over the tubes of paint, test the weight of the paper, tweak the brushes and engage in long discussions about the price and qualities of mediums, paints, stretchers and canvas. There are those inevitable periods of apparent procrastination – cleaning, preening, meeting and greeting (unlike the direct and focused *Scenopoetes dentirostris*), that may not seem part of the process but are in fact essential to marking and preparing for the performance. Then begins the task of constructing the stage.

I lay out the canvas on the floor. I mix liquid paint into jars and line them up, one by one. In this way I construct a stage for myself like a readymade. I start out with some sort of intention but the canvas is already full before I begin. It is the painting before painting. Deleuze notes that between the artist's intention, that is, what s/he wants to do and what s/he does, there is 'necessarily a know-how, a "how to"' (Deleuze 2003: 97). However, this is not the 'how to' of mastery. Whilst composition may be the sole definition of art and what is not composed is not a work of art, what saves the artist from doing what s/he wants to do is precisely the fact of not knowing how to get there.

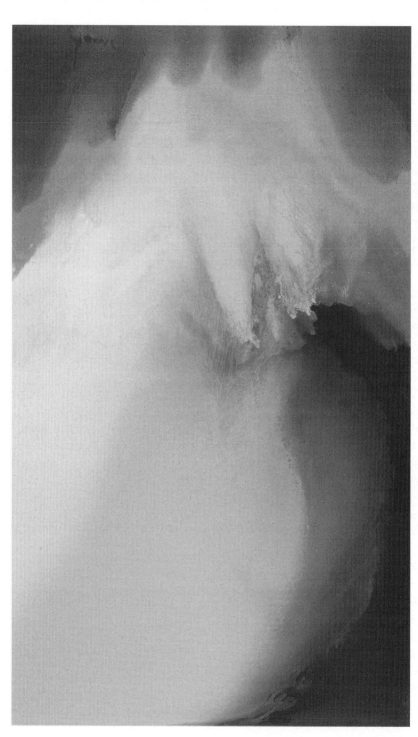

15.1: Barbara Bolt, *Untitled*, 2004, oil stain on canvas, 180 × 120 cm. Image courtesy of the artist.

15.2 and 15.3: Making a Painting 2, 2008. Photos by David Liu and Chris Pahlow.[7]

I position myself above the stage while fluffing out my feathers (the psychic preparation) and prepare to perform. Deleuze and Guattari marvel at the respect, bordering on dread, with which artists approach painting and enter into colour. Without this respect and care, they note, 'painting is nothing, lacking work and thought' (Deleuze and Guattari 1994: 179). It is only through the artist's respectful and careful entering and joining of planes rather than mastery, they say, that the material can ascend into the plane of composition and passes into sensation.[6]

The performance commences. It is a complex assemblage made from the body's gestures, rhythms and speeds in collaboration with those of others to whom this performance is indebted; both human – Morris Louis, Helen Frankenthaler, Dale Frank and Francis Bacon amongst others, and nonhuman, inorganic – the density and fluidity of the paint, the weight of gravity, the vibrancy of the colour, the tautness or slackness of the canvas, the atmospheric pressure and the rhythms and energies filling the room.

The first stain is fairly straightforward: an even wash across the canvas. I lay in paint, watch and wait. Allow the paint to move – wet into wet, wet over dry. I respond to how the paint moves, bleeds, mixes and blisses. I work in the heat of the moment, give over to the paint, the sun, the heat and the fluidity.

I start over again a second stain over the first. It is forty degrees Celsius. It is Australia. The sun starts to move across the surface. Sunlight, wind and heat – the paint moves restlessly in response to the heat and the pull of gravity. It loses surface tension and starts to spread uncontrollably across the surface. It sweats and weeps. Here, in the catastrophe that is the very condition of painting, the plane of material invades the plane of composition. In order to make something true-to-life, Deleuze and Guattari explain, artists necessarily 'go through a catastrophe, or through a conflagration'. Whilst they may pass into chaos, an artist also has to attempt to emerge from it. In doing this, they claim, the artist leaves the trace of this passage on the canvas, on the page or in the plate 'as of the leap that leads them from chaos to composition' (Deleuze and Guattari 1994: 203).

In this ritual and repetitive act, there is the marking out of territory (the delimitation of the territory through the making or buying of the frame), the preparation of the ground (the stretching and priming of the canvas and the preparation of the paints), the positioning above the stage (the psychic preparation) and then the singular performance (the gesture and the unique rhythm that comes with each performance).

The preparation for and the process of making the painting is a becoming house. The painting itself is both territory (marked out by the marking of territory through the process) and the house (a bloc of sensation that is constituted by this marking out of territory). Through this process, the 'technical plane is covered up and absorbed by the aesthetic plane of composition' (Deleuze and Guattari 1994: 195). It is on this condition, Deleuze and Guattari say, that 'matter becomes expressive: either the compound of sensation is realized in the material, or the material passes into the compound, but always in such a

way as to be situated on a specifically aesthetic plane of composition'
(195–6).

Where confused sensation condenses into definite forms in one and
the same movement as the expansive force of the material disrupts form,
the plane of the material can be seen, in Deleuze and Guattari's world,
to ascend irresistibly and invade 'the plane of composition of the sensations themselves to the point of being part of them or indiscernible from
them' (Deleuze and Guattari 1994: 166). While they are quick to point
out that 'sensation is not the same thing as material', they consider that
material plays a critical role in releasing the percept from 'the perception
of objects and the states of a perceiving subject' and 'affect from affection' (167):

> We paint, sculpt, compose and write with sensations. As percepts, sensa-
> tions are not perceptions referring to an object (reference): if they resemble
> something it is with a resemblance produced by their own methods. . . If
> resemblance haunts the work of art, it is because sensation refers only to
> its material: it is the percept or affect of the material itself, the smile of oil,
> the gesture of fired clay, the thrust of metal, the crouch of Romanesque
> stone, and the ascent of Gothic stone. The material is so varied in each case
> (canvas support, paint-brush or equivalent agent, color in the tube) that it
> is difficult to say where in fact the material ends and the sensation begins;
> preparation of the canvas, the track of the brush's hair, and many other
> things beside are obviously part of the sensation. (Deleuze and Guattari
> 1994: 166)

Whilst Deleuze and Guattari argue that the artist must create the syntactical or plastic methods and materials necessary to dissolve representational forms and realise the percept and the affect, they in fact attribute
the power to dissolve form to material. This materialist philosophy of
painting no longer places the artist at the centre, as the one who displays
technical mastery in the handling of the material means, but gives material a privileged position. Whilst the artist may be responsible for casting
a net over chaos and be vigilant to the possibilities that then emerge, art
needs more than the skills of the draughtsman or the eyes of the painter.
It is by means of the material that art is able to wrest the percept from
the perception and the affect from affection.

This is a very different activity than the task normally attributed to
the artist. Plotinsky argues that Deleuze and Guattari's thinking about
art overturns the humanist tradition that would have us see paintings as
objects constructed by human subjects for the pleasure of human subjects. He argues that the ideology of Humanism structures the human
as transcendent and separate from *bios* and *tekhne*. In contrast, he

proposes that Deleuze and Guattari redefine the boundaries between human and animal, and humans and the technological (Plotinsky 2007: 171). The boundary does not totally disappear, but rather becomes 'defined by a potential for a continuous deterritorialization and reterritorialization of both the human itself and of *bios* and *tekhne*' (169). This dynamic relation figures material practice in terms of co-emergence rather than mastery. In a co-emergent practice matter is not impressed upon; rather matter is in process as a dynamic interplay through which meaning and affects emerge.

Movement 3 – Painting Forces

In 1962, David Hockney painted the painting *Picture Emphasising Stillness* (image 15.4). It is an asymmetrical 'composition' in which a leopard appears to leap from the top right-hand corner of the painting towards two men in the left-hand lower quadrant. The two men are in deep conversation, oblivious to the impending onslaught. A diagonal line (a line of text) separates them from the leaping leopard. This line of text reads: 'They are perfectly safe; this is a still.' In the right-hand quadrant, there is a small house-like structure that seems connected to the two figures by a discontinuous plane of dark colour.

In his reflections on this painting, Hockney begins by writing about the work as a narrative:

> From a distance it looks like a leopard leaping on two men who were just having a quite talk, having taken a walk from a little semi-detached house; it looks strange as if the leopard's about to leap on them and eat them, or fight them. And as you walk a little closer to the picture, because you notice a line of type, you read the type first; in a sense this robs the picture of its magic, because you interpret the picture in terms of the written message, which says: They are perfectly safe; this is a still. You realize the leopard will never reach the men. My intention was to force you to go and look closely at the canvas itself, and then in that sense its naughty because it's robbed you of what you were thinking before, and you've to look at it another way. That was the intention. If you put a real message on a painting it is meant to be read, and it will be read. I began the painting without actually knowing its complete subject. Then I realised that what was odd and attractive about it was that, although it looks as though it's full of action, it's a still; a painting cannot have any action. (Hockney 1976: 61)

Hockney is determined that, whilst the painting appears full of action, it is in fact still. 'A painting cannot have any action.' He believes that the

15.4: David Hockney, *Picture Emphasising Stillness*, 1962, oil and Letraset on canvas, 72 × 62 inches © David Hockney.

conceit presented in the line of text 'They are perfectly safe; this is a still', will bring the viewer to their senses so that they realise that this painting is just a picture. The leopard will never reach the men.

On the surface this would seem to make logical sense. In his article 'Pictures Emphasising Stillness', Alan Wood tells us that Hockney's pictures from the '60s are concerned with their status *as* pictures (Wood 1995: 36). Wood suggests that Hockney's paintings are still because they are fictions; static images that have no real time of their own. In this sense, he argues, they are different from photographs. Unlike a 'still' carved from reality, *Picture Emphasising Stillness* is a diagram of an action that never happened. In employing the materiality of paint and the artificiality of the conventions of painting, Hockney demonstrates that 'A picture is not a window on the world; it is an object in the world' (35).

According to an aesthetic regime, where paintings exist as objects to be viewed by human subjects, compositional dynamism may be seen to operate purely within the frame of the work.[8] We are perfectly safe, since it is *only* an image. However, for Deleuze, the function of painting is not re-presentational, if by that we mean a snapshot of the world. Furthermore the event of the painting *is* always more than just an image. Its task is not to illustrate the world, nor is it merely concerned with telling a narrative or story about the world. The common problem for painting, as for all art, observes Deleuze, is that it is 'never a matter of reproducing or inventing forms, but rather a question of capturing forces' (Deleuze 2003: 56). Thus the object of painting is to paint the abstract play of forces. In casting a net over chaos, painting enacts the wresting of the percept from perception and affect from affections (Deleuze and Guattari 1994: 167). Through this athleticism, painting dissolves forms and creates a zone in which subject and object, plane of material and plane of composition are imperceptible. Figured this way, a confrontation with the forces of chaos in painting is not for the faint hearted.

Here we may return to Hockney's *Picture Emphasising Stillness*. In contradiction to Hockney, I suggest it is not *just* a still. We feel the force and the weight of the leaping leopard and its attendants (the shapes and splashes of paint). We become entangled with the leopard (priority of size), become vectors endowed with force and weight in a flight towards the two men who form a stable and seemingly immovable bloc. The line of text becomes a defence shield and we become caught up in the dynamics, as the line deflects us into space. We may be interrupted in this action and, as Hockney suggests, make a counterpoint movement towards the painting, encounter the words as readable text, and actually read them. However, as we move in and out we become caught up again in the pictorial possibilities that this painting, this bloc of sensation, plays out.[9]

The two figures are no longer just two men who have wandered up from the little house and are standing having a chat; together they become inseparable, conjoining as a solid impenetrable square. The right top corner of this square becomes a fulcrum on which the line of text ('They are perfectly safe; this is a still') precariously balances, working as a counterpoint to the forces produced by the leaping leopard and its attendants. For argument's sake, let us engage in some mischief-making to test the sensational affect of such a meeting of forces. What if we were to remove the line of text that has become the figures' defence field? Would we come crashing to the ground, knocking the stuffing out of the two men? And what if we took the little house out of the composition altogether? Would the bloc dissolve and the two men fall out of the picture plane pushed by the force of the leopard and attendants (as shapes with weight, force and direction)? Or would the momentum be dissipated and the shapes slip down the side and dissolve in an ineffectual puddle bringing us to an ignominious halt? Through this interference we become conscious of the forces that populate the picture and make it true-to-life. We are affected, even though we do not necessarily know how. Deleuze and Guattari propose that there is:

> A pictorial possibility that has nothing to do with physical possibility and that endows the most acrobatic postures with the sense of balance. . . Standing up alone does not mean having a top and a bottom or being upright (for even some houses are drunk and askew); it is only the act by which the compound of created sensation is preserved in itself. (Deleuze and Guattari 1994: 164)

Hockney's *Picture Emphasising Stillness* offers precisely this sort of possibility. It is peopled by 'an entire "visualized geometry"' (Deleuze and Guattari 1994: 182). As an object in the world, this painting offers a place where the plane of material rises up and becomes indistinguishable from the plane of composition. It is a 'bloc of percepts and affects' composed of differential speeds, vectors. Paintings are not just spatial. They are a counterpoint of motion. The experiencing of *Picture Emphasising Stillness* affects us and enables us to glimpse the forces beneath perception, affection and especially opinion.

Through this analysis I have demonstrated that the forces operating in *Picture Emphasising Stillness* undermine its representational qualities and question its status *as* a still. The leopard is no longer a leopard but rather a shape with force, direction and weight that, in league with the surrounding patches of paint, becomes a vector cutting a swathe as and through the image. In the meantime, however, the conceptual sense activated by the line of text, 'They're perfectly safe; this is a still', confronts the sensations produced by the forces operating in the picture. The confrontation or interference between the concept and sensation produces a robust athleticism. In *Picture Emphasising Stillness*, concepts and conceptual figures leave the plane of immanence and move amongst sensations and aesthetic figures, whilst conversely sensations and aesthetic figures leave the plane of composition to mingle on the plane of immanence. It is this interference that produces a deframing, that breaks open the image 'onto an infinite cosmos' (Deleuze and Guattari 1994: 197). It is this athleticism that Deleuze and Guattari suggest offers the possibility of a different future of thought.

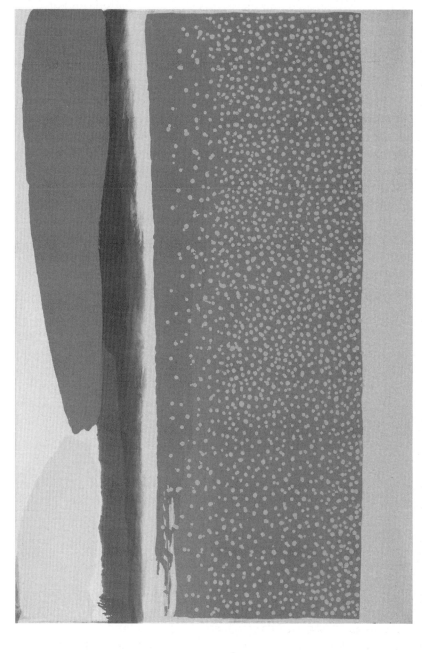

15.5: Barbara Bolt, *Tropical Techno*, 2003–4, oil stain on canvas, 180 × 120 cm. Image courtesy of the artist.

Conclusion

In the three movements of this essay I have demonstrated the athleticism of picturing. Pictures emerge from the positioning of bodies in fields of force. For Deleuze and Guattari, each encounter of the plane of material on a plane of composition involves different intensities, different flows, and different connections so that each repetition is *always* singular. Singularity is not the conscious transgressive act of the artist, but rather it arises in and through re-iteration and citation as the forces of different planes intersect on a plane of composition. Here, an artist's style consists of the rhythms of the lines, the flows and vectors, the eccentric positioning, the material interference and the animated colour, all of which engage in a lively conversation to raise 'lived perception to the percept and lived affection to the affect' (Deleuze and Guattari 1994: 170).

Through mapping the dynamism of material in which colour vibrates and shimmers, lines quiver, and shapes push and shove and topple over, this essay demonstrates the operations of this expansive force. Through returning to the so-called 'formal' language of art and demonstrating how the plane of material rises up into and becomes indistinguishable from the plane of composition of assemblages, my task has been to demonstrate how the expansive force that *is* art undoes 'the image' and produces something true-to-life.

References

Arnheim, R. (1988), *The Power of the Centre: A Study of Composition in the Visual Arts*, Berkeley: University of California Press.

Bogue, R. (1996), 'Gilles Deleuze: The Aesthetics of Force', in P. Patton (ed.), *Deleuze: A Critical Reader*, Oxford: Blackwell.

Boswell, M., M. Makela and C. Lanchner (1997), *The Photomontages of Hannah Höch*, Minneapolis: Walker Art Centre.

De La Croix, H. and R. G. Tansey (1986), *Gardner's Art Through the Ages*, 8th edition, San Diego: Harcourt Brace Jovanovich Publishers.

Deleuze, G. (1989), 'Francis Bacon: The Logic of Sensation', in G. Politi and H. Kontova (eds), *Flash Art: Two Decades of History, XXI Years*, Cambridge: MIT Press.

Deleuze, G. (1993), *The Fold: Leibniz and the Baroque*, trans. T. Conley, Minneapolis: University of Minnesota Press.

Deleuze, G. (1994), *Difference and Repetition*, trans. P. Patton, London: Athlone Press.

Deleuze, G. (2003), *Francis Bacon and the Logic of Sensation*, trans. D. W. Smith, London: Continuum.

Deleuze, G. and F. Guattari (1994), *What is Philosophy?*, trans. H. Tomlinson and G. Burchell, New York: Columbia University Press.

Heidegger, M. (1962), *Being and Time*, trans. J. Macquarrie and E. Robinson, New York: Harper and Row.

Heidegger, M. (1978), 'The Origin of the Work of Art', in *Martin Heidegger: Basic Writings*, trans. D. F. Krell, London: Routledge.

Hockney, D. (1976), *David Hockney by David Hockney: My Early Years*, N. Stangos (ed.), London: Thames and Hudson.

Kress, G. and T. van Leeuwen (2006), *Reading Images: The Grammar of Visual Design*, London and New York, Routledge.

Lauer, D. A. and S. Pentak (1990), *Design Basics*, 4th edition, Fort Worth: Harcourt Brace College Publishers.

Matisse, H. (1995), *Matisse on Art*, trans. Jack D. Flam, Berkeley, New York and London: University of California Press.

Mitchell, W. J. T. (2005), *What Do Pictures Want? The Lives and Loves of Images*, Chicago and London: University of Chicago Press.

Pachnicke, P. and K. Honnef et al. (eds) (1992), *John Heartfield*, New York: H. N. Abrams.

Plotnitsky, A. (2007), '"The Shadow of the 'People to Come'": Chaos, Brain, and Thought in Gilles Deleuze and Félix Guattari's *What is Philosophy?*', in B. Bolt, F. Coleman, G. Jones and A. Woodward (eds), *Sensorium: Aesthetics, Art, Life*, Newcastle, UK: Cambridge Scholars Press.

Solomon, L. J. (1988), 'The Sounds of Silence', available at: http://solomonsmusic. net/4min33se.htm

Stagoll, C. (2005), 'Plane', in A. Parr (ed.), *The Deleuze Dictionary*, Edinburgh: Edinburgh University Press.

Wood, A. (1995), 'Pictures Emphasising Stillness', in P. Melia (ed.), *David Hockney*, Manchester: Manchester University Press.

Notes

1. In a similar vein Heidegger argues that it is art that is the origin of the artwork and of the artist (see Heidegger 1978: 182).
2. Gunter Kress and Theo van Leeuwen's *Reading Images: The Grammar of Visual Design* argues that the visual is a language with syntax and grammar that is combined into meaningful wholes (see Kress and van Leeuwen 2006).
3. In *Difference and Repetition* Deleuze claims not only collage but also Duchamp's readymade for the history of painting. Deleuze observes that 'the history of philosophy should play a role roughly analogous to that of collage in painting. The history of philosophy is the reproduction of philosophy itself' (Deleuze 1994: xxi).
4. Boswell claims that given the violence done in the mutilation of the source material and the obliteration of the representational content, 'it is impossible not to consider these works within the context of Abstract Expressionism and the more gestural manifestations of Art Informel' (Boswell et al. 1997: 20).
5. Larry Solomon writes that the 'magic' of the first performance of *4'33"* was that Cage chose Maverick Concert Hall as the site of the first performance. He left the back door of the Concert Hall open to the surrounding forest so as to allow the sounds of the environment to enter. See http://solomonsmusic.net/4min33se.htm
6. In *Being and Time* Heidegger proposes that 'care' is the fundamental mode of being of Dasein. Our relations with things are characterised by careful and concernful dealings (see Heidegger 1962).
7. These photograph stills were taken during the filming of *Neon Blue*, a film created for the BBC World Service and the Slade School of Fine Art. David Liu and Chris Pahlow directed, produced and edited the film.
8. I am invoking Martin Heidegger's critique of the aesthetic conception of art (see Heidegger 1978: 140–203).

9. Whilst a symmetrical composition induces stasis, an asymmetrical composition is always full of potential action. In a series of drawings and paintings made during this period, Hockney pushes asymmetry to the limit, just pulling back from the chaos that threatens to engulf them.

Chapter 16

BLOODCRYSTALPOLLENSTAR[1]

Neil Chapman and Ola Stahl

Francesco Kulla

Francesco Kulla approaches the lighthouse. Its white crystal eye marks a termination of his journey. And the other, the ruby eye, object of his devotion, was the sign that he should first depart. He has been on the road for years, perhaps decades. In any event, when he tells it, he will exaggerate. Proceeding step by step, always in the same dirt-black suit, always barefoot.[2] Now with a baseball cap, pilfered, its caption: 'Can I buy you a drink or do you just want the cash?' Soiled, his hair beneath it, the same. Without shoes but with head protected. The dissymmetry pleases Kulla. It will give his body a forward momentum demanding no hesitation, one foot and then the next. And he sings.

> . . .*The longest train he ever did ride,*
> *Was a hundred coaches long.*
> *The only man he ever did love,*
> *Is on that train and gone.* . .

Kulla knows the colours. He knows the crystal. He carries it with him in his left trouser pocket. A treasured object. His fingers move across its surface. Ruby red eyes have brought him to the road. (But who's going to shoe Kulla's pretty little foot? Who's going to glove his hand?) Kulla knows the crystalliferious earth. He knows the fertile grounds. Brother's going to shoe Kulla's pretty little foot. Brother's gonna glove his hand. . .

Fransceso Kulla. Kiss his ruby red lips.

Kulla has never seen the sea.

Climbing the stairs to the lighthouse Kulla reaches the platform.[3] There is a vantage point from which he can see the waves breaking against the cliff below, the foam and the ocean's swell marking its force on the rock. The lighthouse's faceted window allows him to see an interior into which there is provided no access. At the centre, a lamp and its prisms. Two panes in the window have been replaced with a glass tinted turquoise. He imagines the beam split, a division within the spread of its rays, sits for a moment, hangs his arms over the balustrade, squints at the horizon. The sun blinks on the water. Kulla rests. His feet carry the dirt of innumerable countries. He inhales. The air tastes different. And as he closes his eyes, the ruby red eyes of Christ are the eyes of sea-birds, are the eyes of the sun and of the moon, are the eyes of his father, and the eyes of the land, the soil, the dust, the molecular-eye; this crystal-liferous aspect.[4]

Kulla leans back and opens his eyes to the autumn sky – these squinting human eyes. The sun reflects in the crystal cylinder of the lighthouse. Kulla counts the steps of the sun; immerses himself in the sun's play on the water. His thoughts canter on the rhythms of light. A momentary lapse in consciousness, but he is alerted, and resurfaces.

Letting his gaze wander, there is another lighthouse, a beacon, situated amongst the cliffs at the water's edge. It too catches rays and sends them refracted through the rays of the other. Interplay. No shadows, only light. Light cutting across the sky, light turning the surface of the water into a plane of infinite variation. Light rendering the universe rhythmical.

He remains on the platform for a moment, hypnotised, counts the sun's descending steps, observes the water: its surface; trying to grasp the nature of the shifting interactions of light. And his attention is drawn to another part of the vista before him. Some yards out to sea, beyond the cliff, piercing the water, a ridge of rock, perfectly round, visible only when the ocean's swell recedes. The water contained within this circular frame forms a pond. A pond in the sea. And for a moment, between the waves, a still surface is revealed – infinitely thin, perfectly blank: mirror in the ocean. With all the attentiveness he can muster, before the next wave, Francesco studies this sight that seems to confound the ocean's fluid mechanics. And he watches the waves' cycle repeat, alternating his attention from one part to another all the better to grasp the whole that will not give itself to the eye's instantaneous apperception.

Allowing himself now to relax, he employs his vision's own rhythmical sensation – no analysis; no reasoning. The light emanating from the crystal cylinders of the two beacons is reflected in the pond in the sea. And beneath the play of lights across its surface, bland and still, a fractured mirror image of the landscape appears. This abundance of fractal universes. Kulla looks up at the sky. The dull circle of his thoughts:

either the images are distributed by the two crystal beacons – cast across distances onto the mirror surface of the pond – or the images are somehow contained by it, disseminated from it.

Francesco Kulla knows well the ruby red eyes that had made him flee in joy, abandoning the confines of a domestic life; that had brought him to the land's end and to this crystal eye submerged in water; microscopic layers constituting the corneas of the optical mechanism of crystal cylinders in a twisted, acrobatic anatomy.

As he descends the steps to make his way towards the beach, something still puzzles Kulla: a question, the answer to which might be his destiny. But his thirst rises and he is lost again to the crystalline ocean.

Bernie N. Galls

The poet's voice splits.

It happens in a way that allows him to mark the moment precisely. He is reciting a line. *Sister's gonna kiss, my ruby red lips.*

Bernie N. Galls' voice split.

It diverged. An alien sensation. There were two voices: one emanating from his larynx – a voice familiar to him – the other from somewhere around his sternum, which caused his clavicle to move, but slightly. The event came with a vague sense of dislocation, but Galls noted it was not unpleasant and so read some more, altering the pace and rhythm of his speech, modifying pitch and tone, toying with prosodies and pronunciations. He transposed his lines into other languages – into foreign tongues he knew, and into those he could barely speak. He noticed again certain turns of phrase seemed to reproduce the voice splitting. Those permutations filled him with pleasure and awkwardness, a non-distinct joy with no reference but the sensation of the sound itself. The pleasure and exhilaration increased with the repetitions. He paced them with his breathing. Mutations appeared. At first, microscopic, slight differences in the pronunciation of a word, changes in the combination or order of phonemes. The mutations became more distinct. New words appeared from the sounds repeated, fractured pieces of syntax.[5]

Bernie N. Galls found the exercise had become part of his routine.[6] He extended his sessions, finding that as he persisted with the longer, more painful sittings, the mutations would take the form of new words. Making a note of these, he found an uncanny similarity between their phonetic content: a certain 'mo-' like sound recurred, as did a long 'ee', and a sound resembling a 'sht' or 'st'. Treating these common roots of the mutations as seeds, Galls made a list of words he could think of in which these sounds played a central role: 'mohair', 'Moscow', 'stick', 'star', 'meek', 'molten'. He focused hard, repeated the words to himself at different paces, tried to visualize them to see if they would allude directly to other texts, images, situations.[7]

Over months, Galls noticed the common roots of the words becoming more substantial. He found himself capable of distinguishing the word 'stone', for instance, in addition to a word resembling 'mould', 'mold', or 'mole', and a word similar to 'beech', 'bleach', or 'beach'. And though he tried to map them out, he could make little sense of the imagery, or of the paths and trajectories engendered. His was a fractured map, a collage drawn together from broken images the relationships between which were uncertain, ambiguous and shifting. Mould and bleach, mould and stone, stone and beach, mole and stone.

Extensive research followed: long sessions in the archives; incessant, silent repetition of word combinations. Galls confined himself, avoided his colleagues, spurned the conversation of friends in preference for an emerging, sub-vocal world of incantation. And gradually, one sequence began to take on weight: 'Molestone Beach'. Shocked by its clarity, Galls surfaced. He wrote his formula on a scrap of paper and took it to the indexes. Two results were returned: punk band, Madrid/ Montevideo (circa. 1981): *Los Moles Tones*; a map reference – a location on the coast 145 miles North-West: Molestone Beach. Population: 1430.

Galls watches from a distance. There are figures on the shore. Something is being done. An operation is being carried out. Or is there only one person? Is the other shape – what he had taken for a body – is that his bucket?

Trouvaille Le Blek

Trouvaille Le Blek has been witnessed before walking with a bag of pebbles. A drawstring bag. Or if not witnessed carrying the container (it must surely equal his own weight) then loading it, or unloading it. He is a figure in the distance. Amongst his skills, Le Blek judges the divide beyond which a witness will see only shapes mutating. But he needs a witness all the same – the other's seeing rendered vague is a component in his operation.

Now stand again. Grasp its gathered opening in two fists. Make a brace with arms and shoulders, but lift from lower. Hold it. Release.

The beach was a mass of grey stones. A jetty, it's railings corroded by the salt air, might once have been frequented by swimmers. Not quite knowing where to begin, Trouvaille Le Blek began to walk. He took 100 steps in a line, struggling to keep his balance across the uneven surface, then stopped to look around the landscape. He turned to walk the 100 steps back. Feeling uncertain, he returned to his room. He sat. He drank (water with a pinch of salt.) Made notes and drawings, pulled out his charts again although he knew them already – every looping contour of the bay's submerged gradient. He played his recordings – the cries of sea-birds; stared at an image in space – followed it with his eye as it drifted.[8] He folded and refolded his drawstring bag, brushed the sand from its folds. But the feeling of an ill-defined uncertainty remained.

Back at the beach, he took the same 100 steps. This time he walked slowly. He tripped, lost his balance, straightened his posture, puzzled over the unaccountable appeal of this place.

The following days passed the same way. He walked in a square formation, repeated it; he walked in rectangles, triangles, circles and oblongs of different dimensions; half-circles, diagonals. He drew a letter, inscribed a numeral; stopped and stood at intervals after a certain number of steps or after intuiting a duration. He got better at walking slowly, crafting each stride, all the while trying to focus on the sensation of the stones, the sounds and smells of the place, the feeling of salt and wind in his face, the cries of birds, engines running in the far distance.[9]

The days passed and he began to notice small lapses in focus. He had developed by now a technique in which he would break each step into several components, and each of these would be executed slowly, with concentration: right heel against stone, roll the sole of the foot across the stones, lift the heel and then toes, raise the left foot, move it forward, left heel against stones, and on. He had developed grace to match his skill, executing his movements whilst maintaining balance and breathing. One day he took his walk barefoot; the next he discarded the rest of his clothes. He experienced the deep interlacing of the materiality of these repeated movements, and the affective relations of stones and feet. Stone sensitised skin. His muscles responded – soft, subtle vibrations. These intensifications did not cause him to lose his focus. But he slipped into a lapse – an apartness from the world. A feeling originating in his belly that spread as an intense heat giving rise to what might have been a temporary unconsciousness, or a profound loss of awareness – he was unsure – whilst not affecting his body, which continued to repeat its movements according to the patterns now established. At first uncomfortable Le Blek began to enjoy this loss of awareness. His periods of apartness were prolonged by graduated steps. He found himself able to retain some vestige of awareness – a third eye? – the capacity of an additional perception with which he could track shifts even within the texture of his apartness.[10]

On his twelfth day, Le Blek had gone through his routines and was about to conclude the activity with one more walk on the stones. 700 steps straight ahead, 70 towards the sea, 700 back, 70 to his starting point, a rectangular path. Leaving his clothes and shoes by the jetty, he made his way slowly along the beach. Through the soles of his feet, the stones; his steps in pace with his breathing, his focus strictly centred upon the activity and the movement. While attempting to maintain a balance, he had slipped or fallen many times. But this time, as the stone under his foot shifted, as he attempted to re-compensate with his weight, something happened. It was as if the imbalance of his posture had, itself, lost its balance. A slip of the slip. He stopped to consider. What he had been doing for the last days had been nothing but an exercise, a preparation, his body passing across and against the stones. The sensations he had experienced had been caused by a conflict between his body, its movements, and the stones; between his path and the uneven surface. Perhaps the hindrance or limit was in his own focus on what now revealed itself to be a battle between matters; perhaps the passage he had been assuming to follow from numbered shapes and figures inscribed on the earth was no passage at all. He gazed at the stones. There was a path. And there was a form of walking against it. But in the implicating disequilibrium of his balance – in the roll of his foot that stretched tendons and brought bones into proximity, there was another walking. This was not a line in resistance to the terrain, nor a blindness to its variety.

It was a twisting line.

It was a line not yet quite twisted, but neither soon to twist.

Barely perceptible slow motion's aim deferred, this was an infinitely fractal twist, a line composed by the stones and by the body there in their mass, a line of a peculiar acrobatics, through the dips, arcing the slopes of the interwoven micro-universes of the terrain. And if the discipline of the procedure was to be embraced – even if only for the sake of grace – there would be here a fluency of a different kind; a virtuosity.

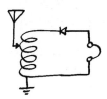

Le Blek walked all through the evening and into the night. As the sun rose spreading a silver film across the bay, a blockhouse came into view. And scanning the ground before him, he took a measure. He saw the paths that others had formed, paths with their destinations clinging to them like bloated fruits on a branch. He saw the gathering and dispersing of the space in these lines, and he walked according to the procedure that had become his method – slow, deconstructed steps drawing a new trajectory between stones, rock formations, and sparse vegetation. Slowing still further, returning to consciousness, he found himself stopped, and staring at an object. Something there at his feet – something familiar, and foreign too in that familiarity. Le Blek looked down at a body – pale, pined away – wasted – a young body prostrate on the stones. Devoid of hair, it was translucent. There were no eyes, only craters for each orifice: no organs, no muscles, but porous grey matter.

Trouvaille Le Blek hesitated. He drew closer and knelt down, reaching out and laying his hand on the forehead. The body was hard and cold, to his astonishment, like marble. In its translucent flesh could be seen an intricate structure. Though devoid of muscular tissue, organs, veins, arteries, the body appeared to contain divisions. Only just visible, these demarcations in the blocks of matter pressed tightly against one another to form a whole. The body appeared to have chambers, to be portioned into rooms and hallways distributed across levels. And as the light struck, its internal pattern was animated as if the divisions were made by mirror glass – rooms within rooms – an entirely different field of perceptions. A hidden architecture within the body's architecture. The stones of the beach as well as the landscape ahead of him and behind were reflected in the body's chambers – the entire beach in the body, contained.[11]

Le Blek looked now neither at the stretch of coast in front of him, nor at the blockhouse. He had arrived with a desire to get to know this place. He no longer had the same desire, but another – the evolution of the first: to get beneath, to penetrate the surface, the earthen element, to relax his muscles and fall back into the land's singular point, its portal, its access to the subterranean.

Le Blek's method, again, his voice now a distant yet intolerably distinct (cuttingly clear, crystal clear, unbearably sharp?) echo (of a code?) in the hollow of his skull: modify path, to the right, now away from the sea, traverse the rock, cushion of vegetation underfoot. Fidelity to the project. A bunker-destination would draw one in a straight line, but the land does not concur. Circle the slab. Ascend. Small changes. Small changes now a distraction. One star blinks in the hazy band above the water. A loss of balance. He falls, his focus dissipated, 80 steps, or less: 70. He shuts his eyes and holds his breath. The boundaries of his body become vague. He gasps.

Venus is a pinprick of brightness low to the horizon. Looking harder, the dim specks of other lights appear. But if you are to focus on the evening star, giving it the attention it demands, it will perform. It will stretch its arms. And with a perfect, integrated movement, will draw them in again while extending vertical limbs. Its mute signals compel further attention, to look longer, to look harder still. Not to imagine other kinds of life, but other lives, with their enigmatic communications, emerge from the bright point's silence. Its mutating centre.

There is a moon in the sky. The sky's dark patches. This heaven an electric void. Its vast expanse. Now a flickering light. Animated in rapture. Its movement, the horizon's pulse. A consuming rhythm. Sudden exhaustion, a transformative potential. And there is blood.

A wound.

But the blood has already congealed. In place of the clot, something different is forming: a cloth. Cloth for clot. Hard, almost transparent. Parchment. The skin beneath the cloth, the body beneath the skin, the stones beneath the body. A reflection of the heavens on its gleaming surface.[12] The body's internal divisions exposed beneath. With rapidly flickering eyelids, and with a quick gesture of the hand, Le Blek rips the blood-cloth from his leg and holds it to the light. In its interior, a room, or a complex of rooms, system of passageways unpopulated, silent, cold – a universe. Le Blek puts the cloth in his mouth.[13] He will ingest it. It has no taste. It will not dissolve. On his leg, already another cloth has formed where the first was removed. He rips again, wedges it between his teeth and cheek, using three fingers to push it into the cavity. He slaps himself hard across the face, inhales deeply, resolves to continue. But to continue now, he will have to find a different way; he no longer has the functioning of his legs. The alternative: to crawl. His pain persists.[14] And he persists, pressing himself now to the stones as he moves, the pattern of these procedures established already – muscle-memorised in limbs that no longer operate, that pass their code to new organs of movement, coextensive with the first, and beyond comparison.

El Topo

The trapdoor to the bunker is disguised by moss gathered from nearby and arranged so as to look natural.[15] Moss is in good supply. The bunker is a subterranean complex. In the past, there must have been more evidence of its extent: a visible platform, the remnants of a rotating turret with apertures for the muzzle of a gun. Likewise, on the opposite side where the ground falls away towards the beach, the bunker's fortifications distinguish themselves from the faces of rock which they seem to mimic all the same. The natural features of the landscape have been taken into account; the building's orientation takes advantage of the slope.

A tangle of fallen branches blocks access to the place where the bunker's platform might still be found. Trees and bushes grow in places that used to be clear.

El Topo knows the passages of the bunker well. Or El Topo does not know the passages of the bunker well.[16] He has walked them, and repeated his walk, in his isolation testing the span of the corridor. He has done so with articulations of his limbs (some natural, some less natural). He has found places to stop, to reside for periods longer than he would be able to reason, where there is no provision for the requirements of a body. He has seen the complex from its anonymous corners. He has watched himself watching, and has made ocular procedures adequate to the task. But if El Topo is familiar with its turns and scattered volumes, his vision of the bunker's extent is confused; with his labour, his knowledge of the passages' convolutions increases, and his picture of their limits becomes less sure.

It does not cross El Topo's mind to consider that this place was built for bodies with dimensions and musculature different from his own.

His appropriation of the blockhouse marks its more recent chapter. In most places the internal walls are damp. And where they are not, to brush one's hand over the surface disturbs a dry residue: a caustic dust that is the concrete's struggle with itself. The dust gathers in crystalline forms around vents, invisible to the eye. These are the concrete's pores. El Topo has seen them. He has done so by listening to the sound of his clothes brushing against the concrete's surface. His legs, part of the soles of his feet, the palms of his hands, a portion of his belly, the left side of his chest, his chin: his encounters with the wall pass through each of these in turn, through all at infinite speed. He knows the density of wall through distributed vibrations. New skin and a new intimacy. El Topo knows his cavernous concrete dwelling, and he knows it not.

But the residue on its inner walls foretells the ruin of the blockhouse.

In conjunction with its steel reinforcement, concrete is unstable. And in its own composition too, over time it transforms. The solid mass expels its interior, becomes a hollow network. Paths across its surface shift as thresholds between the deposits of aggregated dust, the solidus on which the discharged interior collects, and the catastrophic descents of the wall's porosity: each of these compounded by the work of micro-organisms that the hole-complex supports. El Topo has seen it all before inscribed in the stones of the beach.[17] The beach too has testified to the bunker's fate. You just need to know it well enough; take note of the most minute transformations of its surface. El Topo has made their pace part of his own duration; its slowness, the slowness of his movement; the tempo of its modification, his temporal texture against the measured times now abandoned.

He feels the stiff canvas of his jacket in contact with the wall. He brushes from his sleeve some remnants of dust.

He states his tenure.

El Topo is not in residence, but he is close-by and would like to be enjoying its safety again. But there is a more pressing need. The secrecy of its location has been compromised.

He has installed himself at a distance, on the opposite side of the clearing, near the post of a demolished fence, with a view of the bunker's entrance. He has been stationed here long enough that the undergrowth is flattened around him. His movements are slight. But even the warmth and pulse of a body at rest administers to its own comfort. Or in the intangible distance between his crouching, hidden form, and the undergrowth yielding to his weight – in the body's warmth that passes, and then passes back – there is something like sympathy.

But such feelings are forgotten when El Topo is alerted by a sound from nearby. He senses a presence apart from his own. There is no intruder within sight, but he must lie still.

Over his jacket he has wrapped an animal fleece. To maintain the vigil requires him to keep alert. He will imagine his hiding place as if from the vantage point of a third party, plotting himself here in the grass so as to better judge if this position continues to provide advantage. But in the stillness, his mind will wander too. It is odd to have found a transitory security. It is of the same nature, the safety of the hiding place in the bushes and the safety in the deepest cells of the bunker. The same strategy is employed as he hides with a view of the bunker's entrance, secure for a moment, his fur-wrapped body a fortification. But if an enemy becomes aware of his presence, this will happen by the enemy first suspecting it, seeing a fraction of El Topo's disguised form, or by seeing the most imperceptible movement as an anomaly in the field of vision from which the magnitude of the danger that El Topo constitutes for the other can then be inferred. This is the other's advantage: not that the hiding place might be exposed, but that his adversary has a sense of the danger faced while his thinking is not directed exclusively by the spectacle of the danger. Seeing what cannot yet quite be seen, the enemy is made alert beyond his normal capacities. Thinking it through again, El Topo's comfort recedes.

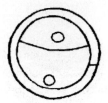

But El Topo has recourse to the same powers. While the necessity to keep still results in the limiting of his view, now his body nested this way realises a new seeing. The fleece in which he is wrapped gives him a vantage of the forest. It is an eye, an insect organ, seeing by touch.[18] His feet – his boots – he would like to draw even closer: they may be visible from the other side of the bush. But it is better not to move. And with this twitch – the impossibility to stay still, the impossibility to move – muscle transmits anxiety of leg's exposure, brain to body's extremity, body's extremity to brain. A carrier wave. Leg-antenna, before he draws it closer. The light is fading. He will sleep here tonight.

Jonah

Jonah's cheeks have grown hollow. He was a wealthy man before this episode. He has been delivered from his trials, yet they weigh heavily on him. Ever since he left the oceans he has suffered an unbearable thirst. Walking barefoot across the city, he has developed scleroderma on the soles of his feet. And on the palms of his hands (he must have crawled, he has no memory), on his chest (lower still to the ground), his chin (beard gathers dust). The rest is burnt by exposure to the light. His hair has grown thin. He can barely see, spends his days squinting at the sun. Its fire is an eternal and overbearing enemy.

Yet those who approach might not notice. He hides his afflictions well. He will not meet another's gaze, offering his profile – a façade fallen into ruins. But the trouble not voiced is written in Jonah's expression all the same, the mote, the plank not in his eye but there about his face somehow. Sunk into his forehead? Or left exposed as roof-joists after walls have caved. If he was to lift himself so that the devastation could be measured, there would be nothing to see. Except in the blink, turning our eyes. And looking back – shocked that the plain arrangement of features should unload the force of its dissymmetry in the diminishing instant of our distraction – we might scrutinise the face's cross again to no avail.

Remnants of a concrete structure scattered on the ground, a fence post, too, sunk into a rough foundation, has survived the catastrophe. This is Jonah's place. He can take from it at least some support for his back. The child comes to visit every day and is here again, stands at a short distance. Jonah will tolerate this chattering visitor. What the child says. Because it is talk not directed at him. It is conceived in his vicinity, sometimes too quiet to hear, a talk that returns, reflected off the surface of things, arriving back as if validated by stones and dried timbers, reorganised by the things from which it is reflected. And this is a gentle relief, to see the ease with which the spoilt conditions might be used, as the faces of an abandoned quarry make an echo chamber. The landscape is doubled by the dull interior of Jonah's skull. This cavity with complexity reduced is worn hollow by the abrasion of pebbles tumbling there. The yellow dust of a peculiar fading, a desert in the desert.[19]

His posture having sunk too, Jonah is led to inspect the patch of earth between his feet. And pushing further in the direction of his sinking body – stretching the ligaments of his back as the curvature allows it – to look at the post's place, where it emerges from the earth, under his arse, where it disappears into its foundation. Bony protrusion, sternum still touches the post at one point – tangent to the curve. But on the ground where his finger has been drawing lines in the dust, there are insect tracks. One tiny hole in the post. Then some more. And surely multitudes of passages for every just-perceptible sign on the surface. Jonah rocks his body. An experiment. To put a little more pressure on the post, sense its flexing, toy with the possibility that it might snap – if not today – somewhere around this segment of the base, at the place were it has become a home for worms.

In the splintered shards in the tracks of elaborate tunnels bored (following the lines of the grain) are there nests already? Clusters of worm-eggs, ovaloid, moist in this interior, protected from the day's dry heat? Protected in a mist of fine threads?[20]

To push at the post Jonah must lift his head. Sunk between his knees in this way he cannot find the force of what's left of the muscles of his thighs. And if he is to lift his head to find traction between the soles of his sandals and the red gravel, he can no longer keep his eye on the wormholes. He must choose one or the other. Lucky that his shoes have been repaired with the rubber of old radials. But how could it occur to him anyway that it might be possible to witness the becoming oval shaped of the wormholes in the base of the post as he flexes it by the pressure of his leaning? Or on the other side for that matter, diminished, the punctures taking on a horizontal orientation as the fibres compress.

Something is glistening in the orifice – a pinprick only. But a burst of light. He looks away. The spot is impressed on his retina. He blinks, looks elsewhere but the spot moves to follow the line of his vision, blotting the centre. Allowing his posture to slump, he looks again. Only the hole stares back, in silence, dark now. Then a pinprick of light. And another spot burned on his retina. Contagion, unholy worm-damage infects his vision each time he looks. Then again, now from several holes. He leans closer, picks up more spots of light that colonise the centre of his focus, grouping themselves like shot-holes. Something is moving between. Microscopic reflections of sunlight. Which divide will they jump next? The holes are connected – wired – a membrane of filaments. This is the fibrous residues of the paths of larvae, or that same filament in consort with fungal growth. No longer even simply the paths of insects, evolving now on lower magnitudes of scale, these are filaments so fine they might capture suns, throw them back to make him suffer again – cast them across the divide by way of a brain-eye mechanism co-opted, annexed, for the malign operations of another.

A tired song in Jonah's hollow of a head, echoing the rattle of the pebbles, wearing him out. A hundred miles. Long as his voyage. His left eye is caught by the wormhole; his right by the sun. Both blinded. The wormhole is the sun is his eye, his damaged retina, is his hardened skin,

is the oceans and the pearl in the belly is that voice he knows so well and the flight he has made his own is water in water is crystalline matter and the crystal cylinder is a perfectly blank surface is the current of an arid river bed is the soles of his feet too

is the incessant chattering of the child is this crystalliferous aspect is stones and rocks and burrows and tunnels and concrete

its pores, is flickering lights is blindness too and death

is a voice split, the blood cloth and the pollen-star and an insect eye, fleece against canvas against skin is the moon submerged in velvet black

is his pain is his anger and its cessation

is the winds always

is

Several days of walking bring Jonah onto the steeper ground of foot-hills. At the mouth of the gorge, the ground descends towards a narrow opening between two imposing rock faces. The quality of the sand underfoot; the way that the cliffs are undercut with sweeping curves; the fields of rounded and polished stones collected along the turns: each of these testifies to the quantities of water that have passed. Now the river bed is dry, a passage towards an ocean that has drained the land, left it thirsty.

It is mid afternoon and this first stretch of the gorge is already in deep shadow. Jonah proceeds to a point where the path turns and the sunlight still penetrates to the canyon floor. Few travellers make it this far. His child finds a smooth rock warmed by the sun on which to sleep. Jonah walks a little further across a bed of large stones, studying them as he goes, judging which one is stable enough to take his weight, allowing his direction to be dictated by the unbroken succession while the falling momentum of his weight demands no hesitation – either one stone or the other. Steady, balanced, technics of movement in his feet, in his ankles: in sinus, muscles and bones.

Amongst these rocks, a result of the floods that come after rain, the broken branches of trees lie trapped. Matted grasses burnt by the winter sun have been caught and collected in the midst of a rapid wash downstream. The dried forms point to involutions in a current deep enough to submerge a man to his waist. But not the brown and muddy torrent of a river in spate: Jonah sees glass, crystal water filling this volume with as many spiralling eddies as there are subtle breaths of air on a still afternoon.

A force, present but almost indiscernible, is the travellers' impetus. Beneath Jonah's hardened soles, and around him as he walks, the water returns, present in the marks cut into the earth. And over the rocks, as this force continues to pull him along the parched riverbed, his thoughts find a new measure with his pace.[21]

Left eye embedded in the earth, right eye caught by the sun (the crystal star, the pollen grain), Jonah continues, each of his steps a paradoxical progress defining, one after the other as they fall, the point from which he never departs at the gyroscopic centre of this horizon's vast hoop.

Notes

1. [Cave: dark. Flickering light. Sand. Grains lodged in mechanical components. Disks spinning. A faint crackling sound. The pods. Fragments of scaly flesh.]

   FIRST VOICE – Do we have company?
   SECOND VOICE – We do. The company of one.
   THIRD VOICE – His name is Williams.
   FIRST VOICE – His business?
   SECOND VOICE – Work. To interrogate the artefacts.
   THIRD VOICE – Shall we offer him something through the lens of our glass?
   FIRST VOICE – Yes. First, details of the wound.
   THIRD VOICE – Will he hear?
   FIRST VOICE – He may not yet hear.

   [Ground discoloured by liquid residue. Patches of charred vegetation in places still burning. A gleam of synthetic light. Rhythmical movement. Expanding and contracting orifices. Metal to metal. Bolted segment upon segment. A desert chill. Winds blowing in from arid surroundings.]

2. Images from Williams' dreams now appear before him although he is awake: The soles of feet, in part crystalline. Wounds contain traces of salt, grains of sand. Little stones lodged in the flesh (in non-crystalline, carnal parts of the

soles). Movement now, with the roll of the foot, a split in the toughened exterior opens to the ground's foreign things, but chooses – sorts from available matter – salt, sand, stones, making a family resemblance in the scale and morphology of heterogeneous matters.

3. [Low rhythmical hum. Power source. High frequency sine tones. Codes in blinking lights. Pods stuck in membranous tissue. Fissures beneath filled with viscous fluid.]

SECOND VOICE - The metal coil wrapped in a desiccated textile that Kulla holds in his fist may have been taken first as beach detritus. . .
THIRD VOICE - But Kulla has never seen the sea.
SECOND VOICE - It is while climbing the stairs to the light-house. He glances to the ground and spots it there – stops and stares for a moment at the thing that stares back at him – stoops to retrieve it. As he walks on, he holds it. An eye for his fist.
THIRD VOICE - Treasures for his pockets. Grit in the wounds of his feet.
FOURTH VOICE - A confounded inlander. . .
SECOND VOICE - Edible seeds too in his trouser pockets.
FOURTH VOICE - . . .vile lump of pined away flesh. . . pre-occupied with black crystal eggs.

[Green surface. Curved. Marbled. Flesh of a kind. Like liquid fat or warm paraffin wax. Transient textures of light connect cave walls in impermanent visibilities. Milliseconds. Pulse.]

FIRST VOICE - These are the signs of turnings.
THIRD VOICE - Does Francesco know it?
SECOND VOICE - His feet crystal, part of his chin too, his hands distinctly crystalline. Francesco has kissed the ruby red eyes – has kissed them twice. The first a kiss of domestic communion; the second a kiss of flight.

[Connection cut. Hollow engulfed in impenetrable black. The code-lights extinguish. . . and resume. Communication ensues.]

THIRD VOICE - Has he a terror of the ocean?
SECOND VOICE - He fears liquidity, matter without division. The infinite expanse of water devouring the texture of the land.
FOURTH VOICE - No man, he, of maritime adventures.

4. FIFTH VOICE - Francesco's passion is an infinite sequence spaced with the ampersand, an organisation of matter, rela-tions and durations in passages. Paths. Universes rendered conjunctive.
SECOND VOICE: The signs of turnings. Knowledge from the gut and the soles of feet.

5. Siringo stubs out his cigarette. Exhales. Williams looks away. The flesh of Siringo's face, its over-articulate flexibility, repulses him. There is no air in the

room. This heat clings to the body. He feels his own skin tighten, thin plastic film wrapped around skeletal physique. No flesh no fat. Light will pass through – a yellowish tinge picked up from its surface. His hair is a mass of reedy strands; chin a patchwork of stubble.

Siringo's pale tongue flicks across thin lips with a lizard's gesture. His skin too: a new dermatological complaint is barely disguised beneath moustache. The dry sands of the desert are advancing. How long, Williams wonders, before both are afflicted?

The ox blood coloured ash tray on the desk needs to be emptied. Siringo directs a sly gaze towards his colleague, provoking Williams to voice his distaste. He scratches his head, sweeps the flakes of dried scalp off the desk's shiny surface and leans back, gripping the buckle of his belt. Beneath Siringo's shirt, the damp spread of a flaccid gut.

Williams stands in the corner, an extended tangle of bones, arachnoid limbs. 'There's something uncanny about the boy, something about his eyes.' Williams gazes vacantly at the boxes. 'His eyes are too large, the jerk of their movements disturbing.'

Siringo's attention returns to the folders. He has said little, but the facts are about to be exposed. Exhaling a plume of smoke, he lifts the recording device towards his mouth, lets it rest on his chin. He presses the record and play buttons, clears his throat. Though Wiliams doesn't move, with the click of the device, his attention is alerted. The tape rolls. Siringo lifts the document from the desk, clears his throat and begins to read:

'*As new words appear the voice emanating from Galls' larynx: 1. fades out; 2. repeats the sequences. In the latter case does the superimposition of prosodies and rhythms create polyvocality (interacting loops)? How does Galls experience this polyvocality as both displacing and intriguing? The vocal split can be explained as a case of acute diplophonia induced by a differential tension of the vocal folds (caused by a cyst or nodule), an archeology of records indicates that the sensation has at an early stage mutated into an entirely distinct experience of two unsynchronised voices. The split voice thus appears to have its reference points partly outside of Galls himself. An "external agent" might be cited, an agent reverberating within him. The preoccupation with sensations of physical "dissolution" seems to support such a thesis. A psychopathology might thus be constructed from the available material; the dissolution of subjective territory opens up to a fugal reconstitution of different subjectification processes involving a play with and between a range of external objects that come to function as signs, incorporated into the construction of a fragmented, polymorphous subjective territory – a territory originating in this initial diplophonic sensation.*'

He pauses, stops the tape, rewinds, plays the recording back, then pulls his notebook towards him:

Tape 3, section one: Addendum: Check references in archive (Galls): 'this iron curtain separating the subject from the object'; 'universe speech', 'matter speech', 'other speech', 'outside speech', 'stone speech'. ALSO: A drawing of a bird with large diamond-shaped eyes protruding from its head, each of which contains meticulously drawn internal structures – like divisions within the consistent matter of a coloured gemstone.

Williams feels another interrogative glance from Siringo; measures his lack of response with care.

FIFTH VOICE – Listen: the universe speaks these shifting fractals, infinite phonetic possibilities: ALLOPOIETIC & FRACTAL 'I' – TO TAKE ONE'S PARTS AND COMPONENTS FROM OUTSIDE ONESELF. . .

6. `. . . From an undisclosed vantage point. Inside? Outside?`
    `Something begins to vibrate. This entity, that entity. An`
    `impersonal third. Not to replicate or represent the sen-`
    `sations of voice splitting, but writing from `<u>`mutagenetic`</u>
    <u>`ground`</u>`.`
    `SIXTH VOICE – Use of ellipses – infinities with meat on`
    `both sides. Chemically induced hysteria, the rant & the`
    `scroll.`

    From whence this echo? Siringo's monotonous dictation duplicates, tripli-
    cates, coming now from three corners, but audible as if through a hum from
    within Williams' own chest cavity?

    With a sigh, Siringo peers at several scraps of paper stuck to the cover of a
    beige cardboard folder titled 'Recovered fragments'.

    Difficulty: at the end of each session Galls cannot recollect particular paths
    between words and phrases. The infinite <u>*impossibilities*</u> *of writing.*
    `THIRD VOICE – The scratching of the pen, a monstrous noise.`
    `The mechanics of the hand a draining effort, the voice`
    `fleeting outside of what can be inscribed. Fever dreams. To`
    `have no language, no loss, no lack.`

    There's something in the air. Williams hears an echo, feels the sound as a
    resonance.

    Siringo: 'To have no language?'
    `SECOND VOICE – To have no language. Such would be a master-`
    `ful advantage. An intimate ally in the sound. All atten-`
    `tion must be directed at the repetitions. From an uncertain`
    `border. 'Limits are what we're inside of (liminal)', Galls`
    `has written.`

    'Ok, Galls' recordings, one through to seven', Siringo's tone is tired.
    'Let's start from the beginning, transcribe them.' Reciting now:
    'This is where we're at. No distinct shifts can be discerned. The material has
    been subjected to several analyses, all of which conclude that there is on the tape
    only one voice, clearly identifiable: my own.'

    He pauses and looks up. The light in the room has shifted. A narrow triangle
    of shadow gives Williams a place to stand. Siringo tries a different approach,
    addresses Williams directly. 'The printed and typed page contain what appears
    to be arbitrary letter combinations, do they not?' With a mute gesture, Williams
    lowers his head. Siringo, clenches his teeth, continues:
    'Still, the fact that Galls records his sessions, remains significant. . .'. he hears the
    lack of conviction in his own voice. . . 'so the question might be: What exactly
    is Galls' relationship to the technological reproduction?'

    Siringo takes his fur felt Stetson Boss of the Plains hat and fans himself gently,
    returns his attention to a passage in Galls' own handwriting:
    Sit down. Close eyes. Strike keys. This interface the site of multiple rhythms:
    fingers against keys, resistance offered, movement of pedals, metal on metal
    music, the ink forced into the fibres. The paper ripped from the roller. A sheet
    sodden with red ink. Ink on the fingers. Hold the paper to the light, Drop it to
    the floor. Clean digits with spittle. Transfer ink residue from finger to tongue.
    With tongue, explore the mouth's internal cavities. Words on the gums. A slap
    of the face to begin again. This <u>*violence*</u>*. When entirely comfortable, repeat twice*
    on inhalation, twice on exhalation.

7. 'Williams!' Siringo shouts, but no reply. Again. 'Williams!' Silence. He stands
    up, puts his cigarettes in his shirt pocket, walks into the hallway, another
    attempt: 'Williams!' Outside on the veranda Williams is squatting, his arms limp

appendages, staring into the barren expanse. 'Williams!' He prods him with the copper tip of his boot. Williams lurches forward, tumbles down the steps and lands in a cloud of yellow dust.

FIRST VOICE – A heap of bones. A body made up of fractures.

'The folder labelled CARTOGRAPHIES. Fetch it from the basement. Quickly.' But hesitating for a moment, Williams' attention is drawn by the dark space beneath the veranda. He peers into it, in his mind still an impression of the landscape persists. Sheltered here, in the lee of the wind it is more devoid of life still; grey with the inexorable dust that filters through the boards as Siringo stamps his weight back and forth.

SECOND VOICE – He is attracted to the cavity, feels the attraction in his bones.

Siringo curses his luck. Is William's mood boredom or lack of incentive? Is it something more? Something methodical?

Williams appears with the folder. Siringo scans the several sketches and the written remarks of an unnamed observer:

Galls is developing a series of arbitrary chains of association with extensive meta-commentary (allusions and analogies; sequences of metaphors; links, paths and passages between different words; geographical references; citations from literature, philosophy, theology, tangents to scientific fields). The remarks in the margins are something short of explanatory. They situate Galls as biographical subject in relation to chains of associations. Various problems to do with poetics, the practice of writing, as well as with personal data are woven into the passages and paths between different words, interspersed with exclamation.

8. THIRD VOICE – Gradually, our subject is building a procedure like that of Le Blek's.

FIRST VOICE – His attention will be given increasingly to the moving image of his thought, that turns itself inside-out in the space in front of him, the common objects of his world refracted through its inverting form.

9. SECOND VOICE – Here again, a refraction of his thought through the material conditions.

FIFTH VOICE – The moon in black water. The lights on the surface. A universe divided in two, one a displaced mirror of the other. A crystalliferous aspect. . .

[Glimmer. Diamondheads. Optical probes penetrate the cavity of the infested rock surface. Communication passes in networks.]

. . . to pass through crystal velvet black. Light shock, numb, lost to all sensation, breath lost in cushioned paralysis.

FIRST VOICE – Entirely aware of his being a profoundly naked surface. He reaches the air and the world above and feels his pores ripped open by the cold, the salt. It is a correspondence between the physical and psychological sense of his dissolution. . .

[Environment collapsed into its own folds. Atrophy. Organic life; annihilated from inside itself.]

```
      . . . Williams will inherit the image, although he knows
   not from where it comes. . .
   THIRD VOICE - From the wall of Le Blek's room?
   FIRST VOICE - . . . squatting low, gazing out through the
   bars of a balustrade, he has felt himself to be below the
   surface but with grace to remain, while he is sustained as
   if by bottled air.
```

10. Siringo dictates from the text into his tape recorder, his voice hoarse:

    'It is clear from the documents studied that during his "lapses", Le Blek is subject to a series of "apparitions", images appearing before him in increasingly rapid succession until he can see only flickering light – an "abstract strobo-scope". See, for instance, the numerous pages of sketches and drawings in the folder entitled EXPERIMENTS.'

11. Now walking in circles, kicking up sand and dust, inexplicable images appear before Siringo: A bird with large eyes of a crystalline quality, a line drawing of a thin female figure, her hands clutching her abdomen; head disproportionately large containing crystalline blocks and complex fractal structures; a fine, milk-white shroud of powder snow; recurring drawings of black eggs; ruptures in the shells, escaping matter, this also crystalline; one side egg, one side crystal. With a wave of the arm he banishes the pictures, reads aloud – shouts to block their return:

    'This relationship with ordinary objects transformed. Stones, rocks, eggs. Semiological contents and expressions?'

    Williams does not look up. He is sitting with his legs folded awkwardly beneath him on the porch counting and categorising the objects in his collection: stones, a feather, a bone – all these found nearby. The thought on his mind: THIS IS A FERTILE GROUND. Meanwhile Siringo circles, his recitation increasingly agitated:

    'Worlds become abundant with signs, each carrying potential to alter the most intimate aspects of what is perceived as destiny.'

12.
```
   FIFTH VOICE - Psychopathology. Obsession with crystal-
   line forms - a passage towards haematological mutation?
   Blood's become crystalline from contact with crystallifer-
   ous aspect.
   SECOND VOICE - And the granular matter sorted and clas-
   sified by Kulla's walking and Kulla's wound appears now
   for Le Blek in the form of the star. Star and pollen
   grain.

   [Exteriorities appearing in patches. Hollows plied
   open.]

   THIRD VOICE - Cosmic star matter, apprehension. Can star's
   arms seize pollen grains?
   FIRST VOICE - The system is plied open, its mutagenetic
   potential rendered with infinite variation.
```

13. Exasperated now, thrusting a sheet in front of Williams' face, Siringo implores:

    'There's something about the notion of the blood-object. . .'. Pause. 'And the way it is retained in his oral cavity. . .'. He reads it aloud, with deliberation:

    'Nt. Psychopathology. Obsession with crystalline forms – a passage towards haematological mutation? Blood's become crystalline from contact with crystal-liferous aspect.'

Then to his astonishment, Williams speaks, completes the sequence, reciting in a voice as placid as the view:

'Nt. pollen grains appear in star, in cloth; cosmic star matter; apprehension – star-arms seize pollen grains, a system plied open; its mutagenetic potential of infinite variation. . . .'.

14. '. . . Mode of Locomotion (Forensic Reconstruction): Conduct an investigation of terrain. Ample evidence of his presence: DNA from blood, urine, faeces. Plot movements of smaller stones.'

SECOND VOICE – Plot movements of smaller stones. Draw up map. Reconstruction shows his difficulties. Due to a wound. . .

'. . . due to a wound, forward movement requires right leg to be held at angle from body. Quadriceps spasm uncontrollably – this again rendering movement impossible, the body's surface contact with stones increases. He moves forward supporting himself with his two arms and his left leg, keeping his right leg straight, stretched back and to the right with his toes against the ground for support and balance. Then first moves his arms forward using his left leg and right foot as support, then left leg forward supported by arms and his right foot, after which he drags his right leg along with him, ending up in original position.'

THIRD VOICE – Why did Le Blek not try to make a provisional crutch from available driftwood?

Staring at his things, Williams speaks the answer to a missing question:

'Le Blek considers the wound yet another "sign" opening up to a series of precise passages. He takes closeness to the stones as datum for the developing method – use of found timber would constitute a "false sign". "We are", he has written, "no longer concerned with the realm of volition or reflection, but with a process of differentiation by which he has been *naturalised* with the stones".'

15. SECOND VOICE – An inventory of all that can be found in the bunker corresponds now to the collection assembled on the grey, sun-bleached boards: traces of animal faeces, a dead bird, egg shells, a metal coil – a radio component resembling an eye wrapped in a fragment of cloth and stored in a cavity in the bunker wall.

[Sequence. Dead lands. Deterioration outwards from the site. Desert rendered emaciated. Merely a thin membrane of sand and parched, burnt matter enfolding the stages where new matter emerges.]

THIRD VOICE – And meanwhile, your colleague stares at the written document and the words blur into abstract marks.
FIRST VOICE – Williams, clean the items of your collection with a toothbrush; polish them with turtle wax.
WILLIAMS – I will polish them with turtle wax.
SECOND VOICE – The desert seems somehow more like a desert now. It's intrinsic quality intensified. What was already dead seems more dead.

Back inside, in the room designated as his office, Siringo surveys the books, reads the titles of the volumes aloud: '*Mammal Burrows*; *The Anxiety of the Scurriers*; *Forehead as Hammering Tool*; *The Wind in The Micro-tunnels*; *The Confounded Entrance and Other Stories*; *Outside in the Inside* and its companion volume; *Dealing with Small Fry, Troubling Sounds and Their Origins*;

Fear of the Larger Beast; The Collapse; Mud on the Claws – Mud on the Snout.'

16. FOURTH VOICE – Vile lump of pined away flesh. 'Or'? 'And?' One or the other? Both? El Topo's passion, an either-or; Francesco's, infinite sequences of &s, universes rendered conjunctive. . .

[Diamondheads. Hard surfaces protrude from pod-membranes. Yellow dust mixes with sand mixes with yellow dust.]

17. Deep in the fortified basement, Siringo has bolted the inner door. Folders, boxes, envelopes and documents lie spread in front of him. Several notebooks open at once, pen in one hand, tape recorder in the other, he reads and records:

    'A watch tower has been constructed. For what form of observation? To monitor what activity?. Boards are suspended between the legs of the structure. (Seats?) Cigarette butts, beer cans, other discarded items, are left beneath the boards. Was the tower constructed before or after the abandonment of the blockhouse? To what desires does it testify, to what impending disaster? To what survey and what frontline? To what discipline and what destiny?'

18. Siringo gathers what he can from the office and carries the laden box into the basement. He will lock himself in, even if there is no need. Williams has been missing for days. Aloud to himself: 'There's some sort of animal living in the bunker.' He chooses at random, but the account provided by the documents seems less and less to be of remote events: it is of these conditions into which he, himself, is being drawn. What is the time of day? With no natural light, he cannot tell. And the temperature is as stable as the dim brightness from his solitary bulb. He pulls his collar tight. Back to work. Pelt. Pelt? He flicks through one of the notebooks:

    'Nt. Presented first with conventional purpose of insulation. Pelt now appears to have been taken for another reason – to invoke animal sensitivity. Hair filaments as sense organs. Issue unresolved.'

19. THIRD VOICE – Exposed, concaved, porous substrate of interior bone face?
    SECOND VOICE – Or what is spotted here is chipped bone in the scull.
    FOURTH VOICE – 'Or, or, or?'
    SECOND VOICE – And. . . and intuited from the body's choreography, the now lost partitions of the prophet's cranial cavity. The internal space reduced to homogenised volume – solid volume simplified through motion of agents of abrasion.
    THIRD VOICE – The pebbles?
    WILLIAMS – The pebbles.

    [Zone: bordered on all sides but expanding. Enter solid mass of bone. Unwrapped now. Virtual archeologies intertwined. Connections tweaked, shifts in pitch.]

    FIRST VOICE – Bits of scull broken off, ground to dust by pebble motion. And the dust gathers in a pattern further indicating the inner absence. While their motion is too quick for viewing there is a rhythm in the pebbles' circulation.
    WILLIAMS – Here is the hodology.

[Bones now dust. Layer upon layer. Inaudible volumes,
refracting code into code. Discordant sounds. Contrasting
oscillations interpenetrating.]

THIRD VOICE - Who are we?
WILLIAMS - Glimmerheads.
VOICES (in unison) - We are the Diamondheads.
WILLIAMS - You glimmer.
VOICES (in unison) - He glimmers.
[Glimmer through dusty film. Sheath.]

THIRD VOICE - Whence do we come? Beyond the stars?
VOICES (in unison) - From the bright point, the star in
the heart of matter.
20. FIFTH VOICE - Contemplate wormhole-distraction.
THIRD VOICE - Something akin to joy?
21. Siringo lights another cigarette. Stubs it out. The resolution of the work will
have to be postponed. The postponement will be indefinite. He speaks into his
recorder:
'Yellow dust. Only yellow dust. And sand.'
And Williams walks on. For the time being – while the temperature control still
operates between the padded, internal layers of his protective suit – he is able
to continue. The soles of his boots expel in rhythmical time their pneumatic
breaths. And the hoarse sound of his own breathing is amplified through the
tubes of his respirator. How long will the life support last? A few days; a week?
Although a prosthetic extension to the body, the rig strapped to his back marks
an inevitable limit. But nothing will sustain him now as effectively as the accumulating mass of artifacts in his sample-vessel.
   Another's footprints are visible in the dust. He records them, notes their
changing character. As he moves along the dried river from the littoral across
the plain he tracks an almost indiscernible evolution. The earlier prints showed
a soft pedature. There were few distinguishing details. Now the prints contain
complex structures more like the imprint of a hard and uneven body-part;
crystalline, replete with differentiations, fractal demarcations and delineations.
Amongst the ground's sharp-faceted, fist-sized lumps of volcanic rock, a fragment of glass catches the light. He stoops to retrieve it. A broken piece of a
technological artifact like the visor of his own helmet? Across its surface there
are scratches like the runes of a foreign alphabet. He hesitates, opens his mouth
as if to sound the marks. And he turns, diverting from his path once more, heads
to the east.

Notes on Contributors

Eric Alliez

Eric Alliez is Professor of Contemporary French Philosophy at the Centre for Research in Modern European Philosophy, Middlesex University, London, UK. He is the author of many books on Deleuze, aesthetics and politics, including *The Signature of the World* (Continuum, 2004), *Capital Times* (University of Minnesota Press, 1996), *L'Œil-Cerveau. Histoires de la peinture moderne*, in collaboration with Jean-Clet Martin (Vrin, 2007), and *La Pensée-Matisse*, with Jean-Claude Bonne (Le Passage / Adam Biro, 2005).

Barbara Bolt

Barbara Bolt is Senior Lecturer in the Theory and Practice of Visual Media in the School of Culture and Communication at The University of Melbourne. She is a practising artist who has also written extensively on the visual arts and their relationship to philosophy. Her publications include a monograph, *Art Beyond Representation: The Performative Power of the Image* (I. B. Tauris, 2004), and two edited publications, *Practice as Research: Approaches to Creative Arts Enquiry* with Estelle Barrett (I. B. Tauris, 2007) and *Sensorium: Aesthetics, Art, Life*, with F. Coleman, G. Jones and A. Woodward (Cambridge Scholars Press, 2007).

David Burrows

David Burrows is Senior Lecturer in Fine Art at Birmingham City University, UK. He is an internationally exhibited artist based in London. Recent shows include *Popnosis*, Chungking Projects, Los Angeles 2005, *Moonage Daydream*, Praz-Dleavallade, Paris 2005, *Mirror Works*,

FA Projects, London 2005, and *New Life*, Chisenhale (and UK tour), London 2005.

Neil Chapman

Neil Chapman is an artist and writer, and a member of The alt.SPACE Network of Artist Research Groups. He studied Fine Art at Duncan of Jordanstone College of Art in Dundee, and Critical Fine Art Practice at Central Saint Martins, London. His work takes various forms, deriving momentum from shifts between disciplines. Collaboratively, Chapman has worked with Anna Best at W139 gallery, Amsterdam, and as co-editor of her book *Occasional Sites* (The Photographer's Gallery). He has worked with artist Steven Claydon, making sculpture and installation, exhibiting at Hoxton Distillery, Greengrassi and the ICA, London. Chapman's book, *The Ring Mechanism* (2004) is published by Book Works. He has recently begun a research scholarship at Reading University.

Gustavo Chirolla Ospina

Gustavo Chirolla Ospina is Professor of Philosophy at Javeriana University, Bogotá and Professor of Aesthetics in the Masters Program in Visual Arts at the National University of Colombia. Some of his recent publications are: *Gilles Deleuze: Inorganic Vitalism as Philosophy of Immanence* (2002), 'El paseo de Orlando: una matriz de subjetivación y de des-subjetivación', in *El cuerpo fábrica del Yo. Producción de subjetividad en el arte de Luis Caballero y Lorenzo Jaramillo* (2005), and 'Hacia una ontología crítica de lo viviente', in *Biopolíticas y formas de vida* (2007).

Robert Garnett

Robert Garnett is an artist, critic and writer. Since the mid '90s he has published in a wide variety of journals and magazines, including *Art Monthly*, *Frieze* and *metropolis m*. He is currently completing a doctoral thesis on humour in contemporary art.

Sue ('Johnny') Golding

Sue Golding is Professor of Philosophy in the Visual Arts and Communication Technologies at the University of Greenwich. She is

Program Leader of the interdisciplinary MA in Media Arts Philosophy and Practice and the author/editor of many books and articles, including *The Eight Technologies of Otherness* (Routledge 1997), and *Gramsci's Democratic Theory* (Toronto 1992).

Maurizio Lazzarato

Maurizio Lazzarato is an independent sociologist and philosopher. He has written numerous books published in French and Italian, including: *Les Revolutions du capitalisme* (2004), *Puissance de l'invention. La psychologie economique de Gabriel Tarde contre l'economie politique* (2002) and *Lavoro immateriale. Forme di vita e produzione di sogget-tivita* (1997).

Claudia Mongini

Claudia Mongini is an artist and independent researcher living in Vienna. She studied physics at the University of Turin, and obtained her doctorate for work applying chaos theory to neuroscience. She subsequently gained a masters degree in fine arts at the Academy of Fine Arts, Vienna. Since 2001 she has dealt with the crossover between art and science, in both artistic practices and theory. In 2008 she conceived and organised the international symposium: *Cartographies of Sensation, between emotion, feeling and affect in art, philosophy and science*. She is member of the Science-Art group of the Austrian Research Association.

Simon O'Sullivan

Simon O'Sullivan is Senior Lecturer in Art History/Visual Culture at Goldsmiths College, University of London, UK. He is the author of *Art Encounters Deleuze and Guattari: Thought Beyond Representation* (Palgrave, 2005) and co-editor (with Stephen Zepke) of *Deleuze, Guattari and the Production of the New* (Continuum, 2008). He is currently working on a forthcoming monograph, *On the Production of Subjectivity* (Palgrave).

Jussi Parikka

Jussi Parikka is Senior Lecturer in Media Studies at Anglia Ruskin University, Cambridge, UK. He is the author of *Cultural Theory in the*

Age of Digital Machines (Koneoppi, in Finnish) and *Digital Contagions: A Media Archaeology of Computer Viruses* (Peter Lang, 2007). He is currently working on a book, *Insect Media*, which focuses on the theoretical and historical interconnections of biology and technology. In addition, two co-edited books are forthcoming: *The Spam Book: On Viruses, Spam, and Other Anomalies from the Dark Side of Digital Culture* (Hampton Press) and *Media Archaeologies*.

Gerald Raunig

Gerald Raunig is University Lecturer at the Institute for Philosophy, University of Klagenfurt, Austria. He lives in Vienna and works at eipcp (European Institute for Progressive Cultural Policies) as coordinator of the transnational research projects *republicart* (http://republicart.net, 2002–5) and *transform* (http://transform.eipcp.net, 2005–8). His recent publications include: *Tausend Maschinen* (Turia+Kant, 2008), *Kunst und Revolution. Künstlerischer Aktivismus im langen 20. Jahrhundert* (Turia+Kant, 2005), translated as *Art and Revolution: Transversal Activism in the Long Twentieth Century* (Semiotext(e)/MIT Press, 2007). He is the editor of *PUBLICUM. Theorien der Öffentlichkeit* (Turia+Kant, 2005), and *Kritik der Kreativität* (Turia+Kant, 2007) (both with Ulf Wuggenig).

Suely Rolnik

Suely Rolnik is a cultural critic, curator, psychoanalyst and Professor at the Universidade Católica de São Paulo, where she conducts the Center of Cross-Disciplinary Studies on Subjectivity. She is also a Professor in the Barcelona Contemporary Art Museum's (MacBa) Independent Studies Program (PEI) and guest researcher at the INHA (Institut Nationale d'Histoire de l'Art) in Paris. She is co-author with Félix Guattari of *Micropolítica. Cartografias do desejo* (1986) which has recently been translated into French (Seuil, 2007) and English (Semiotext(e)/MIT, 2007). She is the creator of the research and activation project of the sensible memory of Lygia Clark's work. She curated the exhibition and edited the catalogue (with C. Diserens), *Nous sommes le moule. A vous de donner le souffle. Lygia Clark, de l'œuvre à l'événement*, at the Musée de Beaux-arts de Nantes (2005) and the Pinacoteca do Estado de São Paulo (2006). She has translated Deleuze and Guattari's *Thousand Plateaus* into Portuguese. She has also published numerous essays in books, journals and art catalogues in Europe and the Americas.

Elisabeth von Samsonow

Elisabeth von Samsonow is Professor of the Philosophy and Historical Anthropology of Art at the Academy of Fine Arts, Vienna, Austria. Her publications include: *Anti Elektra. Totemismus und Schizogamie* (Diaphanes, 2007), *Flusser Lectures. Was ist anorganischer Sex wirklich? Theorie und kurze Geschichte der hypnogenen Subjekte und Objekte* (Verlag der Buchhandlung Walther König, 2005), *Fenster im Papier: Die imaginäre Kollision der Architektur mit der Schrift oder die Gedächtnisrevolution der Renaissance* (Fink, 2001), *Die Erzeugung des Sichtbaren. Die philosophische Begründung naturwissenschaftlicher Wahrheit bei Johannes Kepler* (Fink, 1987). She also exhibits her artwork internationally.

Edgar Schmitz

Edgar Schmitz is an artist and lecturer in the Department of Visual Cultures at Goldsmiths College. He curates for the Curating Architecture research project, Goldsmiths, and is co-director, with Lisa Lefeuvre, of *A Conversation in Many Parts*. Recent exhibitions include *Liam Gillick: 'Edgar Schmitz'* (ICA, 2006), *London Movies* (Bozar, 2005), *Too close is good too* (play, 2005). His book *Ambient Attitudes* is forthcoming with Sternberg Press.

Ola Stahl

Ola Stahl is an artist, writer and lecturer in the Fine Art program at Central Saint Martins College of Art and Design, University of the Arts London. He is a founding member of artist collective C.CRED (Collective CREative Dissent) and The alt.SPACE Network of Artist Research Groups. For three years he was part of the editorial collective of *parallax*, and has published several articles, catalogue essays and reviews in publications including *parallax*, *Angelaki* and *Journal of Visual Culture*. As an artist he has shown widely, both individually and as part of various collaborations, and his work has been included in several biennales, festivals and exhibitions such as *BIG* (Turin, 2002), *BIG Social Game* (Turin, 2002), *ISEA* (Tallinn/Helsinki, 2004), *Urban Festival* (Zagreb, 2005), and *Locally Localized Gravity* (ICA, Philadelphia, 2007).

Stephen Zepke

Stephen Zepke is an independent researcher. His publications include the book *Art as Abstract Machine: Ontology and Aesthetics in Deleuze and Guattari* (Routledge, 2005), and he is co-editor (with Simon O'Sullivan) of *Deleuze, Guattari and the Production of the New* (Continuum, 2008).

Index